THE
COCKER SPANIEL OWNERS'
MEDICAL · MANUAL

Robert M. Brown, D.V.M.

Editor — Carol H. Brouwer

Copyright© 1989 by Robert M. Brown
First Printing 1989
Printed in the United States of America
Cover illustration and design by Jan Kiefhaber

Library of Congress Catalog Card Number 87–71369

ISBN 0-938681-01-X Soft-cover

Breed Manual Publications
3370 Jackson Drive
Jackson, WI 53037
(414) 677–3122

PREFACE

The purpose of *THE COCKER SPANIEL OWNERS' MEDICAL MANUAL* is to serve as a ready reference for medical information about the Cocker Spaniel. While *THE MANUAL* is not designed as an owner's home remedy guide for do-it-yourself treatment, its contents will enhance your understanding of conditions which are common or are hereditary in the Cocker Spaniel. Use this book as a valuable reference to help you understand specific conditions that your veterinarian might diagnose. Whenever you are in doubt or are concerned about your Cocker's health, CONSULT YOUR VETERINARIAN!

THE MEDICAL MANUAL is categorized by body systems: gastrointestinal, cardiopulmonary, skin and related structures, musculoskeletal, blood and blood forming organs, neurological, urogenital, endocrine (hormone), and sensory—eyes, ears, and nose. Poisoning, nutritional management and supplementation, anesthesia and surgery are part of the reference sections. Within each system, topics are arranged alphabetically and then cross-referenced for easier use. All words in **bold** and *italicized* print can be found in the index. The pages listed reference a more complete description of that particular subject.

As the author, I am actively soliciting from my readers any information related to Cocker specific conditions not mentioned in *THE MANUAL*. Your comments on the book are welcomed by both the author and the publisher as we endeavor to improve and update the information in each edition. We are sure that you will enjoy *THE COCKER SPANIEL OWNERS' MEDICAL MANUAL*. Keep it readily available for quick reference!

Robert M. Brown, D.V.M.

TABLE OF CONTENTS

ANESTHESIA AND SURGERY

AMERICAN COLLEGE OF VETERINARY SURGEONS (ACVS):
Established in 1970, the ACVS is recognized as an organization for the advancement of the art and science of veterinary surgery. The more than 250 current members are regarded as experts in veterinary surgery. While most members are employed by veterinary colleges, some members are employed in private practices and see surgery cases on a referral basis. Their level of surgical expertise is much greater than that of the general veterinary practitioner.

ANESTHESIA, DRUG COMBINATIONS AFFECTING: The usage of some drugs just prior to or during surgical procedures may complicate recovery from anesthesia. If the antibiotic *chloramphenicol* is given to a dog under *barbiturate anesthesia*, recovery period up to two times normal length will result. A good safety precaution is the removal of flea collars 24 to 48 hours before the use of barbiturate anesthesia. Some of the insecticides impregnated in flea collars potentiate the activity of injectable anesthetics. The drug *epinephrine*should not be used with the inhalant anesthetic *halothane* because this drug combination predisposes the heart muscle to ventricular fibrillation resulting in *heart failure.* When in doubt, remove all drugs from the dog's body at least 24 hours before any anesthetic is given.

ANESTHESIA, DRUGS USED IN: **Acepromazine maleate** (*Promace*®) is a tranquilizer commonly used prior to surgery. This tranquilizer is also used as the sole method of restraint on a patient for radiography and lab tests or to facilitate the administration of certain medications. The quieting effects last from 4 to 8 hours. Commonly, the third eyelids relax to cover the eyes. Because acepromazine maleate is a *phenothiazine* type tranquilizer, it should never be used to treat *seizures* associated with *chlorinated hydrocarbon poisoning.*

    Atropine sulfate is used in combination with preanesthetic drugs like *Innovar-Vet*® and *Rompun*® to dry up secretions and slow down the GI tract. It blocks the slowing of the heart affect and helps to block potential *laryngospasms* on *intubation* with an *endotracheal catheter.*

    Benzocaine is a topical anesthetic used on mucous membranes.

    Bio-tal® is an ultra-short-acting anesthetic. See *Thiamylal sodium.*

    Brevital® is a short-acting anesthetic. See *Methohexital.*

    Cetacaine® is a topical anesthetic combination of *benzocaine* and *tetracaine* that will deaden mucous membranes when applied by swab or spray.

During endotracheal intubation, it "freezes" the larynx to help prevent *laryngospasms.* See *INTUBATION, ENDOTRACHEAL* and *Tetracaine.*

Demerol® is a narcotic preanesthetic agent. See *Meperidine.*

Diazepam (*Valium*®) is the drug of choice for controlling severe, violent, recurring *epileptic seizures.* Administered intravenously, the drug must be repeated as the effects wear off. Diazepam as an oral sedative is not very effective in dogs.

Enflurane (*Ethrane*®) is a volatile inhalant anesthetic agent. Special equipment is required to administer the combination of enflurane and oxygen necessary to produce *general anesthesia.*

Fentanyl: See *Innovar-Vet*®.

Fluothane® is a volatile general anesthetic agent. See *Halothane.*

Glycopyrrolate (*Robinul-V*®) is a preanesthetic agent used in place of *atropine* to reduce salivary and tracheal secretions. This drug should not be used in pregnant bitches.

Halothane (*Fluothane*®) is a commonly used inhalant general anesthetic agent. Special equipment carries it to the patient in oxygen. Halothane can sometimes cause liver damage or sensitize the heart muscle to *epinephrine* While recovery from halothane anesthesia is rapid, muscle relaxation is poor. Because of halothane's volatile nature, anesthesia can be induced with a face mask.

Innovar-Vet®, the trade name for a combination of the two drugs *fentanyl* and *droperidol,* is used to produce *neuroleptanalgesia* (depression and numbness to pain). While most Cockers do not, some breeds react adversely to the use of Innovar-Vet®. Because little fetal depression results, this drug is commonly used in cesarean sections. *Atropine* is routinely given with Innovar-Vet® to minimize the sting on intramuscular injection and to dry up oral secretions.

Ketamine hydrochloride (Vetalar®, Ketaset®) is a dissociative type of injectable anesthetic approved for use in humans and felines but not in canines because a small percentage of canine patients have *seizures* under the influence of this drug. Owner's consent is required for use on dogs. Ketamine stimulates rather than depresses the cardiac system making it very valuable in old dogs. The drug is given either intramuscularly or, at a much reduced dosage, intravenously. Usual anesthetic monitoring signs cannot be used with this type of anesthesia because of its dissociative nature. Ketamine hydrochloride is ideal for short procedures and as restraint for radiography.

Lidocaine hydrochloride (*Xylocaine*®) is a drug used to "freeze" an area of the body causing *local anesthesia.* The drug is injected under the skin or in the region of a nerve resulting in 45 to 60 minutes of anesthesia. Lidocaine is also injected intravenously in the treatment of some heart irregularities.

Meperidine (*Demerol*®) is a controlled substance used to numb the response to pain. By depressing the cardiopulmonary system, the amount of barbiturate anesthesia needed to produce unconsciousness is greatly reduced.

Methohexital (*Brevital*®) is a barbiturate classified as an ultra-short-acting anesthetic. This drug is given intravenously either alone or in combination. Barbiturates do not produce good *analgesia* (freedom from pain). Anesthesia lasts from 5 to 15 minutes.

Methoxyflurane (*Metofane*®) is a volatile anesthetic administered with oxygen through special anesthesia equipment. The degree of muscle relaxation is excellent during anesthesia. This inhalant agent should not be used in dogs with kidney impairment if surgery is expected to last over two hours. *Analgesia* after removal from the anesthetic machine lasts up to 30 minutes. Recovery from methoxyflurane is longer than from *halothane.*

Morphine sulfate is a controlled substance used as a preanesthetic agent, a pain killer, or an *emetic* (vomit inducer). This narcotic is not commonly used in modern veterinary practices because of the high potential for abuse. Better drugs are available for the same purpose.

Nitrous oxide, also known as *laughing gas* or *giggle gas,* is used with oxygen and another volatile anesthetic agent to produce gaseous *general anesthesia.* Used alone, nitrous oxide cannot produce deep anesthesia. However, when used with other anesthetics, the amount of the volatile anesthesia used is reduced. Therefore, it is particularly valuable in high risk patients. Because nitrous oxide is rapidly excreted by the lungs, pure oxygen must be administered for 5 to 10 minutes following usage of nitrous oxide. Nitrous oxide should not be used during intestinal surgery.

Ophthaine®: See *Proparacaine hydrochloride.*

Pentobarbital sodium *(Nembutal*®), a short-acting injectable anesthetic agent, has effects lasting 30 to 90 minutes. Deep anesthesia causes respiratory and cardiac depression and may also depress kidney function. Pentobarbital should not be used in *cesarean sections* because of extreme neonatal puppy depression. High concentrations of this drug are often used for euthanasia of dogs.

Promace®: See *Acepromazine maleate.*

Proparacaine hydrochloride *(Ophthaine*®) is used topically as a *local anesthetic* in the nose, ear, or eye. Proparacaine hydrochloride does not sting the eye. Onset of anesthesia is rapid, but lasts only approximately 15 minutes.

Robinul-V®: See *Glycopyrrolate.*

Rompun®: See *Xylazine.*

Surital®: See *Thiamylal sodium.*

Telazol® is a non-narcotic, non-barbiturate injectable anesthetic agent composed of a dissociative anesthetic, *tiletamine;* and a tranquilizer, *zolazepam.* Telazol® was recently approved for use in dogs. *Atropine sulfate* is used concurrently to prevent excess salivation. Because Telazol® stimulates the heart rate and cardiac output, it is very useful for minor surgical procedures, restraint, radiography, and in older Cocker Spaniels. The drug is administered intramuscularly. Full recovery should be expected in four hours.

Tetracaine hydrochloride *(Pontocaine*®) is an anesthetic limited to topical usage. It is prepared as a powder for the skin or as a 0.5% solution for use in the eye. The 0.5% solution stings the cornea of the eye without slowing down *corneal ulcer* healing.

Thiamylal sodium *(Surital*®, *Bio-tal*®) is an ultra-short, injectable anesthetic agent used for very short procedures such as radiography or wound suturing, or to allow *tracheal intubation* Surgical anesthesia lasts from 5 to 15 minutes.

Xylazine *(Rompun*®, *Gemini*®) is a non-narcotic sedative and *analgesic* (pain killer). Xylazine produces good muscle relaxation, creating a sleep-like state lasting 30 minutes. However, it can cause severe slowing of the heart rate, respiratory depression, and rarely, a *heart block. Atropine sulfate* is given with xylazine to reduce the side effects on the heart. Xylazine is commonly used as a preanesthetic and as a stimulus for measuring *growth hormone* levels. A dog under the influence of xylazine can still bite!

Xylocaine®: See *Lidocaine hydrochloride.*

ANESTHESIA, TYPES OF: The four methods of anesthesia classified by the area of the body affected are local, regional, topical, and general.

Local anesthesia is the loss of feeling to one specific part of the body.*Lidocaine hydrochloride* or a similar drug, is injected into the area where a nerve supplying that specific part is located. The resulting anesthesia lasts from 45 to 60 minutes. The removal of small tumors and wound suturing is done under local anesthesia.

Regional anesthesia is the loss of sensation to a larger area of the body than with local anesthesia. The most common form is *epidural anesthesia* or *"spinal" anesthesia.* In this procedure, a drug like *lidocaine hydrochloride* is injected into the epidural space around the spinal cord. A loss of sensation occurs in the region behind (or below) the level of the anesthesia. The procedure is useful in anal area surgeries and in *cesarean sections* since the newborn pups are not depressed. The thorax and head must be elevated above the level of the anesthesia injection. If the injected liquid anesthesia gravitates toward the head, respiratory paralysis and death will occur. This form of anesthesia requires a veterinarian who is very familiar with its usage and is adept at the art of its administration.

Topical anesthesia is the loss of sensation to an area of the body surface—either skin, mucous membrane, eye, or ear. Drugs such as *Cetacaine*® *tetracaine,* or *proparacaine* are applied directly to the body surface. Within a few minutes superficial nerves have lost sensation. This anesthesia is useful in the treatment of some painful skin problems, in the control of pain associated with *corneal ulcers,* and in the removal of *foreign bodies* from the *external ear* canal.

General anesthesia or the loss of sensation or awareness to the entire body, is classified into *injectable anesthesia* and *inhalant anesthesia.* A single injectable anesthetic, usually a form of barbituric acid, will create an anesthetic state lasting from five minutes to several hours. Because injectable anesthetics are metabolized by the liver and kidneys, normal hepatic and renal function is essential for safe use of these drugs. The newly approved *dissociative anesthesia, Telazol*® is administered intramuscularly. This drug is appropriate for short procedures and is especially useful in older Cocker Spaniels. Inhalant anesthesia is accomplished when a volatile liquid (one that easily forms a gas in the presence of oxygen) is inhaled causing loss of sensation to the body. The most common volatile anesthetic agents are *methoxyflurane* and *halothane.* Two very new anesthetics that are not yet widely used in veterinary medicine are *enflurane* and *isoflurane.* The veterinarian must weigh the advantages and disadvantages of each agent before deciding how best to utilize them.

ANESTHESIA RECOVERY: Anesthesia recovery is the process of recovering from general anesthesia and the time involved in that recovery. This period varies with the kind of anesthesia used, the size and age of the dog, and the individual idiosyncrasies of the patient. Some recoveries are rather violent. These are lessened by placing the dog in a recovery situation with as little stimuli as possible (e.g. a darkened, quiet environment). The period of freedom from pain on emergence from anesthesia also varies with the kind of anesthesia used and indirectly affects the recovery phase. Generally, injectable anesthetics like *thiamylal sodium* or *sodium pentobarbital* produce longer and more active anesthetic recovery periods than do gas anesthetics like *halothane* or *Metofane*®. Emergence from *Metofane*® takes longer than recovery from halothane.

INTUBATION, ENDOTRACHEAL: When *inhalant anesthetics* are used for *general anesthesia*, an endotracheal tube is usually placed in the trachea (windpipe) to facilitate the administration of the anesthetic-oxygen mixture. Endotracheal tubes can be made of plastic, silicon, or rubber. Placement of the endotracheal tube insures that if the patient vomits, no vomit will enter the respiratory system. The larynx (voice box) is kept open, eliminating the chance of a *laryngospasm* (muscular closing of the laryngeal cartilage preventing air from entering the lungs). An endotracheal tube is necessary in lung or heart surgery because assisted breathing is maintained while the chest cavity is open. Occasionally after the endotracheal tube is removed, hoarseness or coughing is present for a few days but will clear up without medication as the irritation abates. Some endotracheal tubes have cuffs (balloons that blow up around the tube to improve the fit within the trachea) while others fit snugly without cuffs. The latter allows a small amount of anesthesia to escape around the tube when the dog exhales.

SEDATION: Sedation is a mild degree of central nervous system depression in which the dog is awake but calm. Sedative drugs are used to treat fear of thunderstorms and to restraint dogs for procedures such as radiography, anal sac expression, or blood collection.

SURGERY, SECOND OPINIONS PRIOR TO: Seeking a second opinion prior to surgery is much more common today than ten years ago. You have a right to inquire about the expectations of the surgery, the complications anticipated, the cost of the procedure, and the number of similar procedures your veterinarian has done previously. While impossible in emergencies, many procedures can be postponed until a second opinion verifies that the procedure will benefit the patient. A second opinion is unnecessary or unrealistic if the procedure is routine, if you have a long standing, trusting relationship with your veterinarian and he has referred you to specialists in the past, or when the situation is a life-threatening emergency.

SURGERY, STERILE: Absolute sterile surgery eliminates the need for antibacterial agents after the body has been invaded. To achieve sterility, a number of precautions must be taken. All of the surgical instruments and a drape for the area of surgery must be sterilized. Sterilization is accomplished by using high temperature and high pressure as in an autoclave (similar to a pressure cooker), by using a gas like ethylene oxide, or by immersing instruments in an antibacterial solution.

The surgical site must be properly prepared by removing the hair (when possible), scrubbing the area with a germicidal soap, and saturating it with a germicide (*Betadine*® or *Nolvasan*®) The surgeon prepares for surgery by thoroughly scrubbing his arms and fingers with a germicidal soap and by wearing a sterile cap, a mask, gloves, and a gown or scrub suit. Everything used in the surgical procedure must be sterile including the *suture* material and the absorbent gauze sponges. When the entire procedure is carried out with meticulous care, sterile surgery will result.

SURGICAL COMPLICATIONS: Any time an operation is done and anesthesia is used, surgical complications are possible. Fortunately, new anesthetics, new surgical techniques, and skillful surgeons keep complications to a minimum. If the surgical patient is monitored using visual, tactile, or electrical equipment, complications from cardiac and respiratory depression are greatly lessened. In a patient where there is a question about cardiac function and output, use of intravenous fluids to maintain cardiovascular pressure greatly reduces *shock syndromes* both during, and after the procedure. Strict asepsis and judicious use of antibiotics throughout some surgical procedures and recovery(e.g. bowel surgery, bone and joint surgery) greatly reduces post-surgical infection. On rare occasions, post-surgical blood clots (emboli) enter the bloodstream causing fatal results several days after surgery. If the possibility of this problem is anticipated, drugs are used to reduce intravascular clotting. The opposite complication is post-operative hemorrhage. Hemorrhage can occur as a result of poor surgical technique, lack of hemostasis (blood clotting) due to the kind of tissue operated on, or from a clotting defect (e.g. *Von Willebrand's disease* or *hypothyroidism*).

SURGICAL STRESS: Stress is precipitated by both the surgical procedure and the anesthesia. The body attempts to cope with a stressful situation by increasing the secretion of *adrenal corticosteroid hormones* and *epinephrine*. In normal individuals these chemicals are enough to protect the body from the stresses of the procedure. However, in individuals with abnormal immune systems or abnormal adrenal gland function, surgical stress is a very serious problem.

SUTURES: Suture material is classified as absorbable or non-absorbable. The presence of body fluids and chemicals causes absorbable suture material to break down. Non-absorbable suture is not chemically destroyed by the body and lasts for an indefinite period. Different suture materials serve different purposes. For instance, *cat gut suture*, which is absorbable, is useful in tying severed blood vessels, urogenital surgery, and gastrointestinal surgery. However, cat gut is not used on the skin or nerve tissue. The two common types of absorbable suture are surgical gut from the submucosal layer of sheep intestines, (incorrectly called "cat gut") and *polyglycolic acid*, a synthetic absorbable type. Non-absorbable sutures include metals like stainless steel and tantalum, natural sutures like silk and cotton, and synthetic sutures like nylon-braided polyester fiber and polyethylene. Every suture type has its advantages and disadvantages. The veterinary surgeon will use the type and size best suited for the procedure.

TRANQUILIZERS: Tranquilizers are useful in reducing the apprehensive disposition of animals that are being prepared for surgery or are exhibiting fear (such as from thunderstorms). Premedicating surgical patients insures a more stable induction to anesthesia and less excitatory phases on recovery. These drugs are also helpful in radiography and sample collecting for lab procedures. In rare instances, patients react to the normal dose of tranquilizer and remain under its influence for 48 to 72 hours. Extreme drug sensitivity should be mentioned to the veterinarian so that future dosages can be adjusted.

WOUND HEALING: Wounds vary in characteristics as well as location, shape, depth, and degree of infection. The healing process consists of four stages: 1) the inflammation stage, 2) the debridement stage, 3) the repair stage, and 4) the maturation stage. These stages overlap so no exact duration for each exists. Simple tissues, such as connective tissue and fat, heal quickly. Complex tissues, such as the skin and nerves, take much longer. Most simple wounds reach the repair stage of healing by the third to the fifth day after the trauma. The immediate healing phase lasts for over three weeks. The healing wound becomes stronger daily during which time the wound matures and gains strength. The complete healing process may take years.

Many factors affect wound healing. Older dogs wounds heal more slowly. Tissues of obese dogs do not hold sutures well. *Anemia* and *anti-inflammatory drugs* (such as *aspirin*) slow healing. *Steroids* given in medication or released by the body during stress also slow the healing process. Use of *vitamin A* and bandaging speed up healing. *Insulin* is very important to wound healing which explains why *diabetic* dogs have lengthened wound healing times. Temperature, movement of the wound, and radiation also affect the rate of healing. Wounds heal from side to side and not end to end so the length of a wound does not affect the length of the healing time.

BLOOD AND BLOOD FORMING ORGANS

AMERICAN SPANIEL CLUB HEALTH REGISTRY: Thirteen years ago out of a growing concern about hereditary diseases affecting the American Cocker Spaniel and the English Cocker Spaniel, the *American Spaniel Club* established a health registry. The health registrar publishes a compilation of flushing spaniels that have been cleared of one or more of five hereditary disorders: *cataract, progressive retinal atrophy* clotting *Factor X deficiency, hip dysplasia*, and *Von Willebrand's disease* (new in 1988). To obtain the requirements for participation in the registry send your request with a stamped self-addressed envelope to the registrar, Ms. Judith Wright, 2600 Ellsworth Road, Baldwinsville, New York 13027. Membership in the American Spaniel Club is not a requirement for usage of the health registry. Any person interested in the well being of the Cocker Spaniel should consult the registry for information on clear bloodlines and individual dogs. A copy of the annual health registry publication can be purchased from the registrar for $5.00.

ANEMIA: The lack of red blood cells (anemia) is a condition in which the blood is either deficient in hemoglobin within the red blood cell, in the number of red blood cells, or in both. Clinical signs associated with anemia are weakness, loss of consciousness, and pale tongue, gums and lips. The causes of anemia are many and varied generally requiring some lab testing. Commonly performed tests include *hematocrit (packed cell volume), hemoglobin* level, *mean corpuscular volume (MCV), mean corpuscular hemoglobin (MCH), mean corpuscular hemoglobin concentration (MCHC), reticulocyte count, erythrocyte sedimentation rate (ESR)*, *bone marrow biopsy, kidney tests, thyroid test, fecal examination, autoimmune tests (Coombs', ANA, LE Prep)* and *serum iron*.

Three general classes of anemia include less than normal red cell production in response to anemia, increased red cell production but with fewer reaching the circulatory system (rare in dogs), and anemia due to blood loss or blood cell destruction.

Treatment for anemia is directed toward eliminating the underlying cause and when necessary, replacing the lost red blood cells by transfusion. Hereditary hemolytic anemias have been found in several breeds of dogs but to date have not been found in the Cocker Spaniel.

ANEMIA, AUTOIMMUNE HEMOLYTIC (AIHA): Autoimmune hemolytic anemia is an immune-mediated blood disease which occurs by itself (primary or idiopathic) or in association with other diseases or disorders (secondary). A high incidence of AIHA occurs in *systemic lupus erythematosus* and autoimmune *idiopathic thrombocytopenia* (ITP). *Cystitis, pyometra,* and *acute pancreatitis* can be accompanied by autoimmune hemolytic anemia. Some cases also occur following *parvovirus* vaccinations. Cocker Spaniels of all ages and either sex can be affected by this condition. AIHA is frequently found in some bloodlines. Males less than a year old are more likely to be affected while females generally become affected within four years.

Clinical signs of autoimmune hemolytic anemia are fever, *dyspnea* (difficult breathing), staggering, weakness, very pale mucous membranes and tongue, very dark urine, and actual collapse. These signs occur very suddenly. The mortality rate approaches 40%, with a slightly higher death rate for males. The *Coombs' Test* is the most important diagnostic test because it is always positive on either the normal direct test or on the cold agglutinin-type test unless autoagglutination is present. In most cases, the *white blood cell* numbers are elevated.

Conventional treatment involves high doses of *cortisone* or other immunosuppressive drugs (e.g. *azathioprine, Cytoxan*®). A positive response to high doses of *prednisolone* is normally observed within one week. If the *packed cell volume* is not rising within one week, Cytoxan® should be added to the treatment regimen. The entire course of therapy will usually take several months. In rare cases, complete remission takes over a year. Monthly blood counts are necessary as the treatment progresses. In cases with rapidly falling red blood cell levels, *heparin* therapy can be beneficial but remains controversial due to potential bleeding crises. Use of *cyclosporine* (*Sandimmune*® from Sandoz, Inc.) has also reversed some hopeless cases. Removal of the *spleen* is only done as a last resort. With early aggressive therapy, the prognosis is fair to good. However, in those Cockers presented for treatment when the packed cell volume of red blood cells is less than 10 per cent and the *reticulocyte count* production index is less than 2.5, the prognosis is poor.

BIOPSY, BONE MARROW: A bone marrow biopsy provides information on the kinds and numbers of cells present in the bone marrow. In dogs, the iliac crest (hip bone) is the most common site for the removal of marrow material. *Sedation* and *local anesthesia* infiltration of the subcutis and the area around the bone is necessary. Sterile technique is important. Biopsies done at three or four day intervals allow the evaluation of the production and maturation of cell types. Although some danger exists in performing a bone marrow biopsy, the knowledge gained provides important information.

BLEEDING DISORDERS: Hemorrhage can result from a local lesion like a damaged blood vessel that allows blood to escape. A defect in the general clotting mechanism in the body can also contribute. The following three functions are necessary for blood clotting. In the vascular function, injury to a blood vessel causes a local reflex action which contributes to reducing blood loss. During the platelet function, the platelet cell components within the bloodstream are attracted to the site of bleeding. There they release their contents plugging the site of blood loss in the blood vessel. The coagulation function is the stimulation of a systemic effect by releasing and activating various factors associated with clot formation. Defects in any of these three mechanisms lead to blood loss. Causes of defects include lack of bone marrow activity, cancer of the bone marrow, lack of platelets for various reasons, *vitamin deficiency*, severe *liver disease*, poisons like *warfarin*, and numerous inherited coagulation defects. In the Cocker Spaniel, *Factor X deficiency, hemophilia A, hemophilia B*, and*Von Willebrand's disease (VWD)* are the most important inherited coagulation disorders. Refer to each topic individually for a more in depth discussion.

Treatment of bleeding disorders involves identifying and treating the source when possible and eliminating the cause. Whole *blood transfusions* are usually needed. Determining the *blood type* is necessary because multiple transfusions are required throughout the life of a dog with an inherited coagulation defect. If *vitamin K deficiencies* or *warfarin poisoning* are present, *vitamin K* must be administered orally or by injection. If a life-long coagulation defect is discovered, the dog's environment must be modified to minimize accidental injuries that could cause serious bleeding problems. Padded housing surrounded by a smooth wire fence is preferable. The elimination of all parasites, both internal and external, is important. The dog should be fed a soft diet with no bones that might irritate the gums or GI tract. Special precautions should be taken with the use of modified live vaccines and drugs like *aspirin* or *Banamine*® which affect blood coagulation. Under no circumstances should Cocker Spaniels that show clinical signs of blood coagulation disorders be bred.

BLOOD TYPES: A number of blood types and factors that affect the compatibility of one dog's blood to another have been identified. Some confusion exists in the naming of these antigens. They have been assigned the letter names A, B, C, etc. combined with numbers 1, 2, 3, etc. The A antigen is the most important in the alphabetical nomenclature. Of the eight identified numerical antigens, canine erythrocyte antigens (CEA) 1, 2, and 7 are the most important. CEA-1 and CEA-2 are thought to be inherited through a dominant gene. The most desirable blood types for donor dogs are negative CEA-1, CEA-2, and CEA-7 or A negative typing.

BONE MARROW: All of the cell types found in the blood stream are produced by the bone marrow of most bones in the dog's body. The cell types include *leukocytes* (white blood cells), *erythrocytes* (red blood cells), and *thrombocytes* (platelets). Various stages in the development or maturation of these cell types are distinguished on smears of bone marrow material. Abnormalities observed in bone marrow cells give important answers about causes of *anemia, leukemia*, and some *coagulation disorders*.

CHRISTMAS DISEASE: *Hemophilia B* or Christmas disease is a rare sex-linked clotting deficiency observed in parti-colored Cocker Spaniels. Because it is sex-linked, only males are clinically affected. Females carry the defective gene attached to the X sex chromosome. *Clotting factor IX* is deficient. Bleeding episodes are usually severe preventing a normal life for the Cocker. The usual screening tests produce results identical to those of *classic hemophilia*. The *bleeding time* and *one-stage prothrombin time* (*OSPT*) tests are normal and the *APTT* and *ACT* tests are prolonged. Only by identifying a diminished level of *Factor IX* can this be distinguished from *hemophilia A* (classic hemophilia).

COAGULATION DISORDERS, INHERITED: Eight inherited coagulation disorders have been found in dogs. All of these disorders can occur in the Cocker Spaniel. More complete discussion is found under each individual deficiency.

Factor VII deficiency
Factor VIII deficiency (hemophilia A, classic hemophilia)
Factor IX deficiency (hemophilia B, Christmas disease)
Factor X deficiency
Factor XI deficiency
Von Willebrand's Disease
Prothrombin complex deficiency
Fibrinogen deficiency

COMPLETE BLOOD COUNT (CBC): A complete blood count is comprised of a *packed cell volume* (*PCV* or *hematocrit*), *WBC* (*white blood cell count*), and a *differential cell determination*. Blood cell counts determine the amount or number of red and white blood cells. The type and morphology of red cells, white cells, and platelets are determined from the differential part of the count. The counts can be determined by hand or with a Coulter counter.

FACTOR VII DEFICIENCY: Factor VII deficiency is a minor coagulation defect. It is linked to an increased susceptibility to generalized *demodectic mange*.

FACTOR VIII DEFICIENCY: Factor VIII deficiency is present in both *hemophilia A* (*classic hemophilia*) and in *Von Willebrand's disease* See *HEMOPHILIA, CLASSIC* and *VON WILLEBRAND'S DISEASE* for discussion on Factor VIII deficiency as it relates to both diseases.

FACTOR IX DEFICIENCY: Factor IX deficiency causes a rare form of hemophilia called *hemophilia B* or *Christmas Disease*. See *CHRISTMAS DISEASE.*

FACTOR X DEFICIENCY: Factor X deficiency also called *Stuart factor deficiency* is a relatively uncommon clotting disorder that is found mostly in buff colored Cocker Spaniels. It is inherited as an autosomal, incomplete dominant gene with both sexes equally affected. Puppies are more severely affected than older dogs. Those individuals inheriting a very low level (around 5%) of Factor X from both carrier parents will not survive. If the disease is inherited from one parent, the affected puppy can be either a carrier and not clinically affected or mildly to moderately affected by an increased bleeding tendency.

All Cocker Spaniels used for breeding should be tested for Factor X deficiency. Factor X deficiency and *Von Willebrand's disease* testing can be done on specially collected blood samples taken by your veterinarian and shipped on dry ice to the Veterinary Hematology Laboratory—Wadsworth Center for Laboratories and

Research, New York State Department of Health, Empire State Plaza, Albany, NY 12201. Other labs exist that have similar capabilities. However, all results should be verified by the Veterinary Hematology Laboratory in Albany, New York.

Cockers with normal Factor X levels (from 80% to 175%) can be bred without restriction. Dogs with low normal levels (70% to 79%) which could mean a carrier state should only be bred to Factor X normal mates. All offspring of such a breeding should be tested for Factor X levels. All clinically affected dogs and carriers below 70% should not be bred under any circumstances.

FACTOR XI DEFICIENCY: Factor XI deficiency, most commonly found in working and sporting dogs, is transmitted through an incomplete dominant gene.

FIBRINOGEN DEFICIENCY: Fibrinogen deficiency is a rare clotting dyscrasia that is inherited as a autosomal incomplete dominant gene. All clotting test times are prolonged.

HEMOPHILIA A: See *HEMOPHILIA, CLASSIC* and *FACTOR VIII DEFICIENCY*.

HEMOPHILIA B: See *CHRISTMAS DISEASE* and *FACTOR IX DEFICIENCY*.

HEMOPHILIA, CLASSIC: *Classic hemophilia* or *hemophilia A* is caused by a sex-linked, recessive gene resulting in a Factor VIII deficiency. Hemophilia A, the most common coagulation defect in all dogs, is identical to the disease in humans. Females carry the genetic defect on the X sex chromosome but remain unaffected. The affected male Cocker shows an increased tendency to hemorrhage because of poor clotting. The severity of the bleeding predisposition varies greatly.

Screening for hemophilia A is done by measuring the *bleeding time* and the *one-stage prothrombin time, (OSPT)*, which are normal and the *activated partial thromboplastin time (APTT)* and *activated coagulation time (ACT)* which are prolonged. Normal numbers of blood *platelets* are present. A definitive test for classic hemophilia measures Factor VIII activity. Normal levels range from 50 to 200%. Affected males measure about 5% while carrier females have a Factor VIII level under 50% This test is about 90% accurate. Cockers with hemophilia A test normal or above for *Von Willebrand's factor*.

To decrease the incidence of hemophilia A, no affected male dogs should be bred. However, clinically normal males from carrier females can be bred since they do not carry the abnormal bleeding gene. Females from carrier mothers should only be breed to normal males with several generations of clear breeding behind them.

Attempting to maintain a Cocker Spaniel showing clinical signs of *hemophilia A* is very difficult. Only very special homes are able to provide all of the extra care and attention necessary to maintain a hemophiliac. All furniture must be cushioned. The diet must be soft and contain no bones. There should be no other animals in the household to prevent accidental bites or scratches.

LEUKOCYTOSIS: Leukocytosis is an increase in the number of white blood cells in the blood stream. The five different kinds of white blood cells are *neutrophils, eosinophils, basophils, lymphocytes,* and *monocytes.* Any or all of the types may increase in numbers. Knowing which kind of cell has increased and the degree of change is important information.

LEUKOPENIA: A decrease in the number of *white blood cells* in the blood is called leukopenia. The kind and amount of decrease provides important information in determining the cause and treatment of disease processes.

LYAGLUTIN 8 V TEST KIT: Recently, an in-office rapid screening test has been marketed. Information on the *Lyaglutin 8 V test kit* can be obtained from Hemochek Corporation, P.O. Box 15028, Gainesville, Florida 32604. In office VWD screening should be compared to results on VWD testing media developed by Dr. Dodds' laboratory.

POISONING, WARFARIN: Warfarin poisoning is the most common kind of acquired blood coagulation disorder. Warfarin and related compounds (*diphacinone* and *pindone*) are the active ingredients in most rodent poisons. The action mechanism of warfarin inhibits the production of *vitamin K dependent factors* (*VII, II, X, IX*) in the liver causing clotting defects. The degree of bleeding ranges from slight to fatal. The antidote is *vitamin K* and any other support needed to restore normal vascular function. See *WARFARIN POISONING* in Chapter 9 for additional discussion.

POLYCYTHEMIA: This increase in the number of red blood cells, the opposite of *anemia*, is either due to a physiological reaction or a disease process.

PROTHROMBIN COMPLEX DEFICIENCY: *Factor II deficiency* or prothrombin complex deficiency causes mild neonatal bleeding in dogs. This deficiency is transmitted as an autosomal dominant gene. It is not too important as a clotting deficiency.

RED BLOOD CELLS (RBC): Red blood cells carry oxygen in the form of hemoglobin to all of the body tissues. These cells are primarily produced in the *bone marrow.* However, when there are not enough circulating red cells to provide for normal oxygen needs, they are also produced in the *spleen.* The stimulation of red blood cell production is influenced by nutrition (*iron, copper, cobalt, vitamins*), and the *hormones* sex, thyroid, adrenal, pituitary, and *erythropoietin* which regulates the production of erythrocytes (RBC's).

SPLEEN: The spleen, a large ductless organ closely associated with the stomach, lies along the greater curvature of the stomach. Its function is related to the destruction of red blood cells. It is, however, able to store red blood cells and release them into the circulation during times of stress. During the *acute gastric dilatation* (*bloat*) *syndrome*, the spleen may undergo *torsion* (twisting) further complicating the seriousness of that condition. The spleen is the primary site of the *hemangiosarcoma tumor.* Life without a spleen can be relatively normal. Reasons to remove a spleen surgically include splenic tumors, trauma to the spleen, *gastric torsion*, twisting of the blood vessels to the spleen associated with gastric torsion (*volvulus*), and as a last resort to reverse the affects of *autoimmune hemolytic anemia*

STUART FACTOR DEFICIENCY: See *FACTOR X DEFICIENCY.*

TESTS TO EVALUATE CLOTTING DEFECTS: With such a variety of clotting defects, the use of sophisticated tests is necessary to establish the exact cause. A list of tests necessary to diagnose these defects includes *partial thromboplastin time (PTT)*, *activated partial thromboplastin time (APTT)*, *activated coagulation time (ACT)*, *Lee White clotting time, one-stage prothrombin time (OSPT)*, *PF3 release test, autoimmune panel (Coombs' Test, LE Prep, antinuclear antibody test (ANA), Von Willebrand's factor*testing and Factors VIII, IX, and X tests from the Veterinary Hematology Laboratory in Albany, New York. The *toenail cutting bleeding time test* is the most valuable clotting time test in veterinary offices.

THROMBOCYTOPENIA, IDIOPATHIC (ITP): Idiopathic thrombocytopenia purpura is defined as a decrease in the number of blood *platelets* . The cause is unknown. Females are affected more frequently than males. The many pathological states causing ITP include *estrogen toxicity* , *bone marrow* depression, viral diseases, and reactions to drug therapy.

The most common clinical signs are pinpoint hemorrhage on the gums and varying sizes of hemorrhagic spots on the skin which look like red-purple blotches or bruises. The stools from affected dogs are very black. Red blood may be seen in the urine. Weakness and depression are observed in many cases.

Lab tests show less than 10,000 platelets during bleeding episodes. Most dogs have a *regenerative anemia* during the course of the disease. Tests for *immune-mediated anemias* are not generally positive. Only weak *ANA* positive tests are seen and rarely positive *Coombs' tests* occur. *Platelet factor 3(PF3)* is only positive about 25% of the time.

Treatment is variable in its response. Initially, *cortisone* is most commonly used. When necessary, this is followed by *vincristine* or *vinblastine* to stimulate *thrombocyte (platelet)* production. Removal of the *spleen* does not reduce the chance of recurrence. Because of the variable course of the disease, the long term prognosis is difficult to determine. In most cases, treatment will be necessary on an intermittent basis for the life of the dog.

TRANSFUSION, BLOOD: From time to time, canine blood transfusions are necessary. They should be considered when the red blood cell volume is greatly decreased. A decrease occurs rapidly in traumatic blood loss or gradually where blood cell production is impaired. A transfusion is necessary when the total packed red blood cell volume is less than 15%. A single transfusion can be done without crossmatching or worry of a reaction. However, if the potential for multiple transfusions exists, the donor and recipient should be crossmatched to ensure compatibility.

At least eight different factors exist in a dog's blood. Three of these are important in transfusion reactions: canine erythrocyte antigen 1 or (CEA–1), CEA–2, and to some degree CEA–7. Ideally, permanent canine blood donors should be CEA–1, CEA–2, and CEA–7 negative. Dogs can donate blood as frequently as every 7 to 10 days, but an interval of 14 to 21 days is probably best if long term collection is anticipated.

VITAMIN K DEFICIENCY: Vitamin K is essential for proper blood clotting. Deficiencies in vitamin K occur in diseases that cause bile duct obstruction, in diseases where food is not absorbed properly, or in cases where antibiotics have been administered for long periods of time decreasing the bacterial synthesis of this vitamin. Vitamin K is necessary for the production of clotting *Factors II, VII, IX*, and *X* in the liver. Supplemental vitamin K is given orally three times daily or by injection as needed until bleeding tendencies cease. The most active form of vitamin K is K_1 or *phytonadione (AquaMEPHYTON®)*. Response to this form of therapy is evident in 30 to 60 minutes as witnessed by a decrease in hemorrhage.

VON WILLEBRAND'S DISEASE (VWD): Von Willebrand's disease is an inherited coagulation disorder caused by a deficiency of *Factor VIII* and low levels of *Factor VIII related antigen (Von Willebrand's factor)*. Both factors are necessary for proper blood clotting. Von Willebrand's disease is more severe in young Cocker Spaniels and actually diminishes in severity with age. While the incidence of the disease can be high, the mortality rate is rather low. The possible connection to *hypothyroidism* is not currently clear. Those dogs simultaneously affected with hypothyroidism and Von Willebrand's disease have fewer clotting problems if the thyroid levels are brought up to normal with thyroid medication.

The *toenail bleeding time test* which is prolonged is the easiest VWD screening test for a veterinarian to perform. While normal bleeding time varies from 3 seconds to 3 minutes, VWD bleeding times may approach 30 minutes. Definitive testing for *Von Willebrand's factor* and *Factor VIII* is best done at the Veterinary Hematology Laboratory—Wadsworth Center for Laboratories and Research, New York State Dept. of Health, Empire State Plaza, Albany, New York 12201. This lab was formerly administered by Dr. Jean Dodds. Contact the lab for instructions on the method of collecting and freezing the necessary plasma for these tests. Other labs have similar capabilities but the results should be verified with the New York laboratory. An office test kit for VWD, the *Lyaglutin 8 V Test* Kit, was marketed in 1987. Kit results should be checked by the New York lab.

Normal levels of *Factor VIII related antigen (Von Willebrand's factor)* range from 60 to 172%. Cocker Spaniels within these limits can be safely bred. Factor VIII related antigen levels from 50 to 59% are difficult to interpret as they may be borderline normal or carrier dogs. A Cocker within this range should only be bred to Von Willebrand normal dogs. All offspring from this breeding should be tested. Cocker Spaniels with a Factor VIII related antigen level below 50% should only be bred if the dog is not clinically affected with the disease, and then only to VWD normal mates. All offspring should be tested. Under no circumstances should clinically affected Cockers be bred. Puppies from questionable breedings should be tested at 10 weeks of age to determine the level of Factor VIII related antigen (Von Willebrand's factor).

Treatment of *VWD* involves replacing the defective blood elements (platelet function factor and Factor VIII). Transfusion with fresh-frozen plasma will replace the Factor VIII material The platelet function defect can be corrected temporarily by a transfusion of whole blood.

WHITE BLOOD CELL (WBC): Five different cells circulating in the bloodstream are classified as white blood cells (*leukocytes*). Each has a specific function in the body. *Neutrophils* function in the body defense system by engulfing and destroying foreign substances like bacteria. *Eosinophils* increase in inflammatory reactions caused by *parasitic infestations*, *allergies*, and respiratory diseases. *Basophils*, very rare in circulating blood, play a role in the maintenance of the inflammatory reaction. *Monocytes* are important cells in the immune response and in engulfing those particles larger than the neutrophil can handle. Increased numbers of monocytes are seen in *systemic fungal infections* and in chronic infections. Two types of *lymphocytes*, T and B cells, are very important in the development of immunity. These cells have diverse origins and promote different types of immunity.

CARDIOPULMONARY SYSTEM

CANCER, LUNG: *Primary lung tumors*, those that originate in the lung, are uncommon in dogs. Most of these tumors are malignant with a poor prognosis. Dogs older than ten years are most likely affected by this type of cancer. Two forms of *adenocarcinoma* are the most common lung cancers. *Squamous cell carcinoma* of the lung also occurs metastasizing (spreading) very early.

Malignant tumors from other parts of the body commonly spread to the lungs. These tumors may reach the lungs by the blood stream, through the lymph system, or from extension from adjacent tissue. Sometimes the lungs do not become involved until months after tumors are removed from other parts of the body, indicating that small tumor seeds remained in the body after tumor removal.

The common clinical signs of both primary lung cancer and metastatic tumors are *coughing* and *dyspnea*. The severity of the signs depends on the magnitude of the tumor involvement and the degree of mechanical blockage of the airway. The diagnosis of these forms of lung disease is usually made with a physical examination and chest radiographs.

The usual forms of cancer therapy, (chemotherapy, surgery, and radiation therapy) are generally not done in canine lung tumors. However, if some type of treatment is desired, your veterinarian can refer you to a veterinary oncologist for the available options. In most cases of lung cancer, the prognosis is grave.

CARDIOMYOPATHY, CONGESTIVE: The cause of congestive cardiomyopathy is unknown but has been seen as a familial disorder in the English Cocker Spaniel. Cardiomyopathy results in severe degenerative changes in the heart muscle which drastically affect the ability of the heart to pump blood. The first sign is a sudden severe congestive heart failure syndrome. Clinically, either left, right, or generalized heart failure can be observed. The heart beats as fast as 250 times per minute. Sometimes changes in the kidney and liver result from cardiomyopathy. In a number of these cases, the dog is also drastically *hypothyroid*. The significance of concurrent hypothyroidism is not yet clear.

Congestive cardiomyopathy is diagnosed most commonly in young to middle-aged dogs of either sex. Treatment involves the use of low salt diets, oral diuretics, and *digoxin* to slow the heart's electrical conduction. See Heart Diet and H/D® in Chapter 8. The patient should be carefully examined by your veterinarian every one to three months. The prognosis is guarded to poor because the life expectancy varies from days to years.

CARDIOMYOPATHY, HYPERTROPHIC: Hypertrophic cardiomyopathy affects the left ventricle of the heart and occasionally the muscular wall (septum) between the left and right ventricle. The cardiac muscle enlarges making it very inflexible. Many times no clinical signs are observed. Sudden death, especially while the dog is under *general anesthesia* may be the only indication. Sometimes *ECG* tracings indicate abnormal thickening of the ventricular heart muscle. Radiographs indicate left side cardiac enlargement. Treatment can be attempted if the condition is diagnosed. However, use of *digoxin* is contraindicated with a poor prognosis. *Verapamil* and *propranolol* might help in treating the disease.

COUGH: A cough is a reflex action that originates somewhere in the respiratory system. Causes include throat irritation, postnasal drip, swollen lymph nodes, tumors, tracheal (windpipe) collapse, infections of the windpipe (See *TRACHEOBRONCHITIS.*), *heartworm disease*, and *pulmonary edema* from left side *heart failure*. A complete medical history is important when determining the exact cause of a cough. Unless the reason is as obvious as *kennel cough*, testing is necessary to define the problem. A minimum data base includes a *heartworm test*, *CBC*, *fecal examination*, *thoracic radiographs*, and *serum tests*. When necessary, more extensive tests like *bronchography*, pulmonary function tests, ECG, and radioisotope lung scanning can be performed by specialists or at large hospital facilities.

DISCHARGE, NASAL: Nasal discharge can involve one or both nostrils. The discharge is classified as either acute or chronic depending on the length of time it has been present. The nature of the discharge helps to identify the cause. Clear discharge is caused by *allergy*, viral infection, or sometimes foreign particles like dust. Cloudy or pus discharges result from infection, foreign bodies in the nasal cavity, or cancer. Bloody nasal discharge (*epistaxis*) is due to infection, trauma, *clotting disorders*, or cancer. Cancer or foreign bodies are more likely causes if the discharge is from only one nostril. A bilateral discharge (from both nostrils) can come from anywhere in the respiratory system. Causes include clotting disorders, generalized infections, and cancers involving both sides of the nasal septum. The cause of a nasal discharge can be diagnosed by performing a number of tests including radiographs, a *complete blood count*, a chem-panel, and a clotting deficiency profile. Once the diagnosis is made, the cause is eliminated through surgery, antibiotics, or other means of therapy.

DYSPLASIA, MITRAL VALVE: Mitral valve dysplasia is the most common *heart defect* found in Cocker Spaniels. A loud harsh heart murmur is heard in the lower left chest area. No correlation exists between the loudness of the murmur and the severity of the heart valve disease. Both the upper left heart chamber (atrium) and the lower left chamber (*ventricle*) enlarge as the disease progresses. Eventually, the lungs fill with fluid (*pulmonary edema*) resulting in *congestive heart failure*. The most common cause of *mitral valve dysplasia* is fibrosis from some unknown cause. Treatment is symptomatic. The prognosis is fair to poor.

DYSPLASIA, TRICUSPID VALVE: In Cocker Spaniels, tricuspid valve dysplasia is an acquired heart disorder. In larger breeds, the disease is congenital. The right side of the heart (atrium and ventricle) enlarges resulting in a loud, harsh heart murmur heard about mid-thorax. It is not unusual to find *tricuspid valve dysplasia* occurring concomitantly with *mitral valve dysplasia* in middle-aged Cocker Spaniels. Thoracic radiographs show enlargement of the right side of the heart. Electrocardiography will verify right heart involvement. Control of progressive heart failure is very difficult and not very effective.

DYSPNEA: By definition, dyspnea is difficult or labored breathing. Determining in which phase breathing difficulty occurs—while breathing in, breathing out, or all of the time—is important in identifying the cause. Some breeds of dogs with short noses (brachycephalic breeds) commonly have a difficult time with both *inspiration* (breathing in) and *expiration* (breathing out). In general, inspiratory dyspnea occurs in diseases of the upper respiratory system, with fluid accumulation in the thoracic cavity, or with blockage of the trachea. If the breathing difficulty is related to expiration, the problem may involve the lungs. The causes of both inspiratory and expiratory difficulty are chronic bronchitis, *heart disease*, and the presence of tumors in the chest cavity.

EDEMA, PULMONARY: An accumulation of fluid in the lungs is called pulmonary edema. This fluid build-up occurs in the lung tissue or in the terminal spaces of the respiratory apparatus. The common clinical signs include *dyspnea*, *cyanosis*, abnormal lung sounds, and *coughing*. Common causes of edema are *insect bite* hypersensitivity, *drug hypersensitivity*, *chronic heart failure* syndrome, trauma, water in the lungs from drowning, and *electrical shock*. Therapy for pulmonary edema includes cage rest, oxygen administration, use of diuretics to remove interstitial fluid, appropriate cardiac medications if the heart is involved, bronchodilation, and the insertion of an *endotracheal catheter* (tube). With early treatment, pulmonary edema has a good prognosis.

ENDOCARDITIS: Endocarditis is a serious systemic disease which is caused by common bacteria that infect the valves of the heart or inner lining of the heart wall. The most common kinds of bacteria causing this condition are *Staphylococcus*, *Streptococcus* and several gram negative bacteria including *Escherichia coli* and *Pseudomonas aeruginosa*. Male dogs older than four years that have had surgery, IV catheters, immunosuppressive (*cortisone*) therapy, or antibiotic therapy are predisposed to develop endocarditis. The clinical signs are many and diverse. Murmurs and an increased heart rate signal heart involvement. Occasionally signs of *congestive heart failure* are observed as the heart muscle increases in size and fails. A number of signs not related to the heart are seen with endocarditis including chills (fever), lameness, stiffness, depression, and *seizures*.

Proving the presence of bacteria that cause endocarditis is very difficult. Multiple *cultures* from blood or other body fluids are needed. *Echocardiography*, while extremely useful in helping to define the problem, requires equipment not readily available to general veterinary practitioners. This testing must then be done at university settings or veterinary cardiology specialty practices.

Therapy includes very high doses of antibiotics for extended periods of time—at least 5 or 6 weeks. Generally, the initial antibiotics are given by injection or by a combination of injection and oral administration. Sometimes additional supportive therapy is needed. Frequent reexamination is necessary to insure complete elimination of the causative organism.

FLAIL CHEST: The flail chest or flail segment is a life-threatening problem resulting from a car accident or a large dog grabbing a small dog over the chest. In this condition, one or more ribs are broken in two or more places allowing the chest wall to move in and out in an exaggerated manner. On *inspiration*, the fractured segment of the chest is sucked in creating trauma to the lungs and other thoracic structures. On *expiration*, the lungs are blown out against the fractured segment causing hemorrhage and lacerations.

The dog experiences much pain and a great deal of *dyspnea*. Temporary stability may be gained by placing the dog on its side with the fractured ribs DOWN. Immediate veterinary attention is essential. The fracture must be stabilized and any lung contusions treated. Many times, *local anesthesia* is used when stabilizing the fracture. However, if bone pins or wires are needed, *general anesthesia* and positive ventilation from a respirator are necessary.

FUNGI, SYSTEMIC: *Blastomycosis*, a systemic fungal disease caused by *Blastomyces dermatitidis*, is naturally found in the eastern United States, especially the areas drained by river systems. While blastomycosis initially infects the lungs, other tissues of the skin, bones, and eyes are soon affected. The disease is not contagious to other dogs or humans. Thoracic radiographs, direct smears from the skin, and serological tests for increased blastomycosis titer are used to diagnose the condition. Currently, the only approved treatment is *amphotericin B (Fungizone*®, Solvay), a drug that can produce fatal kidney toxicity. Renal function must be continually evaluated during the 6–8 weeks of treatment. If bones are involved, the length of treatment is considerably longer.

Recently, a new antifungal drug, *ketoconazole (Nizoral*®, Janssen Pharmaceutical), has shown promise in the treatment of systemic fungal diseases in dogs. When administered orally, the drug appears to be much less toxic than amphotericin B. However, ketoconazole has been associated with sterility in male dogs. Although no standard dosage has been established, a range of 10 to 30 mg per kilogram three times daily for two to six months is effective. Because ketoconazole is expensive, a definitive diagnosis should be made before treatment is initiated.

Coccidioidomycosis (Valley Fever) is a systemic fungal disease that occurs in the southwest United States, Mexico, and Central America. Valley Fever is not a contagious disease. This fungus found in dry, dusty soils infects dogs when they dig in the dirt.

Two clinical forms of the disease are recognized. The pulmonic form causes coughing and respiratory distress and the disseminated form affects the bones and other body tissues. Dogs with the disseminated form have fevers up to 106° F, weight loss, decreased appetite, and diarrhea. Affected long bones commonly appear swollen or thickened. In rare cases, the neurological system is affected causing *lack of coordination*. The prognosis is guarded to poor depending on the degree of involvement and amount of dissemination to bone tissue. If treatment is attempted, the same drugs are used as for blastomycosis therapy.

Cryptococcosis is a noncontagious systemic fungal disease that affects the lungs, central nervous system, skin, or eyes. This disease is spread in pigeon and other bird droppings. The clinical signs are extremely variable. Many times respiratory signs are not apparent. When the central nervous system and eyes are involved, more dramatic symptoms appear. The prognosis is guarded to poor depending on the degree of involvement. The use of *amphotericin B* or *ketoconazole* could be attempted.

Histoplasmosis is also a noncontagious systemic fungal disease caused by *Histoplasma capsulatum*. This is common in the United States east of the Mississippi River, especially several areas in the Ohio River Valley. The fungal spores are found in soil contaminated with bird droppings. The forms of the disease which occur in dogs are the pulmonary and intestinal forms. Dogs with advanced cases of this disease have high fevers, intractable diarrheas and emaciation. Dogs also experience *dyspnea* and *coughing* with lung involvement. Again, the prognosis is guarded to poor. The treatment is similar to other systemic fungi therapy.

Aspergillosis is a fungal disease classified with the other fungal diseases although it is confined to the upper respiratory tract. A mucus nasal discharge from one or both nostrils, sneezing, and snorting are signs associated with this condition. Very few dogs will show signs of systemic involvement such as loss of appetite and depression. No nasal swelling is apparent. The diagnosis of aspergillosis is made with a *fungal culture* (one week is necessary for growth) or a serological test. A specific serum test for aspergillosis can be run by the Clinical Immunology Laboratory, Veterinary Hospital of the University of Pennsylvania, 3850 Spruce Street, Philadelphia, PA 19104. A 3 ml serum sample is required.

Four types of therapy are available for aspergillosis: 1) the use of *povidone-iodine* (1:10) or *thiabendazole* nasal flushes, 2) systemic therapy with thiabendazole 20 mg/kg/day or *ketoconazole* 10 mg/kg daily for six weeks, 3) surgical debridement of the diseased bone in dogs with nasal turbinate bone involvement and flushing with thiabendazole and 4) the use of immune stimulants. Appropriate therapy over a period of time may justify a fair to good prognosis.

HEART ATTACK: See *HEART FAILURE.*

HEART BASE TUMOR: See *TUMOR, HEART BASE.*

HEART BLOCK, AV: The letters AV represent the atrial (upper) and ventricular (lower) compartments of the heart. Normally, electrical impulses are carried down from the atria through the heart muscle wall into the ventricle, causing the heart muscle to contract and pump blood. An *AV heart block* is a disruption of the electrical impulse so that rhythmic sequential contractions fail to occur some or all of the time.

Three degrees of AV heart blocks are recognized. First degree blocks occur in *cardiomyopathy* from the use of drugs like *digitalis* and *xylazine* and from the administration of the anticancer drug *Adriamycin*®. Second degree heart blocks occur normally in some dogs and also in cardiomyopathy patients. Third degree heart blocks or complete blockages of the electrical impulses occur in cardiomyopathy, cancer, and infections involving the inner lining of the heart (See *ENDOCARDITIS*.).

AV heart block is first treated with a drug like *atropine*. If the problem is not resolved or becomes chronic, the patient may require a *pacemaker* to maintain proper cardiac electrical impulses.

HEART DISEASE, CONGENITAL: Congenital heart disease is an abnormality of the heart present at birth. Eight separate conditions are considered to be congenital in nature. A number are also hereditary. The presence of a *heart murmur* is common to all eight conditions. However, many normal puppies prior to reaching six months may also have an *innocent heart murmur*. If a murmur is detected in a puppy, a veterinary cardiologist should examine the dog thoroughly to determine whether the murmur is innocent or organic. Most general veterinary practitioners do not possess the skills necessary to differentiate between these two conditions. The following is a list of eight congenital heart problems.

• Atrial septal defect (ASD)	Rare
• Mitral Valve Dysplasia	More males
• Patent Ductus Arteriosus (PDA)	More females, Hereditary
• Pulmonic Stenosis	Hereditary
• Subaortic Stenosis (SAS)	Hereditary
• Tetralogy of Fallot	Hereditary
• Tricuspid Valve Dysplasia	More Males
• Ventricular Septal Defect (VSD)	May correct itself by one year of age

HEART FAILURE: Heart failure or *"heart attack"* may occur very suddenly or over a period of time. In sudden cases no cardinal signs of heart disease are seen. A disruption in the electrical impulses carried through the heart muscle is known as a *heart block* which causes heart failure. A sudden lack of blood to the arteries supplying the heart muscle is also a cause. Chronic heart failure is due to partial heart blocks or diminished heart muscle blood supply.

If *heart failure* occurs over a period of time, cardinal signs of heart disease such as coughing, fluid in the chest and/or abdomen, loss of consciousness, bluish tongue color, and fatigue are seen. Prompt treatment may delay death from chronic heart failure. In the case of *heartworm disease*, treatment can be curative.

HEART MURMUR: A heart murmur is heard during a normally quiet period of the heart contraction cycle. These vibrations provide information about the cause and location of heart lesions. Heart murmurs are classified by the time that they occur in the cycle, by the loudness of the murmur, by the place on the chest wall where they are most plainly heard, and by their intensity.

Generally, heart murmurs are described as *functional* and *organic*. Functional murmurs may or may not be due to a disease process. *Innocent murmurs* are a functional type with no underlying disease. *Organic murmurs* are always due to some form of heart disease occurring continually during both the contraction phase and the relaxation phase of the cardiac cycle. The use of murmur determination is important in the identification of cardiac diseases, especially in young animals where congenital heart problems are suspected.

HEART MURMUR, INNOCENT: In a puppy less than six months of age, a murmur is not an abnormal sound when other associated tests (ECG and thoracic radiographs) are normal. The innocent murmur is heard early-to-mid-systolic in the contraction cycle and is very short in duration. These functional murmurs require no treatment or further diagnosis.

HEARTWORM DISEASE: Canine heartworm disease is caused by a filarial worm called *Dirofilaria immitis*. One of several varieties of mosquitoes is necessary for completion of the heartworm life cycle. The heartworm has an affinity for the right side of the dog's cardiovascular system (posterior vena cava, right ventricle, and pulmonary artery). The earliest sign of heartworm disease is a soft cough. In advanced heartworm disease, the signs are those of *heart failure*.

Caval syndrome is a very advanced form in which the accumulation of worms is so great that death occurs rapidly. Both male and female heartworms exist; the presence of their offspring (*microfilaria*) in the bloodstream is the basis for many heartworm tests.

Another filarial worm affects dogs in the United States. *Dipetalonema reconditum* is a parasite that exists asymptomatically under the skin producing microfilaria offspring. Expert clinicians can microscopically differentiate between Dirofilaria and Dipetalonema microfilaria.

Occult heartworm disease occurs in a small percentage of heartworm patients. In these cases, no circulating microfilaria exist. The diagnosis of this form of heartworm disease must be made from immunological blood tests, radiography, and clinical signs. A dog living in a region with a high incidence of heartworm disease that is not receiving heartworm preventive medication and is showing signs of heartworm disease should undergo the above tests. Heartworm preventive drugs are given only after a negative blood test since the presence of both microfilaria and preventive medication in the blood stream simultaneously can cause a fatal shock-like syndrome.

Currently, only two preventive medications are approved—*diethylcarbamazine citrate* (*DEC*) and *ivermectin* marketed by Merck Co. as *Heartgard 30*®. The DEC is given every day from one month before the start of mosquito season to six weeks after the mosquito season ends in the northern United States. Warmer climates require year around preventive medication. Ivermectin is given once monthly through the mosquito season. There have been toxic reactions to ivermectin in

Collie-type dogs and others which might be dose related. If the dog can tolerate the ivermectin prevention, they can be kept relatively free from all parasites except tapeworm with this parasiticide. Heartworm preventive medication does not cause reproductive infertility or tumor proliferation.

Dogs that have heartworm infections are treated by intravenous injections of an *arsenical drug* which kills the adult worms. While drugs like *levamisole* have some effect on adult worms, the only highly effective approved treatment for adult heartworms is arsenic. After arsenical therapy, dogs must be kept very quiet for five to six weeks to minimize the chance of a fatal pulmonary embolism from elevated blood pressure forcing dying worms into the lungs.

After the first phase of therapy, a drug is given to remove microfilaria from the blood stream. Currently, *Dizan*® (*dithiazanine iodide*) is the only approved drug. However, *ivermectin* and *levamisole* are also used but with the disclaimer that they are not officially approved for this purpose.

After two consecutive weekly negative heartworm tests, preventive medication is started. It should be given for the remainder of the heartworm season.

Because the heartworm carrying mosquito does not usually travel more than a mile from its breeding grounds, clusters of the disease occur in small areas. Thus, heartworm preventive medication becomes absolutely mandatory in some areas and less critical in other locations.

HERNIA, DIAPHRAGMATIC: The diaphragm is a fibrous and muscular sheet of tissue that separates the abdomen and its organs from the heart and lungs contained in the chest cavity. Any abnormal opening in this tissue sheet is termed a diaphragmatic hernia. Two types of hernia exist—a congenital form which is present at birth and a traumatic form that occurs after an accident. Until misplaced organs penetrate an opening in the diaphragm, no clinical signs are evident. Difficult breathing is the most common clinical sign. Many dogs with this condition prefer to sit or elevate their front quarters in some manner apparently making breathing easier. A number of chemical changes occur in the body depending on the degree of respiratory embarrassment and the amount of shock present. An x-ray of the junction of the thorax and abdomen will show that the diaphragmatic line cannot be visualized in its entirety. Occasionally, a barium sulfate swallow is needed to outline GI organs in the thoracic cavity. Surgical correction by someone with a high level of surgical and anesthesia expertise is the only effective treatment.

MYOCARDITIS, PARVO INFECTION: When parvovirus surfaced as a new disease in 1978, the virus affected not only the gastrointestinal tract and lymphatic tissue but also the cardiac muscle cells of newborn puppies. Puppies infected with parvovirus before birth or shortly after parturition commonly develop *viral myocarditis*. Because parvovirus affects rapidly growing cells, four to eight week old puppy heart muscle cells are a perfect target.

The overwhelming nature of this viral infection may prevent the development of clinical signs. If present, signs include difficult breathing, depression, crying, and convulsive movements shortly before death. On veterinary examination, the affected pups have *tachycardia* (rapid heart beat), *heart murmurs*, an irregular heart beat, and pink fluid coming from the nose and mouth. Often entire litters are affected. After heart damage, the prognosis for long term survival is poor. Even those puppies that show temporary improvement have severely damaged heart muscle cells and ultimately undergo *congestive heart failure* by six months.

A definite diagnosis of parvovirus myocarditis is made on necropsy (autopsy) when the pathologist finds viral inclusion bodies in the nuclei of the involved heart muscle cells. Serum analysis supports presumptive evidence that parvovirus has caused the problem. At the present time, affected puppies and those that survive the initial parvovirus attack are treated symptomatically.

OBSTRUCTION, TRACHEAL: Tracheal obstruction can result from the accidental ingestion of a large foreign object (a rubber ball). The object becomes lodged at the tracheal-laryngeal junction totally occluding the windpipe. The dog turns blue immediately and may panic as it attempts to breath. The blockage must be removed within five minutes to prevent irreversible brain damage. Rapid attempts to remove the ball or object through the mouth should be limited to three or four minutes. Insertion of a sharp object into the median tracheal membrane below the larynx and positioning an EMPTY ball-point pen case into the trachea may allow enough air to be exchanged to reach proper veterinary care.

Another form of tracheal obstruction occurs if the cartilaginous rings that support the trachea collapse when the dog breathes in. While most severe in toy breeds and short-nosed breeds, collapse can occur in any dog with weak cartilage. See *TRACHEAL COLLAPSE.*

In cases of severe respiratory disease, the trachea becomes completely plugged with thick mucus causing extreme *dyspnea.* The best means of removing thick occluding secretions is with aerosol therapy and the use of expectorants.

PACEMAKER: Pacemakers can add years to the lives of dogs with some heart problems. Heart problems managed by pacemakers include various types of *heart blocks*, sinus *bradycardia*, (slowness of the heartbeat), bradycardia-tachycardia syndrome, and sinus arrest.

Pacemakers have been used in dogs for over twenty years but have not been realistic due to the high cost of the equipment. However, some companies such as Medtronic Corporation of Minneapolis, MN, and some foundations now make old or obsolete equipment available for dog usage. Costs of equipment vary with the complexity of the unit. Those designated VOO and AOO are not programmable making them less expensive than the programmable varieties designated DVI and DDD. At this time, probably only twenty to thirty pacemaker implant operations are done annually in dogs. Many of these dogs are not good surgical risks so extreme care must be taken with the anesthesia.

Almost as important as the surgical technique is the follow-up care. Weekly checks for the first month are necessary, followed by monthly exams for the next six months. The pacemaker battery should last from 16 to 24 months after which a replacement is necessary.

PATENT DUCTUS ARTERIOSUS (PDA): The most common *congenital heart defect* in the Cocker Spaniel is a patent ductus arteriosus (PDA). PDA is twice as common in females as in males. The ductus arteriosus is a functional fetal artery that bypasses the nonfunctional lungs before birth. Several weeks after birth the artery carrying the bypassed blood shrinks and the blood supply to inflated lungs takes over. If the ductus arteriosus remains functional in adult life, serious cardiac insufficiencies develop. A very characteristic *machinery murmur* is audible about halfway up the left side of the thorax making an accurate diagnosis possible with the stethoscope. Should doubt remain, the use of radiographs, ECG's, and *echocardiography* result in a definitive diagnosis. A skilled surgeon with proper anesthesia and ventilator equipment is needed to correct PDA. The prognosis after surgery is good to excellent.

PNEUMONIA: Pneumonia, by definition, is the inflammation of the lungs. Both infectious and noninfectious causes occur. The clinical signs are fever, *coughing, dyspnea* and sometimes spitting up blood.

Infectious pneumonia is caused by bacteria like *Pseudomonas, Bordetella, Klebsiella, Staphylococcus,* and *Streptococcus,* as well as systemic fungi like *blastomycosis, histoplasmosis,* and *coccidioidomycosis,* or by the protozoan parasite *Toxoplasma gondii.* Causes of noninfectious pneumonias are *allergy,* aspiration of vomitus following surgery, and certain swallowing problems.

The exact causes of pneumonia should be ascertained so that proper therapy can be initiated. Aggressive antibacterial therapy is necessary to eliminate bacterial pneumonia before it has done permanent damage to the lungs. Blood counts, serum titers, radiography, and *bacterial* and *fungal cultures* are necessary to determine the cause of pneumonia. Early diagnosis improves the prognosis. With the exception of *aspiration pneumonia,* most have a good prognosis when proper, aggressive therapy is used.

PNEUMOTHORAX: Air in the pleural cavity is called pneumothorax. Classification is made by determining where the air came from and the cause of the injury. For example, air may enter the pleural cavity in the chest from a penetrating external wound or from a tear internally in the tissues associated with the lungs. Pneumothorax also occurs as a result of rib fractures.

The major clinical sign associated with pneumothorax is *dyspnea* with fewer than normal breathing sounds. Radiographs, especially standing side views, will confirm the tentative diagnosis. The primary goal in treating pneumothorax is to reestablish negative pressure in the thoracic cavity. Since pneumothorax occurs frequently after thoracic trauma, other subtle traumatic changes may exist. A ruptured esophagus and *cardiac tamponade,* a condition where the sac around the heart fills with fluid inhibiting heart function are some of these changes.

RESPIRATORY DIFFICULTY, SIGNS OF: A number of signs of respiratory difficulty can be observed without any special equipment. In all cases of respiratory difficulty, the Cocker shows signs of *dyspnea.*

Examination of the mucous membranes, gums, and tongue may show *cyanosis,* a bluish discoloration to the membranes caused by a lack of oxygen in the blood. Respiratory tract obstruction, *pulmonary edema* where fluid has replaced oxygen in the lung air spaces, and a collapsed lung are additional causes of respiratory difficulty. Pale color of the mouth membranes can be caused by severe anemia, shock, or a decreased heart output. In some instances, the membranes take on a brownish cast from the presence of *methemoglobin* in the blood which prevents oxygen from reaching the body tissues. Some kinds of poisons and drug intoxications cause this phenomena.

A patient having great respiratory difficulty shows an extreme level of anxiety with a tendency to panic on handling or manipulation. One should watch the pattern of breathing to determine where the greatest difficulty arises—on *inspiration* (breathing in) or on *expiration* (breathing out). A dog's body temperature may give a clue to the cause of respiratory difficulty. In cases of overheating, the respiratory rate is extremely rapid and inefficient. Extreme shock and low body temperatures also cause respiratory depression. Normal respiratory rates are between 8 and 25 breaths per minute.

SNEEZE: The reflex action of sneezing occurs from irritation of the fine hairs (cilia) that line the nasal passage. Nasal discharge is often present in conjunction with sneezing. Causes include infection, *allergy*, foreign bodies, parasites, tumors, and *osteomyelitis*. Radiographs, blood tests, and cultures are necessary to determine the cause. Treatment is directed at eliminating the irritation.

SUBAORTIC STENOSIS (SAS): Subaortic stenosis is a serious hereditary *congenital heart defect*. Fortunately, it is not common in the Cocker Spaniel. An affected dog will show radiographic evidence of a dilated aorta after reaching six months. The *electrocardiogram* pattern is normal or only slightly altered. A relatively loud *heart murmur* is present about halfway up the thorax on both the left and right sides. Subaortic stenosis has no treatment other than what would be attempted for left side heart failure. Because very few clinical signs exist, subaortic stenosis is most commonly diagnosed on autopsy after a young dog has collapsed and died suddenly.

TETRALOGY OF FALLOT: The tetralogy of Fallot is a hereditary *congenital heart disease* found in several breeds of dogs. A loud *systolic heart murmur* is detected. Actually, four cardiovascular abnormalities are found on autopsy. Radiographs show right heart enlargement and malposition of the aorta. *Electrocardiogram* patterns indicate right ventricle enlargement. Affected dogs fatigue easily, "turn blue," and have a rapid heart beat. No form of treatment is effective although the use of beta blockers like *propranolol hydrochloride* (*Inderal*®, Ayerst Labs) might extend the life of affected dogs.

TRACHEAL COLLAPSE: Tracheal collapse occurs congenitally or develops from a traumatic narrowing of the tracheal opening later in life. In the Cocker Spaniel the most common form is traumatic narrowing of the tracheal opening to an elliptical shape. Removal of the source of trauma causes the elliptical shaped rings to return to their normal circle shaped opening unless the cartilaginous rings have been crushed.

TRACHEOBRONCHITIS (KENNEL COUGH): Infectious tracheobronchitis (*kennel cough*) is a highly contagious respiratory disease of dogs caused by a combination of etiological agents. While *mycoplasma* and a number of viruses and bacteria have been incriminated in the disease, the most important etiological agents are *canine parainfluenza virus (CP1)*, *CAV–2 virus*, and the bacteria *Bordetella bronchiseptica*.

These agents are used in various vaccines against the disease. The bacterial agent has been utilized as an *intranasal vaccine*. Since maternal antibodies do not interfere, intranasal administration of this vaccine may be done as early as two weeks of age. Yearly booster inoculations are recommended. Conventional vaccination with other "*kennel cough*" vaccines is generally undertaken on the same schedule as distemper and hepatitis vaccinations. While yearly booster vaccinations are adequate for distemper and hepatitis, the duration of *parainfluenza vaccine* immunity is only six months.

Dogs exposed to others in kennels, dog shows, and field trials are at higher risk than those that are not exposed to outside environmental challenges. Transmission occurs through respiratory droplets or aerosol spread from the cough of an infected dog. The cough is a very dry, hacking cough that can be elicited by gentle pressure on the trachea just beneath the larynx.

Ten day treatment with a wide spectrum antibiotic like *chloramphenicol* is effective. The use of *antitussives* (cough medicines) minimizes the cough irritation to the tracheal and laryngeal membranes. Sometimes butter or honey is used to coat the pharyngeal membranes as an aid in soothing the throat. Chronic tracheobronchitis cases lead to *pneumonia*. Because kennel cough is very contagious, dogs with coughs should be well segregated from healthy animals.

TUMOR, HEART BASE: A specific tumor that invades the base of the heart near the aorta is called a *chemodectoma*. Heart base tumors are found almost exclusively in short-nosed breeds of dogs. Unfortunately, surgical removal is not realistic since the tumor attacks vital structures. Therefore, treatment is symptomatic as signs of heart failure develop. Since chemotherapy does not help, the prognosis is poor.

VALLEY FEVER: See *FUNGI, SYSTEMIC*.

VENTRICULAR SEPTAL DEFECT (VSD): Ventricular septal defect is caused by the failure of normal fetal shunts (holes) in the wall of the heart to close at birth. Clinically, harsh heart murmur sounds are present well forward on the thoracic wall, especially on the right side. Small septal defects close over during the first year of life. Thoracic radiographs show enlarged *ventricles*. Large openings in the wall of the heart record on the *electrocardiogram* as left ventricular enlargements. An adept cardiac surgeon with the proper equipment can repair ventricular septal defects.

ENDOCRINE SYSTEM

ACROMEGALY: Acromegaly, a chronic hormone irregularity produced by an excess of *growth hormone*, causes an overgrowth of bony structures and soft tissue in adult dogs. Affected dogs show signs of fatigue, increased frequency of urination and water consumption, increased space between incisor teeth, and a tendency toward development of *diabetes*. In an unspayed bitch, an *ovariohysterectomy* will help resolve the condition.

ACTH-DEXAMETHASONE SUPPRESSION TEST: This timed test determines the origin of high resting cortisol (*cortisone*) levels in the body. In normal animals, *ACTH* is a hormone that should stimulate the adrenal gland to produce cortisone. When given in a measured amount, a predictable rise of cortisone in the blood occurs. Two hours after *dexamethasone* (a potent form of cortisone) is given, ACTH-gel administration should have a predictable depressing affect on ACTH production in the pituitary gland. By measuring the change in the blood cortisol level, the veterinarian learns if a suspected cortisone production problem is idiopathic (of unknown causation), in the pituitary gland, or in the adrenal gland.

ADDISON'S DISEASE (HYPOADRENOCORTICISM): In Addison's disease (hypoadrenocorticism), the adrenal glands fail to produce adequate amounts of adrenal hormones. *Glucocorticoids, mineralocorticoids,* or both are deficient. When the cause of Addison's disease is considered as primary, over 90% of the adrenal gland has been destroyed or replaced with tumor cells. Causes of primary hypoadrenocorticism include *autoimmune destruction of adrenal tissue,* tumors of the adrenal gland, granulomatous lesions of the adrenal gland, hemorrhage in the adrenal gland as a result of disease (*distemper, pyometra*), vascular clots in adrenal blood vessels, and *Lysodren*® administration.

When the ACTH hormone from the pituitary gland fails to stimulate the adrenal gland to produce corticosteroid hormones, a secondary form results. Prolonged administration of cortisone by pill or injection is the most common cause of secondary hypoadrenocorticism. This indirectly causes atrophy (shrinkage) of the adrenal gland. To a small degree, tumors involving the pituitary gland may decrease ACTH production.

The clinical signs of Addison's disease include depression, lack of appetite, vomiting and/or diarrhea with abdominal pain, and hypotensive (low blood pressure) shock with weakness and shivering. Primary Addison's disease causes depression of serum *sodium* levels and elevation of serum *potassium* levels. Other serum chemical abnormalities exist to varying degrees. Kidney function is diminished due to decreased blood flow through the kidneys. A very slow heart beat, a weak pulse, and normal to subnormal temperatures are present. The most valuable lab test is a *CBC* (complete blood count) in which the *eosinophil* cells occur in higher than normal numbers. Signs of Addison's disease are related to stressful incidents like boarding, showing, training, and surgery.

Treatment is designed to bring the serum electrolytes (*sodium* and *potassium*) into balance, reverse the shock signs, reestablish kidney function, and then replace the *mineralocorticoids* and *glucocorticoids* that are not being produced in the adrenal gland. Cortisone replacement is accomplished by giving fludrocortisone acetate (*Florinef*®) once daily for life, by giving desoxycorticosterone pivalate (*Doca*®) (Percorten® acetate) intramuscularly every 25 to 30 days, or by having a desoxycorticosterone pivalate (Doca®) (*Percorten*® *pellet*) implanted every 8 to 12 months. These methods will control the condition after the kidney and other body needs have become normal. In addition, salt should be added daily to the diet. If periods of stress are anticipated, the additional administration of glucocorticoids helps to prevent exacerbations of the disease.

ALDOSTERONE: See *HORMONES.*

ALOPECIA, BILATERAL SYMMETRICAL: Equal hair loss on both the left and right sides of the body is termed bilateral symmetrical alopecia. This hair loss pattern is characteristic of hormone disorders.

ANESTRUS: Anestrus is the time in a bitch's *heat cycle* when the body is making a transition into the next cycle. During this 1 to 8 month period, sex hormones are at a low level in the bloodstream.

AZIUM® **(DEXAMETHASONE):** See *CORTISONE.*

BETASONE® **(BETAMETHASONE):** See *CORTISONE.*

CALCINOSIS CUTIS: Calcinosis cutis is a rare condition resulting from the deposition of calcium salts in the skin layers forming a solid plaque in the skin. Most frequently this occurs as a result of *hyperglucocorticoidism* (too much *cortisone*) from any cause. If the excess levels of cortisone are removed from the body, the mineral plaque (calcinosis cutis) disappears in 2 to 6 months. Surgical excision is the treatment of choice if calcinosis cutis is present with normal cortisone levels.

CHEQUE® **(MIBOLERONE):** See *DRUGS, HEAT ALTERING.*

CORTISONE: Cortisone secreted by the adrenal glands is very important in the homeostasis of all body tissues. The secretion of two *glucocorticoids*, cortisol and corticosterone, is regulated by two other hormones, *ACTH* and corticotropin-releasing factor (*CRF*). These hormones are produced by the anterior portion of the pituitary gland and the *hypothalamus*, an organ in the base of the brain. The amount of natural glucocorticoid activity is highest during the hours of greatest activity and stress. *Diurnal rhythm* is important in the principle of medicating with glucocorticoids. Less suppression of the adrenal gland occurs if cortisone medications are given during hours of greatest adrenal activity. In the dog, these are the morning hours.

Glucocorticoids have a profound effect on the metabolism of *glucose, protein,* and *lipids* (fats). Increasing glucose levels in the blood stream are formed from non-sugar sources. Glucocorticoid activity is anti-insulin in nature since tissue utilization of sugar (glucose) is decreased resulting in more sugar being stored in the liver. Regulation of diabetic dogs also receiving glucocorticoid drugs is thus more difficult. Glucocorticoids break down proteins causing muscles to atrophy and skin to become thinner. Fat metabolism is affected with fat abnormally accumulating in the liver. Virtually all of the body organs and cells are affected by glucocorticoids. A partial list of body tissues and the effects of cortisone follows.

Bone—antagonizes *vitamin D* presence and accelerates bone resorption

Cardiovascular System—increases blood pressure

Central Nervous System—euphoria and behavioral changes result and seizure threshold lowers

Gastrointestinal Tract—decreases absorption of *iron* and *calcium* and increases absorption of fats

Hematopoietic System (Blood Cell System)—shrinks lymphoid tissues, decreases numbers of *eosinophils, lymphocytes,* and *monocytes* in the blood stream, decreases clotting time, increases number of *RBC's, platelets,* and *neutrophils* in the blood stream

Kidneys—increases water and salt retention, increases calcium and *potassium* excretion

Reproductive System—may induce birth in later pregnancy; in early pregnancy causes birth defects

Skeletal Muscle—causes weakness and atrophy when given in excess

Skin—excess causes thinning of skin

Because of the listed effects on most organ systems in the body, prolonged or excessive use of glucocorticoids contributes to the following degenerative changes in the dog.

Central Nervous System: nervousness, mood alteration

Dermatologic: *calcinosis cutis,* allergy to cortisone

Digestive System: *pancreatitis,* GI tract ulceration, and liver disease

Endocrine (Hormone): *Cushing's disease* (hyperadrenocorticism), *diabetes mellitus*

Metabolic Effects: general tissue breakdown, increases blood sugar, and growth retardation occurs

Musculoskeletal System: muscle wasting and weakness, *osteoporosis*

Ocular System: *cataract* development

In the search for a better glucocorticoid drug, many different kinds of steroids have become available. All have certain assets and drawbacks. The following list includes some of the most common glucocorticoids with their relative anti-inflammatory potency and duration of action. Trade names appear in parentheses.

GLUCOCORTICOIDS	POTENCY	DURATION OF ACTION
Short-Acting:		
Hydrocortisone	1	less than 12 hours
Intermediate-Acting:		
Prednisone	3.5	12 to 36 hours
Prednisolone	4	12 to 36 hours
Methylprednisolone (Medrol®)	5	12 to 36 hours
Triamcinolone (Vetalog®)	5	12 to 36 hours
Flumethasone (Flucort®)	7.8	12 to 36 hours
Long-Acting:		
Betamethasone (Betasone®)	25	over 48 hours
Dexamethasone (Azium®)	30	over 48 hours

The longer the duration of action the greater the chance of suppressing normal adrenal gland function. Increased anti-inflammatory potency is exchanged for longer or shorter duration of action. Glucocorticoid drugs can be administered orally, intravenously, intramuscularly, and subcutaneously. When long term or high dosage cortisone therapy is anticipated, *alternate day cortisone therapy* should be attempted. In alternate day treatment, the calculated dose is doubled and given every other day in the morning, decreasing the chance of adrenal gland suppression.

If a glucocorticoid drug is used longer than one week, the drug dosage must be lessened daily before completely discontinuing the medication. For example, if your Cocker Spaniel was receiving 10 mg of *prednisolone* once daily over a period of weeks. Then reduce the daily dosage to 5 mg for 7 days. Cut that dosage to 2.5 mg for 14 days, going to the alternate day administration of 2.5 mg for up to 29 additional days before ceasing usage of the drug. The longer the dog has been on *glucocorticoids*, the longer the tapering period should continue before stopping completely.

CUSHING'S DISEASE (HYPERADRENOCORTICISM): *Cushing's syndrome* or Cushing's disease results from an increase in the amount of corticosteroids in the body. The secretion of too much *ACTH* hormone by the pituitary gland in the brain which causes the adrenal glands to produce too much cortisol for normal needs results in Cushing's. Excessive amounts of cortisol can also be produced naturally by hyperplasia (increase in size) of the adrenal gland and by the presence of adrenal gland tumors. *Iatrogenic hyperadrenocorticism* is produced when glucocorticoid drugs are administered over a long period of time.

Polyuria (increased urination), *polydipsia* (increased water consumption), pendulous abdomen, enlarged liver, hair loss, weakness and depression, increased appetite, muscle weakness, obesity, increased panting, and *hyperpigmentation* are all signs of Cushing's syndrome. In a small number of cases, *calcinosis cutis* is observed. To diagnose this condition, a *CBC* (complete blood count), urinalysis, serum chemistry for liver function, and an *ACTH stimulation test* are utilized. If the clinical signs and preliminary testing are highly suspicious of Cushing's, use of the *high dose dexamethasone suppression test* or the combination *ACTH-dexamethasone suppression test* is needed to help determine the origin of the excess cortisone.

Cushing's syndrome is treated by attempting to remove the excessive cortisone from the body. If an adrenal gland tumor is found, surgical removal of the affected adrenal gland is the treatment of choice. Because adrenal gland removal is very delicate surgery, an expert surgeon is required as well as extra care in the monitoring of blood cortisol levels during and immediately after surgery. About 50% of adrenal tumors are malignant resulting in a poor prognosis making euthanasia a consideration. If the cortisol excess is from a pituitary lesion causing an increase in the amount of circulating ACTH, surgical removal of the pituitary gland or of both adrenal glands could relieve the problem. Again, a very accomplished surgeon is required.

Lysodren® (o,p'-DDD or mitotane) causes the adrenal gland to atrophy, decreasing cortisol production. After the initial dose of Lysodren® atrophies the adrenal gland tissue, a lower maintenance level follows for life. Periodic blood tests help determine if the patient is developing any toxicity to Lysodren®.

CYTOBIN®: See *TRIIODOTHYRONINE.*

DEFICIENCY, GROWTH HORMONE: Two clinical syndromes that relate to growth hormone levels occur. The first syndrome is *dwarfism.* The action of *growth hormone* produced in the pituitary gland in the brain is mediated by a substance called *somatomedin (insulin-like growth factor).* A true dwarf is deficient in both growth hormone and somatomedin. Because of a recessive gene, the affected puppy will not grow to full size. Affected puppies appear normal up to the age of three months. The difference between litter mates becomes apparent later as the growth hormone somatomedin deficient puppy stays small retaining a puppy hair coat.

The other form of growth hormone deficiency, more aptly called *growth hormone responsive,* is a *pattern baldness.* The baldness occurs in some small breeds due to a deficiency of growth hormone that is sometimes secondary to *thyroid hormone deficiency.* In this form, a deficiency of thyroid hormone affects growth hormone production and regulation but is readily treated with thyroid replacement. Growth hormone for treatment of primary growth hormone deficiencies is in short supply. Genetically engineered growth hormone should be available within two years for veterinary use.

Growth hormone stimulation tests with *xylazine* or *clonidine* will identify these conditions. Samples must be tested at either the University of Pennsylvania or the University of Tennessee clinical endocrinology labs.

DIABETES INSIPIDUS: Diabetes insipidus is caused by a malfunction involving the posterior part of the pituitary gland. The *antidiuretic hormone* (ADH) is not produced in the pituitary gland nor released for use by the kidneys to promote water conservation. Characterized by consumption of large quantities of water (*polydipsia*) and frequent urination of very dilute urine (*polyuria*), the cause is rarely determined. If the condition is severe, dogs frequently vomit from the large amounts of water consumed, lose weight from reduced food intake, and exhibit *convulsions* and *incoordination*. A urine specific gravity measurement almost equivalent to that of water (1.001 to 1.005) is necessary to prove diabetes insipidus. Also, evidence must indicate that urine cannot be concentrated by withholding water but can be concentrated by giving antidiuretic hormone. Treatment is directed toward supplying ADH. The hormone is given as a long-acting injection, repeated usually in $1^1/_2$ to 3 days as water consumption starts to increase. As a liquid, *desmopressin acetate (APDDV®)* can be dropped into the nasal passage every eight hours. The conjunctival sac of the eye is also used for administration if dogs resist nasal administration. Any treatment will need to be maintained for the life of the dog.

DIABETES MELLITUS: Diabetes mellitus (*sugar diabetes*) is caused by the lack of *insulin* necessary to control the amount of *blood glucose* present. The beta-cells of the *pancreas* produce insulin. Normally, enough insulin is generated to keep the level of sugar below the point that allows passage through the kidneys into the urine.

Diabetes mellitus is diagnosed by finding sugar in the urine and an elevated blood glucose level. Other blood test values may also be abnormal. The extent of the blood sugar elevation is related to the seriousness of the insulin deficiency and the length of time the dog has been diabetic.

Diabetes mellitus is treated by using injectable insulin to lower the blood sugar level. When used in dogs, oral hypoglycemic drugs are neither predictable or particularly effective. Occasionally, a dog that will respond to the oral medication but very rarely. *NPH insulin,* given daily is the most effective kind of insulin. Because the drug's peak insulin activity is about nine hours after injection, the owner must maintain a rigid time schedule for injections, feeding, and exercise. *Heat cycle, pregnancy, cortisone* administration, *thyroid* medication, and exercise all affect the amount of insulin needed. Complicated diabetes occurs when the excess sugar level has been present for a long time. The dog's general metabolism is altered creating a condition called *diabetic ketoacidosis.* Hospitalization with very close scrutiny is necessary to bring the complicated form under control. Inflammation of the pancreas, a life threatening problem, is the most common complication of the ketoacidosis form of diabetes. The enzyme *amylase* is greatly elevated, making that test beneficial in determining the presence of *pancreatitis.*

The prognosis for simple diabetes is excellent providing the dog's feeding, exercise, and insulin administration are maintained on a predictable schedule. The habit of monitoring urine sugar even after the patient has been brought under control is important.

DRUGS, HEAT ALTERING: Currently the FDA has approved *Ovaban®* (*megestrol acetate*) and *Cheque® drops* (*mibolerone*) for the purpose of eliminating, preventing, or controlling the dog's *heat cycle.* Ovaban® given at the rate of 1 mg/lb daily for 8 days if started before the second day of heat is completed will cause the bitch to go out of heat rapidly. An alternate dosage may be given at $1/4$ mg/lb daily for 32 days starting at least one week prior to the onset of *proestrus*.

If the megestrol acetate (Ovaban®) is given late in anestrus, heat will be postponed approximately five to six months. If the drug is started early or in the middle of *anestrus*, usually no postponement of the scheduled heat period occurs. Side effects from Ovaban® include increased appetite, weight gain, decreased activity, and rarely, milk production. Ovaban® is a progestational hormone used in the United States since 1975. Subsequent fertility and heat cycling are not affected by its use.

Cheque® or mibolerone, an androgenic (male) *anabolic steroid*, is approximately 95% effective in inhibiting the heat cycle. Cheque® must be started at least 30 days before *proestrus* bleeding is anticipated to be effective in preventing heat signs. The liquid medication is given daily for an indefinite period. Side effects include mild clitoral enlargement, *vaginitis*, and worsening of any already existing *seborrheic skin condition*. Because of the Cocker Spaniel's *copper hepatitis* tendencies, this drug must be administered with care.

Carnation Pet Foods plans to market a dog food containing mibolerone. Having not yet received final FDA approval, it is not yet commercially available.

Two other drugs are occasionally used to suppress heat cycles. *Testosterone*, a male hormone, has been used but because of side effects is not recommended. *Depo-Provera*®, a long acting time-released progestational hormone used in human medicine, has also been used to keep bitches out of heat. Changes caused in the uterus may lead to *pyometra*. Further predisposition to *mammary tumors* and *diabetes mellitus* also occurs from Depo-Provera® usage. *Depo-Provera*® should not be used in the canine. For additional discussion of heat altering drugs, refer to Chapter 12 on the *UROGENITAL SYSTEM*.

ESTROUS CYCLE: The estrous cycle (*heat cycle*) is the entire process of *proestrus, estrus, metestrus* (*diestrus*) and *anestrus*. The entire process in most Cockers takes approximately six months. If hormonal imbalances are present, the cycle is shortened, lengthened, or non-existent.

ESTRUS: Estrus is that part of the *estrous cycle* (*heat cycle*) when the bitch is receptive to the male dog. Generally lasting 9 days, it may vary from 3 to 21 days. During "*standing heat*" as estrus is commonly called, the bitch will lift her tail, stand with her rear legs firmly planted, and will lift her vulva on stimulation. During estrus, the *estradiol hormone* level has peaked and is starting to decrease while the *progesterone hormone* level is rising. Also during this period, *luteinizing hormone* (*LH*) and *follicle stimulating hormone* (*FSH*) are interacting to bring about ovulation. Ordinarily, ovulation occurs 1 to 3 days after the peak of LH activity.

FLUCORT® (FLUMETHASONE): See *CORTISONE*.

FOLLICLE STIMULATING HORMONE (FSH): See *HORMONES, SEX*.

GLANDS, ADRENAL: The paired glands located at the cranial end of each kidney are the adrenal glands. Essential for the production of *glucocorticoid hormones*, mineralocorticoids (*aldosterone*), and sex hormones (*progesterones, estrogens,* and *androgens*), the adrenal glands are stimulated by the presence of *adrenocorticotrophic hormone (ACTH)* secreted by the pituitary gland. A dog can live without adrenal glands if supplemented with the necessary hormones.

GLANDS, THYROID: The thyroid glands are small paired glands located on either side of the trachea (windpipe) toward the chest from the larynx (voice box). Thyroid hormones are important in the regulation of many body functions.

The four hormones or prohormones produced by the dog's thyroid gland are *thyroxine (T_4), triiodothyronine (T_3) reverse T_3, and 3, 5–diiodothyronine (T_2).* The more potent T_3 is secreted in preference to T_4. Triiodothyronine is the major metabolic hormone associated with the thyroid gland.

The secretion of too much thyroid hormone causes *hyperthyroidism.* Clinically, panting, increased heart rate, and personality agitation are present. While rare in dogs, hyperthyroidism is found with increased frequency in older cats. *Hypothyroidism* (too little circulating thyroid hormone) occurs commonly in the Cocker Spaniel. See *HYPOTHYROIDISM* in this chapter and in Chapter 11 on *SKIN and RELATED STRUCTURES.*

HEAT CYCLE: See *ESTROUS CYCLE*.

HORMONE, FOLLICLE STIMULATING (FSH): See *HORMONES, SEX.*

HORMONE, LUTEINIZING (LH): See *HORMONES, SEX.*

HORMONES: A hormone is a chemical substance produced or secreted by one endocrine organ resulting in an effect on another organ. The following list of endocrine organs either produce the hormones listed or are affected by the hormone listed.

Adrenal glands produce *glucocorticoids* and *mineralocorticoids* (*aldosterone*)

Ovary produces *estrogen* and *progesterone* and is affected by *follicle stimulating hormone (FSH)* and *luteinizing hormone (LH)*

Pancreas produces *insulin* (lowers blood sugar) and *glucagon* (raises blood sugar)

Pituitary gland produces *adrenocorticotrophic hormone (ACTH), antidiuretic hormone, growth hormone, thyroid stimulating hormone (TSH or thyrotropin), thyrotropin releasing hormone (TRH), follicle stimulating hormone (FSH),* and *luteinizing hormone (LH)*

Testes produce *testosterone* and are affected by *follicle stimulating hormone (FSH) and luteinizing hormone (LH)*

Thyroid glands produce *L-thyroxine (T_4), triiodothyronine (T_3), reverse* and *free T_4* and *T_3.*

HORMONES, SEX: Sex hormones, important in the perpetuation of the species, must be produced in proper amounts and in proper sequence for conception to occur.

In the BITCH, the following hormones are part of her reproductive system. *Estrogen* hormones are responsible for the physical signs of *estrus* (*heat*). The most active estrogen hormone, 17–ß-estradiol, occurs in late *proestrus*. *Diethylstilbestrol*, a synthetic female hormone, has been used in older spayed bitches to control *urinary incontinence* and produce *mesalliance* (*mismating*) after a bitch is bred accidently. Prolonged or constant usage of diethylstilbestrol (*DES*) will cause bone marrow depression and contribute to the development of *pyometra*. *FSH (follicle stimulating hormone)*, a hormone produced in the anterior pituitary gland, is responsible for maturation of ovarian follicles in the bitch. The *anestrus* levels of FSH decrease during early *proestrus*. This decrease is followed by a peak level of FSH similar to that found in anestrus. *Luteinizing hormone* (*LH*), also produced in the anterior pituitary gland, stimulates ovulation 24 to 72 hours after the LH peak and initiates a new follicular phase at proestrus. Another pituitary gland hormone, *prolactin*, contributes to the maintenance of normal pregnancy and mammary gland development. *Progesterone hormone* maintains the pregnant uterus and stimulates the development of the mammary milk duct system. Progesterone increases to facilitate behavioral estrus (standing for breeding, "flagging" the tail). About ten days after ovulation, *progesterone* levels peak helping to stimulate mammary glandular development and changing the uterine lining. Because levels in serum progesterone are identical in pregnant and unpregnant bitches, no advantage is gained in pregnancy diagnosis by measuring the level of this hormone in the dog.

The MALE DOG produces *testosterone* from germinal cells in the testes. Testosterone is the hormone responsible for male behavior—leg lifting, territory marking, aggressiveness, larger size, and the development of male behavioral traits such as wandering and protecting his territory. *FSH*, also produced in the male, is thought to be the primary hormone stimulating sperm production. *LH* plays an important part in testosterone hormone production because of its action on the cells of Leydig in the testes.

HYPOTHYROIDISM: The lack of either T_4 (*L-thyroxine*), T_3 (*triiodothyronine*), or thyroid stimulation by *thyrotropin* (*TSH—thyroid stimulating hormone*) causes clinical signs associated with hypothyroidism. Most commonly lethargy, mental depression, either obesity or weight loss, heat seeking, low body temperature, hair loss, *hyperpigmentation*, *seborrhea*, ear infections, muscle and joint weakness, slow heart beat, *infertility*, and several eye conditions are signs of hypothyroidism. Cocker Spaniels do have an increased risk of developing hypothyroidism. Larger breeds of dogs are affected at a younger age than the Cocker Spaniel.

During *lymphocytic thyroiditis* (*Hashimoto's disease*), one of the most common causes of hypothyroidism, the thyroid gland activity is destroyed by the production of auto-antibodies against itself. Another common type is atrophy and necrosis (death) of the thyroid gland functional tissue from unknown causes. Clinical lab findings associated with hypothyroidism are *anemia*, *hypercholesterolemia* (too much cholesterol in the blood), elevated *CPK enzyme test* (creatinine phosphokinase) in over half, possibly low or baseline T_3 and T_4 levels, and a lack of response to *thyroid stimulating hormone.*

Along with measuring baseline T_3 and T_4 levels by radioimmunoassay, a *thyroid stimulation test* should be done with TSH. History, clinical signs, and other lab tests help to substantiate the diagnosis of hypothyroidism. Treatment is for life. In most cases, dogs will respond to T_4 (*L-thyroxine*) administration even though T_3 alone or T_3 and T_4 are low. Most failures in therapy are from administering the wrong products such as desiccated thyroid and T_3, or from giving an inadequate amount of T_4. The correct dosage is 20 µg/kg (0.1 mg/10 lb) two times per day. After response is achieved, the dosage may be lowered to a maintenance level in some dogs.

LUTEINIZING HORMONE (LH): See *HORMONES, SEX.*

L-THYROXINE (T_4): The main secretory product of the thyroid gland is called L-thyroxine or T_4. In some non-thyroid illnesses, T_4 levels are depressed to help the body conserve calories and decrease tissue breakdown processes. Synthetic L-thyroxine is the most widely utilized therapeutic form of thyroid medication. "Name brand" forms of the medication do not seem to be any more effective than some generic forms available at substantial savings. L-thyroxine tablets can either be given two times daily or a double dose once daily. A minimum of three months of therapy should be continued before the clinical changes are evaluated. Dogs with concurrent heart problems should be started at lower amounts and increased gradually over a three or four week period to reach therapeutic levels. Dogs on L-thyroxine therapy require increased doses of *insulin* for *diabetes* and *anticonvulsant* drugs to control *epilepsy.*

METESTRUS (DIESTRUS): Metestrus begins with the refusal of the bitch to allow the stud dog to mate. At this point in the cycle, *progesterone hormone* levels increase for 15 days and then diminish gradually for the next 5 to 6 weeks. Your veterinarian can more accurately estimate when whelping is due by looking under the microscope for the disappearance of superficial vaginal epithelial cells rather than by noting breeding dates or behavior changes. The decline of superficial epithelial cells occurs at the onset of diestrus (metestrus).

OVABAN®️ (MEGESTROL ACETATE): See *DRUGS, HEAT ALTERING.*

PREDNISONE: See *CORTISONE.*

PREDNISOLONE: See *CORTISONE.*

PROESTRUS: The period of the *estrous cycle* when the bitch is attractive to the male but will not stand for breeding is termed proestrus. Clinically, the bitch has a swollen, turgid vulva and passes various amounts of a thin bloody discharge. The average length of proestrus is 9 days but can vary from 2 to 17 days. The level of estradiol hormone is very high during proestrus, decreasing one or two days before the end of the proestrus period.

PROLACTIN: See *HORMONES, SEX.*

SERTOLI CELL TUMOR: The Sertoli cell tumor is a peculiar tumor of the canine testes. While fairly common in undescended testes, normally only one testicle is affected. Sertoli cell tumors produce *estrogen hormone* causing feminine changes in the male dog. Clinically, *hair loss* is evident from both sides of the body, nipples enlarge, and a pendulous prepuce is present. An attraction to other male dogs may be observed. If the cancerous testicle and normal appearing testes are removed early enough, an excellent prognosis results. Long standing Sertoli cell tumors spread to nearby tissues producing high estrogen hormone concentrations which then cause fatal *bone marrow depression.*

STIMULATION TEST, GROWTH HORMONE: The growth hormone stimulation blood test determines if a frank growth hormone deficiency exists. To date, only the University of Pennsylvania and the University of Tennessee endocrinology labs perform this test and then only infrequently. Before undertaking this test, the veterinarian should contact the lab of choice for specific instructions. A baseline plasma sample is obtained after which either *xylazine* (*Rompun*®) at 100 to 300 micrograms/kilogram or *clonidine* at 10 to 30 micrograms/kilogram is given intravenously. A post-stimulation plasma sample is obtained after thirty minutes. This test, which is both difficult and expensive, is valuable in determining true growth hormone deficiencies.

STIMULATION TEST, TSH (THYROID STIMULATING HORMONE): The TSH stimulation test is the most accurate assessment of thyroid gland dysfunction. Because the thyroid stimulating hormone used in the test is very expensive and is in limited supply, the procedure is costly. The testing is simple. A pre-TSH blood sample is taken. Five to ten units of TSH are injected intravenously and a post-TSH injection sample is collected. The samples are tested for T_3, T_4, and reverse T_3. If the response is less than two times the baseline value or if the response fails to reach the normal level, the diagnosis of *hypothyroidism* is justified.

SUGAR DIABETES: See *DIABETES MELLITUS.*

TEST, T_3–T_4: The symbols for a measure of thyroid activity are T_3 and T_4, commonly measured by radioimmunoassay. A measurement of T_3 and T_4 is not enough to confirm the diagnosis of hypothyroidism if the values are borderline. Use of the TSH (thyroid stimulating hormone) stimulation test should be considered. T_3 is *triiodothyronine.* T_4 is *L-thyroxine* which is converted into T_3 for active use in the body. T_3, the more active form in the dog, is secreted preferentially by the thyroid gland. Most dogs can be medicated with either T_3 or T_4 if a deficiency exists.

TESTOSTERONE: See *HORMONES, SEX.*

THORN TEST: The Thorn test, a crude, easily performed adrenal gland measure has been replaced by the radioimmunoassay test. Seven hours after giving a patient ten units of *ACTH* gel intramuscularly, the number of *eosinophils* in the circulating blood stream are counted. A normal response is a 70% reduction of eosinophils in the blood stream. A reduction of less than this indicates a decreased adrenal gland function or *Addison's disease.*

TRIIODOTHYRONINE (T_3): Triiodothyronine is the most active form of thyroid hormone secreted by the thyroid gland or produced by tissue degradation of T_4. The most potent and metabolically active form of thyroid hormone in the dog is T_3. A commercially available form of T_3, *Cytobin*® produced by Norden Laboratories, can be used to treat most thyroid deficiencies. However, its high cost and the fact that it must be given three times a day to be effective are drawbacks.

VAGINAL SMEARS: See Chapter 12 on the *UROGENITAL SYSTEM.*

VETALOG® **(TRIAMCINOLONE):** See *CORTISONE.*

GASTROINTESTINAL TRACT AND RELATED ORGANS

ACHALASIA: Achalasia is a failure of the muscles of the gastrointestinal tract to relax. Two forms of the disease are recognized—*cricopharyngeal achalasia* and *esophageal achalasia.* Only esophageal achalasia has been reported in the Cocker Spaniel. The cardinal sign, frequently recognized at weaning, is persistent vomiting immediately after the ingestion of solid food. In **cricopharyngeal achalasia,** the problem occurs where the pharynx enters the esophagus. Constriction of throat muscles prevents swallowing. Severing these muscles surgically corrects this condition. Recovery is generally rapid and permanent. However, sometimes surgical scarring causes a constriction requiring additional surgery later. **Esophageal achalasia** occurs in the muscle surrounding the esophagus at the entrance to the stomach. A lack of nerve innervation to the esophageal muscle prevents normal *peristalsis.* Eventually, the accumulation of food in the esophagus creates a *megaesophagus.*

Both long term dietary management and surgery are required. Achalasia surgery should be performed by a highly skilled surgeon. Dietary management includes feeding the dog from a high platform to elevate his front feet. Gravity will then help carry the food into the stomach. Feeding a gruel mixture also helps in the long term management of achalasia. Because the disease is hereditary, carriers or affected Cockers should not be used for breeding.

ANI, ATRESIA: *Atresia ani* is a congenital anomaly where no anal orifice or opening exists. At several weeks of age, a puppy will whine and exhibit a progressively distended abdomen. Some of these anomalies lend themselves to simple surgical repair under local anesthesia. Others require general anesthesia and more heroic methods.

ANODONTIA: Anodontia, the absence of teeth from the dental arch, has a genetic basis. Normally one large and one small molar are present on each side in the upper jaw and one large and two small molars on each side in the lower jaw. By seven months, they should have erupted and be in place. Any or all of the small molar teeth can be missing. A common location for anodontia is the upper and lower premolar teeth where the small premolars are not present. The upper jaw has three small premolars and a large fourth premolar tooth. In the lower jaw, four premolars of increasing size between the "fang" and the large molar on each side. All of these should also all be erupted and in place at seven months of age.

Radiographs may determine the presence or absence in the jaw at six months. Rarely, one or several incisors are missing from the six upper or lower teeth in the dental arch between the canine teeth. There is a genetic basis for anodontia.

AORTIC ARCH, PERSISTENT RIGHT: *Persistent right aortic arch* is a common congenital anomaly which causes a stricture of the esophagus followed by *vomiting* within ten minutes after eating solid food. A *barium swallow radiograph* will show dilation of the esophagus anterior to the base of the heart. A ligament or vessel remnant which remains after birth is the reason for the digestive upset. A fibrous cord, the *ligamentum arteriosum*, connects from the left pulmonary artery to the descending aorta completely encircling the esophagus, preventing the esophagus from dilating as food descends.

The treatment involving open chest surgery requires a high degree of surgical expertise and additional ventilation equipment to assist breathing during the procedure. A complication of surgery is failure of the esophagus to dilate after the fibrous cord is severed, resulting in *aspiration pneumonia* and ultimately death. Another complication to the surgery is dilation of the esophagus posterior to the surgical site. If either complication occurs, the prognosis is poor.

BAD BITE: See *MALOCCLUSION.*

BLOAT: By definition, bloat is the accumulation of gas in the stomach resulting in the distention of the abdomen. Bloat in a nursing puppy may be corrected by gentle abdominal massage. Administration of a carbonated beverage like 7-UP™ helps to stimulate burping. On the other hand, treat bloat in an adult deep-chested breed as a true emergency. **Professional care must be found immediately!** Additional information about simple bloat or *gastric dilatation* is found in the section in this chapter under *GASTRIC DILATATION, GASTRIC TORSION, AND INTESTINAL VOLVULUS.*

CIRRHOSIS, LIVER: Cirrhosis of the liver, the end result of *chronic liver disease*, is irreversible. Cirrhosis is a diffuse process characterized by fibrosis (scarring) and conversion of normal liver cells into structurally abnormal nodules. Many different agents affecting the liver over a period of time can cause cirrhosis.

The signs present with cirrhosis vary in intensity. *Icterus* (jaundice), *ascites* (fluid accumulation in the abdomen), and *hepatic encephalopathy* are included. In hepatic encephalopathy, central nervous system signs like *circling, head pressing, convulsions*, and coma are present. Treatment of cirrhosis is generally supportive. Maintenance of electrolyte and fluid balance, control of infections, and prevention of low blood sugar levels are important. The prognosis is poor.

CLEFT PALATE AND LIP: The *cleft palate* is a congenital defect resulting from the improper fusion of both sides of the hard palate in the roof of the mouth. This fusion usually occurs during the first third of pregnancy. The severity of the defect varies from a small "V" in the soft palate to complete separation of the entire length from the soft palate in the back to the lip in the front. While the formation of a cleft palate is considered to be a genetic defect caused by a recessive gene, other causes include stress, dietary deficiencies, infectious diseases, and too much *cortisone* during the first four weeks of pregnancy.

Treatment, if attempted, requires *tube feeding* the puppy. See Chapter 8 under *FEEDING METHODS FOR ANOREXIA*. While acrylic palate prostheses have been utilized to minimize nasal infections caused by milk entering the nasal sinus through the defective palate, surgical correction is the only permanent cure. The older the puppy, the better chance for success with anesthesia and surgery. Antibiotics are also required. However, saving defective puppies where strong evidence of genetic involvement exists, is to be discouraged.

Cleft lip or *hair lip* occurs less frequently in the Cocker Spaniel than do cleft palates. This defect, probably genetic in origin, is not as closely associated with the cleft palate in dogs as in humans. Affected puppies can lead a reasonably normal life and would require surgery for cosmetic reasons only. Any surgery should be postponed for several months to decrease the anesthetic risks. Affected Cockers should not be bred.

COLITIS: Colitis is the inflammation of a portion of the large bowel (colon). Clinically, several characteristics separate large bowel disease from small bowel problems. Frequent attempts to defecate, straining, and the passage of red blood and mucous are signs of colitis. A diagnosis is made from these signs and a *colonic biopsy*. Colonoscopy may be necessary to observe the lining of the colon which is very friable with chronic colitis. Because the colon bleeds easily, areas of ulceration result. Although the cause of colitis is unknown, there may be an immune system relationship. Treatment with *sulfasalazine (Azulfidine®)* and an appropriate diet control the signs. Colitis may recur throughout the dog's life.

COLITIS, HISTIOCYTIC ULCERATIVE: *Histiocytic ulcerative colitis* can occur in any breed. *Whipple's disease* is a similar counterpart in man. A chronic hemorrhagic, mucoid diarrhea is observed before the dog reaches two years. Affected dogs run no fever and initially remain in good body weight. As the disease progresses, weight decreases and the hair coat becomes unthrifty. About 30% of the affected dogs exhibit some vomiting.

A definitive diagnosis is made from a *colonic biopsy* via a proctoscope. A radiograph after a *barium enema* is also useful. Blood tests and *fecal examinations* are commonly negative. The cause is unknown, although both environmental and hereditary factors have been incriminated. Under certain conditions, bacteria or viruses may play a part in the etiology.

Treatment is continuous, concentrating on control not cure. Antibiotics and *Azulfidine®* provide reasonable control. Due to the ulcerative nature of the disease, *cortisone* drugs should not be used unless there has been no response to antibacterial therapy.

CORONAVIRUS: Canine coronavirus produces a highly contagious disease of the gastrointestinal tract. The disease is worldwide with an incidence of up to 30% in some areas. While the virus affects dogs of any age, it is particularly devastating to young puppies. The early clinical signs are a lack of appetite and depression followed by vomiting which may contain blood. The moderate to severe diarrhea that occurs is characterized by a yellow-orange color and foul odor. Dehydration, loss of weight, and death may follow. In some cases, the diarrhea phase may recur up to three weeks later. By maintaining fluid and electrolyte balance, supportive treatment is provided. Until recently, no vaccine existed. Currently, a killed virus vaccine has been marketed by Ft. Dodge Laboratories. Because the vaccine has only been available for a short time, its efficiency in the field is not known.

DIABETES MELLITUS: Diabetes mellitus is a disease of the beta-cells of the *pancreas.* See the *ENDOCRINE SYSTEM* in Chapter 4 for further discussion.

DIARRHEA: Diarrhea is the passage of soft or watery feces. This condition results from greater fluid secretion than absorption from the gut due to increased permeability of the intestine, increased movement or motility of the GI tract, lack of absorption due to disease of the GI tract, and excess secretion without changes in gut permeability. All are caused by malabsorption of fluids. Diarrhea is also caused by impaired digestion due to pancreas and/or bile duct diseases. The exact diagnosis of the cause of diarrhea requires careful study of the history of the case and utilization of specific lab tests. After this is determined, appropriate treatment is initiated. Also see *VOMITING AND/OR DIARRHEA, SIGNS OF* in this chapter.

DISTEMPER: Distemper, a life threatening viral disease of dogs, causes severe diarrhea. Due to the availability of good vaccines, its presence today is not as ominous as in past decades. See Chapter 7 on *NEUROLOGICAL SYSTEM* for further discussion.

DYSPHAGIA: Dysphagia is difficulty in swallowing due to diseases of the throat region that cause mechanical blockage, pain, or a nerve dysfunction.

ENCEPHALOPATHY, HEPATIC: In *hepatic encephalopathy*, the liver fails to adequately detoxify waste products in the blood stream resulting in neurological signs. This problem is the result of several abnormalities: *acute liver failure*, a deficiency in the urea cycle enzyme level in the liver, a congenital *portosystemic vascular shunt* (abnormal blood vessel distribution around instead of through the liver), and chronic liver damage causing the production of new blood vessels which bypass the liver. Most commonly, the congenital *portosystemic vascular shunt* occurs in young female Cocker Spaniels. A hereditary basis for the condition exists. Clinically, affected Cockers are small and thin with scruffy hair coats, and a variety of digestive upsets. They are deficient in albumin and globulin plasma proteins. If untreated, neurological signs associated with hepatic encephalopathy occur.

An accumulation of toxic products either formed or ingested in the gastrointestinal tract produce the clinical signs of hepatic encephalopathy. These signs are primarily neurological in nature. The affected dog may constantly *pace* or *circle*, become disoriented, develop behavior or personality changes, have *seizures*, or become comatose. Non-nervous system signs include stunted growth, lack of appetite, increased water consumption, increased urination, anesthesia intolerance, abdominal fluid build-up, vomiting, and diarrhea.

A single test will not diagnose hepatic encephalopathy. The diagnosis can be made by utilizing combined test data. Combined test data eliminates the need for *electroencephalogram* and *cerebrospinal fluid aspiration*. The five most important tests with their results follow: 1) a *blood ammonia test* showing increased blood ammonia (an unreliable test to do unless a local lab or hospital is closer than 30 minutes away), 2) a *urinalysis* showing the presence of ammonium biurate crystals which look like golden brown thorn apples, 3) a lower than normal *BUN test*, 4) abnormal dye retention in a *BSP test*, 5) a radiograph possibly showing a smaller than normal liver and 6) a *liver biopsy* showing liver pathology.

Treatment of hepatic encephalopathy depends on the underlying cause. Some congenital portal-shunts can be managed surgically by partially occluding the abnormal blood flow, thereby causing more blood to flow through the liver. The surgery requires a high degree of expertise.

Medical treatment of hepatic encephalopathy is complex and must be continued for life. Treatment includes feeding a special diet to reduce ammonia production, prohibiting red meat, and limiting dairy and some plant proteins. The use of $K/D^{®}$ and $U/D^{®}$ prescription foods are helpful. Bacterial production in the colon where ammonia is produced can be controlled with *lactulose* (*Cephulac$^{®}$*), *metronidazole* (*Flagyl$^{®}$*), or the use of antibiotics. Cleansing enemas with *Betadine$^{®}$* are also helpful. *Seizures* must be controlled. Although the prognosis is guarded, dietary management and proper medication may allow the dog with hepatic encephalopathy to lead an almost normal life.

ENTERITIS: Enteritis is inflammation of the intestinal tract in the small intestine. With the exception of *Crohn's disease* (regional enteritis of the colon), the term "enteritis" by itself specifically involves the small intestine (duodenum, jejunum, or ileum). The diagnosis is made from *contrast medium studies*, an examination of the history of the case, and the characteristics of the feces involved. Occasionally, *biopsy* or *laparotomy* (exploratory abdominal surgery) are necessary to specifically identify the location of the inflamed intestinal tract.

ENZYMES AND HORMONES, PANCREATIC: *Amylase,* an enzyme produced by the exocrine portion of the *pancreas,* is responsible for starch digestion. Amylase is also produced by the intestine and liver. The amylase laboratory test measures inflammation of the pancreas. Since canine amylase levels are normally five to ten times higher than those found in man, the clinical laboratory must be familiar with canine values and test protocol. The clinician must decide if the elevated amylase values are significant.

Glucagon is a hormone secreted by the alpha cells of the *pancreas* in response to a reduction in the blood sugar level. Through a complex reaction, more glucose is made available to the blood stream.

Insulin is secreted by the beta cells of the pancreatic islets. Its hormonal function lowers the *blood sugar* level.

Produced by the exocrine portion of the pancreas, *lipase* is an enzyme used to accurately measure increased pancreatic inflammatory activity. Lipase values are more specific reflections of pancreatic activity than are *amylase* values. Of the two tests the *lipase test* is more difficult for a laboratory to perform.

For further discussion, see Chapter 4 on the *ENDOCRINE SYSTEM*.

ESOPHAGUS: Connecting the throat with the stomach, the esophagus is a flexible tube surrounded by muscle. A sphincter muscle at either end of the tube controls the opening and closing of the esophagus. If proper nerve innervation from the vagus nerve is not present to allow normal movement of ingesta (food), the esophagus will stretch and fill up with food creating a *megaesophagus*.

Esophageal surgery warrants several special considerations. Since the last half of this muscular tube is within the chest, the thoracic cavity must be invaded to perform surgery on that part of the organ. Thoracic surgery requires more expertise on the part of the surgeon and the anesthesiologist. The esophagus is very prone to healing by constricting scars. The surgeon must therefore be very careful to minimize scarring. Severe strictures after surgery prevent food from passing into the stomach normally.

FECAL EXAMINATION TECHNIQUES:

Equipment required:
— 1 Microscope with 100X and 400X objectives and light source
— Microscope slides and coverslips
— Paper cups and wooden tongue depressors
— Wire tea strainer
— Either test tubes or commercial kits—Ovassay™, Fecalyzer™ or Ovatector™
— Flotation solution (1 pound granulated sugar, 12 ounces water, 2 teaspoons liquid bleach)
— Centrifuge (optional)

Flotation Technique:
— Suspend 1 teaspoon of feces in flotation solution in paper cup. Mix with tongue depressor.
— Filter into second cup through tea strainer.
— Pour into test tube and centrifuge for 3 minutes –OR– Pour into Ovassay™, Fecalyzer™ or Ovatector™. Fill container with flotation solution. Mix and allow to sit for 15 minutes.
— Take sample from the very top of the solution. Place 2 drops on a clean microscope slide.
— Cover with a coverslip. View under low power (100X) over the entire coverslip area.
Note: *Coccidia* and *tapeworm* eggs are very small and may require 400X magnification.

Direct Smear Technique:
— Suspend small amount of fresh feces in flotation solution on a clean microscope slide.

— Cover with coverslip. View under diminished light, first under 100X, then under 400X.

— Use this technique to observe *Giardia*.

FISTULA, ANAL: *Perianal fistula*, another name for anal fistula, more accurately describes the location of these openings around the anus. Anal fistulas can affect any breed but have a higher incidence in males than females.

Three methods of treatment are available. The conservative approach requires long term antibiotic and *corticosteroid* therapy. With conventional surgery, the diseased tracts around the anus are removed. In cryosurgery, the diseased tissue is frozen with either *nitrous oxide* or liquid nitrogen. Post-surgical complications include strictures and incomplete removal of diseased tissue, necessitating additional surgery. The prognosis for complete recovery is guarded to fair.

GASTRIC DILATATION, GASTRIC TORSION, AND INTESTINAL VOLVULUS: THE SYNDROME OF GASTRIC DILATATION (*BLOAT*), GASTRIC TORSION, AND INTESTINAL VOLVULUS (TWISTING OR TORSION) IS A TRUE EMERGENCY! Seek veterinary care immediately. The veterinary emergency clinics popular in metropolitan areas are probably best equipped to handle these life threatening problems.

If you cannot reach ANY veterinary care facility in less than 60 minutes, you should consider attempting to decompress the gas build-up in the stomach yourself. First, clip away the hair on the lower left anterior abdomen where the "ping" sound is loudest when tapping the abdomen with your fingers. Soak the clipped area with rubbing alcohol. Insert a large gauge needle (at least 20 gauge or preferably an 18 or 16 gauge) to the hub. If blood enters the needle, withdraw it immediately and reevaluate the best location. If gas is expressed, continue to gently press on the abdomen to remove as much as possible over a 15 to 30 minute period. THIS PROCEDURE IS NOT A SUBSTITUTE FOR VETERINARY CARE! However, it may give you the one or two hours of time which could be the difference between life and death.

Gastric dilatation (simple bloat) is the stomach filling with gas. Any breed at any age can be affected. Normally, the gas build-up is relieved by vomiting or by its passing into the intestinal tract. Gastric dilatation results from undergoing abdominal surgery, over eating, *pica* (depraved appetite), spinal injuries, gulping air, vomiting, and giving birth. In older dogs, malignant tumors may precipitate the condition. Non-productive vomiting, swelling in the anterior abdomen, restlessness, and excess salivation are the common signs observed. The diagnosis of the problem is made from observation and an abdominal radiograph.

The gas accumulation from gastric dilatation is relieved by passing a stomach tube. *Anesthesia* or *sedation* may or may not be needed for this procedure. Continual gas build-up can be controlled by the surgical placement of a *pharyngostomy tube* which allows the dog to eat and drink normally. After recovery from gastric dilatation, multiple light broth meals for several days followed by multiple feedings of soft foods are recommended. After a few days, the dog may eat several small normal meals instead of a single large feeding. If a dog is troubled with multiple recurrences of gastric dilatation, changes in management of the environment and additional surgical procedures to speed up the emptying of the stomach should be considered.

Both *gastric torsion* and *volvulus* are much more life threatening than gastric dilatation. By twisting both ends of an long air-filled balloon, one can demonstrate **volvulus** or the twisting of the intestine. The air now trapped in the middle part cannot escape. The clinical signs associated with volvulus are subtly different than those seen with gastric torsion. In volvulus, abdominal swelling is more generalized throughout the abdomen, no salivation is observed, and the vomiting is productive. The diagnosis is easily made by radiographs showing long loops of gas-filled intestines. The treatment for volvulus is surgical correction of the twisting and removal of any devitalized sections of intestine. If removal of intestinal sections is required, the surgeon should have better than average surgical skills. More intensive hospital post-surgical care is also needed. With rapid diagnosis and competent care, both simple gastric dilatation and intestinal volvulus have a reasonably good prognosis.

Gastric torsion complex is a multifaceted, life-threatening problem. The exact way in which it develops is not yet known. Deep-chested dogs are more prone to its development. Most cases are seen at night when exercise follows a large meal with water. A history of *gastritis* (stomach infection) is another contributing factor.

Gastric torsion results from the following sequence of events. A late afternoon feeding with a bulky dog food is followed by a large amount of water. Within one to two hours, the dog is exercised by running. Water expands the food causing it to break down while fermentation produces gas in the stomach. During exercise, the weight of the fluid causes the stomach to turn on itself occluding the esophagus (entry) and the intestine (exit) either partially or completely so that the gas formed cannot escape. The fermentation process continues, enlarging the stomach. As the stomach expands and occupies more abdominal space, it pushes against the diaphragm causing respiratory and cardiac embarrassment. Normal blood flow through the liver and spleen is also disrupted resulting in a deep septic shock. As the stomach enlarges, the wall of the stomach is stretched abnormally causing that tissue to die leading to further complications. Whether this scenario is completely accurate is open to conjecture but the actual events closely follow those described. TIME is of greatest importance! An immediate diagnosis and early treatment are absolutely essential. The earlier the condition is diagnosed, the better the prognosis. If the dog is able walk into the veterinary care facility, the dog has a chance!

Three pre-operative conditions must be treated: 1) *shock* due to reduced blood flow to the heart, 2) electrolyte imbalance from poor blood flow and accumulation of abnormal waste materials in the circulation, and 3) cardiorespiratory embarrassment. The exact sequence or protocol for treatment varies between clinicians. The prognosis, at best, is guarded and is actually fair to poor.

If you are lucky enough to own a dog that has survived gastric torsion, you should reexamine your dog management program. Look into changing the number of daily feedings, the amount of food, the kind of diet fed, and the way in which water and exercise are given. Recently several surgical techniques have been developed which stimulate permanent adhesions between the stomach wall and the abdominal lining to prevent recurrences of torsion. REMEMBER—TIME IS OF UTMOST IMPORTANCE IF YOU HOPE TO BE SUCCESSFUL IN COMBATTING THIS KILLER! Also see *BLOAT* in this chapter for further discussion.

GASTROENTERITIS, EOSINOPHILIC: *Eosinophilic gastroenteritis* causes signs associated with the stomach as well as both the small and large bowel. A chronic liquid diarrhea with occasional vomiting and some weight loss is observed. Any breed can be affected. The cause is unknown. Some have guessed that parasitic involvement or an early phase of *regional enteritis* are the reasons for the high *eosinophil* blood count. Others feel a *food hypersensitivity* is the underlying reason. A specific diagnosis may be determined by *biopsy* and peripheral blood cell counts. This disease, while it is responsive to *corticosteroids*, frequently has relapses.

GINGIVITIS: Gingivitis is inflammation of the gums. If you suspect oral disease, inspect the entire mouth and related structures closely. Inflammation and infection associated with the gums are often related to dental and *periodontal disease*. Large amounts of tartar and loose teeth are present in periodontal disease. See *PERIODONTAL DISEASE* in this chapter for additional discussion. Gingivitis may also be a single sign of a systemic disease problem as diverse as *uremic poisoning* or the *autoimmune disease, pemphigus vulgaris*. A number of diagnostic tests are required to determine the underlying cause of gum inflammation.

GLOSSITIS: Inflammation of the tongue is called glossitis. Like gingivitis, glossitis is a sign of oral disease. A good history, observation of the tongue, and diagnostic tests like *biopsies* and *impression smears* help establish a cause. Once the cause of the glossitis is known, appropriate treatment may be initiated.

HAIR LIP: See *CLEFT PALATE AND LIP*.

HEPATITIS: Hepatitis, the inflammation of the liver, has many causes ranging from viruses (*infectious canine hepatitis*) to toxins (copper, alcohol, drugs, etc.). Because the liver has a large reserve, when clinical signs are finally seen, more than 80% of the liver has already been affected. For further discussion of the clinical signs of liver disease, refer to the specific liver disorders.

HEPATITIS, CHRONIC ACTIVE: Toxic build-up of *copper* in the liver results in chronic active hepatitis seen in Cocker Spaniels. Normally, copper passes through the liver to be excreted in the bile. However, in those Cockers affected by *copper hepatitis*, this accumulation of copper rises to toxic levels. In young dogs, the copper increase does not cause any pathological changes. As years pass, the liver cells retain and accumulate toxic levels of copper causing a detectable *hepatitis* (inflammation of the liver). Even at this time, the dog may not be clinically sick. Not until severe damage is done are clinical *signs of liver disease* observed with a chronic active hepatitis present. The Cocker Spaniel breed is at increased risk to develop copper induced *chronic active hepatitis*. In Cockers, genetic tendencies have not yet been proven but are strongly suspected.

While signs of liver disease and *tests for liver disease*, can indicate *hepatitis*, only measurement of the level of *copper* in the liver can definitely prove copper hepatitis. Normal levels reach about 200 parts per million on a dry weight basis and remain constant. Affected Cocker Spaniels will exceed the normal level by as much as ten times. At the Mayo Clinic in Rochester, Minnesota, the level of copper in the dogs liver can be measured. A *liver biopsy* sample is required for this expensive test. Formalin fixed biopsies can be sent for histopathological diagnosis of copper accumulation in the liver to Liver Registry, Veterinary Medical Diagnostic Laboratory, P.O. Box 6023, Columbia, MO 65205. Family lines with suspected cases should be tested to eliminate the trait.

Treatment of copper induced *chronic active hepatitis* is complicated. Reduction of the amount of copper in the diet and possibly drinking water is necessary. Daily administration of a copper chelator, *penicillamine (Cuprimine®)*, at a rate of 125 to 250 mg per average sized Cocker Spaniel given on an empty stomach eliminates stored *copper* from the body. If vomiting occurs, divide the amount into smaller portions. After sixty days of therapy, liver enzyme levels are measured. If still elevated, the therapy is continued for an additional sixty days. In most Cocker Spaniels showing signs of acute liver cell necrosis (death) from copper toxicity, treatment will not lower the copper level under 2000 parts per million DW. Bimonthly monitoring of liver function is continued for life. *Cuprimine®* therapy is used as needed in addition to a *low copper diet*. See Chapter 8 *COPPER TOXICOSIS, DIETARY MANAGEMENT OF*. The long term prognosis is guarded with death usually resulting from liver failure.

HEPATITIS, INFECTIOUS CANINE: Infectious canine hepatitis is a serious viral disease causing acute destruction of the liver cells, inflammation of blood vessels, and clots throughout the blood stream. Its cause, *adenovirus–I*, has been successfully adapted to a vaccine. Signs of infectious canine hepatitis include those of liver failure, high fever, uncontrolled bleeding, and *white blood cell depression*. On occasion, approximately 10 to 14 days after recovery or following the use of some vaccines, a *"blue eye"* occurs in one or both eyes. The "blue eye" is thought to be an immune reaction in the cornea. The cornea swells and becomes cloudy blue. Some "blue eyes" will clear with or without treatment while others will remain permanently cloudy.

HISTOPLASMOSIS: While the respiratory tract is usually infected by the *systemic fungus Histoplasma capsulatum*, the intestinal tract can become secondarily involved. If the colon is involved, a chronic bloody diarrhea results. Affected dogs show signs such as a cough, emaciation, *anemia*, and generalized lymph node enlargement. A *colonic biopsy* is diagnostic. Occasionally the causative organisms are cultured from the stool. Treatment is unrewarding but may be attempted with *amphotericin B* or *ketoconazole*. At best, the prognosis is guarded.

INTOLERANCE, LACTOSE: Lactose intolerance is caused by a deficiency of the enzyme *lactase* which is necessary to break down the *milk sugar, lactose*, in the small intestine. Usually acquired over a period of months, the condition is most commonly observed in three to six month old puppies. These puppies develop diarrhea after being fed milk or other products high in lactose. Withholding lactose from the diet is curative.

INTUSSUSCEPTION: During intussusception one portion of the intestine has "telescoped" (invaginated) into an adjacent section of gut. The region where the small intestine, cecum, and large intestine meet is most commonly effected. The exact cause is unknown but increased intestinal *peristalsis* is a factor. Associated signs include pain, occasional vomiting, passing blood and mucous from the rectum, and the presence of a mass in the abdomen. A definitive diagnosis requires radiography and exploratory surgery. The surgical resection of the "telescoped" part of the intestine prevents recurrence of the intussusception. After surgery, recovery care is the same as for any intestinal surgery.

LIVER DISEASE, SIGNS OF: The specific signs of liver disease depend to some degree on whether or not the condition is acute or chronic.

Acute liver disease may cause depression, lack of appetite, fever, vomiting, and diarrhea. Specific signs include yellow jaundice, fluid build-up in the abdomen, a painful liver (anterior part of abdomen), and the presence of a coma. Chronic liver problems cause the same set of signs as the acute form. Neurological signs such as behavior changes and *seizures* may also be observed. Signs involving the nervous system are seen most often after eating. With *chronic liver disease*, the liver may actually be smaller than normal. In both acute and chronic liver disease, a lack of normally produced *clotting factors* in the liver creates the tendency for bleeding.

MALOCCLUSION: Teeth positioned in such a manner in both the upper and lower jaw so as to interfere with normal chewing and proper closure of the mouth is malocclusion. The common malocclusions in Cocker Spaniels include *brachygnathia (overshot bite), prognathism (undershot bite),* and *wry mouth.*

When the upper dental arcade is longer than the dental arcade in the jaw, an overshot bite or mouth is observed. An overshot mouth can be due to environmental factors that affect the canine and incisor teeth position during the third to ninth month of life. Genetic limits regulating the length of the jaw can be altered by changing the position of canine and incisor teeth. When these teeth do not meet properly, abnormal length or shortness of the jaw can result. The interlock of the teeth in the upper and lower jaw is the most important consideration in the development of the overshot mouth.

The *undershot mouth (prognathism)* also relates to the loss of interlock of teeth especially the incisors. Traumatic accidents which tilt the lower incisors enough to allow them to push ahead of the incisors in the upper dental arch can cause prognathism. With no lock to keep the lower teeth from pushing forward, the maxilla (lower jaw) grows resulting in an undershot mouth. An undershot mouth may appear for the first time at the age of eight to ten months during sexual maturity when spurts of growth in the jawbones occur. Genetically, the condition might be sex-linked since more males are affected by the undershot mouth than females.

The *wry mouth*, observed as a different rate of growth in both sides of the lower jaw (maxilla), is a complicated abnormality frequently considered to be the most serious form of malocclusion. Breeding affected Cocker Spaniels is not suggested.

MEGACOLON: An abnormal enlargement of the colon is classified as congenital or later in life as a *pseudomegacolon* (*obstipation*). Congenital megacolon occurs when faulty nerve innervation to part of the colon allows stool to accumulate without being evacuated. The pseudomegacolon results from some underlying blockage such as a broken pelvis, enlarged *prostate*, cancer of the colon, or any other cause of chronic constipation. The diagnosis is made with a radiograph and a history of little or no stool passage. Treatment of congenital megacolon is surgical while stool softeners, laxative diets, and frequent exercise will aid pseudomegacolon.

MEGAESOPHAGUS: Megaesophagus is an enlarged esophagus. In puppies, megaesophagus is the result of improper nerve innervation or a stricture preventing a bolus of food from entering the stomach. In older dogs, faulty vagus nerve innervation to the esophagus prevents the passage of food from the throat to the stomach. Management of this condition is difficult as aspiration pneumonia is a common sequelae. Affected dogs should be fed a gruel mixture. Elevation of their food bowls will encourage gravitational passage of food to the stomach. The long term prognosis is guarded.

MISSING TEETH: See *ANODONTIA*.

MOTION SICKNESS, DRUGS USED FOR: While riding, some Cockers are affected by automobile motion causing them to salivate and/or vomit. Drugs like *Dramamine*® (*dimenhydrinate*) used for motion sickness and given at the rate of 25 to 50 mg every eight hours or as needed, aids in controlling these signs. For best results, medicine should be given one hour before the car ride is initiated. *Phenothiazine tranquilizers* like *acepromazine maleate* may also help in controlling motion sickness.

OBSTRUCTION, FOREIGN BODY: The ingestion of non-food objects can cause serious consequences. Young Cocker Spaniels may have *pica* (depraved appetite). They will then eat rocks, metal objects, plastic, or other indigestible materials. As these indigestible objects journey through the gastrointestinal system, they may become lodged in the esophagus, stomach, or intestinal tract. These organs cannot dilate enough to allow continued movement. The location of the lodged object determines the observed clinical signs.

In the esophagus, foreign body obstruction is usually located at the thoracic inlet (where the esophagus enters the chest), at the base of the heart, or at the exit of the esophagus from the thoracic cavity (where the diaphragm separates the chest from the abdomen). When lodged in these locations, salivation, difficulty swallowing, regurgitation of solid food, and retention of liquids is observed.

Complete obstructions of the stomach are rare. Occasionally foreign objects will descend into the stomach and then swell preventing movement into the intestinal tract or regurgitation. These dogs exhibit intermittent *vomiting* and weight loss.

In the intestinal tract, obstructions are classified by the location of the blockage. A *high obstruction* is located where the stomach empties into the small intestine (*pylorus*), the first part of the small intestine (duodenum), and the first portion of the subsequent section of gut (jejunum). High obstruction causes projectile vomiting. If present for a long period of time, severe *dehydration* and *electrolyte imbalance* result. A low obstruction occurs in the last part of the jejunum, the ileum and the entire large bowel (colon and rectum). *Low obstruction* causes the accumulation of gas in the intestinal tract. Over an extended period septic shock and death may occur. Because the dog has a much larger esophagus-intestine ratio than man, a dog can swallow something that cannot pass through its intestine.

Treatment for foreign body obstruction involves reestablishing a normal hydration and electrolyte balance. Only then is removal of the obstruction possible. The surgical procedure may be as simple as making an incision just ahead of the object and removing it or as complicated as removing a devitalized section of gut or esophagus. This second surgical procedure requires more skill and more nursing care. The prognosis is generally good. However, many dogs will repeatedly ingest foreign objects.

PANCREATIC DEFICIENCY, CHRONIC: *Chronic pancreatic deficiency* is a relatively common form of food malassimilation in Cocker Spaniels It is thought to be hereditary through an autosomal recessive trait. Progressive weight loss, an increase in stool volume, and a ravenous appetite are common. The affected dogs are active and alert but may develop *pica* (depraved appetite).

Oral administration of deficient *pancreatic enzymes* in either powdered or tablet form is an effective treatment. Of the two forms, the powdered variety is better utilized. In spite of enzyme replacement, three or four meals daily are necessary as this form of therapy is not efficient in digesting food. Also, a diet low in fat and high in carbohydrates and quality protein is recommended. Treatment is necessary for life.

PANCREATIC DISEASE, SIGNS OF: The signs seen in pancreatic disease vary dramatically. The acute form of pancreatitis is readily distinguished from the chronic form. *Acute pancreatitis* is manifested by a rapid onset of abdominal pain and vomiting. The temperature is either elevated or depressed depending on whether or not shock is present. Rapid loss of body water may cause severe dehydration and depression. Intense abdominal pain causes the dog to walk with a very arched back or assume a "praying" position with its front legs down and rear legs standing.

Signs of *chronic pancreatitis* vary more than those observed with the acute, fulminating form. In general, dogs with chronic pancreatic problems develop *diabetes mellitus*. Diabetes has an entirely different set of clinical signs. The most common signs of chronic pancreatic disease are weight loss with a voracious appetite, poor hair coat, and clay-colored, loose, voluminous stools.

PANCREATITIS, ACUTE: Acute pancreatitis, a rapidly fulminating disease, can cause death. Clinically, the cardinal signs of abdominal pain and *vomiting* are associated with a wide variety of others. Nausea, retching, and salivating are observed if the onset is rapid. An affected dog may attempt to place its painful abdomen on a cool surface or assume a praying posture with the front legs down and the rear legs standing. When these dogs stand, they have an arched back. Most dogs that develop acute pancreatitis are overweight with a history of consuming a large amount of food several hours before the disease process began. The affected dog also shows signs of rapidly progressing toxic shock. The dog's temperature is usually elevated. If severe shock is present, however, the temperature will be below normal.

To help make a definitive diagnosis, both blood work and radiographs are necessary. In many affected individuals, the serum appears cloudy from high levels of fasting lipids (fats). The *white blood cell count* is elevated. Increases in *serum amylase* and *lipase* are normally expected in acute pancreatitis. Treatment of acute pancreatitis involves resting the secretory activity of the pancreas. The dog should receive NOTHING by mouth for at least five days. Intravenous and subcutaneous maintenance fluids and electrolytes are essential. All medications should be given parenterally (IM, IV, or Sub Q) and not orally. The drug *atropine* will decrease pancreatic secretion and stimulation. Broad spectrum antibiotic therapy should be instituted in all cases. If shock occurs, appropriate therapy should be promptly started. Currently, opinion suggests that the benefits of *corticosteroids* outweigh the potential for exacerbation of the condition. They also should be utilized in shock therapy.

The prognosis for acute pancreatitis is guarded since death from shock is always a possibility. Hospitalization with intensive care for up to two weeks is necessary. Recurring attacks are minimized with a strict diet, reducing excess weight, providing adequate exercise, and discouraging the tendency to scavenge for food.

PARASITES, INTESTINAL: Intestinal parasites that affect dogs are either *nematodes* (like *roundworms*), *cestodes* (like *tapeworms*), *flukes*, or protozoans (like *Coccidia* or *Giardia*). Each parasite has a specific life cycle. Understanding the life cycle is important in the management of these diseases in a kennel environment. Some parasites have public health importance since they also cause disease in man. Ascarids cause *visceral larval migrans*. *Ancylostoma* (hookworm) causes *cutaneous larval migrans. Echinococcus* (tapeworm) is the most serious *zoonotic infestation. Dipylidium* (tapeworm) is spread by *fleas*. The ingestion of fleas by people can cause infestation with this species of tapeworm. Whether or not man can be infested with the canine protozoan Giardia species is still unclear.

Ascarids (**roundworms**) consist of two main genera, *Toxocara canis* and *Toxocara cati* and *Toxascaris leonina*. These are the most common internal parasites of dogs and can be differentiated on fecal flotation.

Toxocara canis and *Toxocara cati* have a rough outer shell and show a deeply pigmented center. *Toxascaris leonina* has a very smooth shiny shell and a lighter colored inner structure. *Toxocara canis* has a complex life cycle including larval migration through body tissues and transplacental and lactogenic (milk) transmission to puppies. Bitches infested with *Toxocara canis* give birth to puppies with worms. Puppies also become infected from nursing an infested bitch. Conversely, there is no evidence that *Toxascaris leonina* has this kind of life cycle. Therefore, if these internal parasites are controlled in the bitch, puppies will be born free from them.

Signs of ascarid infections include pot-bellied pups, unthrifty and unkempt hair coat, diarrhea, vomiting, *anemia*, and even the expulsion of parasites in the stool or vomitus.

A bitch should be treated before or during pregnancy to lower her worm burden and eliminate puppy transplacental and lactogenic parasite transfer. The use of *fenbendazole* twice daily for two weeks or once daily from the fortieth day of pregnancy until two weeks after the pups are born will greatly cut the parasite load for bitch and pups. Most wormers have some efficiency against roundworms. *Diethylcarbamazine* for heartworm prevention helps keep the ascarid burden low. *Toxocara canis* should be treated at least two times at three week intervals or until a negative microscopic stool exam is obtained.

After ascarids, **hookworms** are the most common internal parasite. The two species of hookworms in the United States are *Ancylostoma* and *Uncinaria*. The blood-sucking hookworm is devastating to small puppies because of the life threatening *anemia* produced.

The life cycle of Ancylostoma is direct. A free-living phase is necessary for the larval form. A dog becomes infected in one of several ways: lactogenically (through nursing), orally, or through larval penetration of the skin and possibly through the placenta before birth. This parasite flourishes in moist, warm climates with sandy soils where the free living larva mature and become infective. The appearance of puppies affected with hookworm disease is one of *anemia*, bloody diarrhea, and depression. The puppy's tongue and gums appear a pale gray-white.

Treatment with an effective wormer should be repeated in 3 to 4 weeks if a microscopic stool examination indicates the need. In addition, the dog's environment must be treated to eliminate the free living larval form. These larvae will mature and penetrate the unbroken skin causing reinfestation. *VIP Hookworm Concentrate*™ (produced by VIP Products) is used on infested ground to aid in hookworm larva control.

Trichuris infection (**whipworm**) is more serious in some areas of the country than in others. Whipworm lives in the large intestine and cecum causing intermittent hemorrhagic diarrhea, *anemia*, weight loss, and a general loss of condition. Its direct life cycle has no migration through the body tissues. Several newer wormers, including *mebendazole*, *fenbendazole* and *butamisole*, have been shown to have a high degree of efficiency on whipworm. Butamisole is injectable while the first two are given orally on three consecutive days.

Two very common **tapeworms** infest the dog. Another species, Echinococcus, has serious public health ramifications. *Echinococcus* tapeworm is uncommon in most parts of the United States. When ingested by humans, very serious problems develop as it uses man for the intermediate host instead of sheep and rodents. *Bunamidine* and *praziquantel* are used to treat Echinococcus infection. *Dipylidium tapeworm* is common in the dog. The normal intermediate hosts are *fleas* and *lice* although humans become infested by ingesting fleas or lice. This tapeworm is commonly diagnosed by finding "rice granules" (dried tapeworm segments) attached to the hair around the anal orifice. Microscopic *fecal flotation tests* may not identify the presence of tapeworm ova. All tapeworms have eggs that are heavier than most other parasite ova causing them to sink to the bottom of the solution rather than remain on the surface. Control of *Dipylidium* tapeworm involves first eradicating fleas and lice.

Taenia tapeworm , another common kind of canine tapeworm, uses rabbits, rats, and mice as intermediate hosts. If a dog eats any of the intermediate hosts, the dog becomes the final host of this parasite. Treatment for both *Taenia* and *Dipylidium* tapeworms is the same as for *Echinococcus*. The newer tapeworm drugs are much more effective and "more gentle" on the dog's system than the old purgative types. Successful eradication depends on intermediate host control.

Clinical signs of tapeworm infection vary from slight to severe weight loss, mild intestinal upsets, and general unthriftiness. Occasionally, anal itching or rubbing is a sign of tapeworm infestation, but more likely those signs are due to *anal sac impaction.*

The **fluke** *Nanophyetus salmincola* is mentioned here only because of the very serious disease for which it serves as a vector and reservoir. In the Pacific Northwest, the disease *salmon poisoning* is caused by a rickettsial infectious agent *Neorickettsia helminthoeca*. The fluke Nanophyetus is the carrier of this organism. Dogs are infected by eating raw salmon and other fish. The life cycle is somewhat complex and passage through a snail is part of the cycle. The incubation period after ingestion of affected salmon is approximately five days. The clinical signs include severe vomiting, hemorrhagic diarrhea, swollen lymph nodes, and high fever. Death is not uncommon. The disease is diagnosed by finding fluke eggs in the feces and the *rickettsia* on a *lymph node biopsy.* Intravenous fluids and *oxytetracycline* antibiotic offer supportive treatment. Hospitalization is necessary with a guarded prognosis.

Of the *protozoan parasites*, the most common **Coccidiosis** is caused by many species of *Isospora*. Coccidiosis is very serious in young puppies and is capable of mimicking diseases like *canine distemper*. This parasite's life cycle develops both within the body and in the environment.

The signs of coccidiosis, similar to those of other protozoan diseases, are watery or bloody diarrhea, loss of appetite and dehydration. Coccidiosis is more common in crowded environmental conditions. Therefore, a combination of treating both the affected dogs and the environment is necessary to eradicate the disease. The use of *sulfadimethoxine* for two weeks is very effective.

Giardia as a cause of watery diarrhea is somewhat controversial since these motile protozoans are occasionally found in normal stools. Giardia have a direct life cycle. Puppies become infected after eating cysts from contaminated food, water, or stools.

Signs vary from none to an explosive, mucoid diarrhea, depression, weight loss, and loss of appetite. Diagnosing Giardia is done by observing a *direct smear* of stool suspended in saline solution under low microscopic light. *Metronidazole* is given two times daily for three days.

Strongyloides stercoralis is an unusual parasitic infection that causes two different syndromes. In young puppies, the intestinal syndrome may include a blood-tinged diarrhea, *anemia*, and even death. This phase is preceded by coughing, loss of appetite, and a purulent infection of the eyes. The other syndrome seen in older dogs results in very itchy red skin lesions where the Strongyloides larva penetrates the body. These *rhabditiform larvae* are found in the stool. Treatment is with *thiabendazole, dithiazanine,* or *ivermectin.*

PARVOVIRUS, CANINE: Canine parvovirus (CPV) is a new intestinal viral disease of dogs first found in the dog population after 1977. Early history of the disease showed widespread outbreaks were commonly affecting dogs of all ages. A vaccine was rapidly developed now limiting most outbreaks to puppies from 6 to 16 weeks old.

Parvovirus infections are accompanied by a high fever, extreme depression, lack of appetite, vomiting, and the passage of watery or hemorrhagic diarrhea. The degree of depression is profound with a rapid onset. A complicating factor in CPV is the presence of heart involvement in young puppies. Because puppy's heart muscle cells are growing and dividing rapidly, these cells are readily attacked by the parvovirus.

A tentative diagnosis of canine parvovirus is made from a blood count. About 50% of affected dogs have a very low white blood cell count (*leukopenia*), more specifically, a low *lymphocyte* count. A definite diagnosis is made by identifying the stool sample origin virus under an electron microscope. If the dog does not survive, samples of intestine examined under the light microscope may provide certain answers. A number of tests use serum to determine the presence of parvo antibody. While these tests may give one an indication that CPV is or was present, they are not considered to be definitive.

The disease must be treated aggressively. Because of its rapid onset, *dehydration* occurs early and must be dealt with properly. Treatment is supportive, requiring either hospitalization or an IV set up at home for continued supplementation of fluids. Using oral medication is difficult because of the vomiting and extreme diarrhea. Parenteral antibiotics are important because the immune system is depressed. Treatment may continue for upwards of two weeks with a guarded prognosis.

While canine parvovirus is a highly contagious virus, immunization is available. Canine origin *parvo vaccine* gives a more dependable response. Live virus vaccines provide greater immunity than killed vaccines. Puppies must receive a series of vaccinations until they are at least 16 to 18 weeks old.

PERIODONTAL DISEASE: Periodontal disease is common in many Cocker Spaniels because of their mouth chemistry. The premolars and molars in the upper and lower jaw become turned and food accumulates between them. The decay of the food by bacteria in the mouth causes a rapid buildup of plaque and tartar on the teeth and inflammation of the gums and alveoli holding the teeth.

Cockers with crowded teeth require teeth cleaning twice a year and frequent use of antibiotics to maintain a full dentition. Gum infection and periodontal disease lead to *tonsillitis, kidney disease,* and *heart disease* if untreated.

PERISTALSIS: Peristalsis is the worm-like movement by which the intestinal canal uses longitudinal and circular muscle fibers to propel its contents.

SALMON POISONING: See *PARASITES, INTESTINAL.*

STENOSIS, PYLORIC: One cause of delayed stomach emptying is pyloric stenosis, either congenital or acquired. Clinically, the congenital form is seen in young puppies when they vomit undigested food about two to four hours after eating. Over a period of weeks, the puppies become emaciated. The acquired form shows the same signs but is due to a space-occupying lesion or a foreign body. The diagnosis is made from *contrast media x-ray* studies which show delayed stomach emptying.

The congenital form when corrected surgically has a good prognosis. The acquired form also involves surgery. If the obstruction is removed, a good prognosis may also be given.

TEETH ERUPTION, AGE OF: Deciduous (*puppy teeth* or *temporary teeth*) teeth start to erupt at two to three weeks of age. By the end of the first month, a puppy will have four deciduous incisors and two canine teeth in place in each jaw. The outer most incisors are erupted by six weeks. The temporary premolars make their appearance between four and eight weeks. By two months of age, ALL of the *deciduous teeth* should be in place. Puppies have 28 "baby" teeth rather than the 42 adult teeth that will take their place by seven to eight months of age. Almost immediately after the eruption of the deciduous dentition, the roots are reabsorbed in preparation for the replacement by adult teeth. Proper radiographs taken at five to six months will show whether or not all adult teeth are present for eruption.

The schedule of *adult teeth eruption* follows. Six upper and six lower incisor teeth (the teeth located between the large "fangs" on the upper and lower dental arcade) will be in place between three months and five months. The four adult canines ("fangs") erupt at five to six months of age. The first premolar (behind the "fangs") erupt at five to six months; the second and third premolars at six months; and the fourth premolar (the largest in the upper jaw) at four to five months of age. Of the two upper molars on both sides in the upper jaw, the first upper molar erupts from five to six months and the second molar is in place at six to seven months. The lower jaw contains three molars on each side. Eruption is similar to the upper jaw on the first and second while the third molar (the largest in the lower jaw) should be in place by seven`months. If the adult canine teeth have not erupted sufficiently to remove the baby canine teeth by seven months, the retained baby canine teeth should be pulled to allow the adult teeth to be properly placed in the mouth.

TESTS FOR GI, LIVER, AND PANCREATIC DISEASES, DIAGNOSTIC: A number of tests are performed to assist in the diagnosis of GI tract, liver and pancreatic diseases. The following list includes various tests that the clinician may feel are necessary to help define the problem.

BLOOD TESTS

LIVER:

- *Alanine aminotransferase (ALT)*— Formerly known as *serum glutamic pyruvic transaminase (SGPT)*, ALT is the most useful liver disease test in dogs.
- *Serum alkaline phosphatase (SAP)*
- *Total serum bilirubin*
- *Bromsulphalein® retention test (BSP)*
- *Blood ammonia* and *ammonia tolerance test*—Because of the required special handling, blood ammonia is difficult to do.
- *Serum protein*
- *Glucose* (blood)

PANCREAS

- Glucose (blood)
- *Serum lipase*—the most accurate enzyme determination of pancreatic damage
- *Serum amylase*—Results are hard to interpret.
- *Glucose tolerance test*—helpful in diagnosis of *diabetes mellitus*
- *Glucagon tolerance test*—test for pancreatic tumors

GI TRACT:

- *Serum electrolytes*—alterations seen with diarrhea and vomiting
- *Complete blood count* (CBC)

COLONIC BIOPSY: Colonic biopsies are useful in identifying the cause of recurring lower GI tract diarrhea. A colonic biopsy helps to distinguish between bowel tumors, inflammation, allergic reactions and infection. The clinician requires special instrumentation and expertise. Biopsy samples are submitted to a pathologist for microscopic determination of the kind of lesion.

HEPATIC BIOPSY: The hepatic biopsy procedure, although not utilized frequently enough, provides information for a more exact diagnosis from which the clinician can more easily formulate an appropriate treatment plan. Prognostic information for the owner and veterinarian is also acquired from the biopsy.

Each method used in a *liver biopsy* procedure has both advantages and disadvantages. Some techniques require specialized equipment such as a biopsy needle and a laparoscope. *Blood clotting tests* should be performed before the biopsy is done. Knowledge of the status of the liver enzyme and serum protein levels is necessary to determine whether a hepatic biopsy should be done and which is the safest technique. The most common potential complications of a liver biopsy procedure are hemorrhage, bile peritonitis, and infection. The use of a liver biopsy in appropriate situations is an important diagnostic tool for the veterinarian because the information gained generally outweighs the risks of the procedure and *anesthesia* required.

CONTRAST MEDIUM X-RAY STUDY: Barium sulfate, the most common contrast medium, is given as a swallow for upper GI tract studies or as an enema for lower

GI tract studies. *Barium sulfate* itself has a soothing effect on irritated tissues making the test itself somewhat therapeutic. Preparation of the dog before contrast studies is very important. For most studies, the dog should be fasted for 24 hours and have a Fleet® enema eight to twelve hours before the x-rays are taken. Another contrast medium used for GI studies is organic iodide like *Gastrografin*® because it is safely used in stomach or intestinal perforations without fear of foreign body reactions.

ENDOSCOPY: This relatively new diagnostic aid in veterinary medicine requires special instrumentation and expertise in evaluating the results. As the use and availability of this equipment increases, exploratory surgical procedures of the lower bowel and stomach may become obsolete.

FECAL EXAMINATIONS: Two kinds of fecal examinations are done as an aid in diagnosing intestinal parasites. The standard *fecal flotation test* carried out in most veterinary offices involves the suspension of a fecal specimen in a flotation medium such as zinc sulfate, sodium nitrate, or saturated sugar solutions. After centrifuging the specimen forcing the heavy particles to the bottom of the tube, the surface of the flotation medium is examined for parasite eggs. Flotation is effective for all intestinal worms except *tapeworm* and possibly *Strongyloides*. Some *fluke* eggs can be found with this method while others will require specialized techniques. *Direct fecal examination* is necessary if protozoan diseases are suspected. Direct smear technique will help diagnose *Giardia*, *Trichomonas*, and *Balantidium* infections. The direct smear must be examined very quickly after the stool is passed as the protozoan parasites disappear rapidly. Although it is a protozoan parasite, *coccidia* can be found on the routine fecal flotation test.

FECAL TRYPSIN TEST: The trypsin test is important in determining the amount of the enzyme trypsin being produced by the *pancreas*. Most veterinarians are able to perform either the film strip digestion test or the more accurate gelatin tube procedure.

SUDAN III STAIN: This dye, used to demonstrate the presence of fat droplets in the stool, may give presumptive evidence of pancreatic inactivity.

VOMITING: Vomiting is a reflex act that results in the forceful expulsion of stomach contents. Causes of vomiting are classified into two categories— abdominal and non-abdominal. Abdominal causes include blockage of the intestinal tract, inflammatory causes like peritonitis, *pyometra*, and *pancreatitis*, as well as infectious causes like *coronavirus* or *parvovirus* infections and parasitic infestations. Non-abdominal causes include conditions that affect the vomit center in the brain and uremic poisoning.

After identifying the underlying cause, the vomiting is either eliminated or treated. Long term vomiting creates some very serious physiological changes such as *dehydration*, *potassium* and *sodium* depletion, and metabolic alkalosis.

VOMITING AND/OR DIARRHEA, SIGNS OF: In order to help determine the cause of vomiting and/or diarrhea, observe the type, frequency, consistency, and length of time after eating before the condition occurs. Prolonged vomiting will cause serious metabolic upsets. *Sodium*, *potassium*, and *chloride* levels are greatly depleted resulting in a metabolic alkalosis. *Dehydration* occurs from loss of more fluids than are being replaced.

Fluid and electrolyte losses also occur in chronic diarrhea situations. The colon is the portion of the large bowel responsible for fluid absorption. If large amounts of fluids are presented to the short portion of bowel, only a small percentage of the total volume will be reabsorbed into the system. Because of their relatively short colon surface, diarrhea is more common in dogs.

MUSCULOSKELETAL SYSTEM

ACHONDROPLASIA: Achondroplasia, a form of canine *dwarfism* present at birth, is inherited as an autosomal dominant lethal gene. Although achondroplasia has been described in the Cocker Spaniel, distinguishing this form of dwarfism from *chondrodysplasia* is very difficult. See *CHONDRODYSPLASIA* for further discussion on dwarfism. Bone growth of the front and back legs is retarded. The very large, dome-shaped head of a achondroplastic dwarf exhibits an exaggerated stop with a very short nose.

ANURY: The term anury means lack of a tail. Occasionally, Cocker Spaniel puppies are born without any coccygeal vertebrae. Considered a recessive trait, the condition could be lethal if the spinal canal is also underdeveloped. As with many congenital defects, the presence of anury may be only one several defects. Before attempts are made to raise such a pup, a thorough examination is recommended.

ARTHRITIS—OSTEO AND RHEUMATOID: Because a number of classifications of arthritis exist, only the most common forms, *osteoarthritis* and *rheumatoid arthritis*, will be discussed.

Many older dogs suffer from the degenerative joint disease called **osteoarthritis.** This condition exhibits no inflammation in the joint lining nor any systemic signs of joint disease (no fever or increased *white blood cell count*). Fragmenting of the weight bearing surfaces of the bones, a loss of cartilage, and new bone formation are characteristic of this problem.

The most frequent locations of osteoarthritis are the hips, stifles, shoulders, and elbows. While signs of lameness are seen in young adults, it gets progressively worse with age. Stiffness when rising that the dog can "warm" out of as it moves is a clinical sign of degenerative arthritis. After a considerable period of time, stiffness and lameness are almost constant.

Several facets of care are helpful in osteoarthritis therapy. An obese dog should lose weight. *Analgesics* like *aspirin* and *phenylbutazone* may help relieve pain. Periods of properly controlled exercise and periods of rest are important during the day.

Rheumatoid arthritis is an inflammatory, noninfectious form of arthritis with an immunological basis. This disease is very erosive to the joints. Primarily found in young adults of smaller breeds, it occurs as late as eight years of age in any breed.

Signs of rheumatoid arthritis are a shifting lameness and joint swelling, most frequently involving the pastern (wrist) and hock (rear leg) joints. Also seen are fever, depression, lack of appetite, and swollen lymph nodes.

A number of lab tests are used to determine the etiology of the lameness. Radiographs of the swollen joint are helpful. *White blood cell counts* are often elevated. A decrease in *serum albumin protein* and an increase in alpha$_2$ gamma globulin protein can also be present. About 25% of the affected dogs have positive *rheumatoid factor tests*. The cause of this disease is unknown but an immunologic basis is suspected since the disease responds to powerful drugs that suppress the immune system.

Treatment of canine rheumatoid arthritis is started with a *corticosteroid* resulting in a dramatic improvement. However, as further exacerbations occur, the cortisone levels must be increased. Ultimately, even high doses will not cause remission. The best therapy is a combination of either *cyclophosphamide* and *prednisolone* or *azathioprine* and *prednisolone*. Since these drugs suppress blood forming cells, weekly and then monthly blood counts should be done to ensure a good response with minimal side effects. The dosage of the medications is tapered to the lowest maintenance level possible.

ASPIRIN (ACETYLSALICYLIC ACID): See *DRUGS USED FOR LAMENESS*.

ATROPHY, MUSCLE: Muscle atrophy or the shrinking of the muscle mass or number of muscle cells has a number of causes. A cast leg will shrink from disuse. Atrophy may also be generalized as in old age or from the use of long term *corticosteroids*.

BANAMINE® (FLUNIXIN MEGLUMINE): See *DRUGS USED FOR LAMENESS*.

BRACHYURY: The congenital abnormality brachyury, defined as short-tailed, is occasionally seen in the Cocker Spaniel. While not a problem itself, breeding may lead to *anury* (lack of a tail) which could be lethal if the spine is deformed.

BUTAZOLIDIN® (PHENYLBUTAZONE): See *DRUGS USED FOR LAMENESS*.

CHONDRODYSPLASIA (DYSCHONDROPLASIA): Chondrodysplasia (dyschondroplasia) is a pathological condition resulting in abnormal growth of cartilage at the ends of long bone shafts and abnormal cartilage present near the *growth plates*. Clinical signs of *dwarfism* occur equally in both sexes. The body is normal length with bowed legs that are shorter than normal. The chest is flattened from spine to brisket. A radiograph shows vertebrae shorter than normal. This condition is probably genetically transmitted as a simple recessive trait.

Chondrodysplasia is diagnosed by radiographs of affected limbs as early as three weeks of age. In this form of dwarfism, the head appears normal, the body length is normal or only slightly compressed, and the limbs are very short with thickened joint areas. Because no treatment for the condition exists, most affected offspring die prematurely. If they do survive, they have difficulty in reproducing.

CORONOID PROCESS, FRAGMENTED OR UNUNITED: *Coronoid process disease* is a potential cause of *elbow lameness* in sporting and working dogs. Because of loose pieces of cartilage, degenerative joint disease results. It is unclear whether the coronoid process fails to join the adjacent ulna (forearm bone) in its developmental stage or whether some traumatic act has fragmented the process causing the degenerative changes to progress.

Diagnosis of coronoid process disease is difficult, but high quality radiographs taken in different positions will aid the clinician in discovering the problem. Normally the bony process is covered with cartilage and is attached to the ulna bone by fibrocartilage or connective tissue.

Treatment of the coronoid process lameness is surgical. Removal of the unattached or fragmented bony processes will stop the degenerative joint condition and alleviate the pain. Prognosis for recovery of normal gait is good.

CRANIOSCHISIS: Cranioschisis, an uncommon congenital defect seen in newborn Cocker Spaniel pups, appears as an abnormal opening which fails to cover the brain in the bony skull. This defect is inherited as a dominant lethal gene. If born alive, affected puppies are immediately destroyed.

CYTOXAN® (**CYCLOPHOSPHAMIDE**): See *DRUGS USED FOR LAMENESS*.

DRUGS USED FOR LAMENESS:
Aspirin (*acetylsalicylic acid*) is an anti-inflammatory drug commonly used to alleviate the discomfort associated with *osteoarthritis*. Increased gastric acidity associated with aspirin administration may necessitate the use of a buffered product in sensitive dogs. Administration can be from 1 to 3 times daily.

Azathioprine (*Imuran®*) is a cytotoxic drug used in combination with corticosteroids to manage *immune mediated lameness* such as *rheumatoid arthritis* and *systemic lupus erythematosus*. Dosage is given every other day. Its principle toxic side effects are gastrointestinal and hematologic.

Cortisones used to treat lameness include *prednisone, prednisolone* and *triamcinolone*. Corticosteroids are anti-inflammatory agents that depress the adrenal glands when used either at high doses or for long periods of time. In the case of *rheumatoid arthritis*, the initial dramatic relief will disappear with time. Most cases will require combination therapy regimens with Cytoxan® or *Imuran®*.

Cyclophosphamide (*Cytoxan®*) is an anticancer drug sometimes used in combination with *corticosteroids* to treat immune mediated lamenesses. This relative of nitrogen mustard can cause reversible bone marrow depression and *hematuria*. Administration is either oral or intravenous.

Flunixin meglumine (*Banamine®*) is a very potent nonsteroidal analgesic with anti-inflammatory and antipyretic (temperature lowering) activity. Although given to dogs, the FDA clearance for the drug is only for horses. It can be given intravenously, intramuscularly, or orally in granular form. Banamine® should not be used more than 1 or 2 days since longer administration may contribute to the development of fatal gastric perforations.

Phenylbutazone (*Butazolidin*®) is an anti-inflammatory nonsteroidal drug used to treat inflammation and lameness. Given either orally or intravenously, long term usage may cause a *blood dyscrasia*.

DWARFISM: See *PITUITARY DWARfiSM* in Chapter 4 on the ENDOCRINE SYSTEM, *ACHONDROPLASIA*, and *CHONDRODYSPLASIA*.

DYSPLASIA: The term dysplasia is defined as an abnormality in development.

Elbow dysplasia (*ununited anconeal process*) is a developmental disease which causes clinical lameness due to an instability of the elbow joint. This condition which has been observed in the Cocker Spaniel probably has a genetic basis. Lameness occurs because the anconeal process, a beak-like piece of bone, has not united to the ulnar bone in the elbow. In most breeds of dogs, the anconeal process does not have a separate bone growth center. In some dogs, however, the growth of the anconeal process occurs separately from the remainder of the ulna bone and then does not unite to form a stable elbow joint. Normally, closure and unification of the anconeal process is complete when the dog reaches $4^1/_2$ months.

The most common sign is elbow lameness that may elicit pain on flexion and extension of the suspicious limb. Many affected dogs will appear to "toe out" as they walk. The diagnosis is made from a lateral radiograph with the elbow in flexion. The "beak-like" anconeal process is not united with the ulnar bone. Many times the lameness is unilateral even though both elbows are abnormal.

Two surgical procedures are performed to treat *elbow dysplasia*. A surgical screw can be placed in the ununited anconeal process to connect it to the ulna or the anconeal process can be removed. Either type of surgery results in a good prognosis if done before severe degenerative elbow joint changes have occurred. The resulting joint instability is not a problem. Removing the *anconeal process* is technically easier surgery. On the other hand, surgical screw placement requires specialized equipment and a higher degree of surgical skill.

Hip dysplasia is a malformation in the development of one or both ball and socket joints in the hip. The hip joint is composed of the socket formed by the bones of the pelvis and the "ball" (head) of the thigh bone (femur). Normally, this joint is a very tight fitting articulation lined with a smooth, lubricated, articular cartilage. The femoral head is connected to the acetabulum (socket) with a strong ligament.

Hip dysplasia is a multifactorial, genetically based disease which is greatly influenced by environmental factors. No "black or white" exists in predetermining the occurrence of the disease. Normal hipped dogs produce offspring with all degrees of hip dysplasia while dysplastic dogs can produce normal offspring.

Signs of hip dysplasia vary from minimal to severe pain in the hip area accompanied by a pronounced lameness. The disease may be apparent by $3^1/_2$ to 4 months in the early extreme. However in an older dog, only stiffness and a reluctance to walk may be seen. All puppies will appear normal radiographically at or shortly after birth. The degenerative changes occur with growth if the genetic and environmental factors for hip dysplasia are present. Affected dogs may shift their weight forward to remove some pressure from the hip joints. These dogs prefer to sit and as a result will not exercise freely. Subtle disposition changes are also noticed.

A definitive diagnosis is made by pelvic radiograph. Some controversy surrounds the need for *anesthesia* and/or *sedation* in taking pelvic x-rays. Positioning of the dog is very important in determining minor or early changes in the hip joints. Properly positioned dogs lie on their backs with rear legs extended parallel to each other and the tail. Dogs with bony backs, deep-chested dogs, and dogs that have abnormal curvatures to their rear legs are difficult to position correctly. The ideal pelvic radiograph will show both sides of the pelvis as a "mirror image." The thickness of the pelvic bones and the size of the "holes" (foramen) in the bony pelvic girdle will be similar. If the pelvis is tilted, one side of the hip joint will appear shallow while the other side appears very deep.

Another complicating factor in some dogs is *subluxation,* an incomplete or partial dislocation of the hip joint. Dogs with loose hip joints will show some degree of subluxation on a radiograph if they are given an anesthetic or sedative for positioning. Subluxation is of concern in several medical instances. Dogs with subluxation will probably have a greater chance of developing degenerative hip diseases as they age because of the abnormal movement that occurs in the ball and socket joint. These dogs are also more apt to have a dislocated hip if they receive a traumatic blow such as in a car accident.

Treatment of hip dysplasia is directed at alleviation of pain. The use of drugs like *aspirin, phenylbutazone,* or *corticosteroids* are partially effective in pain control. Surgery to relieve the spasm produced by the contraction of the *pectineus muscle* provides pain relief in some affected dogs. The surgical procedure involves cutting the pectineus muscle or its tendon of insertion. Exercise is another important facet of hip dysplasia therapy. With slow, gradual increases in walking exercise, the pelvic and thigh muscles become strengthened. These muscles help support the already weakened hip joints. Affected dogs are reluctant to exercise because of the pain. Lack of exercise weakens the involved muscles which in turn adds to the overall weakness. The snowballing "cause and effect" problem must be handled with slow increases in exercise to increase muscle tone. *Anti-inflammatory drugs* used during the early phases of the exercise program are not needed continually after the muscle tone has improved. Recently, attempts have been made at total hip joint replacement surgery. These techniques replace the entire ball and socket joint on both sides with a stainless steel joint. The success rate of replacement surgery appears to be quite good in breeds the size of Cocker Spaniels. The surgery requires a high degree of skill, is very expensive, and requires a long convalescent period.

Manipulation of environmental factors have been advocated by some people over the years as part of the control of hip dysplasia. These procedures include *pectineus muscle surgery* in young dogs, mega doses of *vitamin C* administered to bitches and their offspring during the formative months, cage confinement of growing puppies, and caloric restriction during puppy growth. These procedures are presented here with no opinion as to their worth.

Hip dysplasia is controlled by radiographing all breeding stock and selecting away from severely affected dogs. The use of dogs with hip dysplasia should be limited to those truly outstanding in other traits important in the breed. The *American Spaniel Club Health Registry* maintains a listing of Cocker Spaniels free from hip dysplasia. The health registrar, Miss Judith Wright, can be reached at 2600 Ellsworth Rd., Baldwinsville, NY 13027. To be included in the health registry for hip dysplasia, an OFA number must be obtained and application must be made to the Health Registry. See the section on the *ORTHOPEDIC FOUNDATION FOR ANIMALS (OFA)* for current statistics on the number of Cocker Spaniels that have been radiographed during a past ten year period and the incidence of hip dysplasia in the breed.

Polyostotic fibrous dysplasia is an uncommon genetically based disease which causes the replacement of normal bone with fibrous tissue and immature bony tissue. The normal bone is lysed, eroded, and seriously weakened by the cystic formation that occurs. The condition has not been observed in the Cocker Spaniel.

FRACTURES: A fracture is defined as a break in the continuity of a bone or cartilage. The break may be partially or completely through the bone. Usually a fracture is accompanied by damage to the tissue surrounding the bone (muscle, connective tissue, blood vessels, and nerves).

The following questions illustrate how fractures are classified. Is there an open wound at the fracture site? How extensive is the damage to the bone? What is the direction and location of the fracture? How stable is the fracture?

A complete list of fractures developed from descriptive questions follows.

Avulsion fracture is the separation of a small amount of bone with its attached tendon, ligament, or muscle. The most common site is the tibial crest of the shin bone where the kneecap tendon attaches.

Closed fracture is a fracture with no break in the skin.

Comminuted fracture is one that fragments into a number of small pieces.

Complete fracture breaks completely through the bone walls (cortex) and is usually accompanied by displacement of the fracture ends.

Compound fracture is another name for an "open fracture" where the fractured bones communicate to the outside of the body. Infection and delayed healing is often a problem.

Fissure fracture cracks the bone wall (cortex) leaving the covering of the bone (periosteum) intact.

Green-stick fracture is a fracture of growing puppies in which one side of the bone wall (cortex) is broken but the opposite side is only bent.

Impacted fractures, generally resulting from falls from high places, are those in which the fragments are forcibly driven into each other.

Multiple fracture is a fracture where three or more pieces have no common meeting point.

Nonunion fracture is a type of fracture that has not healed due to infection, lack of blood supply, lack of nutrients, or instability of the fracture site.

Oblique fracture is a fracture where the fracture line is diagonal to the bone and will slip away from alignment because of muscle contraction without stabilization.

Open fracture—See *Compound fracture.*

Physeal fracture, which occurs in growing puppies, is a separation along a growth plate (epiphyseal line).

Spiral fracture is a break in a curved bone due to inherent instability. Fixation of the fracture is required.

Stable fracture is a break where the bone elements are interlocked and are not movable under normal circumstances.

Transverse fracture is a fracture line at right angles to the long axis of the bone.

Unstable fracture is a movable or unstable break caused from the way the break occurred. Oblique, spiral, and compound fractures are examples of unstable fractures which require fixation to stabilize them.

Pain, crepitus (a crunching sound on palpation), swelling, and deformity are signs of a bone fracture. A definitive diagnosis is made by taking two radiographic views. In the treatment of fractured bones, reduction is attempted to bring the fragmented ends into apposition. Reduction is followed by fixation to keep the ends in position until healing occurs.

Age greatly influences the *rate of fracture healing.* Dogs less than three months old only require 2 to 4 weeks of fixation for clinical union to occur. Three to six month old puppies require anywhere from 4 to 12 weeks. Six to twelve month old puppies need 5 to 20 weeks. Adult dogs require from 2 to 12 months for clinical union of a fracture to occur.

GAIT, DYSFUNCTIONS AND DEFINITIONS OF: The term gait defines the manner or style of moving. Definitions of different kinds and types of gait follow. Complete discussion of movement and reasons for faulty movement is beyond the scope of this manual.

Ataxia—a lack of muscular coordination resulting in a weak and weaving type of gait

Crabbing (side wheeling)—the movement of a dog with its back at an angle to the line of travel

Crossing over (weaving)—the swinging of the legs in an arc crossing each other

Flapping—See *Padding*

Gallop—a fast running gait (two kinds of gallop—single and double suspension gallop)

Goose stepping—See *Hypermetric gait*

Hackney action—the exaggerated, high lifting of the front leg with the pastern and paw pointing downward

Hypermetric gait (goose stepping)—an exaggerated gait indicating central nervous system dysfunction

Hypometric gait—a shuffling, sliding gait due to central nervous system dysfunction

Level gait—a form of movement in which the withers do not rise or fall

Lumbering—a heavy, awkward, clumsy gait

Pace—a gait in which the front and rear left feet are on the ground at the same time that the front and rear right feet are in the air and vice versa—considered to be a lazy gait

Padding—(flapping)—the opposite of the hackney action where the pad actually touches the ground before the normal full forward swing of the front leg occurs

Paddling—a circular motion of front legs like the movement of a canoe paddle

Side wheeler—See *Crabbing*

Single tracking—the movement of the individual paws toward a single imaginary line from the center of the body as the gait speed increases—legs incline inward toward the center line

Trot—a diagonal gait in which the right front and the left rear touch the ground at the same time while the left front and right rear are in the air

Weaving—See *Crossing over*

GROWTH PLATE, AVULSION AND PREMATURE CLOSURE: Growth plates are the areas of the bones in young dogs where elongation (increase in size) takes place. These sections of bone are not as strong as adjacent areas which lack this specialized function. *Avulsion of growth plates* or *physeal fractures* occur in the growth plates above the carpus (pastern). Serious deviation of the paw may result if not treated properly.

Premature growth plate closure can occur throughout the body creating a *dwarf* or *chondrodysplasia* situation. Premature closure in individual bones results in a deformity of the long bone conformation. This condition is illustrated in the foreleg where two bones, the radius and ulna, are growing at the same rate. If the growth plate on the ulna closes and the radial plate remains open, the leg below the pastern will deviate toward the outside. Correction of these problems requires an experienced orthopedic surgeon.

HERNIA: A hernia is defined as a protrusion of body tissue through an abnormal opening. The several types of hernias that occur in the dog are described by the location of the protrusion—*umbilical, inguinal, scrotal,* and *perineal.* The *diaphragmatic hernia* is discussed in Chapter 3.

The **umbilical hernia**, equally common in males and females, occurs as a protrusion of tissue under the umbilical scar on the abdomen. This condition is due to a weakness in the umbilical ring or a lack of closure of the *rectus abdominusmuscles* from each side of the abdomen. Umbilical hernias are due mostly to genetic defects and not trauma during the birthing process. This hernia is probably the most common congenital hereditary defect in the Cocker Spaniel. Many of these hernias will heal spontaneously if the tissue that penetrates the hernial opening is kept in the abdomen. The use of a "belly band" on a puppy with a small umbilical hernia can provide beneficial results. If the hernia has not healed itself by 6 months of age and the hernial ring is larger than 1.25 cm ($^1/_2$ inch) in diameter, surgical intervention should be considered. A large umbilical hernia should be corrected surgically as soon as anesthesia can be safely administered since a loop of intestine can become strangulated in the opening increasing the likelihood of additional serious abdominal surgery.

The **inguinal hernia** occurs predominantly in the female. Present on one or both sides, it frequently enlarges with age. The increase in size is actually due to stresses on the area from obesity, pregnancy, or *mammary tumors* which stretch the opening and cause additional tissue to protrude. The male **scrotal** o r **inguinoscrotal hernia** is the counterpart of the female inguinal hernia. These hernias have a hereditary origin so breeding affected Cocker Spaniels should be discouraged. Depending on the tissues involved, inguinal hernias are classified as either direct or indirect. The surgical repair of these hernias is done through one midline incision allowing the inguinal area of the groin to be inspected on both sides and, if necessary, bilateral reconstruction to be performed. The care of this type of herniation is critical during pregnancy since the pregnant uterus can pass through the hernial ring and be strangulated with catastrophic results.

The **perineal hernia** is exclusively a hernia of older male Cocker Spaniels. All affected males are intact and over 8 years old. The cause of perineal hernias in older male dogs is complex and open to discussion. A number of factors exist including hormonal imbalance, chronic constipation, and a congenital predisposition. To make a case for any of these arguments is easy. An intact male with an enlarged *prostate gland* which leads to constipation has more trouble with this type of hernia. Possibly chronic straining from constipation weakens the tissue in the pelvic diaphragm and ultimately leads to the protrusion of tissue around the anal area. Strangulated perineal hernias often contain the urinary bladder or the *prostate gland* and must be handled immediately. Because most of these cases occur in older dogs, some lab tests are necessary to insure satisfactory results from *anesthesia*. In the case of urinary bladder strangulation, *uremia* is usually present and must be dealt with before the surgical correction is undertaken. The chances of recurrence are directly related to the expertise of the surgeon, the type of the suture material used in the hernial closure, and whether or not the dog has been neutered at the time of the surgical repair. If the owner does not want *castration* at the time of the hernia repair, it should be done as soon as the dog is fully recovered from the previous surgery.

HIP DYSPLASIA: See *DYSPLASIA.*

HOCKS, POPPING: Popping hocks bend forward and/or sideways indicating joint and ligament instability. In many cases, the rear leg conformation does not have enough angulation to keep the hock joint in its proper anatomic relationship. Treatment of severe popping hocks involves the surgical tightening of the ligaments. Straight stifled rear leg conformation cannot be changed.

Magnesium deficiency can cause the skeletal defect *hyperextension of the hock*. In its most serious form, a syndrome in which the rear legs appear reversed is observed. *Reversed rear legs* are rarely treated successfully.

HYPERPARATHYROIDISM (RUBBER JAW): Hyperparathyroidism is a disorder in which the amount of hormone secreted by the *parathyroid gland* is too great. The disease may be primary or secondary to either a nutritional problem or a kidney deficiency.

The most common clinical signs are lameness, multiple fractures in older dogs, and a stiff gait. Other signs are apparent if kidney problems are present. Resorption of bone calcium causes the bones of the face and jaws to become very soft and pliable. Since the jaw does not close properly, the term *rubber jaw* is used. The condition is diagnosed by measuring *blood calcium, phosphorus,* and *alkaline phosphatase* enzyme levels. Radiographs are also helpful.

IMURAN® (AZATHIOPRINE): See *DRUGS USED FOR LAMENESS.*

INTERVERTEBRAL DISC DISEASE: The occurrence of intervertebral disc disease in the Cocker Spaniel is common, most frequently striking dogs three to seven years old. Some affected dogs are reluctant to jump up on the couch. Some won't sit up while others won't go up and down stairs. In the Cocker Spaniel, most disc lesions occur in the thoracolumbar area (back region behind the ribs). However, cervical (neck) intervertebral disc lesions occur in older Cockers and are accompanied by neck pain and leg weakness. Affected dogs are reluctant to turn from side to side. In severe cases, all four legs can be weak or paralyzed.

Thoracolumbar intervertebral (IV) disc disease causes lower back pain and rear leg weakness. In rare instances, acute paralysis can occur affecting everything posterior to the vertebral lesion including disruption of bladder and stool control as well as motor function to the rear legs.

IV disc disease is diagnosed by examining the dog for exaggerated or decreased spinal nerve reflexes. When necessary, *radiographs* of the suspicious region of the spinal cord are taken. In some instances, *myelography* is needed to pinpoint the site of the lesion. Further information on diagnosis and treatment can be found in Chapter 7 under *DISC DISEASE, INTERVERTEBRAL.*

INTRAMUSCULAR INJECTION (IM) TECHNIQUE: Intramuscular injections convey medications to the bloodstream more rapidly than subcutaneous injections and less quickly than the intravenous or intraperitoneal routes. The posterior lateral thigh muscles are commonly used for injections. Lumbar muscles, cervical, or shoulder muscles are also used for *IM injections.*

The technique for administering an IM injection involves grasping the muscular posterior portion of the thigh halfway between the hip and stifle. A sharp needle is introduced into the muscle mass up to a depth of $1/2$ inch. Before injecting into the muscle, the syringe plunger is pulled back (aspirated) to make sure that no blood appears in the needle hub. If blood appears, the needle is pulled out completely and reintroduced into a new area. Aspiration is then repeated. Steady pressure on the syringe plunger conveys the injection into the muscle.

The placement of the medication too close to a nerve can cause temporary or permanent lameness. A sterile abscess can also develop around the material that was injected. Drugs recommended for intramuscular injection include most *antibiotics,* some forms of *steroids,* rabies vaccines, and drugs present in an oil vehicle like hormones and *fat soluble vitamins.*

LAMENESS: Lameness is classified as either weight bearing or non-weight bearing. Joint diseases, fractures, tumors, *bone infections*, muscle inflammation, metabolic bone diseases, neurological diseases, as well as ligament and tendon injuries can all cause lameness. The laboratory aids and tests necessary to diagnose the cause include palpation of the involved area, biochemical tests, radiographs, neurological exams, and blood exams.

LIGAMENT, RUPTURE OF ANTERIOR CRUCIATE: The stifle joint is a complex structure that is stabilized by a number of ligaments, tendons, and the patella (kneecap). One of the major stabilizing forces of the stifle joint is the crossed cruciate ligament pair—anterior and posterior. A higher incidence of rupture of the anterior cruciate ligament occurs in middle-aged heavy females. This injury is common in the Cocker Spaniel.

A history of sudden lameness after exercise, pain on movement of the stifle joint, and loss of use of the leg is suspicious of cruciate ligament rupture. Examination of the stifle joint for the characteristic *"sliding drawer syndrome"* may require *anesthesia* or deep *sedation* because of the pain elicited from manipulation of the affected joint. *Radiographs* may be necessary to determine the degree of instability.

In some cases where total separation of the ligaments is not evident, complete rest for thirty days results in healing. Generally, however, treatment is surgical in nature. Surgical procedures vary from construction of a new ligament to placing a mattress configuration of artificial suture material in the side of the joint tissue to reduce the looseness in the entire stifle region. With proper treatment, the prognosis is good for regaining use of the leg. Problems in treatment can occur if a closed surgical approach is employed because unseen structures may be damaged requiring repair before total clinical soundness is restored.

LUXATION: Luxation is defined as the dislocation of a joint. While luxation occurs in any joint, the four most common locations are the hip, kneecap (patella), elbow, and shoulder.

Hip luxation, the most common form of dislocation in the dog, usually occurs as a result of trauma. If the case is diagnosed within four days, non-surgical closed reduction of the dislocated hip is satisfactory unless severe soft tissue and cartilage damage have occurred. Dogs with *hip dysplasia* are more likely to require open or surgical reduction of a dislocated hip because of their shallow hip socket (acetabulum).

The diagnosis of hip luxation is made from clinical signs and *radiographs.* Pain and crepitus (crunching) are present on manipulation of the hip joint. The affected leg appears shorter than the weight bearing leg. For a definitive diagnosis, x-rays show no fractures exist around the hip joint. The reduced joint is immobilized by a sling for 3 to 10 days allowing the surrounding soft tissue to heal. An additional radiograph to verify the reduction is necessary after the hip is reduced. The open surgical reduction which is necessary in some cases carries with it a more guarded prognosis for recurrence.

Elbow luxations are traumatic in origin and generally occur laterally (outside) because of the structure of the bones and ligaments forming the elbow joint. Clinical signs are a non-weight bearing lameness with the elbow flexed and the radius and ulna (bones of the foreleg) deviated to an extreme degree. Radiographs insure that no fractures or serious ligament damage are evident.

For the reduction of the luxation, *general anesthesia* is necessary. Most can be reduced in a closed manner, but rare instances require open surgical reduction. After reduction, utilization of a modified support splint for several days is required. The elbow joint should be flexed and extended to maintain its range of motion. Restricted activity for several weeks is necessary. If ligament damage necessitates surgery, the healing process will be slower with a less favorable prognosis.

Patellar luxation (*slipped stifle* or *slipped patella*) is a common problem in the Cocker Spaniel. Dislocations of the kneecap (patella) can be to the inside (medial), to the outside (lateral), or in some cases, both ways. The abnormal structure of the stifle joint and associated muscles and tendons above it may cause patellar luxation. The position of the tibial crest on the bone below the stifle joint (the shin bone or tibia) also affects patellar luxation. Patellar luxation can be due to a traumatic accident or to abnormal anatomical structures. *Medial* (inside) *patellar luxation* is more common in bow-legged Cocker Spaniels. Conversely, *lateral* (outside) *patellar luxation* is more common in cow-hocked Cockers.

Four stifle (knee joint) structures are important in maintaining normal patellar function. The quadriceps muscle group on the thigh bone must be in a normal location so the patellar (kneecap) tendon is not pulled abnormally to either side. The kneecap must normally "ride" in a groove in the lower part of the thigh bone. The collateral ligaments that attach to the kneecap from the inside and the outside must not be too long or too short. The bony attachment of the patellar tendon on the shin bone (tibia) must be directly under the kneecap to avoid any abnormal pulling on the tendon. If these above structures are not in their normal positions, the possibility for dislocation of the kneecap exists. Signs of medial (inside) patellar luxation are more apparent as the Cocker turns a corner, suddenly elevating the pivoting leg into a flexed position. Pain is very intense in first time dislocations, but less severe in repeat luxations. Generally, lateral (outward) luxations do not cause the pain response that medial luxations do.

Occasionally, radiographs are used in the diagnosis. However, most are diagnosed by palpation of the suspicious joint structure. Treatment in the acute case is directed toward returning the kneecap to a normal position and massaging the thigh muscles to keep them from contracting, forcing the kneecap out of its normal position. In chronic cases where the patella continually luxates or in cases in which the kneecap does not maintain a normal anatomic position, surgical intervention is necessary. Luxations are graded from 1 to 4. The degree of deviation from the normal dictates the kind and amount of corrective orthopedic surgery. The prognosis after competent surgical repair is good for freedom from pain and use of the leg. Evidence has been found linking the development of medial patellar luxation in family lines. Dogs with *hip dysplasia* have a higher incidence of lateral patellar luxation.

Because **shoulder luxations** in Cocker Spaniels are generally due to traumatic accidents, they are fairly uncommon. The dislocation (luxation) can be either to the inside (medial) or to the outside (lateral).

The diagnosis is made by finding a painful deformed leg exhibiting crepitation (cracking and crunching) on flexion and extension of the joint. *Radiographs* will show an abnormal space in the joint cavity.

Closed reduction done under *general anesthesia* followed by immobilization in a splint for several weeks may be successful. However, many times the shoulder suffers from recurrent dislocation. The most satisfactory treatment for shoulder luxation is surgical open reduction of the dislocation and internal fixation to prevent recurrence. This surgical procedure requires a high degree of surgical skill, but the prognosis for functional normalcy is very good.

MUSCULAR DYSTROPHY: Two forms of muscular dystrophy occur in the dog. The form found in young dogs is characterized by the swelling of the muscles in the neck, back, and shoulders. During muscle swelling, the muscle fibers are actually undergoing degeneration. The muscle cells are being replaced with scar tissue and fat cells. The dog becomes progressively weaker resulting in a more stilted and stiff gait. Specific diagnosis is made by *muscle biopsy* and *electromyography* (EMG). The prognosis is poor since no treatment arrests the insidious nature of the disease.

The other form, which occurs in older dogs, is the form most closely related to muscular dystrophy in man. Except for the lack of muscle swelling, clinical signs are similar to the variety in young dogs. Diagnosis is made by muscle biopsy and *EMG*. Again, the prognosis is poor. Information about the hereditary basis of this disease is sketchy.

MUSCULOSKELETAL SYSTEM DISEASE, TESTS FOR: An **autoimmune panel** is composed of a number of blood or tissue tests necessary in the diagnosis of immunological diseases. Autoimmune diseases which affect the muscles or bones include *systemic lupus erythematosus, polyarthritis/polymyositis syndrome, rheumatoid arthritis,* and possibly *panosteitis* and *myasthenia gravis*. An *anti-nuclear antibody test (ANA)*, an *LE Prep*, a *rheumatoid factor*, and a *Coombs'* (direct and indirect) *test* compose an autoimmune panel.

A **bone biopsy** is technically a difficult procedure requiring an accomplished surgeon with specialized equipment. If a space occupying lesion is situated on the bone, a sample of the bone is necessary. The bone sample must undergo special processing before being examined by a histopathologist. A *bone marrow biopsy* is performed much more easily.

The **creatinine phosphokinase enzyme (CPK) test** is an enzyme test used to determine muscle deterioration. CPK enzyme is normally in high concentrations in skeletal muscle. Increased levels in the blood plasma indicate muscular degeneration. This fact is useful in diagnosing certain kinds of *myositis*.

The **electromyography test** measures electro-potential at the muscle fiber membrane. For this test to be valid, the nervous system must be intact and functioning properly. Normal neuromuscular functions have predictable characteristic waves. Both visual and auditory disorders produce abnormal *EMG* results.

Muscle biopsies are examined microscopically. The muscle sample should not be taken from areas near intramuscular injection sites or EMG sites. After being placed in a biopsy clamp to keep it from contracting, the sample of muscle is preserved in formalin

Radiography (X-ray) is useful in the diagnosis of bone and joint disorders. Views taken from several angles are necessary to adequately diagnose some fractures and joint pathology.

Serum aspartate aminotransferase (AST) (formerly serum glutamic-oxaloacetic transaminase or **SGOT enzyme test** is indicative of muscle damage if the enzyme level is elevated and no other liver enzyme levels are increased. After the liver, skeletal muscle contains the largest amount of the SGOT enzyme. By itself, the *SGOT enzyme test* is of limited value.

MYASTHENIA GRAVIS: Myasthenia gravis is classified as a disease of both the muscular system and the nervous system. The disease is characterized by a deficiency of a chemical that transmits the nerve impulse to the muscle. While this can occur in a generalized state, the muscles of the face and neck are most commonly involved. As the disease progresses, chewing and swallowing become difficult and leg muscles grow weak. Severely affected dogs die from failure of the respiratory muscles.

Myasthenia gravis is diagnosed by clinical signs, *EMG* findings, and a positive response to *Tensilon*®. While not absolute, the use of Tensilon® IV will make an affected dog appear normal within one minute. The effect lasts for about fifteen minutes before the muscle weakness reappears.

Oral doses of *neostigmine* or *pyridostigmine* control the disease but treat only the symptoms. However, since myasthenia gravis may be autoimmune in nature, *steroids* are the chosen treatment. Life long drug therapy is essential to control signs although occasional remissions do occur.

MYOSITIS: Myositis, the inflammation of muscle fiber bundles, has varied causes. Traumatic injury produces severe inflammation of affected muscle groups. Some parasites have an affinity for muscle tissue. In the dog, *Toxoplasma gondii* causes a muscular weakness by initiating a myositis. *Leptospirosis* bacteria also cause a severe myositis.

Three forms of myositis from unknown causes occur in the Cocker Spaniel. The treatment is similar for each. **Eosinophilic myositis** occurs in young adults with a predilection for the muscles of the head. The affected muscles may swell at first but later become painful making eating difficult. This disease is diagnosed by the characteristic bony facial appearance, by a high *eosinophil* cell count, and by a *muscle biopsy* which will also contain eosinophils. The cause is not known. Recurrence is common with muscular control becoming progressively more difficult.

Atrophic myositis also involves the muscles of the face and head initially. As it continues, the shoulder and other body muscle groups are affected. After the initial inflammatory response, affected muscles atrophy. In the case of the head and face, the bony outline of the skull becomes prominent. Little pain is associated with this condition. Diagnosis is made from clinical signs and *muscle biopsy*.

Polymyositis is a generalized muscular inflammation involving a number of muscle groups in the body. While pain is present on acute involvement, the usual clinical sign is weakness. This form of myositis occurs with systemic conditions like *systemic lupus erythematosus, rheumatoid arthritis*, and some malignancies. Diagnosis is made by association with other conditions, *autoimmune panel* testing, *muscle biopsy,* and serum enzyme tests (*CPK* and *SGOT* enzymes). Treatment for the three forms of myositis includes *cortisone* in addition to the removal of any other underlying cause. Exacerbations are common. Therapy is required for life. The prognosis is guarded.

MYOTOMY OR TENOTOMY, PECTINEUS: This surgical procedure is performed to relieve pain associated with the shortening of the pectineus muscle in *hip dysplasia*. The small pectineus muscle originates on the bony pelvis and inserts via a long tendon on the inner surface of the femur (thigh bone). It can be palpated in the groin area near the place the pulse is felt. Normally tube-shaped, the pectineus muscle shortens in cases of hip dysplasia joint instability. The surgery involves completely severing the tendon of insertion on the femur relieving the muscle spasm and associated joint pain. Although the surgical procedure does not change the dysplastic nature of the hip joints, for some dogs this is a salvage operation.

ORTHOPEDIC FOUNDATION FOR ANIMALS (OFA): The OFA has served as a registry for several serious canine orthopedic diseases since 1966. Formerly located at the University of Missouri, their new *OFA address* follows.

Orthopedic Foundation for Animals, Inc.
2300 Nifong Boulevard
Columbia, MO 65201
314 / 442–0418

OFA will read a hip radiograph at any age but will not issue an OFA number unless the dog is 24 months old at the time of the radiograph. The submitted x-ray is read by three independent veterinary radiologists. The majority opinion is then expressed in one of the seven classifications developed by the OFA.

Cocker Spaniels with ratings from 1–3 are given OFA breed numbers. These top-rated Cockers can also be listed in the *American Spaniel Club Health Registry*.
    #1 Excellent Hip Joint Conformation — superior hip joint conformation compared to other individuals of the same breed and age
    #2 Good Hip Joint Conformation — well-formed hip joint conformation compared to other individuals of the same breed and age
    #3 Fair Hip Joint Conformation — minor irregularities of hip joint conformation compared to other individuals of the same breed and age

Ratings from 4–7 are ineligible for OFA breed numbers.

#4 Borderline Hip Joint Conformation — marginal hip joint conformation of indeterminate status with respect to hip dysplasia at the time of the x-ray — repeat study recommended in 6–8 months

#5 Mild Hip Dysplasia — radiographic evidence of minor dysplastic changes of the hip joints

#6 Moderate Hip Dysplasia — well-defined radiographic evidence of dysplastic changes of the hip joints

#7 Severe Hip Dysplasia — radiographic evidence of marked dysplastic changes of the hip joints

Between 1974 and 1984, 475 Cocker Spaniels had hip radiographs rated by OFA. Of these, 7.5% were dysplastic. Bear in mind that many other radiographs were not submitted to OFA.

OFA will also evaluate Cockers for *elbow dysplasia*. Radiographs taken and submitted to OFA become their property. Because of the importance of proper positioning for OFA quality radiographs, chemical restraint is necessary in most cases. The dog must be lying on its back with its rear legs extended and parallel to each other.

OSTEOARTHROPATHY, HYPERTROPHIC PULMONARY (HPOA): This uncommon bone disease is the result of a *lung tumor* or in rare cases, other thoracic conditions like *heartworm disease*. In this disease, new bone is laid down on the lower legs causing a thickened, painful extremity. The cause is unknown.

HPOA is diagnosed by *radiograph*. Signs are lameness with thickened bones in the feet and lower legs. After radiographs of the legs are taken, a lateral chest x-ray is done to look for the thoracic mass that has initiated the leg pathology. The prognosis is poor since in a high number of cases, the accompanying *lung tumor* is inoperable. If, however, the lung pathology is resolved satisfactorily, the new bone proliferation on the legs will be resorbed causing the lameness to disappear.

OSTEOCHONDRITIS DISSECANS (OCD): Osteochondritis dissecans (OCD) refers to the breaking or separation of joint cartilage from the underlying bone resulting in this specific degenerative joint disease. The first description was in the shoulder joint involving the cartilage on the humerus (upper arm bone). Now OCD is found in the elbow, hock, and stifle joints with some regularity.

The clinical signs depend on the location and the degree of cartilage involvement. In general, lameness and possibly swelling of the joint will be evident especially if the hock joint is involved. In the case of the shoulder joint, extension of the leg will elicit pain. A clicking sound is heard in the joint. Clinical signs are first seen around six months of age. In over 70% of the cases, both shoulders or sides will be involved. OCD occurs about five times more frequently in males than females.

The diagnosis of OCD is made by clinical signs, history, and finding radiographic lesions. Positioning of the affected area is very important if a radiographic diagnosis is to be obtained. The shoulder is examined from the side, extending the limb by pulling the shoulder joint forward and away from the neck.

If the lameness is in the elbow, a medial oblique, anterior-posterior radiograph will show the inside condyle of the upper arm where OCD lesions occur. The elbow is extended and rotated outward for proper positioning. Standard positioning is adequate for the diagnosis of OCD in the stifle region. Common practice includes radiographing the opposite leg joint after a lesion is found because many dogs are affected bilaterally.

Treatment is subject to some controversy. The conservative approach rests the dog in confinement for two to three months. Others feel that corrective surgery should be done early before serious degenerative changes have occurred. Before making a decision about treatment, consider that any dog with corrective OCD surgery is no longer eligible for competition in American Kennel Club events. On the other hand, dogs that are confined will probably not cause further damage to their shoulders. If healing does not occur, surgical correction can always be undertaken at a later date. Use of pain killers (*analgesics*) is also questionable. Because the dog feels better during confinement, the dog is more difficult to keep quiet increasing the chances of further damage. Complications from surgery are few, other than the development of seromas (serum pockets) at the site of surgery possibly requiring surgical drainage. The surgical procedure is designed to remove any loose cartilaginous pieces or flaps from the affected area. The resulting defect becomes covered with new cartilage over the next year. If both shoulders are affected, some surgeons advocate surgery on both at the same time so recovery is only necessary once. The post-surgical recovery period lasts from 2 to 8 weeks during which confinement is required.

The prognosis is generally good following either successful conservative therapy or surgery done by a competent surgeon. Whether this condition or tendency toward this condition is inherited remains open to debate. Much evidence points toward a familial tendency but no definitive studies have been done.

OSTEODYSTROPHY, HYPERTROPHIC: Hypertrophic osteodystrophy is also called *canine scurvy* since some think *vitamin C deficiency* is the underlying cause of this obscure long bone disorder. Clinical signs are normally observed between three and seven months in large rapidly growing puppies. The most common site for lesions is in the bones of the forelegs just above the pastern joint. The affected bones are swollen, warm, and painful to the touch. The puppy is depressed, has no appetite, and is reluctant to stand or move around.

Definitive diagnosis of hypertrophic osteodystrophy is made by *radiographs* of the affected bones. Occasionally bones other than the forelegs are affected. Because the exact cause is unknown, symptomatic treatment includes the administration of *aspirin* and *phenylbutazone* for pain relief. Nothing definite is known about hereditary factors.

The prognosis is guarded. Many dogs recover completely but some develop bony degenerative problems and become deformed. Death from hypertrophic osteodystrophy is unusual.

OSTEOMYELITIS: Osteomyelitis is an inflammation of the bone marrow and adjacent bone tissue. Although a number of causes exist for osteomyelitis, a bacterial infection or a mycotic (fungus) infection is normally the underlying cause. *Bacterial osteomyelitis* is frequently the result of a contaminated wound from foreign body penetration, *compound fractures*, or internal bone fixation equipment. *Staphylococcus* or *streptococcus* organisms are usually isolated. Lameness, pain, loss of appetite, and fever are all common signs. Diagnosis is made by radiograph and from bone cultures. Antibiotic therapy is used with the possibility of further surgery to remove any free pieces of infected bone or foreign bodies. The prognosis is good but long term treatment is necessary.

Mycotic osteomyelitis, commonly caused by the systemic fungus disease *coccidioidomycosis*, is also seen in *blastomycosis*, *actinomycosis*, and *nocardiosis*. Treatment is the long term use of *amphotericin B* or *ketoconazole*.

OSTEOPATHY, CRANIOMANDIBULAR: Craniomandibular osteopathy, also called *Lion's Jaw* and *mandibular periostitis*, is a noncancerous, noninflammatory, proliferating bone disease which rarely occurs in Cocker Spaniels. Both mandibles (lower jaws), temporal bones, and occipital bones of the skull are involved. Most cases are recognized between three and six months.

Signs include pain when the mouth is opened, excess salivation, fever, depression, and hard swellings on the lower jaws. Radiographic evidence of the proliferation of bony tissue on the jaws or skull enables diagnosis. Both lateral (side) and ventrodorsal (bottom to top) radiographic views should be taken.

Treatment may be both surgical and medical depending on the number of bones involved. If the dog is unable to open its mouth to eat or drink, the placement of a *pharyngostomy tube* is necessary. The condition is self-limiting. After the skeleton has stopped growing, the disease process may regress and completely disappear. In a very severe condition where supportive therapy cannot buy enough time to allow the skeleton to mature, euthanasia is the only alternative.

The prognosis ranges from guarded to good depending on the degree of involvement. Presently this is believed to have a genetic basis. Suspension of further reproduction of the sire and dam should seriously be considered.

PANOSTEITIS: Panosteitis begins at about six months, more frequently in males (5 to 1). The cause is unknown. Other names include *enostosis*, *eosinophilic panosteitis*, and *wandering lameness*. The clinical signs of this bone disorder are *lameness*, reluctance to walk, occasional inappetence, and fever. If the affected leg is firmly squeezed, pain responses are elicited. In differentiating pain associated with panosteitis from other lameness, isolation of the painful area on the long bone is important. The panosteitis pain area is located in the middle of the bone. Painful areas of *hypertrophic osteodystrophy* and *rheumatoid arthritis* are near the joint. Recurring lameness may involve the same leg or affect another leg. Numerous episodes of lameness occur over several months with each lasting from 1 to 30 days.

Diagnosis is made from history, clinical signs, and radiographic findings. Three phases can be differentiated on x-ray providing the affected bone is included in the radiographic evaluation. Each phase reflects a separate period in the progression of the disease.

Treatment is symptomatic using *aspirin, phenylbutazone,* and *cortisone* for pain relief. *Sulfadimethoxine* at the rate of 25 mg per pound also appears to eliminate the condition. Panosteitis is self-limiting and causes no permanent changes. On occasion, however, pain is severe enough to cause a compensatory deviation in normal movement. Sometimes this deviation remains after the disease has run its course. Panosteitis occurs in certain families. Although inherited traits have not yet been proven, it appears to be passed on through asymptomatic brood bitch carriers.

SLIPPED PATELLA (SLIPPED STIFLE): See *Patellar luxation* under *LUXATION.*

SPONDYLOLISTHESIS: Spondylolisthesis is defined as the subluxation (displacement) of one vertebra in relationship to another. Subluxation in the neck is part of the *wobbler syndrome* and *atlantoaxial luxation.* Surgical stabilization of the vertebra to prevent trauma to the spinal cord is necessary. Conservative forms of treatment fail.

SPONDYLOPATHY, CERVICAL (WOBBLER SYNDROME): Cervical spondylopathy is an abnormality of the cervical (neck) vertebra or associated structures which causes neurological dysfunction. Canine wobbler syndrome (cervical spondylopathy) is seen primarily in large breeds. The cardinal sign is a progressive incoordination of the hind limbs. The forelimbs are not affected or are only minimally affected. Clinical signs appear any time after three months and as late as four to five years old. In cases where the onset of signs is very sudden, the dog may become weak or paralyzed on all four legs. Pain is elicited from manipulation of the neck in acute cases.

A variety of changes occur in this syndrome, including osteochondrosis dissecans of adjacent vertebrae, dislocation (subluxation) of the vertebrae, and deformation of the vertebra and associated cartilage. The most commonly affected vertebrae are the last three cervical (neck) vertebrae: C_5, C_6, and C_7. More than one deformity can occur in the same dog.

The cause of the *wobbler syndrome* is unknown, however, several contributing factors have been incriminated. The most commonly mentioned factors are the presence of a large head, selection toward a long neck, and rapid growth. Possibly over-nutrition in the form of excess protein, *calcium,* and *phosphorus* may induce various skeletal changes that precipitate the wobbler syndrome.

The diagnosis of cervical spondylopathy is made by clinical signs, size of dog, and *radiographs.* Proper positioning for diagnostic radiographs is important. A standard lateral (side) view should be compared to a lateral flexed-cervical radiograph looking for anatomical abnormalities. On occasion, the use of *myelography* is necessary to show the contrast between normal and compressed areas of the cervical spinal cord.

Treatment of cervical spondylopathy is designed to decompress the spinal cord and to stabilize any unstable vertebral structures. In acute cases where the dog is paralyzed or very weak in all four legs, use of *mannitol, steroids,* and surgical procedures to decompress the affected spinal cord must be done very early to achieve satisfactory results. Various surgical procedures for stabilization of the cervical vertebrae exist in the veterinary literature. These procedures require a surgeon with above average skills.

Prognosis for satisfactory resolution of this condition depends on many factors including the surgeon's skill. Affected dogs should not be used in a breeding program until more is known about the possible hereditary implications.

SPONDYLOSIS DEFORMANS: Spondylosis deformans, also called *spondylitis*, has a predisposition for Cocker Spaniels over the age of five. The condition is a slowly developing, noninflammatory degenerative bone disease characterized by the development of excessive bone along the bottom of the vertebrae. When this excess becomes so large, the bone from one vertebra actually fuses with the excess bone from the adjacent vertebral body.

From a clinical standpoint, spondylosis deformans is of minor importance offering it as a diagnosis when no other source of back pain can be found. The common signs usually include stiffness, some back pain, and rarely, rear leg paralysis or reduced movement.

Spondylitis is found when lateral radiographs are taken of the posterior thoracic and lumbar vertebrae. The most common area of the vertebra is T_{9-10} to about L_{3-4}.

If treatment is needed, the use of analgesics and not antiinflammatory drugs like low dose *aspirin* is recommended. *Cortisone* is not necessary since no inflammation is associated with the condition. The prognosis for freedom from pain and normal function is fair to good.

SUPPLEMENTATION, MINERAL: With current high quality balanced dog foods available, the need for mineral supplementation is minimal. In fact, over-supplementation can be detrimental to the dog by creating such problems as *osteoporosis* or *osteopetrosis*. Indiscriminate supplementation of minerals also leads to severe imbalances within the body. Only during times of rapid growth is supplementation needed. *Calcium* requirements must be met during bone and body growth and teething. Deficiencies in *zinc*, sometimes found in growing puppies, necessitate the addition of zinc to the diet.

Essential minerals can be divided into those associated with electrolytes and fluid balance (*sodium, chloride, potassium*), those associated with bones (*calcium, phosphorus*), and the trace minerals (*zinc, copper, selenium, manganese, iodine, cobalt, iron*). Collectively, all of these minerals are called *ash content*.

The amounts for most of the minerals necessary for proper growth and maintenance in dogs have been determined. However, some optimal trace element amounts are still unknown. The established calcium level should exceed phosphorus by 1.2 parts to 1 in the diet. Most name brand commercial dog foods are balanced to meet that ratio.

SWIMMER PUPPY: A congenital problem of the Cocker Spaniel becomes apparent at the age of two to three weeks when the largest puppy in a litter cannot pull its legs under its body. This compresses the body from spine to breast bone (similar to a turtle). As the puppy lies on its belly, heart and lung activity are compromised.

When a swimmer puppy is recognized, taping the right front to the left front and the two rear legs to each other for a period of five to fifteen days is important. This keeps the body in a normal shape until the legs are strong enough to support the weight of the puppy. Moving the puppy to a surface with better traction also helps in correcting this condition.

Frequently, additional abnormalities are found internally in swimmer puppies. However, very normal, long-lived Cocker Spaniels can also result from properly managed swimmers.

SYSTEMIC LUPUS ERYTHEMATOSUS (SLE): Systemic lupus erythematosus (SLE) is a serious *immunologic disease* that affects many body systems. *Lameness* is caused by *arthritis* and muscular weakness. Signs include reluctance to walk, difficulty in rising, a low grade fever, and lack of appetite. If the condition has been present for some time, muscles atrophy. Pain is present when the joints are manipulated. SLE is diagnosed by blood tests (*ANA, LE Prep, Coombs' test*) and a negative *rheumatoid factor test*. If other body systems are involved, additional tests are required. High doses of *cortisone* decreased over a short period of time to establish a maintenance level is the recommended treatment. The prognosis is guarded. Watching for infections during long term cortisone therapy is important.

TETANUS: Tetanus is a bacterial toxin disease classified under either the neurological or the musculoskeletal section. The toxin produced by *Clostridium tetani* acts on the nerve receptors. Tetanus causes muscular rigidity and finally respiratory muscle paralysis and death. Also see *TETANUS* in Chapter 7.

TUMORS, BONE: Of the seven bone tumors mentioned in this section, the four most common are *osteogenic sarcoma, chondrosarcoma, fibrosarcoma,* and *hemangiosarcoma.* Unfortunately, a very high percentage of bone tumors are malignant. Rapid diagnosis and treatment are necessary for a reasonable prognosis. However, in most instances, the tumor has already spread by the time of diagnosis. In those cases, the prognosis is poor.

Most common in large breeds, **osteogenic sarcoma** accounts for at least 85% of the bone tumors in dogs. Males appear to be affected more frequently than females with an average age of seven years at the time of diagnosis. Osteogenic sarcoma has been diagnosed in dogs as young as eight months and as old as fifteen years. The most common locations for the tumor are the front legs just above the pastern joint, near the shoulder joint and in the rear leg bones near the stifle joint, hip joint, or hock joint. The tumor involves the long bones near the above mentioned joints and not the joints themselves.

The first clinical sign observed is pain, followed by *lameness* and swelling at the tumor site. The initial diagnosis is made by radiograph. After a bone tumor has been discerned, the definitive diagnosis is made from a *bone biopsy* examined by a histopathologist.

In spite of advancements in cancer chemotherapy, surgical removal of the affected limb remains the preferred treatment for osteogenic sarcoma. The prognosis, even with amputation, is poor as only 10% of amputees live more than one year after surgery. One must contemplate the following three questions when considering amputation: 1) Has the tumor spread from the leg? (A radiograph of the lungs is a must!) 2) Can the Cocker Spaniel get along on three legs? 3) Is the postoperative period of recovery and learning to use three legs realistic? If you answer these questions affirmatively, have the surgery done as soon as possible.

Ten percent of the bone tumors are **chondrosarcomas**, making it the second most common. Seen most frequently in five to nine year old large breeds, the bones most commonly involved are the ribs, nasal bones, and pelvic bones.

Clinical signs of this tumor depend on the bones involved. For instance, if the nasal bones are affected, *sneezing, nasal discharge* and bleeding occurs. If the ribs are involved, many times the tumor is much larger in the thoracic cavity impeding normal breathing. Other bones would obviously cause pain, swelling, and lameness.

Diagnosis is first made by a *radiograph* although definitely distinguishing an osteogenic sarcoma from a chondrosarcoma on an x-ray is nearly impossible. A *bone biopsy* provides the differential. Surgical removal from accessible bones has a guarded to fair prognosis since chondrosarcomas spread much later than the osteogenic sarcomas. Chondrosarcomas infrequently reappear at or near surgical sites years after surgical removal of the tumor.

Although the **fibrosarcoma** is the third most common form of bone tumor, it is rather rare. About two-thirds of the time this tumor involves the facial and head bones. The other third involves the long bones. Those on the head and face are more highly malignant. Diagnosis is made the same way as other bone tumors, radiograph initially and then biopsy of the affected tissue. If the affected bone can be surgically removed, a long term cure is possible because the tumor spreads slowly.

The **hemangiosarcoma** arises from either bone or from soft tissue like muscle. While uncommon, it occurs in large dogs older than five years but has been diagnosed in dogs as young as two. The most commonly affected places are the ribs and the upper arm near the shoulder joint.

This neoplasm causes *lameness*, pain, and lysis of bone. Radiographs show minimal soft tissue swelling and lysis of the involved bone. Unfortunately, this tumor is always well advanced by the time it is presented for diagnosis. Early metastasis (spreading) makes surgical treatment less than rewarding.

Squamous cell carcinomas, also rather uncommon, occur in dogs past nine years old. The most commonly affected site is the toes causing lameness and swelling. Early surgical resection or amputation of the affected toes increases the chance of survival.

The **synovial cell sarcoma** is very uncommon and is normally located around the stifle joint. Radiographs show soft tissue swelling with tumor cells involving more than one bone. Early amputation may produce over a year of survival since the joint capsule is not normally penetrated.

Another complex tumor that affects bone is **multiple myeloma**. This tumor involves the pelvis, thigh bone, lower spine, or upper arm of aged Cockers (over six years). Typical lytic bone lesions are identified on a radiograph. Additional helpful diagnostic data are the presence of *Bence Jones protein* in urine and a very high *plasma protein* level. Treatment of multiple myeloma includes plasmapheresis, cytotoxic drugs, *antibiotics*, and *cortisones*. The prognosis is guarded to fair.

TUMORS, MUSCLE: Primary tumors of skeletal muscle are uncommon. A benign tumor of skeletal muscle, the **rhabdomyoma**, is encapsulated within muscle tissue. The malignant counterpart, the **rhabdomyosarcoma**, metastasizes (spreads) to the abdominal organs or thoracic structures.

NEUROLOGICAL SYSTEM

ADDISON'S DISEASE (HYPOADRENOCORTICISM): See *DISEASES, METABOLIC, AFFECTING THE NERVOUS SYSTEM.*

ANTIBIOTICS, TOXICITY OF: Antibiotics of the *aminoglycoside* type can cause several neurological reactions if given for an extensive period. *Deafness* is the most common neurological problem from high prolonged doses of *gentamicin, dihydrostreptomycin, kanamycin, neomycin,* and *streptomycin.* These antibiotics can also cause the *vestibular disease, head tilt.* These neurological dysfunctions can occur together or individually. While deafness is usually permanent, the head tilt can correct itself if the drug is discontinued early enough.

ATAXIA: Ataxia or failure of muscular coordination is characterized by a staggering, weaving, swaying gait with either exaggerated or depressed leg movement. Causes of neurological ataxia include loss of balance, loss of sensory function to one or more legs, and motor ataxia in which nerve impulses to the legs are abnormal.

AUDIOMETRY: Audiometry, a neurological test, measures the ability to hear sounds. An *electroencephalogram* performed on a sleeping dog measures changes in brain wave activity in response to sounds. Measurement of hearing ability by observing the dog's response to sound stimulus is more practical making the usefulness of audiometry limited in veterinary medicine.

BEHAVIOR OR PERSONALITY CHANGE: Behavior or personality changes can be due to either physiological, neurological or psychological abnormalities. *Hepatic encephalopathy* and *hyperadrenocorticism* are examples of physiological causes of behavioral changes. Neurological abnormalities affecting personality most commonly arise from the frontal lobe of the brain. These altered personality traits include dementia, the inability to learn, *pacing* or *circling*, lack of owner recognition, and excess sleeping or coma. To determine the origin of the neurological signs, various ancillary neurological tests should be performed.

BLASTOMYCOSIS: Blastomycosis is a *systemic fungus* which can affect the nervous system and eyes. When neurological signs are present, treatment is very difficult. The prognosis is poor. See Chapter 10 on the *SENSORY SYSTEMS.*

BLOOD TESTS FOR NEUROLOGICAL DISEASE: As an aid in the diagnosis of neurological disease, the following blood tests are important. A good gauge of liver activity is provided by **BSP retention**, a measurement of dye excreted by the liver. This test is also useful in the diagnosis of *hepatic encephalopathy*. **Blood ammonia testing** is also valuable in diagnosing hepatic encephalopathy and its associated *seizure* activity. The test is difficult to run because the sample of blood must be iced down and the test performed within 30 minutes of collection. A **complete blood count** (CBC), an essential part of every diagnostic work-up, provides information about *anemia* and *lead poisoning*. **Blood gas tests** determine the degree of acidity or alkalinity of the blood as it reacts to the presence of disease. Although the tests are difficult to have run, the results are meaningful. **Serological tests** (serum titers) determine the presence of protozoan and fungal diseases in the body. **Blood sugar tests** measure the change in the blood glucose level. Both low and high blood sugar levels can cause neurological signs.

BOTULISM: Botulism is a rare disease caused by a neurotoxin from the bacteria *Clostridium botulinum* which is found in spoiled food. Clinical signs similar to those of *tick paralysis* and *coonhound paralysis* are seen 24 to 36 hours after eating the tainted food. Fortunately, dogs are fairly resistant to the affects of botulism neurotoxin. However, if the bacteria is present in large amounts, the clinical signs may progress quickly with death occurring in 24 hours. The most common sign is a flaccid paralysis of all four legs.
    Diagnosis is made from a history of ingesting tainted food, the injection of a sick dog's serum into a lab mouse causing its death, or isolation of the neurotoxin from the stomach contents. Treatment consists of the use of a specific antitoxin during the five days following ingestion, high doses of *penicillin*, and nursing care. Prognosis ranges from poor to fair depending on the amount of botulism toxin ingested. Slightly affected dogs recover in approximately four weeks.

CEREBELLAR DEGENERATION: In three to four week old Cocker Spaniel puppies, cerebellar degeneration has been diagnosed when a pup starts to walk. More than one puppy may be affected in a litter.
    Affected puppies can have head tremors, a very unstable gait and, on occasion, an exaggerated gait of lifting the front feet high before placing them on the floor. The condition is not progressive and has no history of any illness related to the puppies or their mother.
    Making a definitive diagnosis from a live puppy is very difficult because a *cerebellar biopsy* is required. This is not a safe procedure if the puppy is to remain a pet. On autopsy (necropsy), the cerebellum of the brain is usually smaller than normal but some appear normal size.
    No specific therapy for this condition exists. If the deficit is not too debilitating, the affected Cocker Spaniel puppy can make a good pet. Since genetic questions remain unanswered. Repeat breedings should be done carefully.

CEREBROSPINAL FLUID (CSF) ANALYSIS FOR NEUROLOGICAL DISEASE: The brain and spinal cord are suspended in a medium called cerebrospinal fluid (*CSF*) which acts as a cushion for the sensitive nervous tissue. Diseases of the nervous system affect the production of the cerebrospinal fluid, the kind of cells present, and the appearance of the fluid itself.

Because a special spinal needle is necessary for sampling cerebrospinal fluid, some expertise is required for the procedure. Fluid may be obtained at the base of the skull, from the cisterna magna, or from the lower lumbar region in the back. While the risk is minimal, some chance of brain stem injury is present.

The spinal fluid cell content must be evaluated within 20 minutes after collection. Spinal fluid pressure is measured with a spinal fluid manometer while the fluid is collected. Compression of the spinal cord, presence of tumors, and inflammation are all evaluations available from a 2 ml sample of cerebrospinal fluid.

CHLORAMPHENICOL: Chloramphenicol (*Chloromycetin*®) is a broad spectrum bacteriostatic antibiotic that passes the blood-brain barrier and thereby becomes useful in the treatment of bacterial infections in the nervous system. In human medicine, life-threatening side effects make this antibiotic a last resort. Side effects in dogs, even after long term high level doses of chloramphenicol, are very uncommon. Also see *DRUGS USED IN NEUROLOGY* in this chapter.

CIRCLING: Circling is a sign of neurological dysfunction. The neurological lesion is located in the *vestibular apparatus* which controls balance and movement. Circling is toward the side with the disturbed vestibular function. Other vestibular signs such as *head tilt*, jerking of the eyeballs (*nystagmus*), leaning and rolling may accompany this condition.

COONHOUND PARALYSIS: See *POLYRADICULONEURITIS, ACUTE.*

CORTICOSTEROIDS FOR NERVOUS SYSTEM USAGE: *Glucocorticoids* are the drugs recommended for the treatment of acute inflammation of the nervous system. *Dexamethasone*, the preferred glucocorticoid for immediate intravenous usage, can be given orally after the initial critical period has passed. Other useful steroids in the treatment of nervous system inflammation are *prednisolone*, *triamcinolone*, and *methylprednisolone*.

CRYPTOCOCCOSIS: The systemic fungus *Cyptococcus neoformans* can cause central nervous system disease. Manifested initially by a chronic *nasal discharge*, the disease eventually progresses through the nasal bony plates. This area of the nervous system is important for smell and behavior. Eye diseases commonly occur concurrently. Treatment is often difficult resulting in a guarded prognosis at best.

CUSHING'S DISEASE (HYPERADRENOCORTICISM): See *DISEASES, METABOLIC, AFFECTING THE NERVOUS SYSTEM.*

DEAFNESS, CONGENITAL: See Chapter 10 on *SENSORY SYSTEMS.*

DIAZEPAM: Diazepam is the preferred drug for controlling *seizures*, especially those due to *true* (*idiopathic*) *epilepsy*. When given intravenously, diazepam is very effective in controlling seizures. However, the oral form of the drug is not effective in stopping seizures in dogs. A combination of diazepam with another anticonvulsant may benefit dogs with difficult to control seizures. Oral diazepam can provide muscular relaxation in dogs that suffer from disc pain.

Also see *DRUGS, ANTICONVULSANT; EPILEPSY, TRUE and STATUS EPILEPTICUS.* Further discussion is in Chapter 1 on *ANESTHESIA.*

DIPHENYLHYDANTOIN: Diphenylhydantoin (*Dilantin*®), a drug used to control *seizures* in dogs, has one serious side effect. If the antibiotic *chloramphenicol* is administered concurrently with *Dilantin*®, cardiac arrhythmias can occur leading to cardiac arrest. Also see *DRUGS, ANTICONVULSANT.*

DISC DISEASE, INTERVERTEBRAL: Intervertebral disc disease occurs fairly frequently in the Cocker Spaniel between three to seven years old. Most disc disease is due to an upward prolapse of disc material against the spinal cord. The most common place for a disc lesion is between the last thoracic and first lumbar vertebra. Disc protrusions can also occur with some frequency in the neck and other lumbar vertebral spaces.

The clinical signs range from neck pain with a reluctance to move the head to a gradually worsening *ataxic gait* and leg weakness (*paresis*). Severe paralysis of the limbs from cervical (neck) disc disease seldom occurs. Lumbar disc lesions result in pain with varying degrees of leg weakness. Acute rear leg paralysis is accompanied with loss of urinary bladder and anal sphincter control.

Diagnosis of intervertebral disc disease is made with lateral *radiographs* and *myelography.* The offending disc in the Cocker Spaniel is commonly calcified. This prolapsed disc material appears as a white mass at or in the spinal canal. While a narrowed space between two adjacent vertebrae is occasionally seen on radiographs, myelography is sometimes necessary to pinpoint the area for surgical intervention. Using myelography to identify the lesion locations has some risk.

Treatment of intervertebral disc disease can be either medical or surgical. Conservative medical treatment may result in future exacerbations. The surgical removal of disc material requires a high level of skill. If the surgical procedure is successful, the chance of a recurrence at the same site is much less than with medical treatment. Several surgical techniques are used in the repair of cervical disc lesions. Both *cortisone* and *diazepam* are useful post-surgically in controlling inflammation and muscle spasms. Following successful surgical intervention, the prognosis for a normal recovery is good. The earlier the surgery is done, the better the prognosis.

DISCOSPONDYLITIS: Discospondylitis is a bacterial infection of the vertebrae and associated intervertebral discs. More than one area along the vertebral column can be involved simultaneously. Dogs of any age or sex are infected. The most common clinical signs include pain in the area around the affected vertebrae, difficulty in rising, and weight loss. Some dogs are depressed, febrile, and have a poor appetite. Specific neurological signs vary with the extent and location of the infection.

Radiographs are used to confirm the diagnosis of discospondylitis. *Complete blood counts, blood cultures, serological testing* for *Brucella canis,* and *CSF analysis* are helpful in monitoring the progression of treatment. If severe neurological signs are not present, long term antibiotic therapy is the recommended treatment. Anti-inflammatory agents like *phenylbutazone* and *aspirin* are also helpful. *Cortisone* usage with a bacterial infection is not generally recommended. Surgical scraping of the vertebrae and immobilization of the spinal column are necessary when severe neurological signs or failure of conservative antibiotic therapy are present.

The prognosis varies greatly and is dependent on the kind of infection and the degree of neurological involvement. Chronic cases can have recurrences up to a year after apparent cures.

DISEASES, FUNGAL, OF THE CENTRAL NERVOUS SYSTEM: *Histoplasmosis, blastomycosis,* and *cryptococcosis* are the three systemic fungal diseases that may affect the central nervous system. Since several body systems are affected, the signs, treatment, and prognosis are discussed in chapters pertinent to each system. In general, if the central nervous system is affected, the prognosis for recovery is poor.

DISEASES, INFECTIOUS, OF THE NERVOUS SYSTEM: The following infectious diseases can cause dysfunction of the nervous system. Refer to each individual topic for further discussion.

BACTERIAL CAUSE
  Meningitis
  Discospondylitis
FUNGAL CAUSE
  Blastomycosis
  Cryptococcosis
  Histoplasmosis

PROTOZOAL CAUSE
  Toxoplasmosis
VIRAL CAUSE
  Adenovirus 1
  Distemper
  Herpes
  Rabies

DISEASES, METABOLIC, AFFECTING THE NERVOUS SYSTEM: The nervous system is affected by *hypoglycemia, hypocalcemia,* and *hypoadrenocorticism,* and *hyperadrenocorticism.* Even though signs of nervous system dysfunction are observed, correction of the basic metabolic disability is necessary before complete neurological recovery will occur.

Addison's disease (hypoadrenocorticism) can cause a generalized weakness. However, at this time, whether the nerve and muscle weakness is due to an increased *potassium* blood level or to the lack of *cortisone* itself is unclear.

In *Cushing's disease (hyperadrenocorticism),* a generalized stiffness, reluctance to move, and some muscle atrophy are present. The excess cortisone can be from an *adrenal gland tumor* or from tablets taken for skin disease.

Treatment of *cortisone* abnormalities is related to returning the body's corticosteroid level to normal. The neuropathy and myopathy signs will disappear over a period of months.

DISTEMPER, CANINE: Canine distemper, a *paramyxovirus* which affects most of a dog's body tissues, has an affinity for nerve tissue. The disease can occur at any age. Prevention is possible with an appropriate vaccination program including annual booster vaccinations.

The clinical signs observed depend on the affected part of the nervous system. Most young dogs show respiratory and digestive tract signs rather than neurological involvement. Older dogs more commonly show signs of neurological disease early in the course of the problem. In rare instances, postvaccinal neurological signs are seen about 2 to 3 weeks after a dog receives a modified live virus vaccination for canine distemper. While the cause is unknown, *encephalomyelitis* is the result.

Clinical signs of distemper affecting the nervous system include *ataxia*, *chewing gum fits* with excessive salivation, *circling, pacing*, head pressing, and severe *seizures*. One curious manifestation is a self-mutilation syndrome in which the dog constantly chews its legs and tail.

Diagnosis is made from the clinical signs, the presence of viral inclusion bodies in tissue samples, and various *serological tests*. With treatment being symptomatic, months of nursing care are necessary. The prognosis is very guarded to poor.

DMSO USE IN NEUROLOGY: Dimethyl sulfoxide *(DMSO)* is a very hygroscopic (water absorbing) liquid solvent approved for topical use in dogs and horses. In acute spinal cord trauma cases, DMSO has been injected intravenously thereby improving the condition of the spinal cord and decreasing inflammation. Current data, however, shows that intravenous usage does not reduce acute spinal cord inflammation. A gel form of DMSO can be massaged over the back for *lumbar disc neuropathy* (disease).

DRUGS, ANTICONVULSANT: *True epilepsy* is managed by several anticonvulsant drugs. Drug therapy should be initiated if *seizures* occur more frequently than once a month. The three drugs used in seizure prevention are *phenobarbital, primidone,* and *diphenylhydantoin (Dilantin®). Diazepam* and *sodium pentobarbital* will stop seizure activity occurring at the time of their administration.

The suggested treatment for controlling a dog in *status epilepticus* (continual seizures) is intravenous diazepam *(Valium®)*. Once the seizure activity has been controlled, sodium pentobarbital, a short-acting *anesthetic*, keeps the dog under anesthesia until the excessive electrical activity in the brain has diminished. When seizure activity has ceased and consciousness has returned, the dog is given an oral maintenance anticonvulsant.

Phenobarbital is most commonly used in large dogs because it is the least costly of the oral anticonvulsants. The dosage required to control seizures may also cause sedation. Because of its sedative effect, phenobarbital is also highly effective in excitable dogs and is particularly useful in dogs that seizure frequently. The peak activity level is attained about 12 hours after administration.

Primidone, a combination of phenobarbital and several other active ingredients, is expensive for large dogs. Like phenobarbital, primidone also has a sedative effect. Possible side effects include increased appetite and water consumption with the most serious side effect being liver necrosis. For this reason, dogs taking primidone should have yearly *liver function tests*. Seizure control can usually be accomplished with less than the recommended therapeutic dosage. A minimum maintenance dosage should be established that can be increased in the face of a stressful or exciting change in the dog's environment.

Diphenylhydantoin (*Dilantin*®) is the most expensive and the least effective drug used for seizure control. Administration is three times daily while *primidone* and *phenobarbital* are given twice. Because it has little or no sedative effect, diphenylhydantoin is the drug of choice for show and working dogs. A therapeutic level in the blood stream is reached in 7 to 10 days severely limiting its usefulness in clustered seizures.

Anticonvulsant therapy SHOULD NOT be stopped abruptly since this triggers multiple seizure activity. When changing from one drug to another, always taper the dosage of the previous anticonvulsant while concurrently increasing the dosage of the new drug. The use of drugs in combination to control seizure activity is a possibility.

DRUGS USED IN NEUROLOGY: Each of the different drugs used in neurology is discussed in other sections of the book under its individual listing. Refer to the index for the exact page. An alphabetical list of these drugs follows:

- Anticonvulsants	- Corticosteroids
- Diazepam	- DMSO (Dimethyl Sulfoxide)
- Phenobarbital	- 50% Glucose
- Primidone	- Levodopa
- Diphenylhydantoin	- Mannitol
- Sodium Pentobarbital	- Reserpine
- Chloramphenicol	- Tribrissen®

ECLAMPSIA: Eclampsia, also called *periparturient hypocalcemia* because it occurs at whelping time, is generally due to a deficiency in body *calcium*. Bitches in a poor nutritional state are more commonly affected. Muscle twitching, generalized convulsive *seizures*, and an elevated temperature may be present. The diagnosis is made by observed signs and the time proximity to whelping (before, during, or after).

Treatment is the administration of *calcium* intravenously while monitoring the heart sounds and rate. Maintenance is then accomplished by subcutaneous or oral calcium during lactation. Puppies should be removed from the mother and raised as orphans should it recur. Prognosis for recovery is good, but recurrences are common.

ELECTROENCEPHALOGRAM (EEG):   Electroencephalography is a means of recording the electrical activity of the cerebral cortex. The electroencephalogram (EEG) is a technique that can be performed on most dogs. *Sedatives* or *tranquilizers* should not be used to help restrain dogs being examined with an EEG.

For an EEG, the dog is placed on its side in a comfortable, dimly lit area. Five electrodes and eight leads are then attached to the head area. Cotton is placed in both ears and the eyes are covered by a mask. The brain wave activity is then recorded. The EEG by itself is not diagnostic. However, the EEG in combination with a thorough history, clinical signs, and other neurological tests can provide information about specific types of nervous system disorders. This advanced diagnostic equipment is only available at referral hospitals and veterinary colleges.

Some of the neurological disorders that produce abnormal EEG tracings are *hydrocephalus, hypoglycemia, hepatic encephalopathy, organophosphate poisoning* and *lead poisoning*, concussions, cerebral hemorrhage, brain tumors, and the inflammation of the brain due to viral, bacterial, fungal, and protozoan infections. *True epilepsy* does not cause any alteration in the EEG brain wave pattern.

ENCEPHALITIS: The definition of encephalitis is the inflammation of brain tissue. *Encephalomyelitis* is the inflammation of both the brain and the spinal cord. This nervous system inflammation can be caused by trauma, tumor, infection, or the presence of a metabolic abnormality.

ENCEPHALITIS, OLD DOG: Old dog encephalitis, thought to be a form of *canine distemper encephalitis*, is a central nervous system disease of older dogs. Its signs, usually chronic and progressive, are *circling, pacing, blindness*, and *behavior disorders*. Test results on the nervous system are similar to those seen in distemper encephalitis. Treatment is symptomatic and unrewarding with a poor prognosis for recovery.

ENCEPHALOPATHY, HEPATIC: *Hepatic encephalopathy*, one of many causes of seizures, may be congenital in origin or acquired as a result of chronic liver failure. Control of *seizures* caused by hepatic encephalopathy involves lowering the *blood ammonia* level by increasing the liver function, regulating the diet, and using intestinal antibiotics to control bowel ammonia formation. See Chapter 5 on the *GASTROINTESTINAL TRACT* for additional information.

EPILEPSY: Epilepsy is classified as either *acquired* or *true* (*idiopathic*). **Acquired epilepsy** can result from a traumatic injury to the skull. *EEG test* results are often abnormal in acquired epilepsy.

True epilepsy has a strong hereditary tendency, occurring primarily in Cocker Spaniels between six months and three years at the onset. Seen as generalized *seizures* that vary from fairly mild to extremely severe, they last from 30 to 90 seconds. Certain breeds tend to have groups of seizures (*cluster seizures*) which are more difficult to control with *anticonvulsant* medication. Dogs that have had seizures should have both a physical and neurological exam including the necessary ancillary tests. If no cause is found, true (idiopathic) epilepsy should be considered. Anticonvulsant medication should be administered to animals that have more than one seizure per month. In veterinary medicine, the type of seizure is usually not classified.

Frequently, the owner's reaction during an epileptic seizure is one of helplessness. Remember, no dog has died from a single seizure. The dog is not aware of his activity. No attempt should be made to manipulate the dog's tongue during a seizure since he may close his mouth on the hand of the person that is attempting to help him. Instead, position a dog having a seizure on some soft flooring away from any stairs. Make a note of the length and characteristics of the seizure (e.g. paddling on side, urinating, passing stool, foaming at mouth, etc.). Your veterinarian will want to know the duration and type of seizure for diagnostic and treatment purposes. If medication is necessary for seizure control, the choice of drug depends on the size of the dog, the owner's ability to medicate at a given interval, and the cost of the medication. The different anticonvulsants used on dogs are discussed under *DRUGS, ANTICONVULSANT* and individually within this chapter.

The prognosis for managing epileptic seizures is fair to good, depending on the breed. Cocker Spaniels generally respond well to anticonvulsant medication. Control of seizures is a lifelong task. Because of its hereditary nature, Cocker Spaniels affected with epilepsy should not be used for breeding.

FACIAL NERVE PARALYSIS, IDIOPATHIC: Paralysis of the facial nerve occurs with some frequency in either sex of adult Cocker Spaniels. Most affected dogs are over five years old. A similar condition, *Bell's palsy,* occurs in humans. The canine condition develops rapidly involving one or both sides of the face. Clinically, a droopy ear, droopy lip, and a paralyzed eyelid are seen. Further examination reveals a relationship between *otitis media* and facial nerve paralysis in many Cocker Spaniels. When infection or inflammation in that area affects the nerve, damage may occur to branches of the facial nerve in the middle ear. The facial paralysis is usually permanent. No form of therapy alters the course of the disease. Determining the degree of function of the tear glands on the involved side of the face is essential because the glands lubricate the eye. If *Schirmer tear test* results indicate reduced tear flow, daily use of artificial tears keeps the eye moist. About 10% of the Cockers with facial nerve paralysis are also affected with *keratoconjunctivitis sicca (dry eye).*

50% GLUCOSE: To help reduce swelling in the brain and spinal cord, glucose in 50% concentrations can be given orally or intravenously as a diuretic. Glucose can also be used as a source of sugar in treating seizures caused by a low blood sugar level (*hypoglycemia*).

HEAD TILT: A head tilt, often associated with rolling eyes and *circling,* is a sign of neurological dysfunction. They are indicative of a lesion in the vestibular mechanism of the inner ear and cerebellar portion of the brain. Congenital idiopathic disorders, a toxicity to *aminoglycoside* antibiotics, an idiopathic geriatric form of the *vestibular syndrome*, inner ear infections, tumors, and trauma are all possible causes of head tilt.

Treatment for vestibular signs is directed at the underlying cause if one can be found. Various ancillary neurological tests such as *skull radiographs*, *EEG tests*, *CSF analysis*, and a good clinical neurological exam should be done in an attempt to diagnose the cause. Prognosis is variable depending on the exact cause.

HISTOPLASMOSIS: The systemic fungus *Histoplasma capsulatum* which usually affects the bowel or lungs is discussed more fully in Chapter 3, *CARDIOPULMONARY SYSTEM*, and Chapter 5, *GASTROINTESTINAL TRACT*. The central nervous system can also be infected and its presence there is difficult to eliminate. Prognosis of histoplasmosis with neurological signs is poor.

HORNER'S SYNDROME: Horner's syndrome is characterized by three specific neurological signs: *miosis* (pinpoint pupil constriction) of the eye on the affected side, *ptosis* (drooping of the eyelid on the affected side), and *enophthalmos* (sinking in of the eyeball on the affected side).

The presence of Horner's syndrome with other signs of neurological dysfunction helps to identify the location of nerve disease. An interesting condition which occurs in dog-auto accidents involves Horner's syndrome and a paralysis of the foreleg on the same side. Nerve roots that originate in the neck and extend down the leg are severely traumatized. An idiopathic Horner's syndrome also occurs for which no cause can be determined. Many of these will resolve over a period of months with or without treatment. If Horner's syndrome is recognized, a first-rate neurological examination with possible ancillary tests should be scheduled in an attempt to identify any underlying lesions.

HYDROCARBON TOXICITY, CHLORINATED: The ingestion of chlorinated hydrocarbon products either through the skin or orally causes muscle tremors, generalized *seizures*, and an exaggerated response to either noise or manipulation. A diagnosis of chlorinated hydrocarbon toxicity requires a history of exposure to a chlorinated hydrocarbon product and the presence of the neurological signs. Because no antidote is available, treatment is symptomatic. Seizures must be kept under control. *Phenothiazine* type tranquilizers (*Promace*®) should not be used since they can potentiate seizures. The prognosis is guarded, depending on the amount of chlorinated hydrocarbons absorbed into the body and the degree of success achieved in managing the neurological signs.

HYDROCEPHALUS: The most frequent neurological disease of young dogs is hydrocephalus (*water on the brain*). While some puppies are born with *congenital hydrocephalus*, an infection or a parasitic infestation by *Toxoplasma* can affect other puppies early in their development. Some forms of *brain cancer* in adult dogs cause fluid build-up in the brain tissue causing *acquired hydrocephalus*.

Congenital hydrocephalus is usually seen in the smallest puppy in the litter. Many times the skull has a domed appearance. He may exhibit signs of irrational behavior, aggressiveness, *seizures*, and may be unable to be house trained. These behavior abnormalities may not be apparent until the dog is four or five months.

In the acquired form, early clinical signs are similar to other central nervous system disturbances. Affected puppies or dogs may *circle*, exhibit *irrational behavior*, appear *blind*, and cry. A neurological examination with the use of ancillary tests will show abnormal nervous system signs. EEG tracings show changes similar to *adult encephalitis. Skull radiographs* with contrast media demonstrate most cases of hydrocephalus. *CSF analysis* shows changes confirming the presence of infection as a cause of acquired hydrocephalus.

Treatment of hydrocephalus is variable in kind and success. In some cases, surgical removal of fluid from the brain can be beneficial. In the congenital form, frequent *seizures* can be controlled with *anticonvulsant therapy*. An acquired form caused by an infection should be treated with *antibiotics* and possibly *steroids*.

The prognosis to become a normal dog is poor. Some young puppies will stabilize enough to allow them to be reasonably good pets, although their learning ability is markedly impaired. Because of the progressive nature of hydrocephalus, the prognosis is very poor in many young dogs.

HYPOCALCEMIA: A low blood calcium level is a cause of seizure activity. Calcium levels below 7 mg/dl can be due to heavy lactation, *pancreatitis*, and *hypoparathyroidism*. The administration of injectable or oral calcium can generally control seizures and muscle tremors caused by low blood calcium levels. See *ECLAMPSIA*.

HYPOGLYCEMIA: Low *blood sugar* (hypoglycemia) is the most common metabolic cause of *seizures*. Excess stress, overexertion on an empty stomach, insulin overdose, and the presence of an *insulinoma* (tumor) are all causes of low blood sugar levels. All seizure patients should be tested for low blood sugar on admittance to the hospital. A *50% glucose* solution given intravenously will control hypoglycemic seizures but the underlying cause should then be explored. The *glucagon tolerance test* and the *glucose tolerance test* are necessary to identify the exact cause of hypoglycemia.

IMMUNE DISORDERS OF THE NERVOUS SYSTEM: *Coonhound paralysis*, *optic neuritis*, *myasthenia gravis*, *polymyositis*, and *chronic polyradiculoneuritis* are all immune disorders that affect the nervous system. Even though these conditions are immune mediated, ancillary neurological tests should also be conducted since other causes may be found.

INTOXICATIONS AFFECTING THE NERVOUS SYSTEM: A large number of chemical substances have a direct affect on the nervous system causing *seizures* or altering the level of consciousness causing comas. Some chemicals cause muscular twitching while others produce specific neurological signs like *deafness, circling*, and *head tilt*.

If central nervous system signs are observed following exposure to any chemical substance or plant material, immediately call your veterinarian or contact the poison control unit in your area. The ANIMAL TOXICOLOGY HOT LINE can be reached by calling **217 / 333-3611**. In Southeastern United States, call **404 / 542-6751**. Be prepared to give the toxicologist the name of the plant, the chemical name of the substance, or the brand name of the substance you suspect is causing the toxic signs.

KNUCKLING OVER: Knuckling over may be a sign of nervous system dysfunction. Standing upright in a normal manner on all four feet is normal *proprioception*. A simple *proprioceptive test* can be done by placing each foot individually in a knuckled over position and observing how long the dog takes to right itself. From this test, the neurologist can obtain important information about the function of the peripheral sensory nerves and its relationship to the cerebral cortical part of the brain.

LEVODOPA (L-dopa): Levodopa, a drug used for the treatment of Parkinson's disease in humans, has had some success in the prevention of *spinal cord trauma* after injury in canines. Presently, its use is experimental in veterinary medicine.

LOSS OF BALANCE: Loss of balance is a sign of neurological dysfunction in the vestibular area of the inner ear which functions to provide normal balance. This loss of balance results in *head tilting*, *circling*, and rolling. The varied causes of *vestibular dysfunction* include tumors, toxic chemicals, trauma, and infections.

LYSOSOMAL STORAGE DISORDERS: While lysosomal storage disorders are considered rare, several are recognized in the Cocker Spaniel at four to six months of age. As a group of metabolic disorders, lysosomal storage problems are due to enzyme defects in nervous system cells. Because proper metabolic pathways are deficient, normal digestion of lipids, glycoproteins, and mucopolysaccharides does not occur. Disruption of nervous cell function causes the cells to die producing the signs of nervous system disease. Lysosomal storage disorders are transmitted by autosomal recessive genes making both the sire and the dam carriers. These diseases must be differentiated from *multisystem neuronal degeneration* which can only be positively diagnosed by a veterinary pathologist examination of brain tissue after death.

MANNITOL: A drug used to treat swelling in the nervous system is 20% mannitol with its potent diuretic action.

MENINGITIS: Meningitis, the inflammation of the membrane surrounding the spinal cord, is most commonly caused by *Staphylococcus* bacteria and *Cryptococcus* fungus. Signs are neck stiffness and an exaggeratedly stiff walking gait. A fever may also be present without involvement of other body systems.

Analysis and culture from cerebrospinal fluid are important aids in diagnosing meningitis. Prognosis varies from good to poor depending on the cause. Fungal infections have a poor prognosis because of the toxicity of the treatment and the length of time that therapy must be maintained.

MENINGITIS, BACTERIAL: This uncommon disease of the lining around the spinal cord is usually localized in the brain stem (the first part of the spinal cord). The *Staphylococcus* and *Pasteurella* species of bacteria are frequently present in .*bacterial meningitis.*

High fever and increased sensitivity in the neck are the observed signs which reflect the area of the nervous system involved. Diagnosis is made from clinical signs, *blood counts, microscopic examination* of *cerebrospinal fluid,* and isolation of the causative agent from CS fluid. Antibiotics are used in the treatment of bacterial meningitis. The prognosis for complete recovery is fair to good.

MYASTHENIA GRAVIS: Myasthenia gravis can be either congenital or acquired. See the complete discussion in Chapter 6 on the *MUSCULOSKELETAL SYSTEM.*

MYELOGRAPHY: Myelography is a special technique done to pinpoint spinal cord lesions when simple *radiographs* are not diagnostic. Diseases generally diagnosed with myelography include *intervertebral disc disease*, spinal cord compression, *spinal dysraphism*, meningocele, and some tumors of the spinal cord. During the procedure, the contrast substance *metrizamide*, currently the safest, is injected into the cerebrospinal fluid (CSF) at the cisterna magna (the base of the skull) or in the middle lumbar region of the back. The contrast substance mixes with the CSF and flows to the area of the compression or expansion. With the contrast substance present, a radiograph clearly shows the defect. Because some danger is associated with this technique, the risk-benefit ratio must be carefully contemplated. Side effects include increased body temperature, convulsions, and death.

NEURITIS, OPTIC: Optic neuritis, a condition of the central nervous system, impairs the dog's sight due to inflammation of the optic nerves. Some cases of optic neuritis appear to be *immune mediated* while virus infections, tumors, and *vitamin A deficiency* have also been mentioned as causes.

The most common sign is a rapid onset of *blindness* with widely dilated eyes that fail to respond to light. Ancillary tests are not particularly useful in diagnosing optic neuritis. Response to treatment is varied. Some cases respond dramatically to the initial high doses of *corticosteroids*. Other cases show no response to the treatment or experience relapses after an initial response to therapy. Recurrences and the presence of optic nerve atrophy give an overall poor prognosis for recovery.

NEUROLOGICAL DISORDERS, CONGENITAL: "Congenital" means present at birth but is not necessarily hereditary. A list of the congenital neurological disorders follows. More detailed discussion of each can be found under the topical headings.

- Cerebellar degeneration
- Congenital deafness

- Hydrocephalus
- True epilepsy

NEUROLOGICAL DISORDERS, SIGNS OF: The following list of signs of nervous system disease are discussed under each individual heading:

- Ataxia
- Behavior or personality change
- Circling
- Head tilt
- Horner's syndrome
- Knuckling over

- Loss of balance
- Pain perception
- Pupil abnormalities
- Proprioceptive loss
- Seizures
- Visual loss

NEURONAL DEGENERATION, MULTISYSTEM Multisystem neuronal degeneration, a previously undescribed syndrome of red-haired Cocker Spaniels, has been found to have a probable genetic basis. Observed at about six months of age in both sexes, abnormal behavior and loss of house training habits are noticed. Affected dogs become apathetic, have *anorexia*, do not recognize their owners, and become aggressive. All tests of serum, cerebrospinal fluid, and skull radiographs are normal. The disease can only be diagnosed at necropsy (autopsy). The development of progressive *ataxia* and a deteriorating mental state must be differentiated from *cerebellar degeneration* and *lysosomal storage diseases*. Both cerebellar signs (*ataxia*, tremor, *hypermetria*, and difficulty in maintaining balance) and cerebral signs (*circling* and *seizures*) are observed in multisystem neuronal degeneration. Currently only seen in red Cocker Spaniels, there appears to be a familial tendency.

ORGANOPHOSPHATE TOXICITY: The class of chemical compounds referred to as organophosphates is commonly used to kill *parasites*. The chemical may be applied topically (dip or bath) or taken internally as a wormer. When the organophosphate is present in *flea collars*, the dog continually absorbs the insecticide. Excessive amounts of organophosphates can cause nervous system signs like pinpoint pupils, muscle tremors, and *seizures*. Mild signs include excess salivation, vomiting, and diarrhea.

The antidote for organophosphate poisoning is *atropine* and *Protopam*® *chloride* (*2–PAM Chloride*). If *seizures* are occurring, medication to control them must be included in the treatment regimen. Any organophosphate chemicals still present on the skin or hair should be removed to prevent further absorption. Organophosphate poisoning has a fair to good prognosis for recovery.

OVERDOSE, INSULIN: An overdose of insulin can cause severe *hypoglycemia* (low blood sugar) leading to *seizures*. Insulin overdose is caused from the administration of too much insulin in the treatment of *diabetes mellitus* and from the tumors of the insulin producing cells of the pancreas (*insulinoma*). Treatment is in the form of sugar, either orally or intravenously.

PAIN PERCEPTION: Altered pain perception, for example, in the skin over the lower back or neck, is a sign of a central nervous system lesion. A lesion involving the intervertebral discs causes pressure on the nerves or the spinal cord in that region. If the skin is lightly pricked with a pin in the area of the disc lesion, an exaggerated reflex movement of the skin results.

PARALYSIS, TICK: Tick paralysis is a neurological disease produced by a toxin secreted by wood ticks. The toxin produces clinical signs very similar to *coonhound paralysis*, but the treatment and prognosis are considerably different. While mild signs include some rear leg weakness, a flaccid paralysis of all four legs with respiratory and swallowing difficulty is present in more severe cases. *EMG* testing can differentiate tick paralysis from coonhound paralysis.

Thoroughly examine any dog suspected of tick paralysis looking for an engorged female tick and removing any ticks present. General supportive therapy is necessary for 24 to 48 hours. Recovery is rapid. The prognosis for complete recovery from tick paralysis is excellent after the offending ticks are removed.

PERIPHERAL NERVE INJURY: Injury to a peripheral nerve is common in auto accidents. In a traumatic nerve injury, the nerve becomes inflamed and swollen. Early use of *glucocorticoids* like *dexamethasone* cuts down on nervous system inflammation. If edema (swelling) of the nerve exists, *50% glucose* or *mannitol* helps control this undesirable condition. After the injury of a peripheral nerve, five or six weeks may be required for normal function to return. During this period, physical therapy of the affected muscle groups is extremely important. If function has not normalized in six weeks, a permanent neurological deficit can be anticipated.

PHENOBARBITAL: Phenobarbital is the preferred drug in controlling *seizures* created by excitement or in cases where cost is a significant factor. Also see *DRUGS, ANTICONVULSANT.*

POISONING, LEAD: *Lead poisoning* is a common cause of neurological dysfunction in puppies. Teething puppies may chew on items containing lead (rubber boots, golf balls, asphalt roofing, linoleum tile, caulking compounds and some ceramic dog food dishes). Acute lead toxicity will cause decreased *red blood cell* maturation producing *anemia* which then results in the swelling of the brain and neuron degeneration.

The most common signs of lead poisoning are uncontrolled running, screaming, fits, biting, and general hysteria. If the lead intoxication has occurred slowly, signs of *ataxia*, incoordinated movements, or even a total lack of functional movement may be evident. Determining the clinical difference between *distemper*, *rabies*, and lead poisoning is difficult. A *blood lead test* with an elevated lead content is most beneficial. Urine lead levels can also be determined. *Radiographs* of the abdomen may show lead items in the gastrointestinal tract.

The chelating agent calcium disodium ethylenediaminetetraacetic acid (*Calcium EDTA*) diluted in 5% dextrose solution is given subcutaneously four times daily for four to seven days for treatment. If other nervous system signs are observed (e.g. *seizures*), they are treated symptomatically. When the treatment is started early in the course of lead intoxication, the prognosis for recovery is good. However, if the condition is chronic, irreparable brain damage can be present with a poor prognosis for recovery. Additional information is found in Chapter 9 under *LEAD POISONING*.

POISONING, STRYCHNINE: Strychnine poisoning is caused by the ingestion of the chemical strychnine. Strychnine, sometimes used as a poison for varmints, is most frequently used to lace meat by a person intentionally trying to kill a dog.

Somewhat similar to both *tetanus* and *toxaphene poisoning*, the clinical signs of strychnine poisoning are severe muscular rigidity with the head and neck being thrown back to an extreme degree. Any loud noise will cause the affected dog to have muscular spasms and *convulsions*.

If strychnine poisoning is suspected, stomach contents should be saved for analysis. *Seizure* activity must be controlled. Oxygen should be administered as needed. The dog must be kept in a quiet, dark area on soft bedding and turned from side to side every four hours during the recovery phase. The body temperature may be elevated, however, when the excessive muscle twitching is controlled, the temperature returns to normal. The prognosis for recovery is guarded to good depending on when treatment is initiated and if the stomach contents are removed to prevent further absorption of the poison. Additional information is found in Chapter 9 under *STRYCHNINE POISONING*.

POLYRADICULONEURITIS, ACUTE: Acute polyradiculoneuritis, a relatively common neurological disorder of dogs, is believed to have an immune origin. Because it frequently occurs after a raccoon bite, its more common name *coonhound paralysis* has been coined. Acute polyradiculoneuritis, however, is also seen following systemic disease and *vaccinations*.

Dogs are not usually affected before they reach six months. The first sign of rear leg weakness quickly progresses to paralysis of all four legs. The degree of involvement varies. In severe cases, respiratory muscles can become paralyzed causing labored breathing and possible death. The dog not only has difficulty eating and drinking but its bark is also characteristically changed. Diagnosis is from the clinical signs in addition to a history of a raccoon bite or a recent vaccination. When available, an *EMG test* is very helpful.

Extensive nursing care is important for recovery. For 7 to 14 days, assistance with fluid and food intake and aid with excretory functions is necessary. The paralyzed dog should be placed on a water bed or sheepskin to minimize bed sores. To keep blood from stagnating in the lungs, the dog should be turned over every 4 to 6 hours. When adequate nursing care is provided for the required time, prognosis for recovery is good. Recurrences are common with acute polyradiculoneuritis.

PRIMIDONE: Primidone, a drug used in the control of *seizures*, is considered to be the most predictable drug in the anticonvulsant group. However, in some dogs, side affects involving the liver occur. Also see *DRUGS, ANTICONVULSANT*.

PROPRIOCEPTIVE LOSS: *Proprioception* is the ability for a dog to stand on the footpads with the legs under the body in a normal way. A loss of this ability (proprioceptive loss) is a sign of a nervous system lesion. An easy way to test for proprioceptive loss is to place the dog's paw in a knuckled over position and observe the dog to see if he corrects this abnormal posture. Failure to correct this abnormal position is evidence of a proprioceptive loss.

PROTOZOAN INFECTIONS OF THE NERVOUS SYSTEM: *Toxoplasmosis* is the only protozoan infection of the nervous system that affects dogs. See *TOXOPLASMOSIS*.

PSEUDORABIES: Pseudorabies, also called *mad itch* and *Aujeszky's disease*, is a rare, rapidly fatal disease caused by a *herpes virus*. Most commonly seen in swine and cattle, the transmission to dogs requires ingestion of infected tissues. The clinical signs in dogs are an uncontrollable itch, mutilation of the legs and tail, excess salivation, difficulty in swallowing, and death in one or two days. Any dog dying of these signs should be examined for *rabies virus*. Because no treatment or vaccine is available for pseudorabies, the prognosis is hopeless.

PUPIL ABNORMALITIES: The ability of the pupil of the eye to constrict and dilate should be present in normal seeing eyes. The presence of different sized pupils can be an indication of a lesion in the eye, optic nerve, or anterior portion of the brain. This difference is also seen in *Horner's syndrome*. Widely dilated pupils that fail to constrict in response to bright light may indicate blindness. A tightly constricted pupil in both eyes is observed in some *chemical poisons* which affect the nervous system. Pupil constriction is seen in several other disorders of the nervous system.

RABIES: Rabies, a fatal viral disease of all warm-blooded animals, causes a progressive *encephalomyelitis*. The disease can be prevented by timely *rabies vaccinations*. Most states have regulations concerning the frequency with which vaccinations should be administered.

The most consistent sign of rabies infections is its inconsistency. Almost all cases will show a change in disposition and behavior. If the dog is NORMALLY aggressive, it will become friendly; if it is NORMALLY friendly, it will become aggressive and menacing. The variety of signs observed in rabies include fever, excess salivation, difficulty in swallowing, depression, viciousness, paresis, and paralysis of any or all limbs.

The transmission of rabies takes place through a bite from an infected animal. The virus is transmitted from the saliva of the carrier to the bite wound of the victim. The virus travels along nerve endings to the brain where the rapidly fatal encephalomyelitis occurs. Death will occur in three to eight days from the onset of the appearance of clinical signs.

In rare instances, clinical rabies can be induced by a rabies vaccination. This condition is actually an *acute polyradiculoneuritis* and is not fatal as long as *encephalomyelitis* does not occur. The leg where the vaccination was given will be lame and even show signs of paralysis. The inflamed peripheral nerves recover in one or two months in most cases. This type of vaccine-induced disease only occurs when a modified-live virus vaccine is used.

Any dog suspected of having rabies should be handled very carefully and should be placed in a quarantine facility. If any chance of human exposure exists, a qualified diagnostic laboratory must test its brain for the presence of rabies virus after the dog dies.

The prognosis for recovering from clinical signs of rabies is hopeless. A dog that has not been vaccinated and is exposed to the bite of a known rabid animal should be quarantined for six months or destroyed.

RESERPINE: Reserpine (*Sandril®*) is a potent drug used in the treatment of severe spinal cord trauma. When given within twelve hours of the injury, the reduction of hemorrhagic necrosis of the spinal cord is significant.

SEIZURES, CAUSES OF: The causes of seizures listed here are discussed fully under each individual heading:

- Eclampsia
- Encephalitis
- Epilepsy
- Hepatic encephalopathy
- Hydrocephalus
- Hypocalcemia
- Hypoglycemia

- Insulin overdose
- Intoxications (strychnine, organophosphates)
- Lead poisoning
- Pancreatic tumor
- Uremia

SODIUM PENTOBARBITAL: Sodium pentobarbital is a drug used in the control of nervous system *seizures* and as an *anesthetic*. Also see *DRUGS, ANTICONVULSANT* and Chapter 1 on *ANESTHESIA*.

STATUS EPILEPTICUS: Status epilepticus is continuous *seizure* activity never allowing the body to return to a conscious, normal state between episodes. This life-threatening situation requires emergency veterinary care. Because of the continuing seizure activity, the body temperature elevates, greatly altering the body's metabolism. A lack of oxygen causes the brain to swell.

Treatment is directed at stopping the seizure activity. Intravenous *diazepam* and *sodium pentobarbital* are given. If the body temperature remains high, alcohol or ice baths may be necessary. *Mannitol* is used if brain swelling is suspected, followed by *corticosteroids*. Should *hypoglycemia* become a problem, *50% glucose* may be necessary.

The prognosis for the recovery from status epilepticus is fair to good depending on the underlying cause of the seizure activity. Immediate veterinary help should be sought to stop status epilepticus.

TESTS USED IN THE DIAGNOSIS OF NERVOUS SYSTEM DISORDERS:

- Audiometry
- Blood tests
- Cerebrospinal Fluid
  (CSF Analysis)
- Electroencephalography (EEG)

- Food-elicited cataplexy test
- Myelography
- Physostigmine provocative test
- Skull X-ray

TETANUS: Tetanus is a life-threatening disease caused by *Clostridium tetani*, a bacteria which usually occurs in deep, contaminated wounds. Although dogs are more resistant to this toxin than horses, dogs can still be severely affected. Dogs raised around horses should receive tetanus antitoxin and possibly *tetanus toxoid vaccinations* to prevent this serious neuromuscular disease.

The clinical signs of tetanus and *strychnine poisoning* are very similar. Extreme muscle twitching and rigidity are evident in both. Muscular stiffness is generalized. An affected dog walks like a wooden horse. The head and face muscles are characteristically affected. The ears are drawn back over the head, the forehead is wrinkled, and the lips are drawn back tightly. The third eyelids cover the eyeballs. Since all of the body muscles are affected, respiratory and cardiac muscle problems are also apparent. *Seizures* and difficulty in swallowing are common.

Treatment must be continued for as long as thirty days or until all muscle stiffness is gone. Initially, large doses of tetanus antitoxin (assuming no allergic reactions occur) and *penicillin G* are used to kill the bacteria and neutralize the toxin. Other signs are treated symptomatically. All wounds should be cleaned out and disinfected. Finally, the dog must be kept in a quiet, dark place and given extensive nursing care.

The prognosis for recovery is guarded. If the clinical signs become progressively more severe, the prognosis is grave. If the signs are mild, reasonable expectation of recovery after prolonged treatment can be anticipated.

TOXOPLASMOSIS: Toxoplasmosis is a *protozoan disease* that infects many body tissues causing *encephalomyelitis* and *myositis* in any aged dog. Toxoplasmosis is spread in uncooked meats, in fecal material, and by flies and cockroaches. Public health is a definite aspect. No pregnant women should handle any animals diagnosed as having toxoplasmosis because human fetuses may be severely affected by this protozoan parasite.

The signs are typical of any infection involving the brain and related tissues. Toxoplasmosis is very difficult to diagnose. Sampling blood over a two week period and checking for a rising titer to Toxoplasma is the best method.

The prognosis varies. If there is a concurrent immunosuppressive disease (e.g. *canine distemper, leukemia*), toxoplasmosis will spread rapidly in the body making the prognosis poor. However, early treatment of mildly affected dogs provides a much better prognosis.

TRAUMA, HEAD: Head trauma, internal or external, is a cause of various neurological signs. The severity of the neurological signs is determined by the degree of trauma and the injured area of the head. An external blow to the skull can cause swelling within the skull. Internally, either ruptured blood vessels or blood clots can cause head trauma. The prognosis for head injuries is guarded.

TRAUMA, SPINAL: Spinal trauma can occur as a result of manipulation during spinal surgery, a traumatic accident (e.g. car, bad fall), damage from disc and cervical vertebrae instability, or an improper *CSF sampling* technique. The spinal cord is very sensitive to movement and pressure from any source. Hemorrhage around the spinal cord causes necrosis of the nerve tissue. If untreated, necrosis causes the cord to become nonfunctional. However, if spinal cord trauma is properly treated within twelve hours of the injury, some chance of recovery from nerve tissue dysfunction is expected.

TRIBRISSEN®: This antibacterial drug is useful in treating nervous system infections. *Tribrissen®* is composed of two drugs that cross the blood-brain barrier, *sulfadiazine* and *trimethoprim*. Administration, either orally or by injection, is once or twice daily depending on the seriousness of the infection. The antibacterial spectrum for sulfadiazine-trimethoprim is wide. Side effects to Tribrissen® include *"dry eye," optic neuritis,* and *idiopathic thrombocytopenia.*

TUMOR, PANCREATIC: A pancreatic tumor (*insulinoma*) can cause seizures by producing large amounts of *insulin* which lower the blood sugar level creating severe *hypoglycemia.* The recommended treatment which requires above average surgical skill is the removal of the pancreatic tumor or the entire pancreas. In partial pancreas removal, *pancreatitis* is a common post-surgical complication. Most malignant pancreatic tumors have already spread at the time of surgery. The surgeon must be alert in order to remove solitary metastasis (spread tumors). Some malignant pancreatic tumors can be partially controlled by the use of drugs that destroy beta cells and inhibit insulin production.

The prognosis for nonmalignant tumor removal by a qualified surgeon is good. The prognosis for malignant tumor management or removal is poor.

TUMORS OF THE NERVOUS SYSTEM: Any tumor may metastasize (spread) to the nervous system. Discussion of the primary nervous system tumors will follow. Ancillary tests for determining the presence of neoplasms (tumors) include *skull radiographs* and *CSF analysis.* Unfortunately, many tumors are only found on necropsy (autopsy). When nervous system signs are seen in middle and old age dogs, tumors are suspected.

Astrocytomas, primary tumors of the nervous system, are most commonly found in the cerebrum (front part of the brain) and middle portion of the brain. They don't usually metastasize (spread) to other tissues.

Ependymomas   are found primarily in the area of the brain where the cerebrospinal fluid canals are located. They are invasive and cause much damage to surrounding tissue.

Gliomas or *glioblastoma* are tumors of specific functional nerve cells. This type of neoplasm is most commonly found as a circumscribed mass in the front part of the brain. This type of tumor is also hemorrhagic in nature.

Meningiomas are tumors of the meninges which cover the brain and spinal cord. They grow slowly, sometimes becoming calcified and very hard. As they expand toward the brain, neurological signs are observed.

Neurofibrosarcoma, a rare tumor of nervous tissue, can act like a *meningioma*. The vestibular portion of the inner ear region is affected causing *head tilt, circling,* and loss of balance. This progressive lesion will spread to adjacent tissues.

Oligodendrogliomas are primary tumors of the brain, most commonly occurring in the brain stem area. They are seen in middle and old aged dogs. Neurological signs occur which represent the area of the brain involved.

UREMIA: A high level of urea in the blood can cause seizure activity. Most of the dogs that reach this level of uremia are in severe *kidney failure.* The use of *anticonvulsants* in these dogs can produce high lethal levels of the drug in the blood system since most anticonvulsants are excreted through the kidneys. Fluid therapy and *peritoneal dialysis* are the only methods of reducing the uremia level. Kidneys that can resume normal function after the uremia level is reduced produce a better prognosis for control of uremia induced *seizures*. If kidney regeneration is not possible, the prognosis is grave.

VESTIBULAR DYSFUNCTION: See *LOSS OF BALANCE, HEAD TILT,* and *CIRCLING.*

VISUAL LOSS: Visual loss occurs in one or both eyes from either the central nervous system or the eye. In the case of the central nervous system, it is a sign of a nervous system lesion. To determine if the visual imparity originates in the eye or in the brain, a neurological and an ophthalmological examination is performed. The eye is examined for pupil size and symmetry, pupil response to light, and characteristics of the lens, retina, and optic disc. Structures associated with the eye may also be examined. Determination of the cause of the blindness is important in establishing a method of therapy and a prognosis.

WATER ON THE BRAIN: See *HYDROCEPHALUS.*

WOBBLER SYNDROME (CERVICAL VERTEBRAL MALFORMATION): See Chapter 6 on the *MUSCULOSKELETAL SYSTEM.*

X-RAY, SKULL: Radiographs provide valuable information in some nervous system dysfunctions. Usually radiographs must be taken from several different angles. To be normal, when looking down from above the skull should be bilaterally symmetrical (both halves appear similar).

NUTRITION

AAFCO: See *AMERICAN ASSOCIATION OF FEED CONTROL OFFICIALS.*

ADDITIVE-FREE DIETS: Currently a number of additive-free canine diets are being marketed based on the idea that "preservatives" are harmful and can cause disease or cancer when consumed. Close governmental regulation does not allow the use of harmful chemical substances in pet foods. Even "natural preservatives" such as salt and sugar may be harmful at the levels needed to prevent food breakdown and bacterial decomposition. The chance of bacterial contamination is greater in additive-free foods. This kind of food will deteriorate more rapidly than "preserved" dog foods, losing its palatability and wholesomeness. While the idea of feeding an additive-free dog food may primarily be a sales gimmick, feeding this type to a dog is not harmful providing only small amounts of additive-free food are kept on hand.

ADULT DOG, DIETARY MANAGEMENT OF: Adults dogs not under the stress of working, showing, or hunting, and those not being bred or nursing puppies should be fed a quality dog food which will provide all of the *nutrients* necessary to sustain life at a maintenance level. Adult Cocker Spaniels of both sexes weighing about 25 to 30 pounds can be maintained nicely on a quality *dry food* and *water*. Canned food and supplementation is not necessary for normal health. If canned food is added to increase palatability, the amount of dry food in the ration should be decreased to prevent obesity. Adult Cockers have this tendency in later years. Changing food frequently is unnecessary and undesirable because these changes may cause bowel upsets like diarrhea and vomiting.

The aim of an adult maintenance dog food is to maintain optimal weight and health while eliminating excesses of nutrients that are harmful when consumed over a long period. Quality maintenance food should be at least 75% digestible. The *protein* content should be between 18% and 25%, the *fat* content greater than 10%, the *calcium* percentage 0.5% to 0.9%, and the *phosphorus* level between 0.4% and 0.8% on a dry weight basis. The dog food label should indicate that feeding trials show that the diet will maintain adult dogs under average conditions. Do not merely accept the statement that *NRC* minimums have been met.

AMERICAN ASSOCIATION OF FEED CONTROL OFFICIALS (AAFCO): In an attempt to bring some stability to the rules and regulations affecting animal feeds, the American Association of Feed Control Officials (AAFCO) was formed. Representatives from the Food and Drug Administration (FDA), the Federal Trade Commission (FTC), and the U.S. Department of Agriculture (USDA) compose the AAFCO panel that regulates animal feeds. In addition, people from the State Departments of Agriculture and the State Departments of Public Health are included.

Uniform pet food label regulations and a standardized testing procedure of dog food have been established. AAFCO requires that pet foods be *feeding trial* tested on at least 10 dogs of the age specified on the food. These test-fed dogs must then be checked to determine whether the dogs have maintained their weight and health during the feeding trial. AAFCO's feeding trial regulations are much more valid to the pet food buyer than are the *National Research Council (NRC)* standards of minimal nutrient requirements. If AAFCO is not mentioned on the dog food label, write to the company to determine if AAFCO requirements are being met or if only NRC standards are being used. FOR THE HEALTH OF YOUR DOG, ONLY USE DOG FOOD THAT MEETS AAFCO REQUIREMENTS!

AMINO ACIDS, ESSENTIAL AND NON-ESSENTIAL: Amino acids are the structural components of *protein*. The dog's body cannot make *essential amino acids* so they must be provided in the diet. Of the 22 amino acids, ten are essential including arginine, histidine, isoleucine, leucine, lysine, methionine, phenylalanine, threonine, tryptophan, and valine. The greater the quantity of essential amino acids in the dietary protein, the better the *biological value* of that food. A deficiency of arginine in some commercial substitutes for dog's milk can cause *cataracts* in eight week old pups.

ANOREXIA: Anorexia is defined as a lack of appetite or loss of appetite for food. When possible, the cause should be determined so that natural feeding methods may be utilized.

ANOREXIA, FEEDING METHODS FOR: See *FEEDING METHODS FOR ANOREXIA*.

APPETITE STIMULATION: See *FEEDING METHODS FOR ANOREXIA*.

ASCORBIC ACID: See *VITAMIN C*.

ASH: The collective mineral content of dog food is determined by the extraction of *fats*, the acid and alkali digestion of *carbohydrate* and *protein*, and the burning of the food to remove *crude fiber*. What remains after burning is ash (mineral).

AVIDIN: The protein avidin and the vitamin *biotin* are both found in eggs. Avidin is highly concentrated in raw egg white, while biotin is concentrated in the yolk. Feeding raw egg white alone will tie up biotin in the body causing a vitamin deficiency. However, either feeding the entire raw egg (yolk and white) or cooking egg white to denature avidin will prevent an avidin induced *biotin vitamin deficiency*.

B VITAMINS: The B complex group of vitamins consists of *vitamin B1 (thiamine)*, *vitamin B2 (riboflavin)*, *niacin*, *vitamin B6 (pyridoxine)*, *pantothenic acid*, *folic acid*, *biotin*, and *vitamin B12 (cobalamin)*. All are water soluble.

Because all but cobalamin are not stored in the body tissues, overdosing is not a problem. Whole grain cereals, liver, yeast, and egg yolk are all high in B complex vitamins. Each member of the B complex group is discussed separately within the chapter.

Remember that physiological functions which increase fluid removal from the body may also increase the removal of the B complex vitamins resulting in deficiencies. Kidney problems, *diarrhea*, *vomiting*, and prolonged diuretic therapy for *heart failure* may create deficiencies that require B complex supplementation.

BALANCED DIET: A balanced diet contains the correct amount of all the nutrients necessary to maintain a dog at any given age or activity level. A diet for proper puppy growth is balanced when the necessary nutrients for growth are present in the correct amounts to insure optimum development.

Many pet foods which attempt to be all things to all dogs are not balanced diets. A dog has different nutritional needs at every stage of its life cycle. A food balanced for puppy growth is too high in *protein, fat, calcium,* and *phosphorus* for an older dog that is inactive and not raising puppies. Other diets may be unbalanced due to the additional nutrients or vitamins given by the owner. Most commercial pet foods contain too much *sodium* for a dog with a cardiac insufficiency. A high sodium level can lead to hypertension in normal dogs. *Generic dog food* and other inexpensive dog foods do not contain enough of the necessary nutrients to be a balanced diet in spite of the fact that the package boasts of "meeting the minimum requirements of the *National Research Council (NRC)*."

BIOLOGICAL VALUE (BV): Biological value (BV) is the most common measurement of the quality of *protein* in the diet. BV is the percentage calculated from the difference between the amount of a nutrient (protein) absorbed and the amount retained in the body. This measurement is only pertinent if the dog is in a state of good nutrition and has a nonprotein source of calories to meet its food requirements. The following are biological values of some proteins: egg, 100; milk, 92; beef, 78; soybean meal, 67; whole wheat, 48; corn, 45; and gelatin, 0. Gelatin does not contain the essential amino acid tryptophan.

BIOTIN: Biotin is a B complex vitamin sometimes called *vitamin H* or *coenzyme R*. This potent vitamin is required by all forms of life. Health problems do not occur from high levels of biotin but deficiencies may cause skin problems, posterior leg paralysis, *loss of appetite*, and *weakness* from *diarrhea*. Egg yolk is very high in biotin. Raw egg white is high in the biotin antagonist, *avidin*. While eating a whole raw egg will probably not cause a vitamin deficiency, cooking the egg before it is eaten will remove any possibility of a biotin deficiency. Also see *AVIDIN*.

CALCIUM: Because of its contribution to bone, teeth, and cartilage formation, calcium is a very important mineral for normal body function and growth. Calcium is also necessary for normal *heart muscle contraction* and *skeletal muscle* *contraction.* Both deficiencies and excesses of calcium will seriously disrupt normal body function.

Early signs of calcium deficiencies include enlarged joints, splayed feet, stiffness, and *lameness. Hock hyperextension syndrome* may be partially due to a calcium deficiency. Also see *Magnesium.* Long term low calcium levels decrease the appetite and predispose the dog to fractured bones and loose teeth. A rapid loss of calcium will cause the skeletal muscles to have *tetanic contractions.*

Calcium absorption in the gut is associated with *vitamin D* intake. Most deficiencies develop in high meat diets which are high in *phosphorus* but very low in calcium. The proper ratio of calcium to phosphorus in the diet is 1.2 parts calcium for every 1 part of phosphorus. Meat does not have this ratio. As a rule, if a quality growth related diet is maintained during the first year of life, calcium supplementation is not necessary. Some individual circumstances might require the addition of calcium to the diet. Do not add it indiscriminately.

Excess calcium indirectly causes deficiencies in *zinc, iron, copper,* and *phosphorus.* High levels predispose the dog to *bloat* and *decreased thyroid function,* actually decreasing the growth rate.

CALORIES: Calories are the amount of energy produced from food. By definition, a calorie (lower case "c") is the amount of energy needed to raise 1 ml of water 1° centigrade. In nutrition, a calorie is usually expressed as Calorie (upper case "C") or kilocalorie (K calorie) which is 1,000 calories. Dog food diets talk about metabolizable or digestible calories per given amount of food. The energy from the digestible calories is first used for maintenance of normal body functions. If more energy is available, weight is gained. If less than normal energy is available, weight is lost. Certain activities in a dog's life require more calories than those found in a maintenance food. In the following example, multiply maintenance calories by the number indicated for the actual amount of calories needed for that activity.

ACTIVE DOG	1.2
HUNTING (full day in field)	1.1 to 1.4
COLD (below freezing)	1.75
HEAT (hot and humid)	2.5
PREGNANCY	1.0 up to six weeks,
then 1.3 until whelping	
HEAVY LACTATION with large litter	4.0
GROWTH	
to 2 months	3.0
2 to 6 months	2.0
6 to 12 months	1.5

The normal maintenance dietary energy requirements for a mature Cocker Spaniel will be 25 to 30 K calories/pound of body weight/day fed at one meal. The smaller the dog, the more frequent feeding is required to provide caloric needs. Amounts needed for growth, lactation, strenuous exercise or severe environment may be approximated from the above chart.

CARBOHYDRATES: Carbohydrates are simple and complex sugars which compose a good portion of the energy source in dog food. This source of energy is grouped into soluble carbohydrates, those utilized by the body after enzymatic breakdown, and insoluble carbohydrates or *fiber* that adds bulk to the diet for proper intestinal function. Only certain bacteria can break down fiber for absorption and energy usage. These bacteria are not found in the dog's intestinal system. Because carbohydrate fiber cannot be utilized by the dog, adding high fiber to some foods can make them useful as canine diet foods. Cooking increases the digestibility and assimilation of simple sugars from cereal sources of carbohydrates. If more carbohydrates are assimilated than necessary for maintenance, they will then be stored as fat or glycogen.

CHOLINE: Although frequently grouped with vitamins, choline is not a vitamin because it is not needed for metabolism. Choline helps to prevent fat accumulation in the liver and is also necessary for proper nerve impulse transmission. A *deficiency of choline* may result in blood clotting problems, fatty liver formation, and a decrease in *albumin* in the blood stream. Too much choline can cause *diarrhea* and nerve irritability.

COBALAMIN (VITAMIN B$_{12}$): Vitamin B$_{12}$ (*cobalamin*) is one of the *water soluble B complex vitamins* making it non-toxic in large doses. Over a long period of time, deficiencies may contribute to the development of *anemia*. Vitamin B$_{12}$ has been used with some success as an *appetite stimulant*.

COLITIS, DIETARY MANAGEMENT OF: While drugs such as *sulfasalazine* are important in the management of *colitis*, careful regulation of the diet is also paramount to control this troublesome disease.

Prescription Diet® I/D®, dry or canned, is an easy way to feed a highly digestible, easily tolerated diet. The following homemade diet can also be utilized. Both Prescription Diet® I/D® and the homemade diet should be fed in small, frequent meals.

COLITIS DIET

1/2 cup Cream of Wheat (cook to make 2 cups)

1 hard boiled egg	1 teaspoon potassium chloride
2 tablespoons Brewer's yeast	1 teaspoon dicalcium phosphate
3 tablespoons sugar	1 tablespoon corn oil
1 Tums® tablet tablet	1 balanced vitamin-mineral

Cook Cream of Wheat. Cool and add other ingredients and mix well. This recipe prepares 2.2 pounds of food.

COPPER: Copper is a *trace mineral* necessary for normal body function, especially *red blood cell production*. Deficiencies of copper can be produced by excesses in *zinc* or *iron*. Bone deformities, *hair depigmentation*, or *diarrhea* can occur from copper deficiencies. Accumulation of copper in the body causes liver disease.

COPPER TOXICOSIS, DIETARY MANAGEMENT OF: Early dietary management of copper toxicosis in the Cocker Spaniel is important in minimizing liver disease caused by the accumulation of dietary copper. *D-penicillamine (Cuprimine®)* is mixed with the usual low copper diet to increase the excretion of copper in the urine. Puppies younger than nine months can be fed *Prescription Diet® U/D®* supplemented with cooked eggs, hamburger, cottage cheese, and $1/2$ teaspoon of dicalcium phosphate. If the U/D® diet is used, bimonthly blood cell counts should be checked. Maintaining normal red blood cell levels with this ultra-low protein diet is difficult.

The homemade low copper diet follows.

LOW COPPER DIET

2$1/2$ cups of cooked rice	$1/2$ Tums® tablet
1 ounce of corn oil	$1/4$ teaspoon salt
1 cooked egg	1 balanced vitamin-mineral tablet without copper

Cook rice and mix with other ingredients to make one pound. Refrigerate unused portion.

COPROPHAGY (STOOL EATING):   While disgusting, stool eating is usually not harmful. However, *parasites* can be transmitted through this process. The habit of coprophagy evolves primarily from boredom. A *pancreatic enzyme deficiency* may cause a small number of dogs to crave the "extra" ingredients that are obtained from eating stool. Rapid removal of stool from the environment will eliminate the source helping to break this bad habit. Increased exercise helps to alleviate boredom. The addition of Adolph's® Meat Tenderizer to the dog food enzymatically changes the composition of the stool. The use of a highly digestible dog food also helps minimize coprophagy.

CRUDE PROTEIN: Crude protein, the amount of protein present in dog food, is noted on the label. This is an accurate analysis of the quantity but not of the quality. In high quality foods, the digestibility and *biological value* of the *protein* are high. In low quality dog foods, a similar crude protein level will have very low digestibility and biological value.

DIARRHEA, DIETARY MANAGEMENT OF: The dietary management of diarrhea is identical to the management of *colitis* except that within two weeks, normal dog food can gradually be reintroduced in the case of simple diarrhea. The basis for treating diarrhea is feeding a highly digestible, low fiber diet which does not contain disaccharides (table sugar, milk sugar).

DIETARY MANAGEMENT: Each of the following specialized diets are discussed individually within the chapter.

Adult Dog	Obesity
Colitis	Old Dog
Copper Toxicosis	Pancreatitis
Diarrhea	Reproduction and Lactation
Growing Dogs	Stressed Dogs
Heart Disease	Vomiting
Kidney Disease	Weaning
Liver Disease	

DIETS, SPECIALIZED: The following specialized diets are discussed under each individual heading within this chapter.

Additive-Free Diet	Low Mineral Diet
Balanced Diet	Low Protein/Kidney Disease Diet
Food Allergy Diet	Low Sodium/Heart Disease Diet
Formula, Nutritious Puppy	Meat-Free Diet
Lactose-Free Diet	Soy-Free Diet
Low Fat Diet	

DIGESTIBLE PROTEIN: Digestible protein is defined as the percentage of protein absorbed in the body in relation to the amount eaten. A good quality pet food should have protein digestibility of at least 80% in *dry food*, 85% in *soft moist* and *canned ration* forms, and up to 90% in *canned meat* types. Meat-type protein is more digestible than cereal protein.

DOG FOOD, CANNED: Canned dog food is more palatable and more digestible than its dry counterpart. Because of its 75% water content, canned dog food is more expensive than dry food. Of the two varieties of canned dog food, the all-meat gourmet type may contribute to kidney problems and to an appetite for only that diet when used exclusively. The other type is a mix of meat, cereals, and soybean generally balanced nutritionally to create a varied appetite. The mixture is usually less expensive than the gourmet variety. Canned foods provide between 450 K and 600 K calories of utilizable energy per 14 oz can. As with most products, you get what you pay for with canned dog food.

DOG FOOD, COMMERCIAL FORMS: The three basic types of commercial dog food produced are *dry food, canned food,* and *soft-moist dog food.* Each of these types is discussed under its individual heading within this chapter. Remember—good and bad foods exist in all forms. A customer generally gets what he or she pays for.

DOG FOOD, DRY: As with any form of dog food, dry dog food has both advantages and disadvantages. Dry dog food is produced in three forms: meal, kibble, and expanded form. Meal mixes the ingredients together. Kibbles are first baked and then broken into pieces. The expanded form is cooked in an extruder and forced under pressure causing further expansion. Currently, no meal forms of dry food are sold. Most foods available are the extruded type. The cooking process increases digestibility of *carbohydrates*. Fats are added after cooking by spraying them onto the product, helping to increase palatability.

Dry dog food costs less, controls tartar build-up on teeth, and allows the leisure of *free choice feeding*. One disadvantage is the lower palatability of the food. Also, the kind of ingredients that can be used in the dry food process are limited. As an example, muscle meat cannot be used in dry food. Because they are less stable, as a rule, they should be eaten within six months from the time of manufacture.

Acceptable levels of K calories would be 600 K cal per 8 oz cup where the dry food contains 25% fat, 300–400 K cal per 8 oz cup when the fat content is 8% to 24%, and in low-fat dry foods, the K calories per cup are less than 200. Once again, you get what you pay for in dry dog food.

DOG FOOD PALATABILITY: Palatability of dog foods varies but in general, four factors are important in determining how well a dog likes a given diet. The odor of the food, the texture or mouth-feel (dry versus canned), the dog's habits, and the amount of nutrients in the diet contribute to how edible it is. Moistening dog food increases the palatability for most dogs. Adding something to increase the odor of a food may stimulate some dogs to eat more. Habit is a large factor in the eating pattern of a dog. Any changes in the diet should be made gradually by combining the new food with the old.

DOG FOOD, SOFT-MOIST: Soft-moist dog food has the highest level of concentrated digestible energy of any dog food form. The "moistness" is caused by the presence of propylene glycol, corn syrup, and salt, all which attract water. Soft-moist products contain 25% to 35% moisture, 25% to 30% protein, and 10% to 12% fat. Refrigeration is not required to preserve it because propylene glycol and some acids are used to retard bacterial and fungal growth. Providing the packet or pouch has not been opened, these products have a long shelf life. Generally, they are quite palatable. The cost is comparable to canned foods.

ENERGY: Energy as related to foods is expressed in calories. *Protein*, *carbohydrates*, and *fats* provide energy sources. Most of the energy in dog food comes from carbohydrates and fats. Fat provides 2.2 times as much energy as the same amount of carbohydrate or protein. Energy in pet foods, expressed as metabolizable energy, is the amount left after elimination of stool and urine.

FATS: Fats in a dog's diet provide a source of *essential fatty acids. Linoleic acid* is the unsaturated fatty acid necessary for proper fat metabolism in the dog. Fats are essential for proper absorption of the *fat soluble vitamins A, D, E,* and *K*. Fat also enhances the palatability of dog foods. While not an indispensable energy source, fats become the best source of energy in the diet by providing over two times as much energy per unit as either proteins or carbohydrates. Both plant oils (corn, safflower) and animal fat (pork, butter fat) can be used as a source of energy and unsaturated essential fatty acids. High quantities of linoleic acid occur in corn and other vegetable oils. While pork and chicken fat are 25% linoleic acid, only a very small amount is contained in butter fat and beef tallow. Dogs are able to tolerate fat contents up to 40% without suffering from *steatorrhea* (diarrhea from unabsorbed fat). Up to half of the daily caloric (energy) needs can be supplied by fats in the diet. Increased fat in the diet is important during growth, whelping, lactation, and strenuous work.

FATTY ACID DEFICIENCIES: *Linoleic acid* is the only essential fatty acid which must be supplied in the dog's diet. From linoleic acid, the dog's body can make *linolenic* and *arachidonic acid*, the two other fatty acids important for metabolism and health. Therefore, if enough linoleic acid is supplied, no deficiencies will occur. Fatty acids must be present for *prostaglandin* production, hair and skin health, normal *wound healing*, and control of skin water loss. Deficiencies can affect the skin and hair, cause reproductive deficiencies and chronic ear infections, and occasionally result in *hot spots*.

Fatty acids in dog food become rancid with increased humidity, high temperature, or improper storage. Antioxidants such as *vitamin E* are necessary to stabilize the fatty acids in dog food.

FEEDING DOGS, METHODS OF: The three basic methods of feeding dogs are *free choice, meal feeding with food restrictions*, and *meal feeding with a time restriction*. All three methods have both advantages and disadvantages.

Free choice feeding is the easiest form of feeding. The bowl is kept full of fresh dry dog food. This helps discourage *stool eating* and allows a non-aggressive eater time at the food bowl without competition. Because the canned variety will spoil quickly in warm and humid weather, free choice feeding is limited to dry and soft-moist forms of dog food. A dog fed by free choice is more difficult to house train because of the tendency to eat small amounts many times throughout a 24 hour period. However, small frequent feedings are beneficial in the management of some *liver, pancreatic*, and *gastrointestinal diseases.*

Meal feeding with food restriction is done to limit the amount of food consumed at any given time. The dog is given less food than the amount the dog desires so the food is all eaten immediately. Additional feedings of similar portions are done at prescribed times during a twenty-four hour period. This method of never satisfying the dog's appetite can be used to put weight on dogs that seem to stay thin. Frequent feedings of small, high caloric meals may increase weight in poor doers.

Meal feeding with time restriction is a common method of feeding especially for growing puppies and lactating bitches where increased caloric requirements make frequent feedings necessary. The dog is offered all that it will consume in a 20 to 25 minute period. This type of feeding can also be used to manage deep-chested dogs that have a tendency toward *gastric dilatation* or *bloat*.

Combinations of feeding methods may also be useful in other situations. For instance, free choice feeding of dry dog food can be combined with meal time restriction feeding of canned food.

FEEDING METHODS FOR ANOREXIA: At least three methods can be utilized at home for feeding the anorectic dog.

Appetite stimulation should be attempted before other methods are contemplated. The use of a highly palatable canned food either as a sole diet or mixed with normal food may be enough to stimulate an *anorectic* dog to eat. Sick dogs will quickly become deficient in *B vitamins* and *potassium*. B complex and $1/4$ teaspoon of potassium chloride salt substitute should then be given to stimulate the dog's appetite. The drug *diazepam (Valium®)* is a very effective appetite stimulant when given intravenously and may also be effective orally. On occasion, *anabolic steroid drugs* have been used with mixed results as appetite stimulants.

Force-feeding is an effective method of feeding the anorectic dog. By placing the food deep in the throat, the swallow reflex will cause it to move into the stomach. The use of a high quality canned food or a high caloric semi-liquid diet makes force-feeding much easier. Recently, HI-CAL LIQUID®, which contains 2,100 calories per 5 ml (1 teaspoon) has become available through Pan American Pharmaceuticals of Grand Rapids, Michigan. An important part of force-feeding is maintaining adequate vitamins and minerals.

Gavage (tube feeding) is a very easy and rapid method of feeding the anorectic dog. Most commonly, a weak, chilled, or otherwise distressed newborn puppy is fed in this manner. A size 8 French soft rubber or soft plastic infant feeding tube and both a 12 cc and a 35 cc disposable plastic syringe are needed. Refer to *FORMULA, PUPPY NUTRITIOUS* for the most effective bitch milk substitute. Commercial puppy formula will keep the neonatal puppy alive but will not help him to gain weight from birth to the time he is old enough to start lapping from a pan (at approximately two weeks of age).

The following technique is used for *tube-feeding* the newborn. Measure from the mouth to the curvature of the last rib to establish the length of tube that can easily be passed down the esophagus. Before passing the tube, fill the entire length of tubing with warm formula to eliminate the problem of air in the stomach. Pass the tube. If you find that less than half of the tube will pass, remove the tube and repeat the process. A tube incorrectly placed in the lungs will encounter firm resistance after one-third to one-half of the calculated amount of feeding tube has been passed. The formula should be given slowly over several minutes. You will notice the stomach becoming full. The amount of formula that can safely be given will vary. If a puppy has been anorectic for several days, its stomach capacity will be less. As a rule of thumb, start with 5 ml for every eight ounces of puppy weight and feed it six times the first day. Each day, as the puppy gains weight, increase the feedings by 2.5 ml and decrease the frequency to four or five. The warmer the puppy is the less often he requires food. If the abdomen does not become distended with your calculated amount of formula or if the puppy does not gain weight, greater increases should be instituted. After removing the tube, stimulate the puppy to eliminate its urine and stool by gently rubbing the urinary and anal region with a warm, moist piece of cotton.

Several other techniques for tube-feeding older puppies and adult dogs are available but are best utilized in a veterinary hospital setting where long-term force-feeding is anticipated. In one technique, a tube is passed through the nasal cavity into the stomach. Another technique places a tube through a surgically prepared opening in the side of the neck, bypassing the mouth. This *pharyngostomy technique* is particularly useful in broken jaw recovery where manipulation of the jaws is undesirable.

Intravenous (IV) feeding is generally done in a hospital setting. If long-term feeding is required, an indwelling catheter is placed in the jugular vein and sutured to the skin. As the caloric and metabolic needs are determined, various fluids can be given intravenously. The solutions should be warmed, taking care not to overload the cardiorespiratory system.

Feeding the non-eating dog is important and must be done properly to keep the body in a positive balance. Since various methods can be utilized, finding one that is not stressful for either the owner or the dog is desirable.

FEEDING TRIAL, DO-IT-YOURSELF: Two practical feed trials can be conducted by the owner to determine the quality of the dog food. If either trial fails, change foods regardless of what is stated on the food bag label.

FEEDING TRIAL I: (STOOL VOLUME AS A MEASURE OF DIGESTIBILITY AND UTILIZATION)
- Feed a premeasured amount of food daily for six days.
- DO NOT SUPPLEMENT AT ALL!
- Keep exercise level constant during the feed trial.
- Immediately eliminate from further consideration any food that causes diarrhea for more than two days.
- Pick up and save in a plastic bag EVERY stool for the last four days of the feed trial. Refrigerate the stool.
- At the end of the sixth day, weigh the stool and divide the weight of the stool by the weight of the food consumed. The stool should weigh less than 90% of dry food, 70% of soft moist, and 25% of canned food. These are acceptable levels of digestibility.

FEEDING TRIAL II: (THREE WEEK FEEDING TO MAINTAIN ADULT WEIGHT)
- Feed the test food for three weeks free choice.
- Record weight of the animal at the start and again 25 days later.
- Adult unstressed weight should be maintained. If not, eliminate that food from consideration.

FLATULENCE (GAS PRODUCTION): Flatulence (intestinal gas production) is generally due to swallowing or gulping air while eating and to the bacterial fermentation of the food. Some dog food components like soybeans are high in sugars that are not digestible so are likely to undergo the fermentation process. While most gases produced in the intestinal tract are nonodorous, gases produced from spoiled food, high meat diets, and vitamin supplements can be very odoriferous.

Gas production in the gastrointestinal tract can be controlled in several ways. Feeding small amounts of food in a quiet atmosphere helps eliminate the gulping of air. Changing the diet to eliminate soybeans, meat, or a vitamin supplementation will help control flatulence. If all changes have no effect, a physical examination and testing should be done to determine if high levels of fats are present in the stools.

FOLIC ACID: Folic acid is classified as one of the *B complex vitamins*. Being water soluble, overdosage is not a problem. Deficiencies can depress the bone marrow causing *anemia*. Inflammation of the tongue has also been reported in *folic acid deficiencies*. Use of the antibacterial drug *sulfonamide* for long periods can cause folic acid deficiencies.

FOOD ALLERGY, DETERMINATION OF AND DIET FOR: The determination of a food allergy requires the feeding of distilled water and a *hypoallergenic diet* like *Prescription Diet® D/D®* for a three week period. To prepare the dog for this *food allergy* determination, three cleansing enemas should be given at twelve hour intervals during a 48 hour fast. Distilled water is given but no supplements or any forms of food are used. After the 48 hour fast, D/D® Diet is given for a three week period. The signs of suspected food allergy are then compared with the original symptoms. If much improvement is noted, individual food items are added to the diet weekly. Corn Flakes, Wheat Chex®, hamburger, Cheerios™, and Rice Chex® all supply only one food ingredient so can be added weekly while observing signs for food allergy. See Chapter 11, *FOOD ALLERGY.*

FORMULA, PUPPY NUTRITIOUS: Most of the commercially available puppy formulas will keep a puppy alive but will not allow him to gain weight. The following formula will put weight on newborn puppies who do not have bitch's milk available.

PUPPY NUTRITIOUS FORMULA

> 1 can (13 ounce) of condensed milk
> 2 cans (13 ounce can) of water
> 2 packages of Knox® gelatin
> 2 egg yolks
> 1 tablespoon honey
> 1 tablespoon whipping cream

> Blend all ingredients and refrigerate between usage. Note, the formula will become stiff when refrigerated but liquefies when heated.

Follow the directions for *tube feeding
newborn puppies* under *FEEDING METHODS
FOR ANOREXIA.*

GROWING DOGS, DIETARY MANAGEMENT OF: Cocker Spaniel
puppies from weaning to six months should be fed three times daily with a 25
minute time limit at each meal. Between the age of six and twelve months, two
feedings are sufficient for most Cocker puppies. After the first year, only one daily
feeding is necessary.

Providing a good quality growth diet is very important in determining the
kind of start that puppies get in their lives. Food for the growth diet should
consist of 25% *protein* and 17% *fat* and be at least 80% digestible. Each pound of
food should contain approximately 1,750 K calories. The *calcium* to *phosphorus*
ratio should be 1.2:1.

Feeding should consist of one kind of food with no supplementation unless
recommended by your veterinarian. Continually changing brands of food creates a
finicky eater. On the other hand, over-feeding creates fat puppies that have a
tendency toward obesity their entire life.

HEART DISEASE, DIETARY MANAGEMENT OF: The dietary aim in
managing heart disease is to feed the dog a low *sodium* diet. Sodium restriction
helps control the fluid congestion which occurs in *heart failure.* Use only distilled
water for drinking water, avoiding the use of soft water. Commercial canned dog
food has over 1,000 mg of *sodium* per 100 grams of dry matter, soft-moist food
over 850 mg of sodium, and dry food over 500 mg of sodium per 100 grams.
Prepared diets, like *Prescription Diet*® *H/D*® contain 50 to 90 mg of sodium per
100 grams of dry matter. Dogs on restricted sodium diets should also receive extra
B complex vitamins to replace those that are lost in the urine. The following
homemade diet is very low in sodium.

LOW SODIUM DIET

$1/4$ lb lean ground beef
2 cups unsalted cooked rice
1 tablespoon corn oil
2 teaspoons dicalcium phosphate
1 multiple vitamin-mineral tablet

Braise meat retaining the fat. Mix in
remaining ingredients. This makes one
pound of low sodium diet (approximately
660 K calories).

IMBALANCE, PROTEIN: Too much or not enough protein can be detrimental
to a dog's health. Because the kidney must remove the protein waste products from
the body, receiving excess protein for long periods of time subjects the dog to

kidney disease. On the other hand, poor quality or inadequate protein intake causes the body to use both the dietary protein and protein from the body muscle to make energy. Signs of *protein deficiency* include weight loss, stunted hair growth, *ascites* (fluid in the abdomen), and swollen limbs.

IODINE: Iodine is a mineral necessary for normal body and *thyroid gland* functions. While deficiencies are rather common, excess iodine in the body is rare. A deficiency can cause *hair loss, infertility,* and lethargy. *Myxedema* is a complex syndrome which occurs in adult dogs due to thyroid and *growth hormone deficiencies.* Iodine is supplied as a trace mineral in most good quality dog foods.

IRON: Iron, an integral part of *hemoglobin,* is a trace mineral essential to normal *red blood cell* metabolism. Too much iron can cause death in young puppies. However, under normal circumstances this is very unusual. Deficiencies in iron can occur from blood loss or from diets which contain inadequate iron such as milk. Atypical *anemia* results from iron deficiency.

KIDNEY DISEASE, DIETARY MANAGEMENT OF: Diets used to control kidney disease must contain low quantity-high quality protein and low amounts of *phosphorus* and *sodium.* Failing kidneys cannot process large amounts of protein waste nor remove normal levels of phosphorus. The levels of sodium in commercial dog food increase blood pressure which then increase the amount of work that the kidneys must perform. When the kidneys function poorly, *B complex vitamins* are lost in the urine. Therefore, dietary management includes the addition of large amounts of B complex vitamins to the diet.

Both *Prescription Diet*® *K/D*® and *U/D*® Diets are useful in managing *kidney disease.* The following homemade diets are also very good.

LOW PROTEIN AND PHOSPHORUS DIET

$1/4$ pound regular hamburger
1 hard boiled egg
2 cups of cooked, unsalted rice
3 slices of white bread broken into crumbs
1 Tums® tablet
1 multiple vitamin tablet

Cook hamburger to retain fat and mix all ingredients together. Add 4–6 tablespoons of water before serving. This recipe makes $1 1/4$ pounds of diet yielding about 750 K calories per pound.

For dogs with serious *uremic poisoning* and end stage *kidney failure,* the following *ultra-low protein diet* can be used.

VERY LOW PROTEIN DIET

$2^1/_2$ cups cooked rice with $1/_4$ teaspoon
   salt added
2 tablespoons corn oil
1 hard boiled egg
$1/_2$ Tums® tablet
1 multiple vitamin tablet

Cook the rice and mix together all ingredients.
Refrigerate between feedings. This mix will yield $1^1/_{10}$
pounds of diet with about 690 K calories per pound.

LABELS, INTERPRETATION OF PET FOOD: Pet food labeling is
regulated in most states by *AAFCO*. Being able to understand the dog food label
will help you better understand what you are getting for your money.
    The dog food label has two basic parts. The information panel is found to the
right of the display panel. The display panel must contain a statement of identity
which generally includes the product name, brand name, and a statement indicating
the animal for which the product is designed (e.g. "dogs" or "puppies"). The
information panel must declare the quantity of the contents. Optional information
such as a flavor designation indicating the kind of flavor can appear on the display
panel. The flavor source must then be identified in the ingredient list. Any
ingredient making up more than 25% of the total diet must be listed. All meats or
meat by-products other than cattle, pigs, sheep, or goats must be named. This
specifically applies to horse meat. A nutritional statement is found on either the
information panel or on the display panel. Examples of nutritional statements
would be "complete puppy food," or "complete diet for pregnant bitches." By law,
incomplete diets like snacks must carry a statement indicating that the "product is
intended for intermittent or supplemental feeding only."
    The ingredient list, the guaranteed analysis, and the name and address of the
packer, distributor, or manufacturer of the dog food must all appear on the
information panel. The amount or percentage of each of the contents is listed in
decreasing order. The guaranteed analysis which is required states the minimum
amount of crude protein and crude fat and the maximum amount of crude fiber and
water present in the food. Other information may also appear at the manufacturer's
discretion.
    By reading ALL of the information on the label, you will be able to make
more intelligent decisions about dog food purchases.

LACTOSE-FREE DIET: Lactose is the sugar present in milk. Some dogs,
especially puppies, lack *lactase*, the enzyme necessary for splitting lactose into
simple sugars to be utilized by the body. If lactase is not present in sufficient
levels and a diet containing lactose is fed, chronic diarrhea will occur. Many
lactose-free diets are available. Canned *Prescription Diet*® *I/D*®, *K/D*®, *H/D*®,

$U/D^{®}$, $R/D^{®}$, and $D/D^{®}$ can be used. Prescription Diet$^{®}$ dry R/D$^{®}$, I/D$^{®}$, and H/D$^{®}$ are lactose-free as are the homemade low protein and low *sodium* diets.

LIVER DISEASE, DIETARY MANAGEMENT OF: The goals of dietary management of liver disease are four fold: to help replenish the liver glycogen stores, to prevent sodium retention, to keep the ammonia which results from protein breakdown from building up in the blood, and to provide small quantities of high quality protein and an easily used carbohydrate energy source making the job of the liver easier.

For a carbohydrate source, the diet should contain corn starch or dextrose instead of cereal grains. A high quality protein like cottage cheese or eggs instead of meat should be included. *Sodium* should be either moderately or severely restricted depending on the signs. The diet should be fed up to five times throughout the day.

Diets recommended for the treatment of liver disease include Prescription Diet$^{®}$ $K/D^{®}$, $I/D^{®}$ and $H/D^{®}$. The homemade diets for colitis, heart disease, and kidney disease are also beneficial.

LOW FAT DIET: Low fat diets are useful in feeding dogs that need to lose weight. These diets provide bulk with fewer calories than normal. A long-term weight reduction program is superior to a quick, crash diet because good habits are developed by both the owner and the dog. Before initiating a diet program, your veterinarian should perform a physical examination on the dog to determine that a weight reduction program is not dangerous. To check the progress of the diet, weigh the dog monthly. The length of the diet will vary with the amount of weight reduction desired but should be maintained for at least six months.

The prepared *Prescription Diet$^{®}$ R/D$^{®}$* and *W/D$^{®}$* are excellent for weight reduction programs. The following homemade diet can also be utilized.

LOW FAT DIET
$1/4$ pound lean ground beef
$1/2$ cup cottage cheese (not creamed)
2 cups canned green beans
2 cups canned carrots
$1^1/2$ teaspoons dicalcium phosphate
1 vitamin-mineral tablet

Cook and drain fat from beef. Mix all ingredients together when cool. This mixture makes $1^3/4$ pounds of low-fat diet that supplies 250 K calories per pound.

LOW MINERAL DIET: The use of low mineral diets is primarily to dissolve specific *urinary stones* from the bladder and to prevent any recurrences. In some dogs, the chemistry of the urinary tract system predisposes them to the development of *calculi* (stones) in the urinary bladder. Dogs maintained on low mineral diets are less likely to develop stones in the urinary system. The prepared

Prescription Diet® *S/D*® is useful in some cases where urinary bladder stones have already formed. *Prescription Diet*® *K/D*® and *U/D*® and the *low protein homemade diet* are helpful when a low mineral diet is desired.

MAGNESIUM: Magnesium, a mineral essential for proper body functions, helps to maintain fluid balance, structural functions, and acid-base balances. Deficiencies of magnesium in the diet contribute to soft tissue calcification, *seizures*, retarded growth rates, and *hyperextension of the hock* and pastern joints. Excesses of magnesium are unusual but could contribute to the development of chronic diarrhea. Most quality dry dog foods contain adequate amounts of magnesium.

MANGANESE: Manganese is a trace mineral necessary for normal body function. Deficiencies can contribute to *impaired fertility*, joint enlargements, and short, brittle bones. Too much manganese may result in the development of *albinism* and impaired fertility.

MEAT-FREE DIET: Some forms of *kidney disease, meat allergies*, and purine metabolism problems are controlled by meat-free diets. The dry *Prescription Diet*® *K/D*® and *U/D*® are excellent for dogs with these problems. The homemade very *low protein diet* can also be utilized for these conditions.

MINERALS: Although minerals only make up .7% of the body, they play a very important role. Classified by the amount present, *macro-minerals* include *calcium, phosphorus, sodium, potassium,* and *magnesium. Micro-minerals* (trace minerals) include *zinc, selenium, iodine, manganese, cobalt, copper,* and *iron.* The trace minerals function as a part of enzymatic activity while the macro-minerals form bone and are necessary for muscle activity. See *ASH*.

NATIONAL RESEARCH COUNCIL (NRC) NUTRITIONAL REQUIREMENTS FOR DOGS IN 1985:   The National Academy of Sciences National Research Council first established minimum nutritional levels for the dog in 1974. In a study commissioned by a major pet food producer, 65 foods or 83% of the *generic foods* sampled were found to lack at least one essential nutrient. Today, the NRC requirements still do not insure that all dogs will gain or even maintain weight and health while eating these foods.
    The 1985 National Research Council pet food report has made several changes helping to make the pet food labels more meaningful. Now minimum requirements, without allowances, are specified for each nutrient. Substantial changes in protein and mineral level recommendations have been made. Lower levels of these nutrients are suggested. However, if high *calcium* or *phytate* levels are present in the food, increased *zinc* is recommended. *Vitamin E* should be increased in the presence of high levels of *unsaturated fatty acids*. The values are now stated as "available nutrients." Food quantities are expressed in units per 1,000 K calories of *metabolizable energy* available.

As a buyer of dog food, you, the consumer, should only buy foods that have met *AAFCO* guidelines not just NRC minimum levels.

NIACIN: Because of its water soluble nature, niacin is a *B complex vitamin* which in large amounts does not cause serious problems. However, on occasion, high doses may cause skin redness or flushing. Deficiencies of niacin are also uncommon with today's improved nutrition. In the past, a disease called *black tongue* was attributed to a niacin deficiency. Other signs observed from low niacin levels are *anemia* and *hemorrhagic diarrhea*.

NUTRIENT: A nutrient is defined as any food substance that helps to support life. Life support can be accomplished in a number of ways. The six necessary nutrients in order of importance are *water, fats, carbohydrates, protein, minerals*, and *vitamins*. Some nutrients have multiple functions while others, like vitamins, are only required for metabolism.

OBESITY, DIETARY MANAGEMENT OF: The goal in managing obesity is limiting the calorie intake to 50% to 60% of the normal diet. Three to four small feedings daily are superior to one large feeding. The use of *Prescription Diet*® *R/D*® or *W/D*® provide high bulk, low fat dietary needs conveniently. The homemade *low fat diet* is also an excellent low calorie diet.

OLD DOG, DIETARY MANAGEMENT OF: For feeding purposes, all breeds except giant breeds are considered old after the age of seven. Giant breeds are considered old at five years of age. The old dog should receive less *protein, sodium*, and *phosphorus*, and more *unsaturated fatty acids, zinc*, and *vitamins A, C*, and *B complex*. The best diets for the old dog include *Science Diet*® *Senior*®, *Prescription Diet*® *G/D*®, and the homemade diet which is low in protein and phosphorus (kidney diet). Attention should focused on maintaining normal weight levels during the dog's older years.

PANCREATITIS, DIETARY MANAGEMENT OF: Managing pancreatic insufficiency requires a diet with high quality, bland protein sources like eggs and cottage cheese. The addition of *pancreatic enzymes* helps the digestion process. Do not give milk to the dog since the presence of *lactose* (milk sugar) will cause diarrhea. *Prescription Diet*® *I/D*® or the homemade *colitis diet* are the most desirable diets. Both are well-tolerated and digested in the presence of pancreatic enzyme supplementation.

PANTOTHENIC ACID: Pantothenic acid, which is water soluble, is grouped as a vitamin in the B complex group. Toxicities do not occur at high levels. However, deficiencies can produce severe gastroenteritis, *seizures, hypoglycemia*, increased *BUN* levels, and *depressed appetites*.

PET FOOD EXAMINATION FOR WHOLESOMENESS: The wholesomeness and quality of dog food can be determined, in part, by first examining the dog food container (e.g. can, bag) and then by carefully examining the product. *Dry food*, *soft-moist*, and *canned dog food* should meet certain specifications.

Carefully examine the dry food bag for any evidence of grease out (soaking through of fat). The presence of fat-soaked paper will attract rats and mice creating a problem at the distributor's warehouse. Remove a sample of food from the top and the bottom of the bag. Place the samples on paper and examine it for color, odor, and texture. Mold is green, white, or black and smells musty. Spoiling fat is rancid. If numerous fine particles within the sample can be detected as several different ingredients, the overall quality of the product is poor.

Carefully scrutinize the cellophane wrappers in which soft-moist foods are packaged for signs of leakage or vermin contamination. Open the package and examine it for odor, abnormal color of product, and the presence of extra moisture which can cause rapid spoilage. A normal sample of soft-moist food should be soft, spongy, and slick between the fingers. The sample, however, should not be wet. Break open the soft-moist pellet to look for a homogenous mixture of ingredients. Again, the presence of identifiable ingredients denotes lower quality.

Swollen ends on cans of food means bacterial gas production and spoilage. Open both ends of the can, removing the contents by pushing the can lid through the can. Observe the contents for odor, color, and ingredients. Rancidity and spoilage can be determined by smell. A darkened or black area on the food may only mean that charcoal was used to indicate certain ingredients and is not necessarily indicative of spoilage. Spread the canned food out on a plate to examine the ingredients. The ration canned food should be mixed with cereal grains and small amounts of meat tissue. No foreign substances should be present. Wire, paper, feathers, and hair denote a low quality product. The meat-type canned food can be judged by the amount of indigestible protein in the form of blood vessels, tendons, and ligaments present with the chunks of muscle meat.

As is mentioned frequently in this chapter on nutrition, as the consumer, you get what you pay for in dog foods.

PHOSPHORUS: Phosphorus, classified as a *macro-mineral*, is associated with *calcium* in bone formation. Deficiencies of phosphorus can cause depraved appetites and many of the same signs of calcium deficiency. Excesses of phosphorus lead to *kidney disease*. The most immediate affect of high phosphorus levels is to create calcium deficiencies.

PICA: Pica, a craving for unnatural articles of food, can occur in nutritional, neurological, and reproductive situations.

POTASSIUM: The *macro-mineral* potassium will not cause toxicities unless the dog is not urinating. With decreased urination, potassium increases causing *heart toxicities* and death. Deficiencies can result from the use of diuretics, diarrhea, or insufficient dietary intake. If diuretics are used for heart conditions, the blood potassium level should be monitored every three to four weeks. The signs of potassium deficiency include muscle weakness, *wobbling gait*, and paralysis.

PROTEIN: Protein, one of the six nutrients necessary for life, provides *amino acids* for body functions. Structural tissues, hormones, enzymes, and various body secretions all use protein. If the usual energy sources (fats and carbohydrates) are absent, protein can be used as a source of energy.

PROTEIN QUALITY, ESTIMATING: Several methods determine protein quality. Although not practical, the best method of determining protein quality is to compare the amino acid content of the protein in question to the amount of *essential amino acids* needed by the dog to perform a particular function. Probably the most practical method that a dog owner can use to estimate protein quality is a feeding trial in which the dog is closely examined to insure that the protein present in the food meets all of that dog's individual needs.

PYRIDOXINE (VITAMIN B$_6$): Pyridoxine is a water soluble *B complex vitamin*. Toxic levels do not occur. *Anemia* is the most common B deficiency. Severe long term deficiencies result in high levels of blood *iron* and *convulsions*.

REPRODUCTION AND LACTATION, DIETARY MANAGEMENT OF: Since very little growth occurs in the fetuses during the first five to six weeks of pregnancy, supplementation of the maintenance diet is unnecessary. A very good sign of pregnancy is inappetence during the third or fourth week of pregnancy. In most bitches, this lasts for three to five days with each pregnancy. After the sixth week, the ration should be increased until at the time of *whelping* it exceeds the maintenance level by 25%. The diet should be high quality, contain 25% *protein* and 17% *fat*, and be at least 80% digestible. There should be 1,700 to 1,800 K calories/pound of food with more *calcium* than *phosphorus* in the diet. During the last several weeks of pregnancy and through lactation, the bitch should either be fed twice daily or by free choice.

The amount fed to the lactating bitch depends on the size of the litter. A litter of less than four whelps can be raised by a two-fold increase in the bitch's food intake. Litters of up to 10 or 12 pups require at least three times the maintenance amount of food.

Several excellent commercial diets are available for pregnancy and lactation. Science Diet® Growth® is excellent for maintaining the nursing bitch's weight. As puppies are weaned, the bitch's diet should gradually be cut back below the maintenance level to help dry up the milk supply.

RIBOFLAVIN (VITAMIN B$_2$): Riboflavin (vitamin B$_2$) is one of the water soluble B complex group. No toxicities are reported. A wide range of serious problems can occur from deficiencies including *fertility problems*, *pannus* (an eye condition), dermatitis problems, muscle weakness, and death.

SELENIUM: Selenium is a *trace mineral* that must be provided in the diet in small amounts. Too much selenium will result in vomiting, weakness, *pulmonary edema* (fluid in lungs), and death. An overdose through injection is about the only way this kind of toxicity can result. Deficiencies of selenium are associated with a disease in the young called *white muscle disease* which affects both skeletal and cardiac muscles causing stiffness, lameness, and death.

SODIUM: Sodium is a *macro-mineral* which causes either acute or chronic toxicity problems. Acute sodium toxicity occurs only if fresh drinking water is not available. Chronic toxicity can occur from high levels of sodium in pet foods consumed year after year. An increase in *heart disease* and *kidney disease* has been reported with chronic toxicity. Withholding normal levels of sodium can cause *pica*, slow growth, and *increased urinary frequency*.

SOY-FREE DIET: Soybean protein is commonly found in dog food. Some have incriminated the presence of soybean in the diet with the development of *hypothyroidism*. Because some dogs are allergic to soy protein, soy-free diets such as the *Science Diet® Senior®* and *Performance®* and Prescription Diet® canned *K/D®*, *I/D®*, and *G/D®* are available.

SPECIALIZED DIETS: The kind and amount of food fed to a dog should be coordinated with the dog's individual needs. The use of certain diets can substantially lengthen the life of dogs affected with kidney and heart diseases. The following is a list of diets discussed individually within this chapter.

Additive Free Diets	Heart Disease Diet
Adult Dog Maintenance Diet	Kidney Disease Diet
Balanced Diet	Lactose Free Diet
Colitis Diet	Liver Disease Diet
Copper Toxicosis Diet	Low Copper Diet
Diarrhea Diet	Low Fat Diet
Food Allergy Diet	Low Mineral Diet
Formula, Nutritious Puppy	Low Protein Diet
Growing Dog Diet	Low Sodium Diet
Meat Free Diet	Obesity Diet
Old Dog Diet	Soy-Free Diet
Pancreatitis Diet	Stressed Dog Diet
Phosphorus Diet	Vomiting Dog Diet
Reproduction & Lactation Diet	Weaning Diet

STOOL EATING: See *COPROPHAGY*.

STRESSED DOGS, DIETARY MANAGEMENT OF: Stress can take many forms—both physical and emotional. The calories burned up in a stressful situation are much greater than those used in a normal environment. A good diet for stress should contain at least 1,900 K calories per pound, be very digestible, and have at least 25% protein and 23% fat. Ideally, the dog should be fed a very palatable, high energy type diet at least twice a day. Two excellent diets for dogs under stress are *Science Diet® Performance®* and *Prescription Diet® Maximum Stress®*.

THIAMINE (VITAMIN B₁): Thiamine (vitamin B_1) is a water soluble *B complex vitamin.* No toxicity has been observed at high doses however, deficiencies can cause a wide range of clinical signs including loss of appetite, vomiting, paralysis, *seizures,* dehydration, and *heart disorders. Chastek paralysis* is a characteristic downward flexion of the neck from a thiamine deficiency.

TIME-RESTRICTED FEEDING METHOD: The time-restricted method for feeding dogs is useful when house training puppies. With this feeding program, the dog is given 20 to 30 minutes to consume its food. If the entire amount is consumed in less time, no more food is given at that meal. Instead, the next meal is increased by $1/3$ of a portion. Feeding a young, growing puppy is a dynamic situation. The amount being fed to the dog each meal should either be increased or decreased based on its past meal.

TUBE FEEDING (GAVAGE FEEDING): See *ANOREXIA, METHODS OF FEEDING.*

UNSATURATED FATTY ACIDS: Unsaturated fatty acids are discussed under *FATS* and *FATTY ACID DEFICIENCIES.* Remember, the only *essential fatty acid* needed by dogs is linoleic acid found in corn and safflower oil in large quantities. Dogs deficient in unsaturated fatty acids must be supplemented with oil at the rate of 1 teaspoon to every 8 ounces of dry diet.

VITAMIN A: Vitamin A is a *fat soluble vitamin* which is stored in the body. The highest concentrations occur in wheat germ, liver, egg yolk, and animal fat. Because cooking and baking destroys the vitamin, it must be added after dog food has been processed. Great excesses can cause loss of appetite, increased skin sensitivity, and loss of bone *calcium.* A deficiency in vitamin A may cause poor hair coat, skin and eye problems, rear leg weakness, and *reproductive difficulties.* Also see *VITAMIN A DEFICIENCY SKIN DISEASE* in Chapter 11.

VITAMIN B₁: See *THIAMINE.*

VITAMIN B₂: See *RIBOFLAVIN.*

VITAMIN B₆: See *PYRIDOXINE.*

VITAMIN B₁₂: See *COBALAMIN.*

VITAMIN C: Vitamin C (*ascorbic acid*) is a *water soluble vitamin* found predominantly in fresh fruits and vegetables. Vitamin C plays an important role in *wound healing,* in connective tissue integrity, and in the stability of capillary blood vessels. Mega-doses of vitamin C have been used as a method of reducing the incidence of *hip dysplasia.* Those proclaiming this method indicate its action is at the subcellular level. No valid clinical trials have been conducted to prove or disprove this method of joint nutrition. While toxicities from mega-doses of vitamin C have not been reported in the dog, some feel that high levels of vitamin C may increase the possibility of *urinary tract stone* formation.

VITAMIN D: Vitamin D is a *fat soluble vitamin* capable of being stored in the body in high levels. If the amounts stored are above necessary needs, serious physiological problems can result. Natural sources of vitamin D are liver, fish oils, and cereal grain germ. For dogs, vitamin D_2 is the only form necessary. However, some species of animals cannot change D_2 to D_3 so must receive the D_3 form of the vitamin.

Because vitamin D is associated with the assimilation and use of *calcium* and *phosphorus*, deficiencies and excesses are associated with these minerals and their need in teeth and bones. Increased calcium absorption in the presence of large quantities of vitamin D causes organ and *soft tissue calcification* which can result in death. Reversing soft tissue calcification is only partially successful. The use of *cortisone* is necessary during the depletion of stored body vitamin D.

VITAMIN E: Vitamin E is a *fat soluble vitamin* important in reproductive, muscle, and fat normalcy. Vitamin E is the least toxic of the fat soluble vitamins. Being a very unstable vitamin, vitamin E is easily destroyed by storage and heat. Wheat germ contains the vitamin in the natural form. Deficiencies in *alpha-tocopherol* (vitamin E) can cause *pregnancy failures* or *stillbirths*. Muscle cells require the correct level of vitamin E for proper development. Because of its importance in fat metabolism, quantities should be increased as the fat intake level is elevated. Mega-doses have been used in the treatment of *demodectic mange* in South America.

VITAMIN K: Vitamin K is a *fat soluble vitamin* normally produced by bacteria in the intestinal tract. Vitamin K is essential for proper blood clotting. Because the body does not store it, excessive amounts are unlikely. Deficiencies cause *prolonged clotting times* and hemorrhaging.

VITAMINS, FAT SOLUBLE: The four fat soluble vitamins necessary for proper body function are excreted and absorbed with fat. They are all discussed individually within this chapter.

Vitamin A	Vitamin D
Vitamin E	Vitamin K

VITAMINS, WATER SOLUBLE: The water soluble vitamins include vitamin C and all of the B complex vitamins. They are listed here for reference but are discussed separately.

Biotin	Pyridoxine (Vitamin B_6)
Cobalamin (Vitamin B_{12})	Riboflavin (Vitamin B_2)
Folic Acid	Thiamine (Vitamin B_1)
Niacin	Vitamin C
Pantothenic acid	

VOMITING, DIETARY MANAGEMENT OF: The dietary management of *vomiting* is necessary until the cause of vomiting can be determined. Vomiting can cause dehydration and electrolyte or mineral imbalances. While occasional vomiting is normal, repeated or frequent vomiting may cause serious problems. The cause of the repeated vomiting should be sought by the veterinarian.

In the face of persistent vomiting, withhold food and water for 24 hours to help break the drink-vomit cycle. Several ice cubes on five or six occasions during the day will provide small amounts of fluid. With mild dehydration, *Entrolyte*® or Gatorade® given in small amounts replace some of the *electrolytes* lost in the vomitus. This helps to alleviate the weakness and depression caused by fluid imbalances and mineral loss. The mature Cocker Spaniel should receive 2 tablespoons of Entrolyte® every two to three hours for several days. Puppies should receive about $1/2$ tablespoon at the same frequency.

After the 24 hour fast, start small amounts of a very bland, easily digestible diet. See *COLITIS DIET*. Five small feedings are superior to one or two large feedings. Gradually increase fluid consumption using Entrolyte® or Gatorade® as the basic oral fluid for 48 hours then replacing it with increasing amounts of water. Free choice water should be made available when the craving for fluids has ceased.

Identifying the cause of the vomiting is imperative especially if the vomiting continues with a bland diet and restricted fluids.

WATER: Water is the most important nutrient needed to maintain life. The greater the surface area on the dog per unit of weight, the more water required. This means that young puppies have higher water requirements than do adults. Smaller dogs require more than larger dogs.

Three conditions can cause increased water consumption. Puppies that feel the need to compete for water will consume more than is really required. Anything that increases body fluid loss such as *diarrhea*, fever, high outside temperature with high humidity, or nursing bitches increases fluid consumption. The need for water is also greater with increased salt intake.

The form of the dog food eaten plays some role in water consumption. Dry dog food has much less water in it than canned food. Therefore, the amount of water required is less for dogs exclusively eating canned food. If the available water is either too hot or too cold, consumption can be affected. Hard water (water with high mineral levels) is not as palatable as low mineral water. The rule of thumb is that palatable water should be available 24 hours per day unless fluid restriction is indicated in vomiting.

WEANING, DIETARY MANAGEMENT OF: The weaning procedure should take place gradually over a period of two to three weeks. Large litters can start as early as three weeks old or as late as five weeks if the mother has an adequate milk supply and nursing is not detrimental to her. In extraordinary circumstances, weaning could occur as soon as the eyes open (10 to 14 days old). However, this situation should be reserved for orphan pups or pups from mothers with poor or diseased milk supplies.

A gruel is prepared by mixing warm water with a high quality puppy food like *Science Diet® Growth®*. After a short soaking period, the gruel is either rubbed on the pup's mouth or the pup is placed face first in a shallow pan of the mixture. In a short time, the puppies learn to lap from the pan. Start with a once daily feeding and increase feedings to four or five times daily at the time of weaning. After the pups are eating the fluid mixture, gradually decrease the amount of liquid. By five or six weeks, dry food can be fed with water available in a separate bowl.

Remember, when you start feeding the pups, they will take less milk from the lactating bitch. She in turn will then require less water and less food as the *puppy formula* is gradually increased. When this whole process takes 14 to 17 days, weaning is not traumatic for either the bitch or the pups. On the day that you determine weaning is complete, the bitch must be totally separated from the pups. Any nursing stimulation will continue lactation.

All puppies, even puppies weaned as early as five weeks, should be kept together since they need this period of peer interaction to develop well-rounded personalities. As much human contact as possible is also very beneficial to their development.

ZINC: Zinc is classified as a *trace mineral.* High doses will tie up *calcium* and *copper* causing signs associated with deficiencies of calcium and copper. Serious *zinc deficiencies* have been associated with the feeding of *generic dog foods.* Signs of zinc deficiency are a *scaly dermatitis* with inflammation and poor *wound healing.* Also, hair thins out, a poor appetite develops, and the growth rate of puppies slows down. To reverse the signs of zinc deficiency, zinc supplementation must be provided for several years, possibly for life.

POISONING

Many poisonings require immediate attention. Use this chapter as a reference for the treatment of suspected poisoning. First, determine the name of the poison (brand name, if possible), the amount ingested, and the weight of your Cocker Spaniel. Then call either the **ANIMAL TOXICOLOGY HOT LINE** at **(217) 333–3611** (day or night), in Southeastern United States call **(404) 542-6751** or the closest **POISON CONTROL CENTER,** generally located at a metropolitan Children's Hospital. If a specific antidote exists, these people will tell you. Carefully write down the name of the antidote and any recommended supportive treatment. Next, call your veterinarian and request immediate service for the type of poison involved. If you find a home antidote in this chapter for the poison consumed, give the antidote and proceed to your veterinarian's office quickly. The ANIMAL TOXICOLOGY HOT LINE or POISON CONTROL CENTER telephone numbers should be posted near your telephone for ready access.

ACID POISONING, INTERNAL AND EXTERNAL: Acids like sulfuric, nitric, carbolic, hydrochloric, and trichloroacetic acids, used for cleaning and etching procedures are very caustic. A short contact period with any of these acids will destroy the exposed tissue. Changes in the color of the mucous membranes or skin are external signs of acid intoxication. The skin first becomes gray and then black as it is destroyed.

HOME ANTIDOTE FOR EXTERNAL ACID POISONING: Flush affected area with large quantities of water and cover with sodium bicarbonate paste (baking soda). Internal signs of acid intoxication are extreme abdominal pain, bloody vomitus, and rapid breathing. DO NOT MAKE THE DOG VOMIT!

HOME ANTIDOTE FOR INTERNAL ACID POISONING: Mix 3 egg whites and 1 ounce of liquid soap in 8 ounces of water. Orally, give an adult Cocker Spaniel 2 to 3 ounces of the egg white-soap solution. Next, give olive oil (2 teaspoons for an adult Cocker and 1 teaspoon for a puppy) and transport immediately to your veterinarian!

ACONITE (WILD) PLANT POISONING: Serious cardiovascular disturbances are caused by aconite, the toxic principle of wild aconite or monkshood (*Aconitum napellus*). The early signs include nausea, muscular twitching, and *convulsions*. The heart rate becomes very slow and irregular. As breathing becomes labored, the tongue turns blue. Treatment is supportive. If the signs have not yet progressed to convulsions, *gastric lavage* is helpful. Prognosis is guarded and dose related.

ALKALI POISONING, INTERNAL AND EXTERNAL: Alkalis, the opposite of acids, can cause very severe burns both externally and internally. These products are frequently used as degreasers, cleaners, and clothes washing powders. Lye is a common caustic alkali. Signs of external toxicity are very red skin accompanied by pain.

HOME ANTIDOTE FOR EXTERNAL ALKALI POISONING: For external alkali toxicity, flush the area with copious amounts of water. Follow this with vinegar to neutralize the alkali.

Signs of ingestion of a caustic alkali include extreme abdominal pain, blood-tinged vomitus, and difficulty in breathing. DO NOT INDUCE VOMITING!

HOME ANTIDOTE FOR INTERNAL ALKALI POISONING: Attempt to neutralize the alkali by giving dilute vinegar (1:4) or full strength lemon juice orally. Up to 2 ounces may be given to an adult Cocker Spaniel. Then give albumin (3–4 ounces orally of a solution of 5 egg whites dissolved in 1 quart of lukewarm water) or olive oil (2–3 teaspoons). Immediately transport the dog to your veterinarian.

ALKALOID POISONING: This class of drugs includes such diverse members as *atropine*, caffeine, *morphine*, *nicotine*, quinine, and *strychnine*. The potential clinical signs vary greatly from alkaloid to alkaloid. For a broader discussion, refer to the individual alkaloids like *strychnine* included within the chapter.

HOME ANTIDOTE FOR INGESTION OF ALKALOIDS: Inactivate the drug by giving either 1 ml of tincture of iodine in 2 ounces of water orally or 1 to 2 ounces of a 1:400 dilution of strong tea (tannic acid) to an adult Cocker Spaniel. Immediately transport the dog to your veterinarian for additional gastric lavage and supportive treatment. Keep the dog warm on the ride to the hospital.

ALOCASIA PLANT POISONING: Alocasia, a member of the *Arum family*, is normally kept as an ornamental house plant. All parts of the plant are irritating to the internal membranes of the mouth and throat. Vomiting and diarrhea result from the irritation. Generally salivation also increases. Since no systemic toxicity is seen, treatment is oral in the form of milk or olive oil to soothe the irritated tissue. Two teaspoons are usually sufficient for an adult Cocker Spaniel.

AMPHETAMINE POISONING: Amphetamine drugs are tightly controlled by the federal government because of their potential for abuse. The drug, a potent nervous system and cardiovascular stimulator, is only used for treatment of hyperactive children, dieting, and depression. Clinical signs vary from dilated pupils and delirium to convulsions and a very high body temperature and finally to coma and death.

Tranquilizers or an injectable anesthesia controls the *seizures*. Oral lavage with *activated charcoal* removes any amphetamine from the stomach. Acidification of the urine speeds urinary excretion. If the dog lives for six hours after this treatment, the prognosis improves.

ANIMAL TOXICOLOGY HOT LINE: CALL (217) 333–3611. In Southeastern United States, call (404) 542-6751 KEEP THIS NUMBER NEAR YOUR PHONE! Several years ago, as a service to practicing veterinarians and pet owners, the University of Illinois College of Veterinary Medicine established an animal toxicology telephone service. The hot line is answered 24 hours a day, seven days a week. Consultation is designed primarily for the veterinarian, but calls from owners of poisoned pets are accepted. The service attempts to provide antidote information and ideas on the symptomatic care of affected animals. In 1988, a regional center for Southeastern United States became affiliated with the University of Illinois Center. Veterinary toxicological groups in eight other states and two Canadian provinces are working toward regional center status. This network is called the National Animal Poison Information Network or *NAPINet*. If interested, dog owners can receive a quarterly newsletters from NAPINet by supporting them with a $15 fee.

ANT POISONS: *Arsenic* is the active ingredient in most ant poisons. Because of the palatable taste and the slow biodegradable characteristics of arsenic, ant poisons are frequent causes of arsenic poisoning in dogs.

ANTIDOTES (HOME) AGAINST UNABSORBED POISONS: Each of the following poisons has a home antidote which may be partially effective in neutralizing or removing unabsorbed poisons from the stomach of an affected dog. Refer to each poison within this chapter for its particular home antidote.

Acids, Corrosive	Formaldehyde
Alkali, Caustic	Lead
Alkaloids	Mercury
Arsenic	Oxalic Acid
Carbon tetrachloride	Petroleum distillates (Gasoline)
Copper	Phenol and Creosotes
Detergents (Anionic)	Phosphorus
Detergents (Cationic)	Unknown

ANTIFREEZE POISONING: *Ethylene glycol* is the active ingredient in most antifreeze products. This chemical compound becomes more toxic after it is metabolized by the body. Ethylene glycol's sweet taste attracts dogs and cats. Once the diagnosis of antifreeze poisoning is made, very aggressive treatment is required. The minimum lethal dose of ethylene glycol antifreeze for a 25 pound dog is 1-2 ounces. One or two teaspoons of ethylene glycol is lethal for a Cocker puppy. At best, the prognosis is guarded for saving the dog.

If there is to be any chance of saving the Cocker Spaniel, treatment must be started before signs are observed. The earliest signs of antifreeze intoxication are loss of balance and disorientation followed by *seizures* and coma. Affected dogs showing neurological signs usually die within eight hours. If the dog survives the early signs, *congestive heart failure*, kidney pain, and decreased urination may develop within several days. While ethylene glycol causes initial central nervous system signs, later *kidney failure* signs are due to the formation of oxalic acid crystals in the kidney tubules. These effectively destroy kidney function. Treatment first removes any unabsorbed ethylene glycol with activated charcoal, then corrects serious acid-base problems in the body fluids, and finally promotes the excretion of unchanged ethylene glycol through intravenous ethanol. The resulting kidney disease must be treated by maintaining a good flow of urine. If a hospitalized dog can be kept alive for five days, the chances of survival improve considerably. Early treatment is the most important element in saving a Cocker poisoned by ethylene glycol.

ANTU POISONING: *ANTU*, the abbreviation for alpha-naphthyl thiourea, is a very potent chemical used in the past as a *rat poison*. Because of the danger to all life, the use of this poison has diminished dramatically. After a dog ingests a small amount, death from respiratory failure occurs within eight hours . The chemical is irritating to an empty stomach which may result in vomiting. Vomiting is the only chance to save the Cocker's life. No antidote is available. Symptomatic treatment is fruitless.

ARSENIC POISONING: Arsenic is a common ingredient in *ant poison, snail bait, herbicides, insecticides*, and paint. Arsenic trioxide and sodium arsenite are the most poisonous forms. Most commonly, the poisoning is acute. However, repeated low doses can possibly accumulate causing chronic arsenic poisoning. Acute arsenic poisoning signs include extreme abdominal pain, vomiting, and weakness. The vomitus has a garlic odor. Later, bloody diarrhea and circulatory collapse are followed by coma or *convulsions* and death.

　　HOME ANTIDOTE FOR ARSENIC POISONING: Give 2 ounces of evaporated milk mixed with 1 beaten egg white and $1/2$ ounce of strong tea (tannic acid) to an adult Cocker Spaniel. Transport immediately to an animal hospital for intensive treatment.

　　In the hospital, a *gastric lavage* with *activated charcoal* is initiated. As part of the treatment, a heavy metal poisoning antidote, *dimercaprol (BAL)* is given intramuscularly for several days. Aggressive fluid therapy must be maintained for four to eight days. Pain should be controlled during the treatment period.

　　The signs associated with chronic arsenic poisoning are loss of appetite, body fluid loss, and weakness followed by coma and death. If chronic arsenic poisoning is suspected, hair or toenails can be analyzed for the presence of arsenic. Information on heavy metal hair and toenail analysis can be obtained from Micro-Trace Minerals, 915 King Street Suite B–43, Alexandria, VA 22314.

　　The prognosis for arsenic poisoning is guarded. Aggressive hospital treatment is important!

ARUM PLANT FAMILY POISONING: The Arum plant family includes many of the common ornamental house plants—*calla lily, Dieffenbachia, alocasia, caladium,* and *philodendron.* All parts of these plants irritate the gastrointestinal mucous membranes causing vomiting and diarrhea. Affected animals salivate profusely. Oral demulcents such as milk and olive oil provide the best form of therapy. Give 2 to 3 ounces of milk and up to 1 ounce of olive oil for an adult Cocker Spaniel.

ASPIRIN INTOXICATION (SALICYLATE POISONING): Aspirin is tolerated better by dogs than cats but can be abused for fever reduction or arthritic pain alleviation even in the dog. Since children's aspirin is sugar-coated, dogs with sweet tooth tendencies will consume large quantities if given the opportunity.

A wide range of clinical signs are observed in aspirin poisoning. Panting, weakness, and *seizures* are seen acutely. The acid nature of the drug can cause vomiting. *Bone marrow depression*, bleeding under the skin, a nose bleed, and the odor of acetone on the breath are seen in chronic aspirin poisoning. Death results from a high dosage.

After administering a slurry of *activated charcoal*, treatment is directed at emptying the stomach. The metabolic acidosis problem is treated with intravenous fluid containing sodium bicarbonate. Normal body temperature must be maintained. Constant nursing care is necessary for at least 24 to 36 hours. Elimination of the aspirin from the system can be accelerated with *peritoneal dialysis* techniques. The prognosis is guarded to fair depending on the dose and signs observed.

BIRD-OF-PARADISE PLANT POISONING: Ingestion of the seed pod of the bird-of-paradise (*Caesalpinia gilliesii*) can cause severe vomiting and diarrhea. The gastrointestinal signs are usually preceded by nausea. Treatment is directed toward making the patient vomit to remove any unabsorbed pod material. The administration of a mixture of 1 to 2 whole eggs beaten into 2 ounces of milk follows for adults with smaller amounts for puppies. Replacement of fluids lost from the vomiting and diarrhea must be continued for several days. The prognosis depends on how well fluid therapy is maintained and how quickly the GI tract recovers.

BITES: The following bites are discussed individually within the chapter. See each for a more complete explanation.

Black Widow Spider Gila Monster
Brown Recluse Spider Lizard
Common Brown Spider Snake
Coral Snake Tarantula
Fire Ant

BLACK WIDOW SPIDER BITES: The black widow spider is one of two genera of spiders whose venomous bite causes severe damage or death to a dog. The black widow spider (*Latrodectus*) is black with a light colored hour-glass shape on its belly. The bite marks of a spider are often difficult to find. Seeing a spider in close proximity to the dog may provide the circumstantial evidence needed for a diagnosis. After a spider bite, the first sign is localized pain at the bite site. Neurological signs like muscle spasms, jerking convulsions, and flaccid paralysis follow. Hours or days later, difficulty in breathing is observed. Heart irregularities are also seen.

A specific antivenin is available but must be given early to be very effective. *Corticosteroids* are given along with fluid therapy. Antibiotics and various pain medications are also utilized. If the Cocker survives for three or four days, the chances of recovery are good.

BLEACH INTOXICATION: Bleaches are household cleaners that disinfect by an oxidizing action. In concentrated strengths, they are caustic to skin and mucous membranes. Diluted forms, if consumed orally, cause a gastrointestinal upset. Immediate treatment is directed at emptying the stomach by vomiting or lavage. Then, give up to 2 egg whites or 1 ounce of olive oil orally to soothe and coat the irritated tissues. If the bleach was highly concentrated, sodium thiosulfate is given to neutralize the bleach solution. Generally, the prognosis for recovery is good providing the bleach was not too concentrated.

BLUE TAIL LIZARD POISONING: See *NEUROTOXINS.*

BOTULINUM TOXIN: The toxin from *Clostridium botulinum* bacteria found in some spoiled foods is a very potent and fatal toxin which causes motor paralysis and coma, followed by death. Fortunately, dogs are fairly resistant to the affects of the toxin. Only the early administration of a specific antitoxin will insure success in controlling the disease progression. Also see Chapter 7 on the *NEUROLOGICAL SYSTEM.*

BROWN RECLUSE AND COMMON BROWN SPIDER BITES: The brown recluse and common brown spiders (*Loxosceles*) are long-legged spiders with a dark colored violin-shaped marking on their backs. Their bite is capable of causing extreme tissue and skin necrosis. Immediately following the bite, little pain is present. However, after several hours the area around the bite swells, becoming red and blistered. The tissue surrounding the bite becomes necrotic and dies over a one to two week period. In a very susceptible dog, systemic signs are observed ranging from fever and vomiting to convulsions and poor blood clotting. Early surgical removal of affected tissue is the primary treatment. Antibiotics and *corticosteroids* are also used, especially if severe systemic signs are seen.

BUCKEYE POISONING: The seeds from the buckeye (*horse chestnut*) tree cause gastrointestinal upsets if ingested. The active ingredient, saponin, causes salivation, vomiting, nausea, and finally diarrhea. Generally abdominal pain is present. Treatment is directed toward removal of the seed material by vomiting, followed by symptomatic management of the gastrointestinal signs. When these signs are managed aggressively, the prognosis is fair to good.

BUFO TOAD POISONING: The Bufo toad species was introduced in the southern United States forty years ago for insect control. The parotid salivary glands of the toad produce a very potent, lethal toxin. Dogs may mouth the toad as it emerges and becomes active at dusk. The toad toxin is a very complex chemical compound capable of producing different clinical signs depending somewhat on the age and condition of the dog. Old dogs with cardiac and asthmatic conditions are very severely affected. Where the poisoning takes place in the United States effects the death rate in dogs. While Florida mortality rates approach 95%, Texas and Hawaii are as low as 10%. Apparently the strength of the toxin varies with different strains of the Bufo toads.

Signs vary from slight salivation to convulsive *seizures*. The dog may have difficulty breathing to the point that its tongue turns blue. Flushing the mouth and gums with copious amounts of water to remove the waxy thick toxin that sticks to the mucous membranes is one of the oldest and best forms of treatment. Induction of vomiting helps protect the exposed dog. While no specific antidote is available, proper medical treatment will increase the chances of the dog's survival. Several drugs have been used to treat affected dogs. *Atropine* dries the mouth and decreases respiratory tract secretions. *Pentobarbital anesthesia* and *tranquilizers* may increase the ability of the dog to combat lethal doses of the toad toxin.

The heart rhythm is frequently altered by the toxin. In dogs not previously affected with bronchial asthma, the use of a heart medication called "beta-blockers" may result in spectacular reversal of heart irregularities. *Propranolol hydrochloride* is also very effective in these instances. Aggressive treatment is necessary to counteract the affects of the complex toxin.

CALADIUM PLANT POISONING: The caladium is an ornamental house plant from the *Arum family*. The sap and various other parts of the plant are irritating to the mucosal lining of the digestive tract. Intoxication causes severe salivation, vomiting, and diarrhea. Treatment is the use of emollients such as olive oil or milk to soothe the irritated tissues. The prognosis is generally good.

CARBAMATE POISONING: Carbamate compounds are used in many insecticide treatments for dogs. This effective flea, tick, and louse killer is classified as a cholinesterase inhibitor because of the way it kills insects. This compound also causes the toxic signs seen when the dog has received an overdose of the drug. Clinical signs of carbamate poisoning are pinpoint pupil constriction, excessive salivation with vomiting, and diarrhea. As the poisoning becomes more severe, muscle twitching and a *wobbly gait* are seen. Death is usually due to paralysis of the respiratory muscles.

The treatment of choice for carbamate poisoning is *atropine*, both IV and sub Q. Other therapy such as artificial respiration may be needed until respiratory paralysis is reversed. The administration of *2-PAM* is contraindicated in carbamate poisoning. The prognosis is guarded and depends on aggressive treatment and the amount of carbamates absorbed.

CARBON MONOXIDE POISONING: Carbon monoxide poisoning most commonly occurs in dogs transported in vans with defective exhaust systems, dogs transported in car trunks, and in animals housed near faulty space heaters. Affected dogs are depressed, undergo *convulsions*, and have an elevated temperature accompanied by very red mucous membranes and dilated pupils.

Treatment involves the removal of the dog from the source, pure oxygen administration, and *50% glucose* intravenously. Dogs should be hospitalized for at least two days for observation. The prognosis is guarded to fair. Elimination of the source of carbon monoxide is a must!

CARBON TETRACHLORIDE POISONING: Carbon tetrachloride, commonly used in fire extinguishers and cleaning solutions, is a very potent liver poison. Poisoning can occur from topical administration or oral ingestion of the chemical. Signs of nausea and diarrhea will precede those of acute liver failure. Death follows *acute liver failure*. If the skin has been saturated with carbon tetrachloride, flush it with copious amounts of water. Fresh air or oxygen therapy should be sought. If ingestion has occurred, the stomach should be evacuated and *activated charcoal* should be used to absorb any remaining poison in the gut. Intravenous fluid therapy is important.

HOME ANTIDOTE FOR CARBON TETRACHLORIDE POISONING: Feed a high quality protein and carbohydrate diet to help protect the liver. The high quality diet is NOT a substitute for the veterinary care necessary to treat potential *acute liver failure*. Prognosis for recovery is guarded at best.

CHARCOAL, ACTIVATED: Activated charcoal is widely used in treating unabsorbed poisons. Vegetable origin activated charcoal is much more effective than either animal or mineral origin charcoal. Many different poisons, including *ethylene glycol, strychnine, morphine*, and *mercuric chloride*, can be tied up with activated charcoal. However it is ineffective against *cyanide*. While activated charcoal will prevent the absorption, the poison is not detoxified. To remove the charcoal mix from the stomach, an *emetic* (vomit stimulator) or *gastric lavage* is used.

CHERRY SEED TOXICITY: The seeds of the cherry tree contain a potent chemical, amygdalin, which will cause *cyanide poisoning* when chewed by a dog. The clinical signs which include muscular twitching and convulsive *seizures* occur rapidly. The odor of almonds on the breath and respiratory distress followed by coma and death are also signs of cherry seed toxicity.

Because the clinical progress is so rapid, treatment is not usually undertaken. If time is available to initiate therapy, sodium nitrite is given intravenously, followed immediately by sodium thiosulfate and repeated as needed. Oxygen is administered either in an oxygen cage or by mask. Oral *activated charcoal* is also given. The prognosis is poor to guarded depending on the number of seeds chewed and the severity of the signs when treatment began. Also see *CYANIDE*.

CHLORINATED HYDROCARBON TOXICITY: Chlorinated hydrocarbons are a class of chemicals found in *insecticides* such as lindane, aldrin, and chlordane. They cause convulsive *seizures* and neurological irritation that must be differentiated from *strychnine, metaldehyde, 1080*, and *lead poisoning*.

Clinically, the affected dog becomes restless, its muscles twitch, its legs become wobbly, and it may convulse. Its temperature rises and breathing difficulties result. Death follows shortly.

Certain groups of dogs are more susceptible to chlorinated hydrocarbon toxicity than others. Thin dogs are more severely affected than those in prime condition. Young dogs suffer more than older dogs. Animals with a full stomach are not as severely affected as those with an empty stomach.

Chlorinated hydrocarbon toxicity has no specific antidote. If the poison was applied externally, wash the dog completely with soap and water. Internal poisoning is treated by using an *emetic* (vomit stimulator) and *activated charcoal* in the stomach. *Diazepam* or *sodium pentobarbital* control the *seizures*. Aggressive supportive therapy is needed to eliminate toxic signs and maintain respiration. The general prognosis is guarded to poor. However, if the dog lives for two days, the chances for recovery increase.

CHOCOLATE POISONING: Poisoning from the ingestion of large amounts of chocolate candy or Baker's® chocolate is actually due to xanthine compounds present in the chocolate. Most of the signs are related to nervous system irritation which vary from restlessness and excitability to general seizures. Large increases in the amount of urine excreted are also observed. If the ingestion is discovered within thirty minutes, stimulate vomiting. The administration of oral aluminum hydroxide gel (like *Amphojel*® by Wyeth Laboratories) is important in addition to general supportive care. The prognosis depends on the amount of chocolate ingested and the time that has passed before treatment is initiated.

CHRYSANTHEMUM TOXICITY: The resin found in the chrysanthemum flower can cause an external skin irritation. The irritative properties of the flower produce exudative dermatitis. The only treatment necessary is thoroughly washing the affected area and applying a steroid cream like *Panalog*®.

COMMON BROWN SPIDER BITES: See *BROWN RECLUSE AND COMMON BROWN SPIDER BITES.*

COPPER POISONING: If actual copper is ingested in toxic amounts, treatment should be directed toward preventing its absorption by giving 1 or 2 egg whites and sodium ferrocyanide in a $1/2$ pint of water to adult Cocker Spaniels and one quarter of that amount to small puppies. If the copper has been absorbed into the system, *Cuprimine*® is used for long periods to eliminate the copper from the body.

CORAL SNAKE BITE: The coral snake found in southern states is the only poisonous snake in the United States that possesses a *neurotoxin*. The pit viper family of rattlesnakes, copperheads, and cotton-mouthed water moccasins are totally unrelated.

Since there is little pain at the onset of the bite, one may not be aware of the bite. Signs of the neurotoxin poisoning may not appear for one or two hours. On dogs with dense hair coats, the fang marks may not be apparent. The initial signs are difficulty in swallowing and depression. These signs progress to skeletal muscle paralysis and finally death by respiratory paralysis.

Treatment includes intravenous administration of specific coral snake antivenin obtained through the State Board of Health, at some zoos, or directly from Wyeth Laboratories, Radnor, Pennsylvania. If possible, a tourniquet should be placed between the bite and the heart and left in place for up to two hours. The dog MUST be kept absolutely quiet to keep circulation of the poison in the blood to a minimum. Part of the treatment is directed at controlling shock and anaphylactoid (allergic) reactions. The tissue containing the venom should be cut away when possible. Time is of great importance! Obtaining coral snake antivenin is the only realistic chance in treating the dog successfully.

The prognosis is poor to fair. The amount of time that has passed between the bite and the administration of the antivenin, the amount of venom injected, and the location of the bite all determine the severity of the case.

CREOSOTE POISONING: Creosote is a *phenol* derivative used for preserving fence posts. Topical applications of this chemical may cause skin or mucous membranes to blanch (turn white). If creosote is ingested, the odor of phenol can be detected on the breath and serious abdominal pain with vomiting occurs. After several days, signs of kidney and liver failure are observed.

HOME ANTIDOTE FOR CREOSOTE POISONING: After the injured tissues are bathed with soap and water or with alcohol rinses, treatment should include bicarbonate of soda dressings. Either 2 to 3 ounces of milk containing 1 egg white or 1 ounce of olive oil are given orally to adult Cocker Spaniels and one ounce of milk with one egg white or two teaspoons of olive oil to Cocker puppies. Rush the dog to your veterinarian immediately for further treatment and observation. Your vet will probably give *activated charcoal* and establish an IV drip to treat shock and promote diuresis (urine formation). The prognosis is good with treatment for topical poisoning and guarded with oral ingestion of this toxic chemical.

CROW FOOT FAMILY PLANT POISONING: All parts of the crow foot plant are toxic if ingested. A severe gastroenteritis with vomiting and diarrhea occur. Most dogs will become weak and develop convulsive *seizures.* Treatment is directed at removing the plant parts from the stomach and then maintaining blood pressure and oxygenation of the body tissues. The prognosis is guarded to fair depending on the amount swallowed and the observed signs.

CYANIDE POISONING: Cyanide, one of the most potent protoplasmic poisons known, is used in herbicides and other fumigants. Cyanide is found naturally in *cherry seeds* and *hydrangea plants.* Because it is a very rapid killer, many times treatment is too little too late. If treatment is initiated, it involves intensive care with intermittent intravenous sodium nitrite followed by sodium thiosulfate. This procedure is repeated as needed. Concurrent oxygen therapy is a must! *Activated charcoal* is not very useful in preventing the absorption of cyanide products. The prognosis is poor to fair because death occurs so rapidly.

DETERGENT (ANIONIC) POISONING: Anionic detergents are salts of sodium, ammonium, or potassium, usually found in Class I or Class II, light-duty or all-purpose types of detergents. Uncolored, unperfumed soaps are relatively non-toxic even in large quantities. However, the addition of perfume and coloring agents can cause gastrointestinal upsets.

HOME ANTIDOTE FOR ANIONIC POISONING: Administer water or milk followed by demulcents like 1 ounce of olive oil and 1 egg white for an adult Cocker Spaniel. Before giving the fluid and the demulcent, vomiting should be induced unless the poison is a strong *alkali*. NOTE: Remember that some laundering agents contain strong alkalis such as lye. If this is the case, DO NOT INDUCE VOMITING! Follow instructions under *HOME ANTIDOTE FOR ALKALIS* instead. After administering the home antidote, take the dog to your veterinarian for further treatment. Provide the doctor with as much information about the product as possible.

DETERGENT (CATIONIC) POISONING: Cationic detergents are those that contain chlorides and iodides. While most of the highly caustic detergents are anionic in nature, the same principle applies to cationic poisoning that applies to anionic. DO NOT induce vomiting if a strong *alkali* is present!

HOME ANTIDOTE FOR CATIONIC POISONING: Give large quantities of Castile soap dissolved in hot water. If an *alkali* is present, give egg whites in large quantities. Seek veterinary care after the home antidote has been given.

DIEFFENBACHIA PLANT POISONING: Dieffenbachia (*dumbcane*) is an ornamental plant that causes mouth and throat irritations if consumed. Signs include profuse salivation and some swelling in the throat and esophageal region. The use of demulcents like an ounce of milk or an ounce of olive oil are usually sufficient to soothe the irritated tissues until they become less inflamed. Since systemic signs are rare, the prognosis for recovery is good.

DIGITALIS POISONING: Digitalis and digitalis derivatives are widely used in the treatment of cardiac insufficiencies. Naturally occurring digitalis-like compounds are found in *foxglove*, *mistletoe*, *lily of the valley*, and *oleander* ornamental plants. The mistletoe berries are especially toxic when consumed.

Two distinct sets of signs are observed. The first signs are those of a gastrointestinal disturbance with vomiting and abdominal pain. This then leads into a very slow heart rate with disturbances in the heart rhythm.

Treatment for plant digitalis poisoning would be similar to one for a drug overdose of *digitalis*. First, *potassium* is administered followed by *atropine*. The dog is also placed in an oxygen cage. Occasionally *beta-blocker drugs* are used to correct irregular heart beats. If the dog lives for 24 hours, the chances of survival are quite good.

DRUG OVERDOSES (MARIJUANA, AMPHETAMINE, TRANQUILIZER): Drugs subject to abuse are called controlled substances. When dogs are accidently exposed to these products, the veterinarian must know which drug or compound the animal has been exposed if the owner has that knowledge. Rapid treatment may save your Cocker's life if you let your vet know the nature of the drug overdose. Because your veterinarian is bound to confidentiality by the doctor-patient relationship, you will not be reported to the authorities even if the drug is illicit.

Other individual drugs are discussed throughout this chapter. Refer to each under its own heading.

ETHYLENE GLYCOL INTOXICATION: See *ANTIFREEZE POISONING.*

FINGER CHERRY POISONING: The fruit from the plant referred to as the finger cherry (*Rhodomyrtus macrocarpa*) is very toxic. Permanent total *blindness* will result within 24 hours after ingestion. Treatment is directed at removal of the ingesta by inducing vomiting. No specific antidote is known. The prognosis is guarded at best.

FIRE ANT BITES: The fire ant which resides in the southern part of the United States is capable of producing a painful, inflamed bite or sting. In a dog previously bitten by a fire ant, *anaphylactic allergic reactions* can occur. These can be fatal if not promptly treated by a veterinarian. Hundreds of bites simultaneously can also cause a shock-like syndrome that could be life threatening. If anaphylaxis is not a consideration, the use of injectable and topical *corticosteroids* cuts down the severe inflammation that occurs. With proper treatment, the prognosis is good.

FLUOROACETATE POISONING: *Sodium fluoroacetate (1080)* is a very poisonous *rodenticide* currently used only by licensed exterminators. Its use as a predator control measure is tightly regulated today because of its extreme toxicity and the chance for accidental poisoning.

The clinical signs must be differentiated from those of the *chlorinated hydrocarbon, toxaphene.* Signs may be seen as early as one hour after ingestion of 1080. Early vomiting and mucoid diarrhea with evidence of abdominal pain are observed. The affected dog howls, appears agitated, and runs aimlessly. Salivation increases and *tetanic seizures* occur with the dog lying on its side. During the seizure activity, the tongue and membranes are blue. Loud noises do not intensify the seizures caused by 1080 as in seizures caused by *strychnine*. Since no antidote exists, treatment is symptomatic. *Pentobarbital anesthesia* is of little use in the treatment of 1080 poisoning. Calcium gluconate is given both orally and intravenously. Once *seizures* have started, treatment is unsuccessful in most cases. The prognosis is poor, but in rare cases dogs have recovered.

FORMALDEHYDE POISONING: Used in taxidermy and in some photography procedures, formaldehyde is an uncommon poison source. Because of its acid composition, VOMITING IS NOT INDUCED. If the formaldehyde has been applied externally, copious amounts of water should be used to flush the area. Orally, a 0.2% ammonia water or a 1% ammonium acetate is administered. At home, 1 to 2 ounces of gelatin in water or starch water may also be given orally to an adult Cocker Spaniel before transporting the dog to the veterinary hospital for further treatment and observation. The prognosis is fair to good depending on the amount ingested and the speed at which the antidotes and other therapy are initiated.

GARBAGE TOXINS: The significant garbage-produced toxins come from *Staphylococcus* and *Salmonella* bacteria and *Clostridium botulinum.* Staph and Salmonella food poisoning are due to the putrefaction of certain foods like ham, milk, chicken, and some vegetables. There is a proliferation of exotoxins and endotoxins capable of causing gastric distress and death. *Botulism poisoning* is fortunately very uncommon in the dog. A more complete discussion can be found under *BOTULISM* in Chapter 7.

The signs of *garbage intoxication* are vomiting, nausea, abdominal pain, and often mucoid bloody diarrhea. Garbage poisoning has a rapid onset but is usually not lethal. A more serious form of this type of intoxication occurs with the *Staph lethal toxin* which causes initial signs within 30 minutes and violent convulsions and death in 24 hours.

Treatment is symptomatic. Vomiting should be induced. The stomach should be lavaged to empty all contents. Intravenous fluids are very important in overcoming this intoxication. The prognosis for Staph toxin poisoning is good. For the Staph lethal toxin ingestion, the prognosis is guarded depending on when emesis (vomiting) is induced and the intensity of supportive treatment.

GASOLINE (PETROLEUM DISTILLATES) POISONING: Gasoline poisoning occurs in three ways: by externally exposing large areas of the skin to gasoline, by breathing gasoline vapors, and by swallowing gasoline. If large surface areas of skin are saturated with gasoline, the signs are similar to inhalation poisoning. Areas of skin that have come in contact with gasoline may be more susceptible to infection in the future because gasoline has been absorbed through the skin and removed fats from the subcutis area. Treatment of this level of toxicity involves cleaning the affected area with soap and water, followed by general supportive therapy.

If large areas of the skin are saturated with gasoline or if the vapors are inhaled, signs of a stumbling gait and stupor occur. If the dog is given fresh air and the gasoline is washed from the skin, recovery may take place. However, some dogs progress to dilated pupils, muscle twitches, and then convulsive *seizures.* At this point, treatment is probably of little value. Treatment is supportive through oxygen therapy and support of kidney and cardiovascular function.

Oral ingestion of gasoline is rather irritating causing salivation, vomiting, and diarrhea. Treatment is *gastric lavage* with mineral or olive oil to try to prevent absorption into the body. This is followed by copious amounts of warm water. Veterinary supportive care is absolutely necessary. The prognosis is good if the gasoline can be removed from the body before muscle twitching and convulsions are observed. If the product has been absorbed into the body, signs of muscle twitching and convulsions signal a poor prognosis.

GASTRIC LAVAGE: See *STOMACH PUMPING PROCEDURE.*

GASTROINTESTINAL UPSETS, POISONS CAUSING: A number of substances can cause GI upsets as part or all of the observed signs. Each of the following listings is discussed individually within the chapter.

Acids	Garbage Toxins
Alkalis	Gasoline Poisoning
Aconite (Wild) Plant Poisoning	Holly Poisoning
Alocasia Plant Poisoning	Household Cleaners Poisoning
Arsenic Poisoning	Insecticide Toxicity
Arum Plant Family	Iris Plant Poisoning
Bird of Paradise Plant Poisoning	Lily Plant Poisoning
Bleach	Mistletoe Poisoning
Buckeye Poisoning	Mushroom Poisoning
Caladium Plant Poisoning	Philodendron Poisoning
Carbamate Poisoning	Poinsettia Poisoning
Carbon Tetrachloride Poisoning	Privet Plant Poisoning
Creosote Poisoning	Rayless Goldenrod Poisoning
Crow Foot Plant Poisoning	Rhubarb Poisoning
Detergent Poisoning (Anionic)	Thallium Poisoning
Detergent Poisoning (Cationic)	Wisteria Plant Poisoning
Digitalis Poisoning	Yew Plant Poisoning
Fluoroacetate (1080) Poisoning	

GILA MONSTER BITE: The Gila monster (*Heloderma suspectum*) is one of two poisonous lizards located in the United States. They reside in the arid Southwest. Because the Gila monster is not particularly aggressive, dog bites are rare. However, if a bite occurs, the lizard has a tendency to attach itself at the bite site. To release its grip, gently pry the lizard's mouth open or light a fire under the lower jaw to stimulate it to release its grip. Do not shake it loose because teeth may break off in the multiple puncture wounds.

If venom was injected in the bite, pain at the bite site will occur within a few minutes. The venom appears to have some affect on the cardiovascular system but does not affect blood coagulation. If enough venom is injected in the bite wounds, shock and circulatory collapse may occur within hours. There is NO specific antivenin but symptomatic treatment will produce good results if shock and circulatory collapse can be controlled. The wounds should be flushed with a saline-antibiotic solution, *tetanus antitoxin* should be given, and systemic antibiotics used to control potential infections.

HERBICIDE POISONING: Two classes of herbicides are especially poisonous for dogs: the dipyridilium group which includes paraquat and diquot and the phenoxy group which includes TCDD, HCDD, 2,4–D, and 2,4,5–T. The most poisonous form of these herbicides is the concentrate prior to mixing it to spray on weeds.

Signs of toxicity to the dipyridal group (paraquat, diquot) become most severe after the majority of the chemical has been excreted. These clinical signs include severe gastrointestinal upset, vomiting, diarrhea, loss of coordination, and convulsive *seizures*. As the toxic process continues, respiratory difficulty becomes apparent and a gurgling sound of fluid is heard with each breath. Treatment is not rewarding. The prognosis is poor.

The signs of phenoxy-type herbicide poisoning include depression, loss of appetite, vomiting, bloody stools, muscle weakness and incoordination, and finally coma and death. A seven day period may elapse from the time that clinical signs are first observed until death occurs. The only treatment is symptomatic support of kidney and liver function as the herbicide is eliminated over several days. The prognosis is poor to fair depending on the amount of the chemical ingested.

HEXACHLOROPHENE POISONING: Hexachlorophene is a phenolic chemical that, because of its antibacterial properties, was included in hospital-type bathing soaps. However, the compound can be absorbed through the skin causing *phenol poisoning*. Currently, hexachlorophene has been removed from all over the counter antibacterial cleaners and is no longer widely used for elimination of bacteria from the skin. Signs of hexachlorophene poisoning are similar to those caused by *phenol, creosote*, and other phenol derivatives.

HOLLY POISONING: The berries of English holly (*Ilex aquifolium*) cause extreme gastrointestinal irritation resulting in vomiting, abdominal discomfort, and diarrhea. Also, a neurological affect causes stupor or loss of awareness of surroundings. The treatment is directed at removal of the berries from the GI tract by vomiting followed by *gastric lavage*. The treatment is symptomatic. If the neurological signs are not too extreme, a good recovery is anticipated.

HOME REMEDIES: Home remedies can be found under their individual titles within this chapter. Home remedies for the following poisons are included.

Acid Poisoning (External)	Carbon Tetrachloride Poisoning
Acid Poisoning (Internal)	Creosote Poisoning
Alkali Poisoning (External)	Detergents (Anionic) Poisoning
Alkali Poisoning (Internal)	Detergents (Cationic) Poisoning
Arsenic Poisoning	Mercury Poisoning

HOUSEHOLD CLEANER POISONING: Most household cleaning agents are classified as bleaches or anionic and cationic detergents. Discussion of household cleaner poisoning is found under each specific kind of cleaning agent. With supportive treatment, most cleaner poisonings have a good prognosis for recovery.

HYDRANGEA POISONING: All parts of the ornamental plant hydrangea (*Hydrangea macrophylla*) contain *cyanide* producing substances and are highly toxic to a dog. The clinical signs are the same as those of *cyanide poisoning*. The prognosis for recovery is poor but is generally related to the amount consumed.

INDIAN TOBACCO POISONING: All parts of Indian tobacco (*Lobelia inflata*) contain the toxic substance lobeline, a nicotine-like chemical. Salivation and vomiting are followed by CNS depression, pinpoint pupils, weakness, disorientation, and finally, loss of consciousness. Treatment is to stimulate vomiting followed by *gastric lavage* to remove any unabsorbed toxic principle. General supportive treatment includes artificial respiration when necessary. *Atropine* is given to counteract some of the signs that appear. The prognosis is dose related, ranging from good to poor.

INSECTICIDE POISONING: Three groups of chemical compounds are used for insecticide treatments: *carbamates, chlorinated hydrocarbons*, and *organophosphates*. Since *flea collars* and flea medallions contain insecticides that are constantly being released into the hair of the dog, exposure to additional insecticides may cause a toxic accumulation. Each group of chemical compounds is discussed under its own heading.

IRIS PLANT POISONING: The root of the flag iris (*Iris*) contains a resin that severely irritates the gastrointestinal tract. Signs include vomiting, abdominal discomfort, and diarrhea. Removal of the root material from the stomach by stimulation of *emesis* (vomiting) and *gastric lavage* will cure the irritation. Intestinal protectants like kaolin and pectin soothe the gut in severe cases. The prognosis for recovery is good following treatment.

JASMINE PLANT POISONING: All parts of the jasmine plant (*asminim sempervirens*) contain a number of alkaloid chemicals capable of causing a diverse number of clinical signs. Signs commonly seen are dilated pupils, dry mouth, generalized weakness followed by convulsions, and respiratory failure. Occasionally, signs of gastrointestinal disturbance appear early after ingestion of this poison. Treatment is induction of vomiting followed by symptomatic therapy which includes artificial respiration. The prognosis is guarded to fair depending on the amount ingested.

LAUREL PLANT POISONING: The mountain laurel (*Kalmia latifolia*) contains the resinoid, andromedotoxin, that can cause severe gastrointestinal upsets which progress to paralysis or convulsions. Although all parts of the laurel contain the resinoid, the leaves are especially toxic. The induction of vomiting will remove the toxic element from the stomach. Supportive therapy follows until signs subside. Prognosis is fair if treated early and if the dose ingested was not extremely large.

LEAD POISONING: Some of the many articles in our environment containing various forms of lead are paint, batteries, linoleum, caulking compound, and various plumbing supplies. If lead is present in the GI tract over an extended period, toxic amounts may be absorbed in the blood stream.

Both gastrointestinal upsets and central nervous system signs can be seen. The GI signs include poor appetite, occasional diarrhea, vomiting, and abdominal pain. The nervous system signs are personality changes, *seizures, blindness*, and hysteria. This type of poisoning is diagnosed by clinical signs, by blood lead levels over 40 mg/dl, and by *radiograph* by finding opaque objects within the intestinal tract.

Effective treatment involves the prevention of absorption of any more lead. Enemas or emetics can help remove any residual lead. The treatment of choice for lead poisoning is *calcium versenate* given four times daily for five days. If neurological signs occur, adjunctive treatment for seizures may be needed. The prognosis for complete recovery is very good.

LETHAL STAPH TOXIN: See *GARBAGE TOXIN.*

LILY PLANT POISONING: Several different plants use the name lily as part of their common name—*calla lily, glory lily,* and *lily of the valley.* The **calla lily** causes irritation to the mouth and gastrointestinal tract. The signs accordingly are salivation, vomiting, and diarrhea. The use of milk or olive oil to soothe the irritation is the only treatment necessary.

The **glory lily** produces the chemical colchicine. This causes abdominal discomfort, delayed vomiting, and finally diarrhea. Treatment is removal of the toxic substance and symptomatic therapy until signs subside.

Lily of the valley produces signs of *digitalis poisoning.* See *DIGITALIS POISONING* for further discussion.

LIZARD BITES: Three lizards in the United States are considered poisonous: the *blue tail lizard,* the Gila monster (*Heloderma suspectum*), and the Mexican beaded lizard (*Heloderma horridum*). See *GILA MONSTER BITES* and *NEUROTOXIN POISONING* for further discussion. The clinical signs and treatment principles would be different for blue tail lizards.

LUPINE PLANT POISONING: Lupine and other alkaloids are found in all parts of the lupine plant but are especially concentrated in the berries. Ingestion of this plant causes convulsions and general cardiorespiratory failure. Many affected animals will appear paralyzed. The treatment is symptomatic after vomiting is induced. Respiration must be supported and convulsive *seizures* controlled. The prognosis is guarded.

MANCHINEEL PLANT POISONING: The sap from the manchineel plant (*Hippomane mancinella*) is very irritating to the skin and mucous membranes. Skin that comes in contact with the sap will blister and peel. Removal of the sap from the skin with soap and water or alcohol comprises the treatment. If severe blistering has occurred, secondary infection must be prevented until new skin has formed.

MARIJUANA POISONING: Marijuana poisoning is becoming much more common in veterinary medicine as pets get into the owner's supply of marijuana or hashish. The toxic principle in marijuana is tetrahydrocannabinol. As the owner of a dog that may have been poisoned with marijuana, you must convey this information to your veterinarian so that he can provide expert treatment for the problem. Doctor-patient confidentiality enables you to trust your vet.

The clinical signs are rapidly changeable. Either excitement or depression is seen. The dog is wobbly, weak, and confused. Treatment is supportive in nature. If the poisoning is discovered within 90 minutes, vomiting should be induced to remove any residual marijuana from the stomach. Two to three days may pass before the dog returns to normalcy. Usually recovery is complete.

MERCURY POISONING: The sources of mercury poisoning are vague. Some is found as a residue from burning fossil fuels while other is used as a fumigant on farms. Heavy metal poisoning is the result primarily affecting the central nervous system. The signs associated with central nervous system toxicity are exaggerated gait, *blindness*, rear leg stiffness, a wobbly weak gait, and convulsions.

Since there is no specific antidote, the **HOME ANTIDOTE FOR MERCURY POISONING** should be given if it can be administered within an hour of ingestion of the poison. Give $1/2$ pint of milk with 1 beaten egg white. Magnesium oxide may be helpful. Starch (1 part to 15 parts hot water) aids in detoxifying the mercury. Between 25 and 35 grams of *activated charcoal* helps prevent absorption of the poison. These amounts are based on adult weight for the Cocker Spaniel. Divide the amount by four or five for puppy doses. Further treatment is directed at controlling the central nervous system signs and convulsions by tying up the mercury after it gets into the blood stream. *BAL* (*dimercaprol*) is an injectable antidote used in heavy metal poisonings. The dog is hospitalized so that necessary treatment and antidotes can be administered. The prognosis is guarded when central nervous system signs are seen.

METALDEHYDE POISONING: Metaldehyde, a polymer of acetaldehyde, is widely used as a slug and *snail bait* for gardens. When combined with *arsenic*, it becomes a *rodenticide*. In recent years, chemical baits have been altered making them less attractive to pets. Because muscle tremors and salivation are characteristic in all of three poisons, distinguishing metaldehyde poisoning from *strychnine* and *toxaphene poisonings* is essential.

The group of clinical signs seen in metaldehyde poisoning is due to the extreme acidosis which occurs after the chemical is ingested. A very rapid heart beat is present and muscular twitching results in muscle spasms. Early in the intoxication, the dog is extremely agitated, pants continually, and appears anxious. The body temperature may become seriously elevated (over 105°F) because of the muscle twitching, panting, and rapid heart rate. In a few individuals after what appears to be a recovery from the central nervous system signs, the dog will die of *liver failure*. Liver failure occurs when the liver attempts to metabolize the metaldehyde poison resulting in the degeneration of the liver tissue.

Treatment consists of removal of any unabsorbed metaldehyde by *gastric lavage* or vomit induction. Muscle tremors or convulsions are controlled by *diazepam* or *general anesthesia*. The metabolic acidosis is corrected with bicarbonate fluid therapy. Occasionally, muscle tremors can be controlled with *Robaxin®*. Anesthesia treatment may be needed for two or three days. With intensive therapy, the prognosis is guarded to fair. The use of *liver function blood tests* is helpful four to five days after recovery to determine whether permanent liver damage has occurred.

MISTLETOE POISONING: All parts of the ornamental plant mistletoe (*Phoradendron flavescens*) contain a *digitalis-like* toxic principle. The concentration of this toxic ingredient is especially high in the mistletoe berries. The signs of mistletoe poisoning are similar to other *digitalis poisoning*.

MUSHROOM POISONING: The toxins produced by the Amanita species of mushrooms cause different symptoms. *Amanita muscaria* produces an alkaloid that causes lethal affects in minutes. The fungus *Amanita pantherina* causes central nervous system signs very rapidly. However, the poison produced by *Amanita phalloides* may not cause signs for up to 12 hours with symptoms lasting for weeks.

The early signs seen are severe gastrointestinal involvement, cramping, vomiting, bloody mucoid diarrhea, pupil constriction, salivation, cardiovascular collapse, severe agitation, coma, and death. In the types of amanita toxins that have delayed affects, both liver and kidney failure signs occur.

No antidote is available for this potent toxin. Therefore, the treatment is symptomatic. Rapid gastric lavage with tannic acid (1:400) or activated charcoal may help to keep the toxin from being absorbed. If no central nervous system signs are observed, *atropine* can be helpful. A prolonged course of therapy is essential to keep the liver and kidneys from complete failure. *Sedatives* are also necessary if the central nervous system is involved. The prognosis for mushroom poisoning is poor to guarded depending on the type and the amount of ingested toxin

NEUROTOXIN POISONING (SNAKE, LIZARD, TOAD):   The *coral snake*, a member of the cobra family, is the only snake in the United States that produces a neurotoxin. *Bufo toad* neurotoxin is discussed more fully under the *BUFO TOAD* heading. A neurotoxin is also produced by the *blue tail lizard* living in the southeastern United States.

The clinical signs involve the central nervous system including agitation, salivation, twisting of the neck, incoordination, and death. Treatment is only symptomatic because no antidote is available. Gastric lavage and control of nervous system signs with sedatives and anesthesia are necessary. The prognosis is guarded.

NEUROLOGICAL POISONING, LIST OF CAUSES:

Aconite (Wild) Plant Poisoning	Blue Tail Lizard Poisoning
Alkaloids	Botulinum Toxin
Amphetamine Poisoning	Brown Recluse Spider Bite
Antifreeze	Bufo Toad Poisoning
Arsenic Poisoning	Carbamate Poisoning
Aspirin Toxicity	Carbon Monoxide Poisoning
Black Widow Spider	Cherry Seed Toxicity

Chlorinated Hydrocarbon
Toxicity
Chocolate Poisoning
Coral Snake Bite
Cyanide Poisoning
Finger Cherry Poisoning
Fluoroacetate (1080) Poisoning
Gasoline (Petroleum Distillates)
Hydrangea Poisoning
Herbicide Poisoning
Holly Poisoning
Indian Tobacco Poisoning
Insecticide Poisoning
Jessamine Plant Poisoning
Laurel Plant Poisoning

Lead Poisoning
Lupine Plant Poisoning
Marijuana Poisoning
Mercury Poisoning
Metaldehyde Poisoning
Mushroom Poisoning
Organophosphate Poisoning
Peas
Phenol and Creosote Poisoning
Plant Poisoning
Rodenticide
Strychnine Poisoning
Thallium Poisoning
Tranquilizer Overdose

Each of these poisons is discussed separately within the chapter.

NON-PLANT POISONING:

Acid
Alkali
Alkaloid
Amphetamine
Antifreeze
ANTU
Arsenic
Aspirin
Blue Tail Lizard
Bufo Toad
Carbonate
Carbon Monoxide
Carbon Tetrachloride
Chocolate
Copper
Creosote
Cyanide
Strychnine
Thallium
Tranquilizer

Detergents (Anionic)
Detergents (Cationic)
Fluoroacetate
Formaldehyde
Gasoline
Herbicide
Hexachlorophene
Household Cleaner
Insecticide
Lead
Mercury
Metaldehyde
Organophosphate
Oxalic Acid
Petroleum Distillate Products
Phenol and Creosol
Phosphorus
Vacor
Warfarin
Zinc Phosphide

Each of these non-plant poisons is discussed individually within the chapter.

OLEANDER PLANT POISONING: The toxic principle oleandrin, found in all parts of the ornamental plant oleander (*Nerium oleander*), contains *digitalis-like* properties toxic to the cardiovascular system.

COCKER SPANIEL OWNERS'

ORGANOPHOSPHATE INSECTICIDE POISONING: Organophosphates, classified as acetylcholinesterase inhibitor chemicals, are found in *insecticides* and in some *parasiticides*. Dichlorvos, diazinon, ronnel, malathion, trichlorfon, and ciodrin are some of the common chemical names from this group.

These chemicals most commonly affect the central nervous system but can also cause vomiting and diarrhea. Salivation, pinpoint pupils, muscle tremors, incoordinated gait, and *convulsions* are observed. Respiratory involvement may be evident because of excessive bronchial secretions making breathing difficult, causing a bluish tint in the mucous membranes, and causing death.

The antidote for organophosphate poisoning is *2-PAM* and *atropine* intravenously. Any residual poison should be removed from the skin with soap and water. When swallowed, gastric lavage and a saline (salt) cathartic (laxative) will aid in the elimination of the chemicals. After these measures, residual signs such as respiratory difficulty and convulsions must be treated symptomatically. Remember—*phenothiazine tranquilizers* are CONTRAINDICATED in organophosphate poisoning! They actually increase the clinical signs of poisoning. Common phenothiazine tranquilizers are *acepromazine*, *Sparine*®, and *Tran-Vet*®. The prognosis is guarded to fair depending on the amount of poison assimilated and the quality of treatment.

OXALIC ACID POISONING: Oxalic acid is found naturally in *rhubarb* leaves as well as chemically in many cleaning agents. This acid should not be neutralized by alkalis since all alkalis except calcium hydroxide are too soluble and will cause the build-up of oxalates in the kidneys. Oxalates will quickly destroy the functional tissue of the kidney tubules.

Early clinical signs are those typical of caustic acids. Initial signs include excessive salivation and ulcerations of the mouth and throat followed by bloody vomiting and diarrhea. If the oxalic acid is absorbed, *uremia* and signs of *kidney failure* will be seen.

The antidote for oxalic acid toxicity is calcium given as calcium hydroxide (0.15%), chalk, or as other calcium salts. Magnesium sulfate is given orally for its laxative effect. If absorption of oxalic acid has occurred, intravenous fluids should be given to stimulate urine flow and prevent calcium salts from developing in the kidneys. Sodium bicarbonate is administered for the extreme acidosis build-up in the body. *Antifreeze (ethylene glycol) poisoning* is also due to the accumulation of oxalate crystals in the kidneys. The prognosis is guarded depending on the amount of oxalic acid that was absorbed and the affect on the kidney tissue.

PEAS PLANT POISONING: Peas (*Lathyrus*) can cause poisoning if ingested. The entire plant is poisonous, but the seeds are the most toxic. The clinical signs are primarily neurological including paralysis and convulsions. Respiratory embarrassment and a weakened pulse are also seen. Treatment is only symptomatic. Following *gastric lavage*, the dog is supported as needed. *Seizures* must be controlled and occasionally respiration must be supported. Prognosis is guarded depending on the severity of the convulsions occurring.

PHENOL AND CREOSOL POISONING: Phenolic compounds vary from wood tar and wood preservatives to antibacterials like phenol and *hexachlorophene.* While cats are especially sensitive to phenolic compounds, dogs can also be poisoned. Signs observed from these compounds include necrosis of mucous membranes and skin, swelling of the brain, and a variety of liver and kidney degenerations. The dog may merely show depression or it may be comatose. Its skin and mucous membranes can turn yellow. Signs of *uremia* may develop. Treatment is supportive. The compounds must be washed from the skin and mucous membranes. Once signs of toxicity are observed, the prognosis is guarded, at best. Also see *CREOSOTE POISONING.*

PHILODENDRON PLANT POISONING: The philodendron is a member of the Arum plant family. See *ARUM PLANT FAMILY POISONING* for further discussion.

PHOSPHORUS POISONING: Phosphorus, the active ingredient in various roach and *rat poison*, is also found in matches and fireworks. Vomiting and diarrhea with considerable abdominal distress accompany phosphorus poisoning. After the initial recovery, liver degeneration and hemorrhage can occur.

The treatment is *gastric lavage* with a .4% copper sulfate solution. *Activated charcoal* will help absorb the phosphorus. Mineral oil can be given as a cathartic. Intravenous *dextrose* will help to spare the liver and protect it from the affects of phosphorus. DO NOT give vegetable oil! Also, remove all fats from the diet. The prognosis is fair to guarded depending on the amount of liver pathology.

PLANT POISONING, LISTING:

Aconite (Wild)	Lily
Alocasia	Lupine
Arum Plant Family	Manchineel
Bird of Paradise	Marijuana
Buckeye	Mistletoe
Caladium	Mushroom
Cherry Seed	Oleander
Chrysanthemum	Peas
Crow Foot Family	Philodendron
Dieffenbachia	Poinsettia
Finger Cherry	Primrose
Holly	Privet
Hydrangea	Rayless Goldenrod
Indian Tobacco	Rhubarb
Iris	Wisteria
Jessamine	Yew
Laurel	

The plants listed can cause toxic reactions when parts or all of the plant are consumed by a dog. Each listed plant is discussed separately in this chapter.

POINSETTIA PLANT POISONING: The ornamental holiday season plant, the poinsettia (*Euphorbia pulcherrima*), can cause both skin and gastrointestinal irritation. The sap, leaves, and stems all contain irritating material capable of producing clinical signs. If the skin is exposed to sap, blistering and redness occur. The blisters break resulting in ulcerated areas. If the leaves or sap are eaten, irritation to the mucous membranes of the gastrointestinal tract will result in vomiting and diarrhea.

The treatment of poinsettia ingestion is to remove any remaining plant from the digestive tract by giving an *emetic* (vomit inducer). Any remaining sap on the skin can be removed with soap and water. Additional treatment with protectants and demulcents like milk soothe the irritated membranes. The prognosis is good with proper treatment.

POISON CONTROL CENTER: The number for the Poison Center in your area is listed in the front pages of your telephone book. In large metropolitan areas, most poison centers are located in Children's Hospitals. While their focus is primarily as a service to human poisoning, they are also very helpful in cases of dog poisoning. Do not hesitate to call the number of the poison center nearest you when confronted with poisoning. You must provide as much information as possible about the kind, name, and amount of the poison consumed. The Poison Control Center and the *Animal Toxicology Hot Line* telephone numbers should be posted near your telephone.

POISON NEUTRALIZATION, PRINCIPLES OF: The following guidelines are general and will only supplement the specific instruction given by Hot Line personnel or your veterinarian.

On discovery of a possible poisoning, calmly carry out the following steps:
- Write down the brand name, active ingredient(s), and approximate amount missing.
- Look for clinical signs of toxicity: red or blistered skin, salivation, vomiting, depression, garlic or almond odor to breath, diarrhea, muscle tremors, seizures, labored breathing, cardiorespiratory collapse, unusual tongue color (blue, white, gray, brick red,), altered consciousness (agitated or stupor).
- Call the **Animal Toxicology Hot Line** at **217 / 333–3611**, in Southeastern United States, **404 / 542-6751** or call the Poison Center listed in the front of your phone book.
- Call your veterinarian for immediate instructions and to advise him/her of the emergency nature of your visit.
- Give home antidote as per instructions from Animal Toxicology Hot Line and your veterinarian. Do not waste time! TRANSPORT IMMEDIATELY!
- Immediately wash away any external poison with copious amounts of water. DO NOT TOUCH the poisoned area with bare flesh. Wear rubber gloves if you must touch red blistered areas.

DO NOT ATTEMPT TO STIMULATE VOMITING IN ANY OF THE FOLLOWING SITUATIONS

- If the dog is unconscious or severely depressed
- If petroleum distillates (e.g. gasoline) have been ingested
- If acids have been ingested
- If alkalis have been ingested
- If tranquilizers or other antiemetics (vomit prevention) has been consumed
- If the poison was ingested more than 90 minutes earlier

Many *emetics* (vomit inducers) may be relatively ineffective and can actually cause more harm than good. When in doubt, give up to $1/2$ pint of milk with 2 beaten egg whites depending on the age of the Cocker Spaniel. *Activated charcoal*, an important part of poison treatment, should be given by your veterinarian as part of the *gastric lavage* procedure.

Mineral oil is an excellent *cathartic* (bowel evacuator). Because it has no taste, mineral oil does not stimulate a swallow reflex so requires care with its use. Mineral oil is helpful in fat soluble poisons. Vegetable oils like olive oil can be used but will be absorbed to some degree. If the poison is soluble in oil or fat, it may aggravate the situation. Approximately 30 minutes after the oil is given, a saline (salt) laxative should be given to stimulate emptying of the bowel.

Treatment of poisons must be done quickly and expertly. If you follow the instructions outlined in this section, the prognosis may improve due to your rapid, intelligent action.

PRIMROSE PLANT POISONING: Primrose leaves and stems contain a contact irritant which makes skin red and blistered. This stimulates the dog to scratch, sometimes resulting in the self-mutilation of the involved skin surface. Since this plant is so irritating, the toxic affects are limited to topical application. The irritating substance is removed with soap and water. The inflamed area may be soothed with rubbing alcohol. Following treatment, the prognosis for complete recovery is good.

PRIVET PLANT POISONING: The toxic substance contained in the leaves and berries of the privet plant (*Ligustrum vulgare*) can cause gastrointestinal irritation. Later, signs of kidney damage occur if the toxic substance has been absorbed in any quantity. The treatment consists of removing the privet by stimulating emesis (vomiting) and following this with *gastric lavage. Kidney function tests* and *urinalysis* should be performed for two to four days after apparent recovery to ascertain any damage to the kidneys. The prognosis is fair to good depending on the absorption of the toxin and subsequent kidney compromise.

RAYLESS GOLDENROD PLANT POISONING: All parts of rayless goldenrod (*Happlopappus heterophyllus*) contain the toxic chemical tremetol which causes gastrointestinal upsets followed by liver and kidney damage. Signs are those of liver damage: jaundice, *ascites*, and a shutdown of urine production associated with kidney damage. In treatment, the liver and kidney function must be supported. The recovery and prognosis depend on the amount of damage done to these organs. The prognosis is guarded.

RHUBARB PLANT POISONING: Rhubarb leaves are rich in *oxalic acid*. For further discussion, see *OXALIC ACID POISONING*.

RODENTICIDES, LISTING OF:

ANTU	Thallium
Arsenic	Vacor
Fluoroacetate (1080)	Warfarin
Red Squill	Zinc phosphide
Strychnine	

Many of the items on this list are currently used or have been previously used in rat poisons. Some are so toxic that they are not now available (e.g. *thallium*) or are only available to professional exterminators. See each topic individually within the chapter for further discussion.

SKIN IRRITATION, POISONS CAUSING:

Acids	Gasoline (Petroleum Distillates)
Alkalis	Gila Monster Bite
Black Widow Spider	Manchineel
Bleaches	Phenol & Creosote
Brown Recluse Spider	Poinsettia
Chrysanthemum	Primrose
Creosote Poisoning	Snake Bites
Fire Ant Bites	Tarantula Bite
Formaldehyde	

SNAKE BITE: The *coral snake* is the only poisonous snake related to the cobra family in the United States. All snakes in the cobra family produce a *neurotoxin* Further treatment principles are discussed under *CORAL SNAKE BITE*.

All other poisonous snakes in the United States belong to the *pit viper family* including the *copperhead*, the *cotton-mouthed water moccasin*, and all species of *rattlesnakes*. These snakes produce a *hematoxic venom*. Soon after a bite, the bite site swells causing small blood vessels to rupture as tissue destruction continues. Systemic signs like bloody stool, bloody urine, vomiting, convulsions, and death follow. Antivenin-polyvalent produced by Fort Dodge Laboratories, Fort Dodge, Iowa, can be used to neutralize pit viper family venom. If treatment is postponed for longer than three to four hours, the prognosis for recovery is very poor.

SPIDER BITES: The bites of four spiders are considered toxic or poisonous: the *black widow spider*, the *brown recluse*, the *common brown spider*, and the *tarantula*. The docile tarantula is not apt to bite unless seriously provoked. Refer to each spider individually for further discussion.

STOMACH PUMPING PROCEDURE (GASTRIC LAVAGE): The removal of toxic substances by gastric lavage (stomach pumping) should only be done by your veterinarian. This procedure is very effective for the removal of some poisons before they are absorbed into the body. To be successful, however, gastric lavage should be done within an hour of the consumption of the poison. The administration of *activated charcoal* is a useful complement to gastric lavage. Extra care must be taken if the stomach wall has been weakened from caustic material. Remember, a veterinarian must perform this procedure because *anesthesia* is required.

The affected dog should be lightly anesthetized or unconscious for this procedure. A cuffed endotracheal catheter is inserted in the windpipe to prevent aspiration of the lavage solution. A stomach tube about the same diameter as the endotracheal catheter is passed to the level of the last rib. The lavage solution is administered at the rate of 5 ml (teaspoon) per pound of body weight (a little more than $1/3$ pint for a mature Cocker Spaniel). Extreme pressure should be avoided in placing the lavage solution in the stomach since it could be forced into the small intestine. The lavage solution is then removed from the stomach with a bulb suction syringe. The procedure is repeated up to 15 times or until the solution returns clear. A slurry of activated charcoal is included in the last two to four lavage procedures.

STRYCHNINE POISONING: Strychnine is a substance found in some *rodenticide* and predator baits. Most of the commercial baits contain several times more strychnine than is needed to kill an average-sized Cocker Spaniel.

Signs of toxicity occur as quickly as 15 minutes after ingestion or as long as two hours later. Early signs are nervousness and agitation. These signs rapidly change into seizures and extreme muscle rigidity with the legs extended out in "saw horse" fashion. The head and neck are thrown back at an extreme angle. In a characteristic appearance, the ears and lips are drawn back. When *seizures* begin, periods of relaxation will occur. As the poison circulates, the muscular rigidity becomes almost continual. This depresses respiration leading to an elevated body temperature. Characteristic strychnine seizures may be initiated by sound or touch, differentiating them from *toxaphene* insecticide *seizures* which are not initiated by external stimuli.

The use of gas or *barbiturate anesthesia* controls the seizures while the poison is being removed from the stomach by *gastric lavage* and *activated charcoal* and while it is being metabolized by the liver. Between six and twelve hours of intensive care are required to metabolize the strychnine absorbed and to stop the seizures. Watching for respiratory depression during this period is very important.

The prognosis is somewhat dependent on when treatment is initiated and the amount of strychnine ingested. If lavage and intensive care are started within an hour of ingestion of the poison, the prognosis is guarded to good. The prognosis is less favorable if severe *tetanic seizures* have already begun.

TARANTULA SPIDER BITE: The tarantula (*Eurypelma*) is capable of a venomous bite. However, most are not very aggressive and do not seem to become agitated easily. Because the principles for managing a *tarantula* bite are similar to those for other spiders, see *BLACK WIDOW SPIDER BITES* or *BROWN RECLUSE AND COMMON BROWN SPIDER BITES* for further discussion.

TAR REMOVAL FROM HAIR COAT: Some people want to use petroleum distillates or gasoline on the hair coat and skin of a dog to remove road tar. UNDER NO CIRCUMSTANCES SHOULD *PETROLEUM PRODUCTS* BE USED TO REMOVE TAR!!!! Instead, the following procedure should be followed.

- Cut away any tar on the hair without cutting the skin.
- Saturate the area covered with tar in vegetable or mineral oil. The area should be covered with the oil for 24 hours.
- After 24 hours, wipe away as much tar as possible using several towels.
- Bathe the hair coat and skin in a mild detergent to remove the final traces of tar.
- Observe the skin for 24 hours for signs of redness and irritation. If irritation occurs, it may be treated with *steroid* creams and ointments.

THALLIUM POISONING: Because *ant poison, rat poison,* and roach baits are more strictly regulated today, thallium poisoning is not as common as in the past. However, old baits placed on farms over the years can serve as a source for current intoxications. Thallium can either kill very quickly or be chronic, taking months to cause death.

Early signs are salivation and very severe stomach pains. The gait becomes weak and wobbly, followed by paralysis, coma, and death. This whole syndrome can occur in one or two days. If the dog lingers, hemorrhages on its gums and skin are observed. *Pneumonia* frequently develops. The chronic form most commonly affects the skin and mucous membranes. The skin becomes inflamed and ulcerated causing most of the hair to fall out. Ulcerated areas are also seen under the front legs and around the anus, mouth, eyelids.

Treatment must be aggressive but with the realization that chances for recovery are slim. Following repeated *gastric lavages* with *activated charcoal*, Prussian blue is given orally three times daily to bind thallium and carry it out of the GI tract. The prognosis is poor to fair depending on whether the case is acute or chronic.

Poisoning

TOXINS: The following toxins are discussed in detail within this chapter under each individual heading.

Botulism Toxin
Garbage Toxin
Lethal Staph Toxin

TRANQUILIZER POISONING: Tranquilizer poisoning usually results from the dog gaining access to a prescription drug. The two clinical signs seen most frequently are extreme depression and a coma with very low blood pressure. If the dog is seen before the depression starts, *gastric lavage* is indicated. If depression has begun, do not attempt gastric lavage. If supportive care treatment can be maintained while the drug is metabolized, the prognosis is good.

UNKNOWN POISON—ANTIDOTE: In the case where poisoning is suspected but the cause is unknown, the best home antidote is large quantities of milk ($1/2$ pint) with 2 beaten egg whites for an adult Cocker Spaniel and one-fourth as much for puppies. This procedure is helpful in nearly all cases of poisoning. The use of *activated charcoal* in gelatin capsules can also be very helpful where poisoning is suspected. A *cathartic* or an *emetic* (vomit inducer) should follow. Even if these measures are taken, they do not eliminate the need for professional care. In most types of poisoning, supportive care is needed until the absorbed poison is metabolized.

VACOR POISONING: *Vacor,* a *rodenticide* available as a bait or as a powder, is classified as a nicotinamide vitamin B antagonist. Clinical signs are vomiting, abdominal discomfort, muscle quivering, dilated pupils followed by collapse, coma, and death. Treatment is *gastric lavage* followed by intramuscular injections of the *B vitamin, nicotinamide,* for about two weeks after the early signs have ceased. Other forms of supportive treatment are used as needed. The prognosis, which is somewhat dose related, is guarded to good.

VOMITING, INDUCTION OF: In many kinds of poisoning, the stimulation of *emesis* (vomiting) is a very important part of the treatment. However, in cases where strong caustics like *acids* and *alkalis* have been ingested, vomiting should NOT be stimulated since the caustic will burn on the way up as it did on the way down. *Petroleum products* should not be forcefully vomited. Also unconscious or very depressed dogs should not be stimulated to vomit. As a rule of thumb, induction of vomiting is worthwhile up to 90 minutes after a poison has been ingested.

The products available at home that may be used to induce vomiting are 2 teaspoons of hydrogen peroxide (adult Cocker dose), copper sulfate, warm salty water, and *syrup of ipecac.* Syrup of ipecac is a gastric irritant that is effective at the rate of 1 ounce (2 tablespoons) per 30 pounds of body weight. If *activated charcoal* is to be used as part of the treatment regimen, syrup of ipecac should not be used because it reduces the effective absorption of activated charcoal. Your

158   COCKER SPANIEL OWNERS'

veterinarian may have *apomorphine* available which is an excellent *emetic* (vomit inducer).

WARFARIN POISONING: Warfarin, the most common over-the-counter *rat poison*, contains *Coumadin*® which interferes with the production of *vitamin K* in the liver. Vitamin K is essential for proper blood clotting. Several second generation anticoagulant rat poisons have become popular in the past six years. The toxic principle of these is usually *brodifacoum* which is very toxic to dogs. Toxic signs include hemorrhaging which occurs almost anywhere in the body. Other clinical signs such as labored breathing, lameness, or central nervous system signs are related to the hemorrhagic tendencies. Treatment is fresh, whole blood transfused when *anemia* becomes life threatening. Intramuscular and oral use of vitamin K is also necessary. While five to seven days is a sufficient length of treatment with vitamin K for warfarin, three or four weeks of oral and injectable vitamin K is needed with second generation anticoagulant rat poisons. Any other signs must be treated by supportive therapy. The prognosis is very good to excellent in most cases if treatment is initiated before blood loss becomes critical.

WISTERIA PLANT POISONING: All parts of the wisteria plant can produce toxic consequences. The usual signs are digestive upset and vomiting. Treatment is symptomatic and supportive in nature. Early treatment will usually insure a satisfactory outcome.

YEW PLANT POISONING: The yew is one of several species of ornamental trees that can cause poisoning. The wood, bark, leaves, and seeds contain the toxic substance taxine which causes intestinal irritation and upset and later, cardiovascular disturbances. Initially, the dog appears nauseous and has abdominal cramps. Vomiting and dilated pupils then occur. As the cardiovascular system becomes involved, weakness, shock-like signs, irregular heart beat, and death result. Treatment for yew tree poisoning is similar to the treatment for *DIGITALIS POISONING*. The prognosis is guarded.

ZINC PHOSPHIDE POISONING: Zinc phosphide is a highly toxic *rodenticide*. The early signs are severe gastrointestinal upset with pain, vomiting, and diarrhea. The next phase of toxicity is fluid accumulation in the lungs and great difficulty breathing. Further affects are in the central nervous system with extreme restlessness, convulsions, coma, and death. The treatment is supportive and generally not effective. Oxygen is given to assist breathing difficulties. *Seizures* must also be controlled. The prognosis is poor to fair.

SENSORY SYSTEMS

ACUTE ANTERIOR UVEITIS: Acute anterior uveitis is an EYE EMERGENCY that should immediately be seen by a veterinarian. As an owner, look for severe pain, excessive tearing, redness, excessive blinking, and pupil constriction. Other emergency eye problems may also present similar signs. Most importantly, remember that veterinary attention is absolutely essential.

With acute anterior uveitis, the area around the iris (the colored part of the eye around the pupil) and the tissue that supports the iris become inflamed. Causes of anterior uveitis include trauma to the eye, either internal or external infections, *systemic fungal diseases*, and *heartworm infestation*. This may also occur after a hepatitis vaccination or be associated with *toxoplasmosis*. Acute anterior uveitis may also come as a sequelae to intraocular (*cataract*) surgery, as part of *canine brucellosis*, or as a result of *infectious canine hepatitis*.

The usual ophthalmic tests (*tonometry, fluorescein dye test, ophthalmoscopic exam*), and a complete systemic work-up (*CBC*, chest *x-rays, biochemical serum tests*, lymph node aspiration) may be necessary for an accurate diagnosis. Anterior uveitis may be a symptom of a systemic disease or of some form of cancer.

Treatment is dependent on whether or not a systemic cause is found. Appropriate action must be initiated quickly since vision will be lost if treatment is delayed. Generally, *atropine* helps to dilate the eyes. Then either *aspirin* or *steroids* are used to minimize inflammation. If an infection is suspected, appropriate antibiotics are utilized. The systemic problem must be resolved for uveitis therapy to be successful. With quick action, the prognosis is good to excellent for complete recovery.

ACUTE BLINDNESS: True acute blindness is an optic emergency. Early diagnosis and treatment by a veterinarian are necessary for any chance of visual recovery. If you suspect that your Cocker Spaniel is not seeing, observe the dog in unfamiliar surroundings. With bilateral (both eyes) blindness, the dog will have difficulty moving around without running into furnishings. Do not assume that pupils which respond to light indicate a sighted dog! Some forms of blindness occur at higher levels in the brain.

Provide your veterinarian with an accurate history of the dog's past seven to fourteen days. Recent vaccination history, excessive tearing, continual blinking, and red eyes are important facts. Neurological signs like *circling* and *head tilt* are also significant. Signs attributed to generalized illness such as fever, excessive water consumption, and digestive upset may provide clues as to the cause of acute blindness.

Optic neuritis and *retinal detachment* are the two most common causes of acute blindness. The underlying causes of these conditions are discussed fully under each individual topic.

Use of *steroids* in treating some forms of acute blindness can result in the return of sight provided that the medication was initiated early enough and at the proper dosage level. If steroids are effective, improvement is seen within two weeks. If absolute blindness is still present after two weeks of therapy, don't anticipate the return of vision.

The cause of visual loss, the proper use of medication, the length of time between blindness and the start of therapy are all relevant factors. Prognosis for recovery of vision is guarded.

ACUTE CORNEAL ULCER: The cornea, a clear window through which we see, has five layers. Normally the cornea is devoid of a blood supply but does have a generous network of nerves. Because of the nerve supply, ulceration of the cornea causes signs of a painful eye like excess tearing, rubbing, redness, and blinking.

The rapid ulceration of the corneal tissue by enzymes cause it to dissolve resulting in a very serious EYE EMERGENCY. A grayish mucoid exudate is present on and around the cornea when the enzymes are digesting the tissue. These proteolytic enzymes are produced by bacteria like *Pseudomonas*. In a matter of HOURS, these potent enzymes erode the entire five layers of the cornea causing perforation of the eye with subsequent infection of inner structures of the eye. The usual signs of eye pain are present. IMMEDIATE treatment is mandatory!

The treatment of this acute ulcerative process must occur HOURLY until the enzymatic degeneration is brought under control. From six hours to two or three days may be required. *Gentamicin* and *tobramycin* are the two most effective antibiotic ophthalmic medications for this condition. In addition to this treatment, *10% Mucomyst*® drops should be administered every two hours to deactivate the enzymes. *Atropine* drops are also needed to keep the eye dilated. Systemic antibiotics are given to help support internal eye structures during this battle. If the battle is lost and perforation of the eye occurs, vision in that eye will probably be lost. Immediate diagnosis and intensive care are necessary to keep this eye condition from becoming a disaster. While cultures from an eye ulcer are usually taken, treatment must begin before those results are received. The choice of antibiotics can be modified when culture results are known. The prognosis is guarded.

AMERICAN COLLEGE OF VETERINARY OPHTHALMOLOGISTS: The American College of Veterinary Ophthalmologists (*ACVO*), established approximately 20 years ago, currently includes about 105 members. The five objectives of the ACVO are to encourage education, training, and research in veterinary ophthalmology, to establish standards for training and experience in the field, to aid in the development of methods of residency graduate training in veterinary ophthalmology, to recognize qualified individuals with certification, and to advise veterinarians desiring certification and training in the field.

Members of the ACVO are recognized as experts in the diagnosis, treatment, and surgery of veterinary eye problems. If a perplexing canine eye problem arises, your local veterinarian can refer you to the nearest member of the ACVO. While most members are in academic situations, some also maintain private referral practices in ophthalmology. Dr. John D. Lavach, 10661 Ellis Avenue, Suite A, Fountain Valley, CA 92708 is the 1988-89 secretary-treasurer.

AMERICAN SPANIEL CLUB, INC. HEALTH REGISTRY: Because of the concern over two very serious eye diseases in Cocker Spaniels, the American Spaniel Club established a registry for Cocker's clear of *cataracts* and *progressive retinal atrophy*. Eye examinations must be performed by members of the *ACVO* (*American College of Veterinary Ophthalmologists*). To be listed in the Health Registry, a Cocker Spaniel must be two years old at the time of the eye exam. The listing, which is maintained for a year, certifies that the dog was clear at the time of the examination. Because the average age for cataract incidence in the Cocker Spaniel is 4 to $6^1/_2$ years of age, permanent eye registration is open to eight year old living Cocker Spaniels. *CERF* eye examinations also qualify for the registry since they are performed by ACVO diplomates. Information on the American Spaniel Club Health Registry can be obtained from Miss Judith Wright, 2600 Ellsworth Road, Baldwinsville, NY 13027, the registrar.

ANTERIOR LENS LUXATION: The anterior luxation of the lens of the eye is a TRUE EYE EMERGENCY. The lens, after coming out of its normal place, pushes forward blocking the normal drain openings for the liquid within the eye (aqueous humor). This blockage causes the eye to swell with a *secondary glaucoma*.

Clinical signs are a painful eye that appears cloudy and red. The only effective treatment for this condition is the surgical removal of the misplaced lens. Because the lens is in an abnormal location, the performing surgeon should have above average expertise in dealing with eye problems. The prognosis for retaining vision is guarded, depending on how long secondary glaucoma was present before the lens was removed.

APPLANATION: Applanation is a method of *tonometry* which measures the intraocular pressure of the eye. At lower pressures, this technique is more accurate than *Schiotz's tonometry*. Specialized equipment and some degree of expertise in interpreting the results are required for this procedure.

AURAL HEMATOMA: The presence of free blood between the skin and the cartilage of the external ear is called an aural hematoma. The ear flap appears swollen and spongy. The dog shakes its head because of an unbalanced feeling created by the swollen ear.

In most cases, an underlying cause exists for the capillary blood vessel rupture that fills the ear with blood. Violent head shaking from an ear canal infection, a clotting defect such as *Von Willebrand's disease*, or a liver deficiency that prolongs the clotting time could all contribute. The Japanese have presented the theory that an immune reaction causes the capillary rupture. Evidence that this may be true relates to the effectiveness of *cortisone* at high doses in treating aural hematomas. Conventional treatment is directed at removing the blood and clots from the subcutaneous tissue compartment. Stapling or gluing the skin to the cartilage eliminates the compartment. Some techniques utilize Silastic® tubes placed under the skin to drain off any further blood as healing progresses. With any procedure, the underlying cause must be treated when possible. The treated ear should be taped to the side of the head to keep it from being shaken while undergoing healing.

The prognosis for recovery is excellent. The amount of scar tissue (thickening) in the healed ear is usually related to the surgeon's expertise. Some increase in thickness of the ear should be anticipated.

BLINDNESS: Blindness is described as an inability to see. In dogs, assessing partial loss of sight is impossible. When a dog is placed in a familiar environment, it can move around with no trouble even though totally blind. In unfamiliar surroundings, the dog will have difficulty finding his way. Loss of sight can happen for many reasons. Some causes of blindness are hereditary. The blindness may be permanent or correctable with treatment.

Sensory impulses normally occur in the retina at the back of the eye and then travel the optic nerve to register in the brain. However, if the clear cornea is covered or cloudy or if the lens is cloudy or out of position, sensory impulses are not perceived rendering the dog blind. If blindness is suspected, the dog should be thoroughly examined by a veterinary ophthalmologist since some cases can be corrected.

BLOOD IN THE EYE: The presence of *red blood cells* in the anterior chamber between the lens and the cornea is termed *hyphema*. While the presence of blood in the eye is a debatable ocular emergency, a serious traumatic or systemic condition is indicated. Early veterinary attention should be received. Blood in the anterior chamber of the eye comes from the iris, its associated ciliary body, or the vascular layer under the retina. The causes of hyphema include trauma to the eye, *detached retina*, *bleeding disorders*, cancer, infections, and some of undetermined origin.

The cause usually dictates the treatment. If the blood is from an *anterior uveitis*, *atropine* and *steroids* are used. If anterior uveitis is not a problem, *pilocarpine* drops are used to increase the emptying of the fluid from the anterior chamber of the eye. Therefore, in the presence of an identifiable clotting disorder, clotting therapy should be instituted. After the *hyphema* has lessened, atropine and steroids can be used. The use of *vitamin K* is of questionable value. An important adjunct to treatment is very quiet, confined rest for 10 to 14 days. If hyphema recurs, the presence of a tumor somewhere in the eye should be suspected.

BLOODY NOSE: *Epistaxis* (a bloody nose) is the loss of blood from one or both nostrils. The history is important in determining the cause of the nasal hemorrhage. A traumatic blow to the muzzle can cause capillary hemorrhage. Violent sneezing may produce clots of blood. Certain systemic diseases and poisons have been known to cause epistaxis. Nasal cavity tumors which are more common in long-nosed dogs can cause nosebleeds from one or both sides. Persistent nasal hemorrhage with no traumatic history requires a thorough diagnostic work-up including *radiographs* of the nasal cavity, *cultures*, and *serum lab tests*. The treatment and prognosis depend on the cause. Early identification of any cause improves the chances for successful treatment.

BLUE EYE: Blue eye is the common name given to the presence of a hazy, gray-blue opacity which usually appears in only one eye. In a severely affected eye, the iris color is not visible. This phenomena is most frequently a reaction to *canine hepatitis virus*—either after an infection or a vaccination. The time between exposure and development of the ocular lesion is seven to ten days. This ocular reaction has not been found after vaccination with *adenovirus–2*. Canine hepatitis is *adenovirus–1*.

In actuality, the developing eye problem is an *anterior uveitis*. The blue color is due to the accumulation of fluid between the layers of the cornea. The eye is sensitive, tears excessively, and may also appear inflamed as the blue color develops.

Treatment is controversial. Some advocate no treatment while others recommend anterior uveitis therapy. See *ACUTE ANTERIOR UVEITIS* in this chapter. Most cases will resolve satisfactorily within two weeks. However, a small percentage may sustain permanent blindness.

BULGING EYE: The bulging eye is unilaterally swollen. In comparison to the other eye, the swollen eye appears larger and redder and may appear to be looking in a different direction. Pain often accompanies a bulging eye early in its development.

Increased intraocular fluid pressure (*glaucoma*) increases the size of the eyeball causing a bulging eye. *Tonometry* and an ophthalmic examination will diagnose this condition. Early glaucoma treatment will save the sight in the affected eye.

Traumatic proptosis (popping out of the eyeball) causes the affected eye to appear larger than the normally placed eye. THIS IS AN OPTIC EMERGENCY! Early replacement of the eye is essential for the sight to be saved. A third cause of bulging eyes is a retrobulbar lesion, usually in the form of an abscess or a tumor. The lesion located behind the eye pushes the eye outward giving the eyeball an enlarged appearance. A *retrobulbar abscess* causes pain and reluctance to open the mouth. A tumor, however, is slow growing with no pain sensation.

The cause dictates the treatment for bulging eyes. A diagnostic work-up is necessary to determine the feasibility of treatment and the prognosis.

CANINE EYE REGISTRATION FOUNDATION: See *CERF*.

CATARACTS;:   A cataract, the partial or total opacity of the lens and capsule within an eye, occurs in one or both eyes. Cataracts are grouped by their cause, by the age at occurrence, and by the location within the lens. By age, *congenital cataracts* can be present at birth. Hereditary *developmental cataracts* occur in the American Cocker Spaniel. Although the average age is from $4^1/_2$ to $6^1/_2$ years, cataracts have been observed between 8 weeks and 7 years old. This type of cataract is transmitted to offspring by an autosomal recessive gene. Located in the anterior and posterior cortical (outer shell) region of the lens, the cataract becomes progressively more dense with time. Old dogs can develop *senile cataracts*. *Nuclear sclerosis* is a normal phenomena of the aging process which changes the opacity of the lens protein. Even though the lenses appear cloudy, sight is not impaired with nuclear sclerosis. Cataracts can also form as the result of other disease processes or from traumatic injury to the lens or capsule. *Diabetes mellitus* and other infectious diseases can initiate the mechanisms that cause cataracts to form. In some breeds of dogs, cataract formation is present with other serious eye disorders (e.g. *retinal atrophy, retinal dysplasia*).

A variety of cataract medical treatments have been tried. Short of surgical removal of the lens, no universal cure or treatment for cataracts exists. Consider three factors when contemplating cataract surgery: 1) the ability of the owner to treat and control the cataract patient, 2) the age and general health of the dog, and 3) the possibility of the presence of concurrent blindness from another cause resulting in surgical failure to provide vision.

With dense cataracts, evaluating the retina behind the lens is impossible. If significant retinal degeneration is present, cataract surgery is not indicated. Cataract surgery is expensive. Only after a discussion with an experienced ophthalmologist weighing all of the pros and cons should the surgery be performed. Possible post-operative complications to cataract surgery include severe *anterior uveitis, secondary glaucoma*, adhesions of the iris to the lens capsule, and persistent cloudiness to the cornea from surgical trauma. Occasionally, retinal detachments may occur post-operatively. Consider all aspects before making the decision for cataract surgery.

CERF: The *Canine Eye Registration Foundation* (CERF) was founded in 1974 to function as a registry for clear-eyed dogs of all breeds. The examination of eyes for CERF certification must be performed by a member of the *American College of Veterinary Ophthalmologists* (ACVO). Within 15 minutes after dilating the eyes with drops, they are examined with a slit lamp for corneal and lens abnormalities. An *indirect ophthalmoscope* is then used to examine the retina and associated structures. The examined dog is classified into one of three groups: 1) clear of hereditary eye disease at the time of examination, 2) affected with hereditary eye disease, or 3) suspicious or cannot judge properly. If a suspicious rating is given, the dog should be re-examined in six months.

American Cocker Spaniels can be certified after 24 months of age. A CERF certification is good for 12 months for an initial registration fee of $5.00. Recertification may then be obtained following a subsequent examination for a $3.00 fee. Effective January 1, 1988, the CERF registry has moved to Purdue University as part of the Veterinary Medical Data Program (VMDP) which maintains a computerized data bank on many canine health disorders. CERF eye registrations can be sent to VETERINARY MEDICAL DATA PROGRAM (VMDP), c/o Alan Warble, South Campus Courts, Building C, Purdue University, West Lafayette, IN 47907, (317) 494–8179.

CHEMICAL KERATITIS: Chemical keratitis is a TRUE OCULAR EMERGENCY! A foreign substance has irritated the cornea causing it to become inflamed (*keratitis*). Shampoo from bathing the dog is the most common cause of chemical keratitis. To guard against this problem, place a small amount of eye ointment, petroleum, or mineral oil in each eye prior to a bath. More serious sequelae result from *strong acids* or *alkalis*. Acids are not as severe a problem as alkalis because acids are neutralized on contact. Alkalis stimulate the migration of *neutrophilic blood cells* to the damaged area resulting in severe *corneal ulceration* with possible corneal penetration.

Immediately after exposure to a strong chemical, the eye should be irrigated with tap water for 30 minutes. The dog should then be transported directly to your veterinarian for follow-up treatment. While the prognosis for recovery from soap in the eye is excellent, it is guarded following alkali damage.

CHERRY EYE: Cherry eye is characterized by the presence of a red mass at the inner lower edge of the upper and lower eyelid junction. Excessive tearing and conjunctival inflammation accompany this condition. A prolapse of the glandular structure located on the inside of the membrane nictitans (third eyelid) causes this problem. The American Cocker Spaniel has a common hereditary weakness in the fibrous tissue which keeps the gland from being hidden under the third eyelid.

In the past, the accepted form of treatment has been to surgically remove the gland. Recently, a connection between the development of *dry eye* (*keratoconjunctivitis sicca*) and the removal of the third eyelid gland was discovered. The third eyelid gland is one of the primary sources of tear formation. Cockers having *Schirmer tear test* levels below 18 mm should not have this form of surgery. A new surgical technique preserves the gland, replacing it in a cosmetically acceptable method. Before surgery, ask the veterinarian which technique will be performed to correct the gland prolapse. This procedure may either be done as a one day or overnight stay in the hospital. Prognosis is excellent for normal recovery.

CLOUDY EYE: A cloudy eye, one which has a bluish or gray colored cornea, signifies an eye problem involving at least the cornea. If the entire cornea is involved, the iris or any of the internal eye structures can not be seen. Cloudy eyes are associated with a number of more complex eye problems such as *glaucoma, descemetocele, corneal laceration*, and *anterior uveitis*. The *blue eye syndrome* following exposure to *canine hepatitis virus* is another example of a cloudy eye.

The layers of the cornea take on fluid disrupting the normal cell continuity of the cornea. As the eye condition returns to normal, the corneal fluid level diminishes and the tissue clears. However, if edema (fluid) remains in the cornea, permanent blindness results.

CONJUNCTIVITIS: Conjunctivitis, the most common eye problem in dogs, is inflammation of the mucous membranes around the eye. These membranes attach to the cornea on the eyeball and to the membranes inside both eyelids including both surfaces of the third eyelid.

A myriad of causes exist for conjunctivitis. Irritants such as dust and pollen can result in an *irritant conjunctivitis*. *Staph* and other bacteria are capable of creating an infectious conjunctivitis. *Canine distemper, adenovirus (canine hepatitis)*, and other viral diseases can cause *viral conjunctivitis*. The clinical signs vary. Some dogs show very little reaction while others exhibit a thick mucopurulent discharge from the eyes. Swelling of the affected mucous membranes is common. Little or no pain is felt with pure conjunctivitis. However, if a concurrent *corneal ulcer* is present, much pain will be exhibited.

The preferred treatment is the application of a wide spectrum antibacterial ointment three or four times daily for 7 to 10 days. Unless the case is complicated, it should be under control within that period. Complicated cases may require bacterial culture and antibiotic sensitivity tests because resistant *Staphylococcus* can be a therapeutic nightmare. The prognosis is generally good to excellent.

CONTACT LENSES: The use of soft hydrophilic contact lenses can be helpful in cases of chronic *corneal ulcers*. All forms of medical and surgical therapy appear to be fruitless in such cases. Soft contact lenses provide protection for diseased corneal tissue. They do not correct vision problems. Several difficulties are associated with the use of soft contact lenses. Even a very calm Cocker Spaniel will try to avoid the placement of the contact lens thus requiring at least two assistants. Use of a *topical anesthetic* on the eye can help to minimize the objection. The third eyelid has a tendency to close over the eye as soon as the eye is touched with the lens. Again, use of a topical anesthetic helps to cut down on the over activity of the third eyelid. Several companies make soft contact lenses that can have animal usage. Optech Company makes three different sizes for usage in dogs and Vifilcon-A™ hydrophilic contact lenses can be obtained from American Optical Corporation, Framingham, MA 01701.

The major problem in the use of soft contact lenses in dogs is the loss of lenses requiring frequent replacement. However, in cases where the lens remained in place for 10 days, healing occurred in 92% of the dogs. The loss of the contact lens is generally attributed to either the movement of the third eyelid, a poor fit, or the presence of a bulging eye as seen in some short-nosed breeds.

CORNEAL DISEASES: The cornea can be affected with a primary disease or secondarily to other conditions such as acute *corneal ulcer*, *corneal dystrophy* and *pannus*. Changes in the transparency of the cornea with pain manifested by squinting, excess tearing, and closed eyelids are the most consistent signs of corneal disease. Application of a topical anesthetic like *Ophthaine*® can eliminate pain related to the cornea helping to differentiate corneal pain from *glaucoma* and *uveitis* pain. Because of the loss of transparency of the cornea, a decrease in sight occurs in dogs. Total blindness, however, is not a result of corneal disease.

Keratitis is the inflammation of the cornea. *Pannus* is an unusual nonulcerous form of keratitis. Acute corneal ulcers (*ulcerative keratitis*) are discussed earlier in the chapter. Also see *KERATITIS, PUNCTATE ULCERATIVE* and *KERATITIS, PIGMENTARY*. While assorted organisms are the cause of infectious types of keratitis, the most common fungal types are *Aspergillus* and *Candida*, a yeast.

Several congenital conditions such as *microcornea* (smaller than normal cornea), *megalocornea* (larger than normal cornea), and corneal dermoids, affect the cornea. A *dermoid* is the presence of a piece of tissue containing hair, an eyelash, or other epithelial elements on the normally clear cornea. The cornea can be partly occluded by a *persistent pupillary membrane* which adhered to the inner surface of the cornea and did not degenerate at birth.

Other corneal diseases include *corneal dystrophy* and corneal degeneration. Corneal degenerations are associated with an inflammatory process affecting only one eye. They are often part of a systemic disease process which must also be treated.

An accurate diagnosis is necessary for proper treatment of corneal disorders. Many can have a good prognosis with early and accurate therapy. Also see *CORNEAL DYSTROPHY, PANNUS,* and *ACUTE CORNEAL ULCER*.

CORNEAL DYSTROPHY: By definition, corneal dystrophy is a deficiency in the growth and nutrition of the cornea. The American Cocker Spaniel has a high incidence of corneal dystrophy. Most dystrophic areas are round or oval and coalesce to form white dots or lines in the corneal stroma (tissue). The outward appearance is either ground glass in appearance or concentric rings of white in the cornea. Both eyes are equally affected with corneal dystrophy. The condition, which is not part of any systemic disease, is not inflammatory nor progressive in its development. Because corneal dystrophy is frequently seen in young puppies, there may be some hereditary basis.

An ophthalmologist with special lighting equipment should examine the eyes. The axis of the cornea will show some steamy opacities which interfere only slightly with vision. These opacities in the subepithelial portion of the cornea are not painful. No treatment is indicated since corneal dystrophy does not interfere with sight and in most cases does not progress from its early appearance.

CORNEAL LACERATION: A corneal laceration (tear) is an OCULAR EMERGENCY! If a traumatic injury to the eye is apparent, veterinary care must be found immediately. Initially, moist pressure bandages control hemorrhaging from a protruding, bleeding iris. The moist bandage also prevents self-trauma to the eye. Each corneal laceration must be evaluated independently. The faster competent surgical repair can be accomplished, the more satisfactory the results.

CORNEAL ULCER: See *ACUTE CORNEAL ULCER*.

DEAFNESS: Deafness, either partial or complete, is the inability to hear. Since the normal hearing range for dogs is different than humans, evaluation of partial hearing loss is difficult. Deafness can be congenital (present at birth) or acquired. In the Cocker Spaniel, *congenital deafness* is due to the inherited lack of development of the organ of Corti in the inner ear. Since deafness is not treatable, dogs deaf from birth present special problems in adapting to their environment. Maintaining a deaf dog and small children in the same household can be difficult. Young children may touch the deaf dog before showing themselves resulting in a startled bite response from the dog.

Acquired deafness may be due to either external or middle ear disease resulting in a nonfunctional ear drum (tympanic membrane). If the hearing loss is due to a traumatic *rupture of the ear drum*, hearing will return after the ear drum has repaired itself. However, if the ear drum is permanently damaged by infection or proliferative tissue, hearing ability may remain impaired.

Aging causes fusion of the small bones that carry sound to the inner ear resulting in acquired deafness. With senility (old age) comes a decrease in the sound carrying ability of three small bones that vibrate and transmit sound waves to the inner ear. This loss in the ability to perceive sound occurs gradually and is both irreversible and untreatable in dogs.

DESCEMETOCELE: A descemetocele is an EYE EMERGENCY which requires immediate veterinary care! This *corneal ulcer* has eroded down to the level of the elastic Descemet's membrane. The pressure of the aqueous humor fluid in the eye causes the elastic membrane to protrude through the ulcer and bulge above the outer level of the corneal surface. A descemetocele is one layer away from having the eyeball rupture!

Vigorous aggressive medical treatment is necessary to reverse the ulcerative process present in a descemetocele. The dog must be hospitalized for the application of timely medication and the administration of any other care necessary to keep the eyeball from rupturing. If medical therapy fails to reverse the process, surgical intervention is necessary. Post-operatively, the eye is treated with *atropine* and antibiotics until healing is complete. With aggressive treatment and timely surgery, the prognosis is excellent for saving the sight in the eye.

DIRECT OPHTHALMOSCOPE: The direct ophthalmoscope is the most common piece of eye examination equipment present in veterinary clinics. The cornea, iris, lens, vitreous, and retina can be examined with a hand held direct ophthalmoscope. This instrument has a moderate cost, is easy to use, gives great magnification of the retina, and allows one to determine the size of lesions found in the eye. However, the depth of the eye field seen is very small as is the area examined. Dilating the eyes of a dog is usually necessary to perform a thorough examination of all of the components of the eye.

DISTICHIASIS: Distichiasis, a source of eye irritation and excessive tearing, is hereditary in Cocker Spaniels. An affected dog should not be used for breeding.

If present for a long period of time, corneal damage and ulceration result. Pigment is produced to protect the irritated area of the cornea. Clinically, this condition is due to cilia (fine hairs) or eyelashes abnormally located along the eyelid edge. Normally, the hairs are directed outward away from the eye itself. In distichiasis, the hairs are directed toward the corneal surface stimulating excess tearing, conjunctival irritation, and a mucoid discharge. Continual irritation will also cause *corneal ulceration*.

Recommended treatment depends on the number of hairs causing the problem. If a small number are misdirected, electroepilation is the most efficient method of treatment. Repeat electroepilation may be necessary if the entire hair follicle is not destroyed the first time. While this method can cause scarring on the eyelid, the scarring is not serious if only a few hairs are treated. However, if a large number of hairs are involved, delicate eyelid splitting surgery will give the best results. This surgery requires above average ophthalmologic surgery skills so is best handled by a specialist.

DRY EYE: Dry eye is the common name for *keratoconjunctivitis sicca (KCS)*. Cocker Spaniels of either sex are commonly predisposed. Many Cockers will suffer concurrently from severe cases of *seborrhea* and KCS. Although the exact cause is unknown, KCS can be part of the following systemic disease complexes: *hypothyroidism, Cushing's disease, diabetes mellitus, demodectic mange, canine distemper, systemic lupus erythematosus,* and occasionally *vitamin A deficiency.* If the *KCS* is associated with *autoimmune hemolytic anemia, rheumatoid arthritis,* or *chronic active hepatitis,* an *autoimmune panel* will explore the immune competence of the Cocker Spaniel. In some cases, KCS will occur while dogs are receiving sulfa drugs (*dapsone,* sulfadiazine, *Tribrissen*®, trimeth-sulfa, *Azulfidine*®) or *atropine* eye drops. If the third eyelid glands have been removed due to *cherry eye,* a Cocker will have a much greater chance of developing dry eye.

Dry eye is commonly misdiagnosed as chronic recurring *corneal ulcers* with allergic or bacterial *conjunctivitis.* Early in the course of the condition, the white tissue around the eye (the conjunctiva) becomes inflamed. Corneal ulceration follows from lack of lubricating tears. Ulceration causes pain indicated by blinking and pawing at the face. In cases that become chronic, the cornea becomes thickened, pigmented, misshapen, and covered with stringy mucus.

The diagnosis is made by the *Schirmer tear test.* A normal Schirmer reading is between 15 mm and 25 mm per minute. Any dog under 10 mm/minute has a positive dry eye test. Most will be under 5 mm/minute.

Treatment lubricates the cornea and conjunctiva so that the eyelid movement friction doesn't damage the epithelial tissue surface. Artificial tears are the best medical means to increase the lubrication effects. To be effective, they must be applied every two to three hours. The minimum application rate would be four times daily. Some artificial tear ointments can be used in conjunction with drops for overnight application when more frequent applications are not possible. Recently, the combination of *Equron*® (hyaluronate sodium) and artificial tears (*Tears Naturale*®) has been found to decrease the application frequency. The protocol is designed to gradually lengthen the time interval between the drops administration In some cases, once a day application is achieved.

Cyclosporine topically in the affected eye provides another promising new therapy for dry eye. *Optimmune*®, a commercially packaged cyclosporine, effectively increases tear production while decreasing corneal inflammation in about three weeks. This medication used once daily can sometimes be tapered to every other day.

If any residual tear secreting gland is present, *pilocarpine* drops can be used orally to stimulate tear formation. Some Cockers do not tolerate pilocarpine well and will vomit, salivate, and develop diarrhea. However, if tolerated satisfactorily, pilocarpine is an excellent alternative to frequent artificial tear administration. If all else fails, a surgical procedure may help selected dogs. The parotid salivary gland duct is transplanted from its normal opening in the cheek to the outer corner of the eye. This procedure requires above average surgical skill and could be expected to approach a 90% success rate. With any form of treatment, use of antibiotics is occasionally necessary to minimize infection. The overall prognosis ranges from fair to good.

EAR CULTURE: The ear culture is important in the battle against chronic ear infections in Cocker Spaniels. Because the technique is not difficult, your veterinarian can routinely perform this procedure. If a culture is anticipated, the ear should be left "as is." No medication or ear cleaner should be used to make it look better for your veterinarian. In 24 to 48 hours, a culture can grow both yeast and bacteria for results. Once the organism causing the infection is identified, an *antibiotic sensitivity test* should be done.

EAR DISCHARGE: The exudate (discharge) present in the ear of a Cocker Spaniel is important in determining the type of ear infection. When observing the quantity and kind of exudate, knowing what is normal is important. Normal ceruminous (ear wax) material is a yellow-brown color, shiny, and reasonably devoid of odor. Each dog has its own rate of *cerumen* (ear wax) accumulation. Until the interval for wax removal is determined, inspect the ears weekly.

The presence of abnormal ear wax is indicative of a pathological process. Your veterinarian should diagnose and treat this condition immediately. Black-brown, dry, gritty wax is characteristic of *ear mite infestation*. With a magnifying glass and with the heat from a good light, ear mites can be seen moving as gray-white dots in the gritty wax. A yellow, moist, and foul smelling discharge indicates a purulent (pus producing) infection. These discharges are very ulcerative to the ears causing a great degree of pain. Dark, sweet-smelling copious waxy discharge indicates a pure yeast infection. See *YEAST INFECTION IN THE EAR* for more information.

EAR MARGIN SEBORRHEA: The build-up of scale and crusts with occasional cracks on both surfaces of the ear and the edges of the pendulous portion of the ear is termed ear margin *seborrhea*. While not uncommon in the Cocker Spaniel, the cause is unknown. Although discomfort is not present, its presence is displeasing to see and touch. The condition is controlled with antiseborrheic shampoos.

EAR MITES: Ear mites (*Otodectes cynotis*) can contribute to inflamed ear canals. This parasitic mite burrows into the epidermal layer of the external ear canal resulting in inflammation and infection. In most cases, a characteristic gritty dark wax is present . Ear mites are not only contagious to other dogs and cats but will also cause itchy red "bites" on people.

Treatment is necessary to prevent its spread and keep human lesions to a minimum. To break the three week life cycle, the affected ears must be treated at least that long. Today, *Xenodine*® drops once weekly for five weeks or *Tresaderm*® drops twice daily for 10 days and once daily for 20 days are the most effective treatments. While one injection of *ivermectin* is a very effective treatment for ear mites, this drug is not government approved for this use in dogs.

In rare instances, dipping the dog in a mange dip to keep the mites from traveling to other parts of the body is necessary. The prognosis for recovery is excellent if treatment is maintained long enough.

ECTROPION: Ectropion is the outward rolling or drooping of the eyelid usually present only in the lower lid. Sometimes this rolling will be present in the middle of the lid when both ends of the lower lid are turned inward (*entropion*). Because the cornea and lower conjunctival tissue around the eye are exposed to more debris and dust, chronic irritation occurs. Ectropion is very common in the Cocker Spaniel.

Mildly irritated eyes are managed with cortisone-antibiotic ophthalmic ointments as needed. Dusty places should be avoided. Severely affected eyes require surgery. Some eyes require more than one surgical procedure because of the complexity of the involvement of the eyelids. While the prognosis following surgery is excellent, any Cocker with this problem should not be used for breeding purposes unless the ectropion was due to a traumatic injury to the eyelid.

ELECTRORETINOGRAPHY (ERG):   The use of electroretinography in diagnosing disease of the posterior portion of the eye (the ocular fundus) is available at some universities and veterinary ophthalmologist specialty practices. The ERG is especially valuable in diagnosing *progressive retinal atrophy*. A clinical electroretinogram consists of three wave-forms termed a-wave, b-wave, and c-wave. The height of the wave and the time of reaction from the onset of the light stimulus are the important features in determining retinal disease. Many factors affect the ERG. Each electroretinography system must establish a normal standards for its procedure before abnormal changes can be interpreted. In veterinary medicine, dogs undergoing ERG testing have their eyes dilated and are placed under general anesthesia with either *sodium thiamylal* or a gas like *methoxyflurane* or *halothane* before the testing is done.

Progressive retinal atrophy produces a retinogram with decreased wave amplitudes and increased time intervals. With this procedure, a diagnosis can be made at a much earlier age. For additional information, see *PROGRESSIVE RETINAL ATROPHY*.

ENTROPION: Entropion is much less common than ectropion in the Cocker Spaniel. With entropion, all or part of the upper or lower eyelid turns inward. The cilia and eyelashes touch the cornea or, in extreme cases, the eyelids may touch the cornea. Irritation to the cornea elicits tearing, squinting, and the formation of *corneal ulcers*.

The presence of an entropion should be treated medically first. Spastic contraction of eyelid muscles can cause the lid to turn inward. If the spasm can be eliminated with medication, the entropion will disappear. Other entropions disappear as puppy head's mature. However, a severe entropion can rapidly ulcerate an eye so must be watched closely. Surgery may be the only method of correcting a major entropion. The surgeon will determine which surgical technique should be utilized after the extent of the problem is determined. The prognosis for normal sight is very good unless serious corneal scarring occurs. Many entropions are hereditary and breeding should be discouraged.

ENUCLEATION OF EYES: Enucleation of the eye is the surgical removal of the entire globe of the eye. Reasons for eye enucleation include congenital sightless small eye (*microphthalmus*), an infection within the eye that has not responded to medical treatment in which sight has been lost, conditions of non-responsive inflammatory changes with blindness, a tumor within the eye that cannot be removed, severe irreparable damage to the globe of the eye, and prolapse of the eye with permanent muscle, optic nerve, and blood vessel damage.

Several surgical techniques can be used at the discretion of the surgeon. Early post-operative complications include hemorrhage and infection. If the tear duct apparatus is not removed, a draining wound may develop several months after the surgery. Also, inadvertent damage to the zygomatic salivary gland may become apparent several months post-operatively. After the surgery, bloody serum drainage may be present for a few days but will resolve itself.

This surgery performed for any of the mentioned reasons is probably done more frequently than necessary. Owners must be aware that the surgery involves suturing the eyelids closed resulting in an obvious indentation where the eyeball had been. Sometimes this is not cosmetically acceptable. Dog owners should be aware of the alternate solution of having a prosthetic eyeball placed in the globe for cosmetic reasons. A more complete discussion of the *FALSE EYE* (prosthesis) is found within this chapter.

EVERSION OF THIRD EYELID: The third eyelid (nictitating membrane) contains a cartilaginous form that can roll forward or backward causing irritation to the eye structures. A cosmetically unacceptable appearance results. Eversion can occur in one or both eyes. Swelling appears in the inner corner of the eye accompanied by excessive tearing or a mucoid discharge from the irritation.

Surgical removal of the curled cartilage without removing the third eyelid is the best treatment. Aftercare is instillation of antibiotic ointment during the week of healing. This defect seen in young dogs is genetically transmitted as a simple recessive gene. Affected dogs should not be used for breeding purposes.

EXTERNAL EAR INFECTION: One of the most common reasons for an American Cocker Spaniel to visit the veterinarian is for inflammation of the external ear (*otitis externa*). The external ear includes the *pinna* (ear flap) and the ear canal down to the ear drum. Because the external ear canal slopes downward and inward to the ear drum, water and debris fail to drain properly making moisture a predisposing factor in external ear canal disease.

Clinical signs of otitis externa begin with head shaking and scratching around the ear. Depending on the underlying cause, foul smelling exudates or progressive swelling of the tissues can be found in the ear canal.

Primary factors which cause otitis externa include foreign bodies (fox tails), parasites (*ear mites*), hypersensitivity diseases (*food allergy* or *atopy*), disorders in keratinization (Cocker Spaniel *seborrhea*), and *autoimmune disease* (*pemphigus* varieties, *systemic lupus erythematosus*). Predisposing factors include the pendulous ears of the Cocker Spaniel which restrict free air circulation, increased moisture in the ear canal, very warm moist climates, any condition in which the ear canal is occluded or smaller than normal, and an elevated body temperature. *Anal sac diseases* for some unknown reason cause *otitis externa* in some dogs. The three most common perpetuating factors, those that maintain otitis externa once the normal environment of the ear canal has been altered, are bacteria, yeasts, and a continuing problem with *otitis media* The same bacteria can exist in normal and diseased ears. However, *Pseudomonas*; and *Proteus;* infections are most commonly found in chronic ulcerative ear infections that have been treated with antibiotics over a long period of time. The yeast *Malassezia canis* is found in some normal ears but causes stubborn, chronic infections with sweet-smelling dark ear canal discharge. See *YEAST INFECTION IN THE EAR* for more information. When the ear drum is ruptured, a *middle ear infection* (*otitis media;*) can keep an external ear infection smoldering. Until the middle ear infection is effectively treated, the external ear will not heal. See *MIDDLE EAR INFECTION* for more information.

The management of external ear infection is dependent on the factors mentioned. Because external ear problems are so common in the Cocker Spaniel, especially in the blond Cocker, aggressive, vigilant maintenance of normal ear canal conditions is absolutely mandatory. Timely ear canal cleaning removing wax, drying the ear canal medicinally when excess moisture is present, as well as controlling and treating other body dysfunctions like *anal sac infection*, fevers, and systemic disease are essential in suppressing the development of external ear disease.

EYE COLOR: Eye color is derived from the pigmentary cells present in the iris surrounding the black pupil opening. Eye color is hereditary and related to the color of the coat. A yellow iris color has a tendency to occur with a diluted coat color. Yellow eye color is one step away from blue or walleye color. Blue eyes are one step removed from pink eyes which occur in true albinos. No visual deficit is related to any of the various iris colors. However, strong sunlight should be avoided when *albinism* is present. *Heterochromia* is the presence of two or more colors either in the same iris or in the same dog. This is undesirable in the Cocker Spaniel. Selection should be away from this condition. Occasionally, pigment spots or *iris freckles* are seen. They cause no problem and need no treatment but may be cosmetically objectionable.

EYE EMERGENCIES: The listed conditions are considered to be TRUE EYE EMERGENCIES. Each is discussed individually within the chapter. All of these situations require the immediate treatment by a competent veterinarian. **DO NOT LET THEM GO OVERNIGHT OR THROUGH THE WEEKEND!** If your veterinarian is not available, find someone else to provide the needed help.

Acute Anterior Uveitis	Bulging Eye
Acute Corneal Ulcer	Chemical Keratitis
Acute Blindness	Corneal Laceration
Anterior Lens Luxation	Descemetocele
Blood in Eye	Eye Foreign Body

Glaucoma   Traumatic Proptosis
Optic Neuritis

EYE PAIN, SIGNS OF: Since dogs are unable to tell us if and where it hurts, we must be aware of signs indicating acute eye pain such as excessive tearing, the presence of increased redness, increased blinking or closing of the eye. Many painful eyes appear sunken in the eye orbit and may also be partially covered by the third eyelid. If pain is intense, behavioral changes such as agitation or even snapping may be observed.

EYE TESTS: To determine the cause of eye abnormalities, various eye tests are necessary. Each test is discussed individually within the chapter. Since specialists have other types of equipment and tests available, this list includes tests available in most well-equipped veterinary clinics.

Applanation—tonometry test   Indirect ophthalmoscopy
Direct ophthalmoscopy   Rose Bengal test
Electroretinography   Schiotz tonometry
Fluorescein dye test   Schirmer tear test
Gonioscopy test   Slit lamp examination

EYE TUMORS: Eye tumors can be grouped by the affected tissues. Your veterinarian must determine if the tumor is a primary eye tumor or one that has spread to the eye from somewhere else.
   Tumors of the eyelids have a very low malignancy potential. Most involve the various glandular structures of the eyelids causing irritation to the eye. The *sebaceous gland adenoma* is the most common tumor. Depending on the extent of the tumor, eyelid tumors can be treated by excision, cryosurgery, or observation. Tumors of the third eyelid are relatively uncommon but must be differentiated from "*cherry eye.*"
   Tumors of the tissues around the orbit of the eye present special problems. Most of these tumors are malignant. Their location makes them very difficult to remove surgically. The prognosis is guarded, at best. Although tumors occurring within the eye as a primary neoplasm are rather rare, when they do occur, they cause a number of signs of ocular disease. In depth examination of an eye suspected of having a tumor requires a specialist with sophisticated diagnostic aids. Because clinical signs of primary and secondary tumors of the eye are similar, it necessary to perform a complete work-up for the entire body to determine the chances of metastasis (spreading). A chest radiograph should be included. The *uveal melanoma* which grows as a black mass from the iris is one of the more common intraocular tumors in dogs. This neoplasm, more common in young dogs, is a rather benign type of tumor. A *melanoma* found in an older dog's eyes is more invasive causing deterioration of multiple tissues within the eye.

EYELASH ABNORMALITIES: In Cocker Spaniels most eyelash abnormalities are congenital and possibly hereditary in nature. *Distichiasis* and *trichiasis* are two types of eyelash abnormalities discussed individually within the chapter. *Ectopic cilia*, the least important kind of abnormality, are fine hairs that are directed through the eyelid toward the surface of the cornea. Their abnormal location causes a great degree of irritation with signs of *epiphora (excess tearing)*, blinking, and redness. Ectopic cilia can be diagnosed by a veterinarian through magnification with strong light. Surgical removal of the tissue containing the cilia is the most effective treatment. One week of antibiotic-*steroid* ointment follows.

EYELID ABNORMALITIES: The two eyelid abnormalities which occur in the dog are *ectropion* and *entropion*. Both conditions may be hereditary so breeding affected dogs is not advised. Each is discussed more fully under its own heading.

FALSE EYES: False (prosthetic) eyes are more widely accepted than *enucleation* of the eye. In a sightless eye in which the disease process is not progressive like a tumor or infection, the installation of a false eye should be considered. The results are more cosmetically acceptable. The degree of surgical skill needed for this procedure is not much greater than that needed to remove the globe of the eye completely. However, special instrumentation and implants are required. Inert silicon implants are well tolerated by the dog after the initial surgical recovery period. Post-operatively, some swelling and irritation may exist for two to three days. Warm compresses, analgesics, and possibly topical antibiotics can relieve this condition. Within two weeks of the surgery, the eye has usually healed giving pleasing results to both patient and owner.

Implants are available from Jardon Plastics Research Corporation, Southfield, MI 48076. The special instrumentation can be obtained from Storz Instruments, St. Louis, MO.

FLUORESCEIN DYE TEST: Fluorescein dye has several uses in eye-related conditions. Instillation into both eyes determines patency of the lacrimal (tear) ducts. The tear ducts drain from the inner corner of each eye through a small tube under the skin which empties at the opening in the nose. If the ducts are open, dye placed in the eye should be evident at the end of the nose within one to five minutes.

The primary usage of fluorescein dye is in the detection of *corneal ulcers*. Normal corneal epithelium (covering) is resistant to the yellow-orange stain. However, when the epithelial lining is ulcerated, the stain enters the corneal tissue and colors it green indicating corneal ulceration.

FOREIGN BODY—EAR, EYE, NOSE: A foreign body is the abnormal presence of a material in its current location. The body reacts vigorously trying to wall off or remove anything that does not belong. This inflammatory response is marked by swelling, redness, fever, and the presence of *white blood cells*.

The presence of a foreign body in the ear can cause acute violent head shaking. The head is generally tilted to one side. The affected ear canal is inflamed and very sensitive. Foreign bodies take the form of dirt, plant material, kid's toys, or even medication that has dried in the ear canal. In areas like California, the plant awn of the foxtail is a major source of ear foreign bodies. Usually deep *sedation* or *anesthesia* is required to examine and treat one of these painful ears. The prognosis for recovery is excellent providing the problem is not chronic.

The presence of a foreign body in the eye is an EMERGENCY requiring immediate veterinary attention. These are classified as penetrating or non-penetrating depending on their location in the eye tissue. A foreign body that penetrates the cornea will cause intense pain. The presence of pain makes anesthesia necessary in order to perform a thorough examination of the eye. Each foreign body wound in the eye must be evaluated on its own merit to determine if removal is feasible, needed, and in the best interest of the patient. Antibiotics are used to prevent infection and surgery can be anticipated. The prognosis is guarded to good depending on the kind of foreign body, the location of the lesion, and the damage done.

The presence of a foreign body in the nasal cavity is manifested by the existence of a one-sided nasal discharge. The discharge contains pus and some blood. An affected dog paws at his nose and exhibits signs of discomfort in other ways. *Anesthesia* is necessary to examine and diagnose this condition. Occasionally, *bacterial cultures* and *antibiotic sensitivity tests* are needed to diagnose concurrent infections. The use of *radiographs* may be necessary to differentiate foreign bodies from tumors or *fungal infections* of the nasal cavity. Since removal may be difficult or may require a major surgical procedure, the prognosis is fair to good for recovery.

FOREIGN SUBSTANCE IN EYE: This category differentiates between foreign bodies that have been traumatically introduced into the eye and the presence of foreign substances that are not normal in a healthy eye. Some of the foreign substances which occur within the eye are blood, pus, tumors, *persistent pupillary membrane*, hyaloid remnants, *asteroid hyalosis*, and the *Thelazia worm*. Some of these require treatment and removal. Others do not need any attention because vision is not appreciably affected.

GLAUCOMA: Glaucoma is a disease of the orbit of the eye in which the intraocular pressure (pressure within the eye) greatly increases causing the degeneration of many structures within the eye. In the American Cocker Spaniel, hereditary glaucoma is classified as a closed angle *primary glaucoma*. Primary means no other eye abnormality is present. The angle is formed by the cornea and the small ligaments holding the base of the iris to the cornea. If the ligaments are shortened or not visible, the type of glaucoma is called a closed or *narrow angle glaucoma*. The fluid produced in the anterior portion of the eye cannot flow out of the eye through normal passages to the venous system. Pressure builds-up and unfortunately symptoms are not apparent until extensive eye damage is done.*Secondary glaucoma* affects the Cocker Spaniel when a swollen lens decreases or eliminates the angle formed by the iris and the cornea thereby impeding the outflow of fluid.

The most practical of the several methods for the classification of glaucoma is based on the stage of the disease. The four levels considered are Class I—enlarged, blind eye; Class II—normal-sized blind eye; Class III—recent attack of congestive glaucoma; and Class IV—very early glaucoma.

The only treatment for Class I is to eliminate the pain of increased pressure. Since the eye is blind, implanting a prosthesis (*false eye*), using cyclocryosurgery to lower the pressure, or enucleation of the eye are the only available choices. Class II treatment options include intense medical therapy, cyclocryosurgery, and the implant of a prosthesis (false eye). The blindness is probably permanent even in Class II.

In both Class III and IV, intense medical therapy has a chance to save the vision. Long term control with medications is unlikely in the dog. The surgical procedures that should be considered are designed to either decrease intraocular fluid production or to increase the outflow of the intraocular fluid. In any case, these surgical procedures coupled with appropriate medical therapy may be successful in controlling the intraocular pressure in one or both eyes. Be aware that early, aggressive treatment is essential to save an eye with increased intraocular pressure.

Acute glaucoma is considered an OCULAR EMERGENCY requiring immediate veterinary attention! *Gonioscopy*; and *tonometry* tests will evaluate the degree and the kind of glaucoma present. For additional information on these tests see *GONIOSCOPY, APPLANATION*, and *SCHIOTZ'S TONOMETRY*. Signs of acute glaucoma include a hazy bluish cornea, a reddened eye, a pupil which may or may not be responsive to light, a slightly enlarged eye, and eye pain.

GONIOSCOPY: Gonioscopy is an eye test which measures the angle of filtration for the removal of fluid from within the eye. The angle is formed by the pectinate ligaments that meet the cornea at the base of the iris. Specialized equipment, magnification, and a light source are required. Only this test can definitely diagnose hereditary narrow or *closed-angle glaucoma* in the American Cocker Spaniel. With the special lens, the veterinary ophthalmologist can also see if the iris is adhering to the eye lens.

HEMERALOPIA: The hereditary condition of hemeralopia (*day blindness*) is passed on by a simple autosomal recessive gene. This condition becomes apparent at three or four months of age. Night vision remains normal. No ophthalmologic lesions are visible on examination. However, the electroretinogram can be used to diagnose hemeralopia by demonstrating that only the presence of rods necessary for night vision are present. The cones necessary for day vision are absent or severely degenerated. Rods and cones exist in the retina on the back portion of the eye and receive the light stimulus that is ultimately sent to the brain via the optic nerve. To date, day blindness has not been diagnosed in the American Cocker Spaniel.

HYPOPYON: Hypopyon is an accumulation of pus in the anterior chamber of the eye, the area between the lens and the cornea. This is fairly uncommon and is usually a sequelae to very severe corneal disease. Occasionally aggressive antibiotic therapy and surgical drainage are required to resolve the problem.

INDIRECT OPHTHALMOSCOPY: Because a larger area of the eye is visible, an indirect ophthalmoscope gives the ophthalmologist a great deal of information in a short period of time. The stronger light used in this ocular test is also able to penetrate a diseased cornea. The fact that the room must be dark, the pupils must be dilated, the image is magnified one-third of the amount of the direct ophthalmoscopy image, and all of the observed images are upside down are all drawbacks of this examination.

This instrumentation is available in either monocular or binocular models. The technique is not easy to learn. Indirect ophthalmoscopy does provides valuable information quickly. This equipment is usually found in a referral practice or in a veterinary clinic with a special interest in eyes.

INDOLENT ULCER: The indolent ulcer usually occurs in one eye in middle-aged to old Cocker Spaniels. While the cause is unknown, a lack of tissue regeneration from the deep part of the cornea is suspected. Very little pain, tearing, and discomfort exist with this eye disorder. A positive *fluorescein dye test* exhibits the center of the ulcer absorbing a deeper stain than the periphery. Treatment of this disease is time consuming. The possibility of recurrence or development of a similar ulcer on the opposite eye exists. Following topical anesthesia to the eye, debridement (scraping) of the ulcerated area of the cornea with a sterile Q-tip® removes the diseased covering from the ulcer. After debridement, the size of the ulcer will be up to ten times larger. The fresh ulcer is cauterized with 7% iodine. A protective collar is put in place to keep the Cocker from rubbing the eye. Occasionally in large ulcers, the cautery is repeated as many as three times. After healing is underway, *cortisone* drops can be beneficial in this troublesome type of eye ulcer.

INNER EAR INFECTION: The inner ear is part of the *vestibular system*. The brain stem is connected to the vestibular function by the inner ear. Infections involving the inner ear must be treated aggressively. Signs of an inner ear infection include *head tilt, circling*, loss of balance, fever, and sometimes other neurological dysfunctions.

Radiographs may show lesions in the middle ear if the problem is an extension from that region. With the aid of an otoscope, blood can sometimes be observed through a *broken ear drum*. Inner ear infections are treated with systemic antibiotics for extended periods. If the middle ear is seriously involved, surgical drainage is required on occasion. If caught early, the prognosis is fair.

IRIS ATROPHY: The most common sign of iris atrophy is an irregular shape to the pupil of the eye. The condition is observed with advancing age. Closer inspection shows that fragments of the iris are present which might cause a slow or incomplete pupillary response to light. A number of holes can occur in one iris and if it is severe enough, the dog may be sensitive to light (photophobic). Iris atrophy occurs in old dogs as a senile aging change. No treatment is necessary because sight is not affected.

KERATITIS, PIGMENTARY: Pigmentary keratitis refers to the presence of pigment in the cornea resulting from inflammation to the cornea. The protruding eyes in some Cockers are predisposed to the development of pigmentary keratitis.

In other situations, chronic infection in the tissues around the eye stimulate the deposition of the pigment.

Treatment is only effective with the removal of the inciting cause of pigment deposition. Attempts to surgically remove pigment in the cornea are limited to totally blind Cockers. The use of *steroid* drops or ointments in the eyes decreases the amount of pigment in the corneal layers. Unless the primary cause of pigment production is eliminated, the prognosis is only fair for resolution of the problem.

KERATITIS, PUNCTATE ULCERATIVE: Although the exact cause of punctate ulcerative keratitis is unknown, viruses are suspected. An increased incidence of this eye disorder is observed in the Cocker Spaniel. Eye pain is intense. Clinically, the dog squints, excess tearing is present, and the third eyelid is over the eyeball. The white part of the eye is very red. Multiple small white pinpoint opaque dots which appear on the cornea result in a positive *fluorescein dye test.*

Cortisone drops every four hours are recommended. With aggressive treatment, the eye returns to normal in three or four days as evidenced by a negative dye test and lack of pain.

KERATOCONJUNCTIVITIS SICCA (KCS): See *DRY EYE.*

MICROPHTHALMUS: Microphthalmus, a congenital condition in which all structures associated with the eye are smaller than normal, is often associated with any number of other eye abnormalities. Either one eye or more commonly both eyes may be affected.

MIDDLE EAR INFECTION: A middle ear infection originates from either a broken ear drum or via the blood stream. Many times the infection settles in the bony bullae just inside the ear drum. Systemic antibiotics are used for two weeks. If control is not achieved, the dog is placed under *anesthesia* and the middle ear is gently flushed until the fluid is clear. Generally, one flushing session is sufficient. However, in rare instances, an additional flushing session is needed if the ear drum has not healed. If the bony bullae are infected, surgical drainage is possible. The prognosis for recovery is fair to good.

NASAL DISCHARGE: The presence of a nasal discharge can either mean that any of a number of disease processes are underway or that the tear ducts are open and draining properly. Characterizing the kind of discharge present is important. Observe the discharge to determine if it is serous (clear and watery), mucus, bloody, or a combination. Is the discharge from one or both nostrils? Attempt also to determine the amount of drainage present.

Many of the causes for different kinds of nasal discharges follows. Nasal discharges must be diagnosed as accurately as possible since the prognosis and treatment possibilities are so variable.

COCKER SPANIEL OWNERS'

SEROUS DISCHARGE (Clear)
Viral infection
Normal tear drainage
Early tumor (in old dogs)
Extension of dental disease to nasal sinus
Nasal mites, Pneumonyssus
Nasal worm, Linguatula

BLOODY NOSE
Clotting defect
Warfarin poisoning
Tumor
Nasal worm
Aspergillus infection
Foreign body

MUCOPURULENT DISCHARGE (Cloudy)

Chronic nasal infection	Mature tumor
Cryptococcus infection	Foreign body
Aspergillus infection	Trauma sinuses

NASAL SWELLING: Nasal swelling can occur in conjunction with nasal discharge, sneezing, pawing at the face, and with systemic signs like fever and depression. The cause should be determined as accurately as possible. *Radiographs, fungal cultures, bacterial cultures, serology tests,* and other blood tests are often necessary to establish the exact cause of nasal swelling. The location of the swelling on the nose also helps to focus on the cause. For instance, a swelling located just below the eye in the presence of a broken upper fourth premolar tooth is good evidence of a bacterial sinusitis (infection in a bony sinus). This case should respond to tooth extraction and antibiotic therapy.

Early diagnosis is important if treatment is to be successful. The prognosis in nasal swelling is related to cause and length of time the swelling has been present.

NASOLACRIMAL PUNCTA ATRESIA: See *TEAR DUCT BLOCKAGE.*

NOSE BLEED: See *BLOODY NOSE.*

NOSE DEPIGMENTATION: The causes of nasal depigmentation are generally idiopathic (unknown). Some plastic food bowls cause depigmentation of the lips and nose. "*Snow nose*" is the fading of the pigment in the winter. The lack of sunlight and presence of cold temperatures may contribute to this fading nasal pigmentation. Another syndrome that causes nasal hypopigmentation is similar to *Vogt-Koyanagi-Harada syndrome.* Additional information on the V-K-H syndrome is found in Chapter 11 on the skin. Other proposed causes of nasal depigmentation are immune mediated diseases like *discoid lupus erythematosus*, trauma to the nose "leather," and nutritional mineral deficiencies (specifically *iodine*).

OPTIC NERVE HYPOPLASIA: Optic nerve hypoplasia is a congenital, probably hereditary, lesion. While this condition can occur with other eye disorders, the degree of severity and symmetry varies. Blindness can result in a severely affected eye while the other eye remains less involved maintaining its sight. In mild cases, sight and pupil response to light are not affected. If both eyes are severely and equally affected, the eyes appear dilated with no pupillary light response and a cross-eyed appearance to the face. These dogs are blind.

Optic nerve hypoplasia can be diagnosed with an *ophthalmoscope*. Affected eyes show normal retinal blood vessels and variable sizes of optic disks. No treatment for the condition exists currently. Affected dogs should not be used for breeding.

OPTIC NEURITIS: Optic neuritis is the inflammation in the optic nerve. If inflammation is located where the nerve enters the retina, it can be seen on eye examination. Otherwise, the eye exam shows nothing but a dilated blind eye. While it can occur in just one eye, normally both eyes are affected.

Optic neuritis has a number of both known and unknown causes. *Brain tumors, systemic fungi, canine distemper virus*, toxic chemicals, trauma to the eye, and reticulosis are among the known causes. Determining the cause is important. Without infection, the suggested treatment is *cortisone*; which prevents demyelination of the optic nerve. If cortisone therapy is effective, improvement is seen within one week. If no sight has been restored in 14 days, further therapy is futile.

Early treatment is important to prevent permanent damage to the optic nerve. However, relapses can occur when treatment is discontinued. The prognosis for return of sight is guarded to fair.

OTITIS EXTERNA: See *EXTERNAL EAR INFECTION*.

OTITIS INTERNA: See *INNER EAR INFECTION*.

OTITIS MEDIA: See *MIDDLE EAR INFECTION*.

PANNUS: Pannus is a severe *immune-mediated* degenerative condition of the cornea. The upper outer edge of the cornea is first affected. If untreated, the entire eye, third eyelid, and cornea become covered with pigmented, fibrous tissue. The only effective treatment is topical and/or systemic *cortisone* drugs. This is control, not cure. Surgery is occasionally recommended to remove the thickened pigmented tissue covering the cornea. However, surgery is probably not necessary if compliance with *steroids* is good.

PERSISTENT PUPILLARY MEMBRANE;:   Before birth, the pupil of the fetal eyes are covered with a thin membrane. Just prior to birth, this membranous tissue and associated blood vessels are absorbed. Within ten days after birth, the eyes can react to light and movement. Occasionally, part of the pupillary membrane is not absorbed creating a "cobweb" appearance when a light is shined into the eye. This persistent pupillary membrane does not interfere with vision. The condition may be hereditary in development. No treatment is necessary.

PHOTOPHOBIA: Photophobia, an abnormal intolerance of light, is a sign present in some systemic diseases like *canine distemper*. The signs signaling ocular disease include blinking and attempting to shield the eyes from bright light.

RED EYE: Redness in one or both eyes is a sign of ocular disease. The location of the redness is important in determining the affected parts of the eye. The eyes will look red if the normal blood vessels are unusually prominent, if the blood vessels on the normally white sclera are congested, if new blood vessels are growing out on the cornea, and if solid red masses are on or around the eye. In a healthy situation, a prominent blood vessel lies on the top of the white of the eye, appearing to approach the cornea. This large blood vessel is normal!

Causes for red eye include *anterior uveitis, acute glaucoma, ulcerative keratitis, dry eye,* hemorrhage around the eye, and *retrobulbar abscess (tumor).* Because some of these conditions are considered emergencies, seek veterinary care immediately when you see a red eye to determine its urgency.

Some of the tests used to ascertain the cause of the red eye are the *Schirmer tear test, fluorescein dye test, tonometry,* and *direct* or *indirect ophthalmoscopy.* The prognosis depends on the cause and available treatment. Having a red eye diagnosed early improves the chance of resolving the problem satisfactorily.

RETINAL ATROPHY: Retinal atrophy is a gradual deterioration of the retina's ability to carry images to the optic nerve and on the brain. The hereditary aspects are of great concern to breeders because evidence of the condition may not show up in Cocker Spaniels until they are six or seven years old, long after they have sired or borne puppies. Two types of retinal atrophy are diagnosed.

Progressive retinal atrophy (PRA) is characterized by progressive *night blindness* and increased reflectivity of the retina. In the Cocker Spaniel, whether PRA is rod-cone dysplasia (early forming), rod dysplasia and cone degeneration (occurring at 1 to 3 years of age), or rod-cone degeneration (occurring as late as seven years) is unclear. Possibly all subclassifications exist in the breed. Early in the course of the disease, the dog will bump into things in dim light. Dilation of the eyes shows a greater yellow-green reflectivity in diminished light. As the condition progresses, day vision is affected and total blindness results. Because *cataracts* often occur in dogs with PRA, *electroretinograms* should be undertaken before performing cataract surgery in a Cocker that would remain blind from PRA. The mode of inheritance is probably an autosomal recessively transmitted disease.

Two methods of early diagnosis exist for breeders. If a facility with *ERG* equipment is near and cost is no object, examination of puppies with the ERG is a useful tool. Others choose to test breed and sacrifice the litter for histopathology. The presence of PRA lesions can also be determined before they are observed either clinically or by usual ophthalmoscopic methods. Breeding to dogs registered with the *American Spaniel Club Health Registry* or *CERF* is also helpful in reducing the incidence of this serious eye disease in Cocker Spaniels. No treatment is currently available.

Central retinal atrophy (CRA) occurs in a number of breeds as a hereditary disease. Day vision is the first sight affected, followed by the inability to see stationary objects. Increased pigmentation in the retina is evident, followed late in the disease by retinal hyper-reflectivity. Blindness may be the end result. However, this condition may not progress to that extreme. No treatment exists.

RETINAL DETACHMENT: Causes for retinal detachment are grouped into three categories. The first group includes detachments due to pushing the retina away from the reflective part of the eye. This type of detachment generally is caused by infections, parasitic worms, and tumors. The second group of detachments occurs when the retina is pulled forward away from its attachments. A blood clot within the eye is the principle cause of this type. As the clot shrinks, the retina is pulled away from the wall of the eyeball. The third group of detachments occurs when the semi-solid mass in the center of the eyeball (the vitreous body) is lost. Without support of the vitreous material, the retina can detach from the eyeball wall. This can occur after intraocular surgery or from a penetrating injury.

Small retinal detachments are not noticed because the eye is not yet blind. Only massive detachments that cause sudden blindness are apparent to owners. A detached retina can be observed with the use of a pen-light. A veil-like structure appears behind the lens. In many cases, only one eye is involved. A comparison may alert one to an abnormality. Some detached retinas can be treated effectively with *steroids* and antibiotic therapy for a period of 30 days. The prognosis is guarded to fair depending on the origin of the retinal detachment. Lasers are used in humans to reattach some detached retinas.

RETINAL DYSPLASIA: Multiple small areas of retinal dysplasia can be found in young American Cocker Spaniels. Both eyes are affected. The diseased folds of retinal tissue are located on both the reflective and nonreflective parts of the retina. The lesions in an eye can number up to more than one hundred. While these areas are nonfunctional for sight, the overall vision of the Cocker is unaffected as long as no other visual deficit is present. Retinal dysplasia is thought to be genetically transmitted as a recessive trait.

RETROBULBAR ABSCESS AND TUMOR: Retrobulbar abscesses and tumors clinically appear very similar. Because the space behind the globe of the eye becomes occupied, it displaces the eye causing redness, third eyelid protrusion, and bulging. In the majority of cases, only one eye is involved. The cause of this eyeball protrusion may be an abscess (cellulitis) behind the eye, a space occupying tumor, or the presence of a foreign body that has penetrated the roof of the mouth near the back teeth.

A *general anesthetic* is usually necessary in order to open the mouth enough to inspect the area behind the molar teeth for a foreign body or abscess. While abscesses develop quickly and are painful, tumors develop more slowly and are not painful. The use of *blood counts* and skull *radiographs* may be necessary as aids in the diagnosis of the cause. Fine needle aspirations will help with tumor prognosis.

Abscesses and foreign body removal are generally treated through the mouth. They respond quickly to drainage, removal, and antibiotic therapy resulting in a good prognosis. Tumor treatment prognosis is guarded depending on the type of neoplasia (tumor) present.

ROSE BENGAL TEST: The rose bengal test instills a red stain in the eye to color diseased and dying cells on the cornea and conjunctiva. The test is well-suited for use in the diagnosis of *"dry eye"* (*KCS*). Because rose bengal dye 1% is irritating to the eye, the stain is better tolerated if a drop of *topical anesthesia* is placed in the eye before beginning the dye test. Excess dye should be removed with a saline or artificial tear wash.

ROUTINE EAR CLEANING: Ear wax is normally produced in varying amounts in all dogs. Breeds and individuals will differ in the amount of wax that forms in the external ear canal. Until you determine how often ear wax needs to be removed from your own Cocker, inspect the ears weekly. A few dogs will accumulate a significant amount of wax on a weekly basis. Most Cocker Spaniels will require wax removal monthly. Normal wax is a yellow-brown glistening material located in the external ear canal. If the wax in the ear canals is present with no redness and no offensive odor, the ears can be safely cleaned without veterinary supervision.

Rubbing alcohol and cotton balls are needed to clean normal Cocker ears. Do not use baby oil, peroxide, or mineral oil! Do not place cotton-tipped applicators in the ear canal!

The cleaning procedure is quick and simple. Saturate a cotton ball with rubbing alcohol, squeezing it as you place it in the ear canal. With your other hand, massage the base of the ear to work the alcohol into all "nooks and crannies" of the external ear canal. Using clean dry cotton balls, now remove the alcohol and the loosened wax from the ear canal. Repeat the procedure until the cotton ball comes out clean with no yellow-brown wax on it. Follow the same procedure in the other ear. If all of the alcohol is not removed, it will evaporate causing no further problem.

NOTE: DO NOT use alcohol in an inflamed ear! Seek veterinary help in treating all ear infections!

RUPTURED EAR DRUM: A ruptured tympanic membrane (ear drum) will not cause permanent deafness. The introduction of foreign objects (cotton applicators, fox tails) into the horizontal external ear canal can cause ruptured ear drums. *Middle ear infections* which create pressure on the tympanic membrane causing it to break and overzealous flushing of the ear canal are also reasons for ruptured ear drums. If infection is not present, the ear drum heals in seven to ten days forming scar tissue. If hearing is diminished, it will return. If infection is present in the middle ear, antibiotic medication and flushes are necessary. Extension of middle ear infection to the external ear canal can occur through ruptured ear drums.

SCHIOTZ'S TONOMETRY: The Schiotz tonometer is the most common indirect tonometric method for determining intraocular pressure. This instrument is used to diagnose *glaucoma*. A small, weighted plunger is placed on the cornea measuring the degree of indentation on a numerical scale. The normal values for the dog are lower than 25 mm of Hg The instrument is designed for the human eye so a built-in error exists when used on dogs. Calibrations for compensating for this error are available in the 1976 proceedings of the .*American College of Veterinary Ophthalmologists*, pages 47–73.

SCHIRMER TEAR TEST: The amount of tear formation from the dog's eye can be measured by the Schirmer tear test. Both eyes are tested individually without placing any drops or *anesthesia* in the eyes topically. A piece of filter paper is placed in the lower eyelid for one minute. The amount of tear formation found on the paper is measured in millimeters. The normal tear flow for a dog is at least 15 to 25 mm in one minute. Any reading under 10 mm is very suspicious of *dry eye (KCS)*.

SNEEZING: Sneezing is a sign of acute or chronic nasal passage irritation. As a reflex act, it occurs from irritation of the fine hairs (cilia) that line the nose. Since this clinical sign may indicate a more serious problem, a diagnostic work-up is needed to determine the cause. Allergies, the presence of a *foreign body*, an infectious disease, parasites, or an injury to the nasal passages can all cause sneezing.

SWELLING OF EAR CANAL: In ears that have been infected or inflamed for a long time, the tissue lining of the external ear canal will swell. This tissue swelling may be so extensive that the ear canal cannot be seen by normal methods. Since the ear canal is occluded, medicating the diseased canal is very difficult. This hyperplastic tissue can be treated by two methods. The medical use of *cortisone* and *dimethyl sulfoxide* in a topical mixture will shrink the swollen ear canals over a period of time. A surgical procedure removing the lateral (outer wall) of the ear canal allows deeper involved tissues to be medicated with appropriate antibiotics. Either procedure is effective and can be part of any ongoing treatment for chronic ear problems.

SWOLLEN EYES: Swollen eyes are actually swollen eyelids. The eyes are very puffy with the tissue around the eye appearing red and swollen. The eye itself may be difficult to see. Swollen eyelids should be seen by your veterinarian to determine what treatment should be initiated.

The cause of swollen eyelids varies. In newborn puppies, a serious infection called *ophthalmia neonatorum* occurs before the eyelids have opened. If this condition is diagnosed, the eyelids must be quickly opened and wide spectrum antibiotic ophthalmic ointment instilled frequently. Trauma can cause eyelids to swell. Cold packs minimize any damage in these cases. *Insect bites* and some *food allergies* can cause *angioneurotic edema* (fluid accumulation in the eyelids). The use of *cortisone* parenterally will control this problem. The prognosis with treatment is good.

TEAR DUCT BLOCKAGE: Tear duct blockage occurs later in life either from congenital causes or from infection. An absence of a lower opening in the tear duct called *nasolacrimal puncta atresia* results in tear duct blockage in the Cocker

Spaniel. Also, a malalignment of the lower opening hindering natural drainage presents similar problems. In both congenital causes, tears overflow staining the side of the face. The most common acquired type of blockage is due to infection in the tear duct canal causing accumulation of debris, ductal swelling, and canal occlusion. After the cause is determined, the veterinarian can use medical or surgical procedures to correct the problem. If the blockage recurs, a Silastic® tube may be inserted in the tear duct for three or four weeks while antibiotic drops are administered.

TEARING: *Epiphora*, an excessive amount of tearing, is evidenced by moisture and debris extending from the eye down the side of the face. In light haired dogs, the fur is stained with a reddish discoloration from the excess moisture. This discoloration is especially noticeable in light colored Cocker Spaniels A specific cause of epiphora should be determined. Some of the conditions that cause excessive tearing are pain within the eye like *glaucoma*, pain from irritation or ulceration of the cornea, inflammation of the tear gland, defects in the lacrimal duct system (see *TEAR DUCT BLOCKAGE*), an abnormal number or placement of eyelashes or cilia, and turned in eyelids (*entropion*). A complete eye examination with ancillary tests may be needed to ascertain the cause of epiphora. In cases where a cause for the excess tearing cannot be determined, the use of *tetracycline* antibiotic at the rate of 50 mg per day in a Cocker Spaniel will eliminate the staining of the hair. This therapy can be used indefinitely but should not be initiated until all of the adult teeth have erupted. The prognosis for recovery is excellent if a specific cause can be found.

TRAUMATIC PROPTOSIS: Traumatic proptosis is an OCULAR EMERGENCY! In this condition, the eyeball protrudes or hangs outside of the eyelids. Because of the relatively full, slightly protruding eye, the problem can occur in the Cocker Spaniel. In dogs with normally bulging eyes, this is common after a fight or a car accident. It is a genuine emergency! Immediately place a cold compress over the exposed eye and call for veterinary service!

The veterinarian will attempt to replace the eyeball in its socket. This procedure may require *general anesthesia*. Before any anesthesia is given, determine whether the cornea is ulcerated and whether the pupil responds to light. Having a constricted pupil is a better sign than one that is widely dilated or normal in size but unresponsive.

The healing from traumatic proptosis can take four to six weeks. During that period, several surgical procedures may be necessary. If the eyeball is hanging or has collapsed, *enucleation* is recommended. The prognosis depends on the degree of damage and the length of time before veterinary care is obtained. At best, it is guarded.

TRICHIASIS: Trichiasis is an eyelash abnormality in which the hairs arise from normal follicles coming in contact with either the cornea or the conjunctiva (white part of the eyeball). These hairs act as an irritant causing the dog to blink and tear excessively. This congenital condition is usually a hereditary defect which is secondary to another underlying cause such as *entropion* or a *dermoid growth*.

Temporary relief can be obtained by protecting the eye with an eye ointment. The only permanent cure is to remove the cause of the irritant usually through surgery. The prognosis with treatment is good. However, the breeding of affected individuals should be discouraged.

YEAST INFECTION IN EAR: A great deal of controversy exists as to the role that yeasts play in *otitis externa* (external ear canal infections). The two yeasts found in infections of the ear canal are *Candida* and *Malassezia canis* (*Pityrosporum*). What complicates the situation is the presence of *Malassezia* or *Pityrosporum* in about 40% of the normal ears. Some investigators feel that dogs that frequently get water in the ear canals are more prone to yeast infections. If severe overgrowth of yeast occurs in a diseased ear canal, the veterinarian should be suspicious of an *immune deficiency* or a possible *diabetes* complication.

A culture of stubborn ear infections is absolutely necessary since most *antibiotics* are not effective against yeasts. From the results, other forms of medication can be prescribed to bring the otitis under control. With proper therapy, the prognosis is fair to good if no complicating immune deficiencies exist.

SKIN AND RELATED STRUCTURES

ACANTHOSIS NIGRICANS: Acanthosis nigricans is an uncommon skin disorder. The characteristic skin lesions are manifested as a thickened blackening of the skin in both armpits (axillae). In chronic cases, the ears and even inner surface of the rear legs are involved. The cause is unknown but some think that the hormone regulation of melanin pigmentation is disrupted. Secondarily, acanthosis nigricans can occur due to rubbing the legs against the chest, to hormone disruptions, or as a response to *allergies*. In secondary forms of the disease, resolution occurs when the underlying cause is treated.

The prognosis depends on the cause. In primary acanthosis nigricans, control rather than cure is sought. Treatments include the use of *melatonin*, a *pineal gland hormone* available from Rickards Research Foundation, 18235 Euclid Avenue, Cleveland, OH 44112. *Cortisone* and antibiotics combined with weight reduction programs are also helpful.

ACNE: Canine acne is not an unusual problem in the Cocker Spaniel. Bumps, pustules, and blackheads (*comedones*) appear on the chin and lips most commonly between the ages of three and twelve months. Many cases clear up at sexual maturity (about 12 months old). Some cases, however, continue into adulthood and are difficult to handle. The usual treatment is the daily application of benzoyl peroxide gel with twice weekly benzoyl peroxide shampoo baths. Bathing will control all but the most stubborn cases. In cases of follicle infection, the use of anti-*staphylococcus* antibiotics are indicated. The prognosis is guarded since the condition can recur over a long period of time. Acute flare-ups should be treated because permanent scarring can result.

ACRAL LICK: The acral lick, also incorrectly called *lick granuloma*;, is classified as a *psychogenic dermatosis*. A higher incidence of this condition occurs in emotional high-strung Cocker Spaniels. Reasons range from lack of human companionship to stressful or boring life styles. Many of the dogs that develop acral licks are shy and/or nervous. Male Cocker Spaniels over the age of five seem to be affected more than females.

The lesion appears on the front leg near the carpus (wrist) or on the rear leg near the hock joint. The skin lesion is round, raised, thickened, hairless, and darker than normal. In most cases, only one lesion is apparent. On occasion, the skin lesion looks like a slow healing ulcer.

The treatment is complex. The dog's routine must be changed by exercising it at a different time, feeding it differently, and giving it new toys. Anything that gives the dog something else to think about helps. The lesion should be covered for 30 days while the life style is altered, providing the Cocker will leave a bandage in place. Breaking the itch-lick cycle is the most important part of the treatment. Recently, a combination of *Synotic*® and *Banamine*® applied daily for three weeks has shown much promise. The prognosis depends on the success of changing the life style and on the appropriate use of medication to break the itch-lick cycle. Recurrences are common if the life style is not varied from time to time.

ACUTE MOIST DERMATITIS: *Moist eczema, pyotraumatic derma:itis,* and *hot spots* are among the names given to acute moist dermatitis. Pyotraumatic dermatitis is the most accurate because this skin problem occurs secondary to a primary irritation. Hot spots are common in Cocker Spaniels, especially in the summer. Inciting causes can be *anal sac infections, external ear infections,* a dirty dead hair-coat, and pain in the area where *hip dysplasia* lesions are found. The development of lesions is very rapid. What may appear as a small oozing, hairless, red, ulcerated lesion will grow to an area three to four times as large in less than two hours.

To minimize the dog's discomfort, vigorous treatment is necessary early in the course of this condition. Often, *sedation (anesthesia)* is necessary in order to clip hair from around the lesion to initially treat the oozing painful dermatitis. An excellent astringent for this problem is a mixture of 5% tannic acid, 5% salicylic acid, and 70% alcohol. This solution is applied two to three times daily until the skin starts to crust. The use of *cortisone* may be necessary. In all cases, the primary cause should be treated or eliminated. Prognosis for recovery is excellent. The more aggressive the therapy, the earlier the recovery. The missing hair will grow back because the hair follicles are not destroyed.

ALLERGY: A dog may develop allergies to many proteins in his surroundings. Cocker Spaniels are more prone to inhalant and food allergies than many other breeds. The following allergies are discussed individually within this chapter.

Atopy (inhalant allergies)	Hives
Bacterial hypersensitivity	Hormone hypersensitivity
Drug allergy	Irritant contact dermatitis
Food allergy	

ALLERGY TESTING: An alternative to *cortisone* for *atopy (inhalant allergy)* is the use of skin testing and *immunotherapy (hyposensitization)* to desensitize the body to the inhalant allergens. The best results in allergy testing are achieved when individual antigens are used. These antigens should be regionalized to your area of the United States. The veterinarian who performs the test should have a good deal of experience in reading test results since some interpretation is required.

An area of skin is prepared for the test by shaving and marking a spot where each intradermal injection is to be made. The dog may or may not be sedated for the test procedure. Normally 40 to 60 antigens are tested at one time, including a positive and negative control. The test results are read after 15 minutes and after one hour to determine allergic skin reactions. A number of factors can alter the test results. Prior to the allergy test, dogs should be free from orally administered cortisone for three to four weeks and from injectable *cortisone* for seven to eight weeks. Some allergens test more strongly at certain times of the year. For example, ragweed is a late summer and early fall allergen. Its skin reaction will be stronger then than in the spring of the year. Allergy testing and treatment are 60% to 80% successful in the hands of a competent veterinary dermatologist.

ALOPECIA: Alopecia (*hair loss*) can develop normally or be due to a wide number of disease processes. Hair grows in a cyclic pattern. During the growth period (anagen), hair grows in length by cell division (mitosis). At the end of anagen, a transitional period or catagen takes place. The hair bulb where growth occurs constricts causing the area above the hair bulb to thicken. After a variable length of time, the resting period or telogen starts. Weeks or months later, the whole cycle begins again.

Cocker Spaniel hair is classified as a long silky variety coat. Because of its rate of growth, the Cocker Spaniel's coat is clipped or stripped several times a year. See additional information under *CONGENITAL ALOPECIA* and *ENDOCRINE ALOPECIA*.

ANA TEST: The ANA (*antinuclear antibody*) test is done when *immune mediated skin diseases* are suspected. The ANA test is most useful when *systemic lupus erythematosus* is suspected. Accurate test results can be obtained on dogs receiving *cortisone*. However, many drugs and diseases can create positive ANA tests. The test is done on a serum sample. The titer and staining pattern are the most important factors in interpreting the test results.

ANAL SAC DISEASES: The anal sacs open to the outside through small ducts at the junction of the anal tissue and the skin. They are located at 8 o'clock and 4 o'clock in relation to the anal opening. Anal sacs are customarily emptied during grooming. Most groomers attempt to empty the sacs by applying pressure to both sides of the anus squeezing the sacs against each other. However, to completely empty each anal sac, insert a gloved finger into the anus and squeeze each sac individually.

Treatment of anal sac disorders involves expressing the sac material, infusing antibiotic ointment into the sacs, and on occasion, surgically removing the sacs. Impaction, chronic infection, and acute infection or abscess formation are the three disease processes associated with the anal sacs.

Anal sac impaction is a chronic process which fills the sacs with a black, dry odorless material. This substance is difficult to express with a bowel movement or by digital expression. After removal of the impacted material, the sacs are filled with an antibiotic ointment.

Acute anal sac infection is a very active process which enlarges the infected sac and ruptures through the skin. This infection responds to both local and systemical antibiotic therapy. In the acute infection, the thin, bloody discharge is accompanied with some pus and a fetid odor.

Chronic anal sac infections produce a thicker reddish paste which has a fetid odor. After the sacs are expressed, antibiotic ointment is placed daily in the sacs for a period of time.

ATOPY: Inhaling environmental allergens causes canine atopy (*allergic inhalant dermatitis*), a common itch-causing dermatitis. Inhalant allergies in principally white and buff colored Cockers are rather common. At one to three years, the first outbreak occurs between the spring and fall seasons. More females than males are affected. Genetic predisposition contributes to atopy.

Generalized itching initially begins without the presence of skin lesions. In chronic cases, the skin becomes very flaky, blackened, and thickened. Affected dogs lick their feet and rub their faces. Diagnosis is made by the clinical signs, from the time of year, and conclusively, by *intradermal skin testing*.

The treatment involves a combination of any or all of three forms of therapy. First, avoidance of the allergen will stop the observed signs. This, however, is sometimes impossible. Second, the use of systemic *cortisone* will stop the itching. When the offending allergens are in the air a relatively short time, cortisone provides excellent control. However, if the allergy season is longer than one month or if the dog is very sensitive to cortisone, *hyposensitization* or *immunotherapy* is recommended. In this form of treatment the allergen is administered in increasingly larger doses over a period of time with the hope that the body will become desensitized to the foreign protein. Dogs do not respond to antihistamine therapy for inhalant allergies as humans do.

Atopy can be controlled after the offending allergens are identified. Occasionally, the use of both cortisone and immunotherapy are necessary to provide relief from pruritus (itching).

AUTOIMMUNE SKIN DISEASES: Autoimmune skin diseases are uncommon skin disorders characterized by blistering and ulceration of the skin and mucous membranes. A variable amount of *pruritus* (itching) is present.

Four varieties of *pemphigus* are diagnosed in the dog. The most common, *pemphigus foliaceus*, involves general ulceration over the body. Often the foot pads become hardened and thickened. *Pemphigus erythematosus* is thought to be a more benign form of pemphigus foliaceus. The most virulent form is *pemphigus vulgaris* which usually produces lesions involving the skin, the oral cavity, and other mucous membranes. Its benign counterpart is *pemphigus vegetans*. *Bullous pemphigoid* is a closely related disorder. The diagnosis, clinical signs, and treatment are similar for all of the pemphigus diseases.

Two other autoimmune diseases seen in the dog are *systemic lupus erythematosus* and *discoid lupus erythematosus*. Systemic lupus is a very complex disease involving multiple organ systems such as the skin, kidneys, joints, and heart. Discoid lupus is always limited to skin lesions on the nose, face, and ears.

The diagnosis of autoimmune skin disease requires *biopsies, direct immunofluorescence testing*, ANA tests, and *direct smears* from lesions. These, coupled with history and clinical signs, formulate a diagnosis. All of these diseases are treated with very high levels of cortisone, anticancer drugs like *azathioprine* and *cyclophosphamide*, and *gold salt therapy*. Some cases require long courses of treatment with flare-ups being common. With the exceptions of discoid lupus and pemphigus erythematosus, the prognosis for these skin diseases is guarded for long term control.

BACTERIAL HYPERSENSITIVITY: Bacterial hypersensitivity is a very pruritic (itchy) skin disorder caused by a hypersensitivity to the antigens of the *Staphylococcus* bacteria. The swollen red pustules are very itchy. Many dogs with bacterial hypersensitivity are also *hypothyroid, atopic,* or allergic to some foods. The disease can be diagnosed by reading an *intradermal skin test* 24 to 72 hours after the test injection.

Management of this skin problem requires a combination of antibiotic therapy and injections of increasing amounts of Staph antigens. The most commonly used antigen products are Staphoid A & B® and Staphage Lysate (SPL)®. Good control can be obtained if the owner is diligent in the treatment of bacterial hypersensitivity.

BASAL CELL CARCINOMA: The basal cell carcinoma, more correctly termed basal cell tumor, is one of the most common benign tumors of the skin. This tumor is an ulcerated solitary nodule generally occurring on the dog's head and neck after the age of seven. Basal cell tumors are managed by any number of surgical removal methods. Since the tumor is benign, the prognosis is excellent.

BIOPSY, SKIN: The biopsy of skin aids in the understanding of skin diseases. A razor-sharp punch provides a circular 6 mm sample of the skin. In the case of a tumor, an excisional biopsy removes the entire growth. After the sample is removed, it is fixed in a preservative for further processing. Samples are prepared for routine microscopic examinations with formalin. Michel's media or freezing are used for *direct immunofluorescence testing.*

While biopsies may or may not provide definitive answers to the cause or diagnosis of skin disease, they do provide the clinician with an assessment of the current status of the skin. Biopsies can be taken by freezing the skin with a *local anesthetic.* However, samples from the nose and mouth require *general anesthesia.*

BULLOUS PEMPHIGOID: See *AUTOIMMUNE SKIN DISEASES.*

BURNS: Both full thickness and partial thickness burns occur in the dog. In a partial thickness burn, the entire thickness of the skin has not been destroyed making healing faster and complications less likely. Full thickness burns destroy the underlying nerves and connective tissue as well. The underlying tissues are subject to massive bacterial infections. The major secondary problems from full thickness burns include infection, *kidney failure,* respiratory difficulty, shock, and *anemia.* Even when the complications are successfully managed, healing is a long painful process. The amount of nursing care for a burn patient is tremendous. Extensive burns require costly, time-consuming periods of healing.

The prognosis for full thickness burns covering 25% or more of the body is poor to fair. Partial thickness burns have a better prognosis and depend to some degree on the amount of burned tissue present.

CALCINOSIS CUTIS: Calcinosis cutis is a rare skin disorder usually associated with too much circulating *cortisone* or *diabetes mellitus*. The causes can, however, range from cancer to kidney disease. Clinically, inflamed bumps which feel gritty appear in the skin. Some infection may be evident around the gritty plaques. These raised areas are calcium salts that have been mistakenly deposited in the skin tissues. Calcinosis cutis can be reversed when the underlying cause is controlled or eliminated. Two to four months are required for the calcium plaques to be resorbed. See *CUSHING'S DISEASE* and *CALCINOSIS CUTIS* in Chapter 4.

CALLUS: Callus formation is a normal body reaction to trauma over pressure points. The most commonly affected areas are elbows, hocks, and breast bone. If trauma continues, the callus becomes infected as the thickened tissue cracks and ulcerates.

The hard surface causing the trauma should be removed. Cushions, water beds, and padded chest and elbow wraps are helpful in correcting callus build-ups. Daily applications of Vitamin A and D ointment help to soften the calluses. In rare instances, surgery is required to remove the callus. Potential complications to this surgery include hemorrhaging, sutures that don't hold well, and difficulty in immobilizing the affected area which slows down healing.

CHEYLETIELLA MANGE (WALKING DANDRUFF): Dogs, cats, humans, and rabbits are all affected by Cheyletiella mange caused by a large mite. Because owners may also complain of red, itching welts, this condition is of public health significance. The mite does not burrow through the skin layers but lives on the dead skin surface keratin. Puppies will exhibit a yellow scurf over the entire length of the back with variable degrees of itching. This mite can live its entire life on one dog and remain alive off the host for three or four days.

The condition is diagnosed by observed signs and finding the mite on superficial *skin scrapings* from the dog. This form of mange is easily treated with three weekly insecticide shampoo baths. During the bathing process, the environment should also be treated to remove any free living mites. Prognosis for recovery is excellent.

CHIGGERS: About twenty species of chigger mites are capable of causing dermatologic disease. In most cases, they are a seasonal problem of late summer and fall. These mites are orange-brown in color and can be seen by the naked eye. The affected areas are very itchy with raised red bumps.

Treatment consists of the use of various insecticide products over a two or three week period. The dog should not be returned to the environment from which the chigger infestation was obtained until later in the fall season. On occasion, *cortisone* is used for several days to minimize the itching during insecticide treatment. Prognosis for a full recovery is excellent.

CONGENITAL ALOPECIA: Congenital alopecia is hair loss at birth or shortly after birth. Color mutant alopecia is part of this group of hair loss conditions. Occasionally in puppies, balding patterns are related to hair color. In dogs with black and white hair coats, the black hair becomes sparse while the skin becomes scaly.

CULTURE, BACTERIAL AND FUNGAL: Obtaining bacterial and fungal cultures is part of any thorough dermatologic case work-up. *Bacterial cultures* are taken with sterile swabs from pustules and from under crusts or other lesions. The swab is either placed in a transport media or streaked on appropriate culture media. After the sample is incubated, any growth is identified. An *antibiotic sensitivity test* is then prepared from the culture growth. The time necessary to do a bacterial culture and antibiotic sensitivity test ranges from 36 to 72 hours. Most bacteria grow out in 18 to 36 hours. A second culture is necessary for the antibiotic sensitivity test portion.

Fungal cultures are taken from diseased hair and scale near the edge of a skin lesion. They are inoculated in an appropriate media and incubated at room temperature for a period of up to four weeks. Most of the common *dermatophytes* (skin disease producing fungi) start to grow in four to seven days, but since some uncommon varieties have a longer incubation period, the culture is routinely kept for the full four weeks.

CUTANEOUS LEISHMANIASIS: Cutaneous leishmaniasis is common in the temperate Mediterranean region and in Africa. Although a rare disease in the United States, it has been diagnosed in Florida and Oklahoma. A *protozoan parasite* spreads the disease to susceptible dogs by an insect bite. The clinical lesions are itchy, red, or ulcerated nodules commonly on the abdomen, inner thighs, head, and ears. The diagnosis is made from a *skin biopsy* and a *serological blood test*. The standard treatment for leishmaniasis is an *antimony* compound given intramuscularly. Because these drugs are not routinely used in the United States, they must be ordered through the Parasitic Diseases Drug Service of the Center for Disease Control in Atlanta, GA (404 / 329–3670). Treatment periods of six weeks are not uncommon. The prognosis for a cure is good if the disease is diagnosed early in its development.

CUTANEOUS LYMPHOSARCOMA: Cutaneous lymphosarcoma is a rare form of fatal skin cancer in either sex of older dogs. Some breed predilection has been found. Cutaneous lymphosarcoma may consist of a solitary nodule or, more commonly, as multicentric lesions with generalized red, scaly, itchy skin. While some cases advance rapidly, others become more chronic in nature. In either case, a fatal outcome will result unless an individual nodule can be successfully removed.

Cutaneous lymphosarcoma is usually diagnosed by repeated *skin biopsies*. *Mycosis fungoides*, one form of the disease, requires multiple biopsies to diagnose. While no treatment will cure the cancer, nitrogen mustard has been used to prolong life. If this compound is used, gloves must be worn by the owner when handling the dog. The prognosis for long term recovery is poor.

DANDRUFF: See *SEBORRHEA*.

DEMODICOSIS (RED MANGE): Demodicosis is an inflammatory skin disease characterized by an *immune deficiency* condition and a larger than usual number of *Demodex mange mites* on the skin. A few demodectic mites are found on normal skin. One of the two types of demodicosis is localized involving a small, scaly, hairless area of skin. These lesions, commonly found on the legs or face, do not seem to itch very much. Clinical features of localized mange are circumscribed, scaly, red areas that may or may not itch. The majority of these cases will regress once any stress is over. However, a small percentage will become generalized if not treated. For this reason, all cases must be treated even if spontaneous regression is anticipated.

Generalized demodicosis has three subtypes: juvenile onset (3 to 12 months), adult onset, and chronic *pododemodicosis (foot mange)*. Most adult onset generalized cases of mange have either cancer or a serious systemic disease as a predisposing factor. The Cocker Spaniel rarely contracts generalized demodectic mange.

Generalized demodicosis is a very severe inflammatory skin disease which results in much *hair loss, pyoderma*, severe crusting on the skin, and deep infections in the hair follicles. The most severe lesions appear on the head and neck. Because of the tremendous inflammatory feature of this disease, many owners choose euthanasia.

The disease is diagnosed by *skin scrapings*. All cases of *seborrhea* and generalized skin disease should have a number of skin scrapings done to determine if demodicosis is present. All swollen foot lesions should be scraped.

The treatment and prognosis depend on the form of the disease. Most local cases will respond to *Goodwinol*® ointment applied daily to the lesions for several weeks. The prognosis is excellent if no new lesions are observed during treatment. Generalized demodicosis is treated with antibiotics for the secondary *pyoderma* and either weekly *Mitaban*® dips or the use of Scott's solution over a long period of time. Some generalized cases can only be controlled and not cured. If diligent treatment over a four month period has not resulted in a clinical cure, the *Demodex mites* will only be controlled in that individual. In those cases of stubborn *Demodex* infection involving the feet, *Mitaban*® should be added to mineral oil submersing the feet in the mineral oil-Mitaban® mix daily for 30 days. Recently, a report from Brazil indicated that 5,000 international units of *vitamin E* daily resulted in total cures of generalized demodicosis. Vitamin E therapy is unproven in the United States. Because the dogs are already immunosuppressed, under no circumstances should any kind of *cortisone* be given to dogs with generalized demodicosis! The prognosis for demodicosis has improved with the advent of Mitaban® (amitraz), but much supportive care is needed in seriously infected generalized cases.

DERMATITIS: A word that is widely misused, dermatitis itself actually means inflammation of the skin. In order to use the word properly, dermatitis must be modified with a descriptive term.

DERMATOPHYTOSIS: Dermatophytosis is a fungus infection of skin cells, nails, or hair caused by fungi of the species *Microsporum, Trichophyton*, or

Epidermophyton. The term *dermatomycosis* is sometimes used incorrectly yet interchangeably with dermatophytosis. Dermatomycosis is caused by fungi that are not members of the mentioned species of fungi.

The clinical appearance of a superficial fungus infection is extremely variable. Some forms of the dermatophytes (fungi) cause inflammation, hair loss, crusting, and scaling of the skin. In other cases, only a mild "breaking" of hairs and slight balding are observed. The term *ring worm* was so named because the fungus would attack the hair causing it to fall out as the fungus spread to the periphery of the circle. After a period of time, the hair in the center would start to grow in giving the appearance of a ring.

The superficial fungal diseases are best diagnosed by *fungal culture* and occasionally by direct observation of diseased hair under the microscope. Since fungi grow slowly, all fungal cultures are maintained for 28 days before being discarded as negative. A few dermatophytes fluoresce under the *UV light* of the Wood's lamp. However, less than 50% of the *Microsporum canis* species do this. A negative Wood's lamp reading is not reason enough for rejecting a diagnosis of superficial fungus infection.

If only a few small circumscribed areas are present on the Cocker, treatment of superficial fungus infections can be topical. *Miconazole nitrate, clotrimazole,* 1:20 *Captan* dips, and *Weladol*® shampoo are effective topical fungicidal agents. If a generalized fungus infection is present, oral systemic medication is needed to eliminate the dermatophytosis. *Griseofulvin* in the microcrystalline form is recommended. The gut absorption of the griseofulvin is enhanced with a high fat meal. **Under no circumstances** should griseofulvin be given to pregnant dogs because it causes fetal abnormalities. At least two weeks are required for this drug to reach the hair shaft, making quick cures impossible. A cure can vary from four weeks to nine months. The drug should always be given for two weeks longer than clinically deemed necessary. *Ketoconazole*, a new antifungal drug used to treat dermatophyte infections, may have some effect on a dog's fertility. Because of its expense, use is limited to cases where griseofulvin is found to be ineffective.

With the exception of fungus infections of the claw, the prognosis for curing superficial infections is good. *Nail bed infections* may require systemic griseofulvin for as long as a year to effect a cure. In rare cases, the surgical removal of the claw is necessary to cure the fungus infection.

DIRECT IMMUNOFLUORESCENCE TESTING: Direct immunofluorescence testing is done on *skin biopsy* samples to determine if an *autoimmune skin disease* is present. Biopsy samples are submitted in *Michel's media*. A positive DIT will reinforce the diagnosis of an autoimmune skin disease. This very complicated test is currently done in only a few testing labs.

DISCOID LUPUS ERYTHEMATOSUS (DLE): Lesions of discoid lupus erythematosus are confined to the face, most commonly involving the nose. Many dogs previously diagnosed as having *"Collie nose"* are probably discoid lupus cases. Scarring is common. Ultraviolet light rays aggravate the condition.

Solar screens are helpful in the treatment. *Vitamin E* oil has also been used successfully. *Cortisone* preparations help to control the condition. The response to treatment is good but therapy must be maintained for as long as the life of the dog. Also see *AUTOIMMUNE SKIN DISEASE.*

DRUG ALLERGY: A drug allergy can also be termed a *drug idiosyncrasy.* Individual dogs react to *penicillin* in an allergic manner requiring prompt treatment. Some breeds show increased sensitivity to certain drugs. *Trimeth-sulfa,* for instance, causes *dry eye, polyarthropathy,* and *thrombocytopenia,* among other things.

ECZEMA: For a long time the word eczema has been misused by referring to any deviation from normal skin as eczema. The actual definition is an inflammatory, superficial skin disease that, in its early stages, is red, swollen, oozing, and crusting, and later becomes scaly, red-purple, thickened, and possibly pigmented.

ENDOCRINE ALOPECIA: The hormone (endocrine) system in the body has a profound affect on skin and hair coat health. Most hormone disturbances affect the skin by causing a symmetrical baldness. Usually the remaining hair coat becomes dry and brittle and is easily pulled out. The clipped coat will not regrow in an affected dog. Generally, increased pigment is observed in the bald areas on the skin. Most hormone skin disturbances are not itchy. However, exceptions do occur when other factors complicate the clinical signs.

ENDOCRINE DERMATOPATHIES: The following is a list of endocrine dermatopathies. Each is discussed individually with the text of the book.

Cushing's disease (hyperadrenocorticism)   Ovarian imbalance, type I & II
Diabetes mellitus   Pituitary dwarfism
Growth hormone responsive dermatosis   Sertoli cell tumor
Hypothyroidism   Testosterone—responsive dermatosis
Male feminizing syndrome

ERYTHEMA: Erythema is a redness of the skin produced by congested capillaries.

EXTERNAL PARASITES OF THE SKIN: The following is a list of the external parasites of the skin. Each is discussed within the chapter unless otherwise indicated.

Cheyletiella mange   Hookworm dermatitis
Chiggers   Lice
Demodicosis   Pelodera Strongyloides
Ear mite otitis—See Chapter 10   Scabies
Fleas   Spiders—See Chapter 9
Flies   Ticks—Also see Chapter 7

FATTY ACID DEFICIENCY: The signs of a fatty acid deficiency are most common in dogs fed only people foods and those exclusively on a dry dog food diet. While most dog foods have the proper amount of essential fatty acids present at the time of manufacture, the product can deteriorate in storage. The food must be stored in a cool area to prevent rapid oxidation of the added fat. Long term storage, however, can cause the fat coating of dry dog food to decompose. The presence of antioxidants like *vitamin E* are important to prevent rancidity. Within six months from time of production, the fat coating is no longer nutritious.

Several months of low essential fatty acid intake will cause dermatological changes. The hair coat becomes dry and dull. The hair falls out. The skin becomes thicker with evidence of itching and scaling. Fatty acid deficient dogs have a greater tendency to develop *hot spots*. The skin and ears become greasy, filling with wax more frequently. Because the normal lipid film on the skin changes, a dog deficient in essential fatty acids is more prone to the development of *pyoderma*.

Providing *essential fatty acids* is important to good skin health. The dog can convert linoleic acid into all of the fatty acids needed. At 70%, safflower oil provides the greatest amount of unsaturated essential fatty acids. Other fats provide the following percentages: corn oil, 59%; pork fat, 30%; chicken fat, 24%; and beef tallow or butter, 3%. Pet Tab® FA with zinc-liquid and EFA-Z Plus® are two superior commercial products. Both products are better balanced than vegetable and animal fats alone. Each can be obtained from veterinarians. Three weeks to three months of essential fatty acid supplementation are required before a change is seen in the skin. The prognosis is excellent with continued supplementation. Also see Chapter 8 on *NUTRITIONAL MANAGEMENT*.

FIBROSARCOMA: Fibrosarcomas originate from the subcutaneous or dermal connective tissue (under the skin layer). These tumors are usually solitary, poorly defined, rapidly growing ulcerated masses appearing anywhere on the body and rapidly infiltrating the surrounding tissues. About 25% will metastasize (spread) to other areas of the body. Wide surgical excision is recommended. Chemotherapy and radiotherapy are of limited value. About 30% of excised tumors will recur locally. Fibrosarcomas are common in older female Cocker Spaniels.

FLEA COLLAR DERMATITIS: The most common cause of flea collar dermatitis is the tightness of the collar around the neck. A minimum of a two fingers distance is essential between the collar and the skin. This type of dermatosis is more common in very short-coated breeds. Some dogs are very sensitive to the polyvinyl plastic collars while others are irritated by the insecticide chemical impregnated in the collar.

These red, raised, ulcerated areas appear near or under the collar initially, becoming thickened and crusty in chronic cases. The lesions can spread over the entire body.

The treatment involves removing the flea collar and treating any signs of insecticide toxicity. See *INSECTICIDE POISONING* in Chapter 9. The acute skin lesions are treated with wet dressings or astringents. Use of *cortisone* ointments is helpful. In severe cases, hospitalization and intensive therapy are required.

Recovery is usually complete although occasional scarring can be evident in Cocker Spaniels. Other forms of flea control are more reliable.

FLEAS: Fleas are small wingless insects that live up to a year in an optimum environment consisting of a suitable host (the dog) and high temperature with humidity. The higher the temperature and humidity, the more efficient the flea life cycle becomes, completing itself in as little as two weeks. The flea is incriminated in the transmission of a *tapeworm* in the dog. Fleas do not live in altitudes over 5,000 feet above sea level.

The flea also causes *flea bite dermatitis (flea hypersensitivity)*, the most common skin problem observed in dogs. A dog not sensitive to the flea saliva will not acknowledge the presence of fleas. No irritation or itching is present until the dog becomes sensitized to the flea saliva. The hypersensitive state usually develops between three and six years of age but with proper exposure can occur as early as the first year. At that time, a hypersensitive state is produced in which the dog reacts with severe itching. A raised, crusty skin lesion most commonly found on the posterior part of the back near the tail, on the back part of the thighs, and on the belly is seen. This intense *pruritus* (itching) also initiates *acute moist dermatitis (hot spots)* with hair loss and scaling. Flea allergy dermatitis is seasonal in climates with cold winters and on outside dogs. Dogs from warm climates and those that live in the house exhibit the problem through the entire year.

The diagnosis of the flea bite allergy is made from the location and appearance of the skin lesions and by finding evidence of fleas. This evidence may be an actual flea or the presence of flea dirt. Flea dirt is actually flea excrement (dried blood) that appears on the skin as a black, gritty material. An easy test for flea dirt is the placement of several particles of black grit on a white piece of paper. Add a small drop of water and rub with a toothpick. Since it is actually dried blood, genuine "flea dirt" turns the water red. Once the diagnosis of flea bite dermatitis (allergy) is made, the treatment is directed toward eliminating the fleas from the environment and the dog. Since fleas only spend about 10% of their life on the dog feeding, the environmental treatment is very important. While the flea population is being brought under control, use of *cortisone* may be necessary to relieve the allergic signs present in the dog. Some dermatologists and veterinary allergists have good luck desensitizing dogs to flea antigen. Most, however, don't feel the hyposensitization therapy works well in flea allergy.

Flea control must be individualized to each dog and environmental situation. The following are general observations about various flea control products and procedures. Flea shampoos are generally worthless because they lack any residual activity. Some flea dips with residual activity lose it rapidly if the dog gets wet. *Brewer's yeast* and *vitamin B_1* are not effective in flea control. Generally, *flea collars* are ineffective on most dogs. *Spotton®* is used in the Southern United States for flea control. Most effective at a concentration of 20%, it is dangerous and is not government approved for use on dogs. Humans may have toxic reactions to the treatment. *Pro-Spot®*, the counterpart of Spotton®, is cleared for use in dogs but its lower concentration makes it less effective.

The most effective management of fleas involves the use of premise sprays and foggers at timely intervals coupled with the use of a good insecticide spray on the dog EACH time it goes outside. Many flea sprays contain pyrethrums which are effective flea killers. Pyrethrum is derived from the chrysanthemum, a member of the ragweed family. Some dogs have *inhalant allergies* to ragweed that will cross react with pyrethrum flea products causing increased itching and redness.

FLY BITE DERMATITIS: Several types of dermatological problems occur from fly bites. A problem common in late summer in young puppies is the presence of a circular hole surrounded by a swollen area beneath the skin. The *Cuterebra fly larva* can be seen moving through the skin opening. The hole is enlarged to remove the larva with a forceps without crushing it. Serious inflammatory reactions can result from crushed larva.

More common are stable fly bites on the nose and ear tips. The inflamed crusted areas on the ear tips are usually seen in the summer. The flies can be seen landing on the ears or nose. The lesions are treated with an anti-inflammatory cream or ointment. A repelling insecticide gel like Pet Guard® gel is applied as needed during the fly season.

FLY STRIKE (MAGGOT INFESTATION): Fly strike (maggot infestation), a disease of negligence, is much more common in long-haired dogs that have soiled the area under their tails with stool and urine. This damp dark area is an ideal environment for flies to lay eggs which hatch into larvae (maggots) that feed on the skin. The skin has a punched out appearance as the maggots quickly proliferate. The dog becomes systemically ill from the degenerating toxic skin products poisoning their system.

Treatment requires veterinary care for complete removal of all maggots, to clip the hair from the affected area, and for topical and systemic treatment of the severely diseased skin. Prognosis for recovery is good if treatment is started early and maggot removal is complete.

FOLLICULITIS: Folliculitis is an inflammation within the hair follicle. The pruritic superficial form has a very itchy yet superficial clinical feature. This form is very common in the Cocker Spaniel.

This itchy disease is detected by the presence of pustules with hair growing out of the pustule. The area around the lesion can be severely inflamed. As the lesion ages, a target or bull's-eye pattern is formed. The outer circle is red with a scaly inner region and a darkly pigmented center.

The exact cause of this disease varies from *bacterial hypersensitivity* to nutritional deficiency to hormone imbalances like *hypothyroidism*. The diagnostic test work-up includes *skin biopsies, staphylococcal antigen skin testing, skin scrapings,* and *bacterial cultures* and *fungal cultures.*

The management of folliculitis can be troublesome because of its tendency to recur. If bacterial allergy is found, hyposensitization or elimination of the bacterial cause should be attempted. *Cortisone* is contraindicated because it cuts down on sebum (skin oil) production further aggravating the condition. Antibiotic therapy is used at full dosage for one to two months. Bathing with a good quality follicle-flushing shampoo is done weekly during treatment. If relapses occur following the cessation of antibiotic therapy, *hyposensitization* for the Staph antigens should be considered. Prognosis for complete recovery is guarded. Many cases will require occasional bathing, nutritional supplementation, and antibiotic therapy.

FOOD ALLERGY: Food allergy (hypersensitivity) is an uncommon problem causing nonseasonal itching in any aged dog. Puppies as young as six months are affected. More commonly, these allergies are seen in dogs that have been on the same diet for over two years. A food allergic reaction to any kind of meat, milk, eggs, cereal grains, fish, potatoes, rice, and soybean can develop. The dog must have had previous exposure to the offending food in order to develop hypersensitivity to it.

The diagnosis for this cause of itching skin is made by placing the dog on a *hypoallergenic diet.* This is a single form of food to which the dog has had little or no previous exposure. This diet must be strictly maintained for three weeks. The dog should drink only distilled water. The whole diagnostic procedure may yield faster results if three cleansing enemas are administered during the 48 hour fast at the beginning of the three week diet. A commercially prepared hypoallergenic diet called *D/D*® diet or a homemade lamb or mutton and rice mixture can be used to feed the affected dog. During the test period, no supplements, vitamins, or heartworm chewable tablets are given. Results (less itching) are observed in five to seven days in many cases. However, in some cases, up to fourteen days may pass before a significant decrease in itching and red skin lesions is noticed. If at the end of the three week feed trial the itching decreases significantly, an individual food item is added weekly. For instance, Wheat Chex® could be added to the hypoallergenic diet as a source of wheat. After one week with no increase in itching, Cheerios™ could be added as a source of oats. Each addition is tested for one week. By following this procedure, a list of nutrients that do not cause food hypersensitivity can be compiled and used in an every day diet.

The prognosis for controlling food allergy is good providing the offending allergen can be identified. Many food allergy problems are poorly responsive to *cortisone.* Because *prednisolone* does not control an itchy food allergy dog very well, identifying the cause of the hypersensitive state is more effective.

FOOT DISEASES: Diseases involving the feet, foot pads, and nails are very difficult to control or cure. If a well thought out treatment program is to be undertaken, making a definite diagnosis is important. The following conditions involve the feet, interdigital (between the toes) areas, and the foot pads: *atopy, contact dermatitis, demodicosis, dermatophytosis, hookworm dermatitis, interdigital foreign bodies, rhabditic larvae dermatitis, pemphigus,* and *pododermatitis.* See each topic individually for a complete discussion.

FROST BITE: Cockers that are either not acclimated to a very cold climate or have been left outside for several hours in sub-zero temperatures are most likely to suffer frost bite.

The signs of frost bite vary. A mild case is evidenced by a very light redness and scaling. Total death of the cells at the ear tips results in necrotic sloughing of the tissue and very slow healing. Hair near the affected areas can turn white in response to extreme cold.

If the ear tips are pale and cold to the touch, they should be gently bathed in warm water to return the tissues to a normal temperature as quickly as possible. Severe loss of tissue may necessitate the surgical removal of dead flesh and plastic repair of unsightly defects. Surgery should not be done too quickly because more tissue may be saved than originally anticipated.

FUNGUS INFECTIONS: Fungus infections of the skin are classified as *dermatophytosis* (superficial fungal infections) and *deep fungal infections.* Deep fungal infections are primary infections of other body organs, secondarily involving the skin. These primary infections include *blastomycosis, cryptococcosis, mycetoma, sporotrichosis,* and *phaeohyphomycosis.* A more complete discussion of most of these conditions can be found within the book.

GENERIC DOG FOOD SKIN DISEASE: With the advent of generic dog foods, a specific skin disease related to nutritionally deficient generic food has been observed. Signs of the disease are similar to *zinc deficiency skin disease.* A bilateral symmetrical loss of hair with crusting on the nose, pressure points (elbows), and on the feet becomes apparent. Severely affected dogs run a fever and have swollen lymph nodes. A rapid clinical response is seen when the dog is fed a good quality dog food instead of the generic dry food. Changes are observed within one week. The prognosis for recovery is excellent providing the good quality food is continued.

GROOMING: The methods of grooming Cocker Spaniels for show are beyond the scope of this book. Many good references for this information are available. Personal communication with individuals involved in dog showing can also provide many helpful insights.

To keep a Cocker pet looking its best, clipping should be done every three to four months. The necessary tools for Cocker grooming of a pet include an electric clipper with several different blades, a natural bristle brush, steel combs, and scissors. Because the skin under the tail is very sensitive, only a scissors should be used in that area. A soothing lotion like Vaseline® Intensive Care® lotion is very helpful in avoiding serious burns associated with grooming. Dead woolly undercoat should be removed with a brush and comb before bathing to avoid the formation of a felt-like mat of the undercoat. Daily brushing is beneficial in maintaining a healthy Cocker Spaniel coat.

GROWTH HORMONE SKIN DISEASE: Although the Cocker Spaniel has not been diagnosed with growth hormone skin disease, it can occur in any breed. Found more frequently in male dogs, this condition is usually first observed between the ages of one and three years. Except for the presence of skin disease, the dog is normal.

The signs are typical of a hormonal skin problem with bilateral symmetrical hair loss, generally no itching, soft skin, and hair left on the head and legs. The skin is *hyperpigmented* and any hair left in affected areas of the body is easily epilated (pulled out). The condition can be diagnosed by *growth hormone stimulation tests* using the drugs *xylazine* or *clonidine* to stimulate growth hormone release from the pituitary gland.

Treatment is growth hormone replacement which is in short supply today. However, growth hormone replacement is being genetically engineered and will be more readily available within five years. Treatment is usually for life with periodic injections. Some dogs treated with growth hormone will develop *diabetes mellitus* as a side effect to the growth hormone therapy.

HAIR DISEASE: Signs of diseases involving the hair coat can exhibit any of the following four clinical changes: change in the color of the hair, broken hair shafts, easily removed hair (can be pulled out of skin with no effort), and loss of sheen to the hair shaft. Certain nutritional deficiencies alter the color of the hair coat or can change the type and consistency of the protein in the hair.

HAIR LOSS: See *ALOPECIA.*

HEMANGIOPERICYTOMA: Female Cocker Spaniels over the age of six are affected by hemangiopericytoma (*spindle-cell sarcoma*), a common benign skin tumor. Appearing on the limbs as solitary well-circumscribed nodules, they range in size from 1 to 10 inches (2 to 25 cm) in diameter. Surgical excision is the preferred treatment. Within four years, about 25% will recur at the site of incision.

HISTIOCYTOMA: The histiocytoma is a rapidly growing benign skin tumor in young adult dogs. An orange button-like growth appears on the head, ears, and legs. When examined by a human pathologist, a malignant diagnosis is given. Veterinary pathologists recognize that although the tumor appears malignant, the growth is benign and will regress and disappear with no treatment.

Surgical removal is optional. After approximately four to six months the tumor will completely disappear on its own, leaving no scar. Cocker Spaniels have a predisposition to histiocytomas.

HIVES (ANGIOEDEMA): Hives (*urticarial angioedema*) is an uncommon hypersensitive reaction which can occur in dogs. Swelling within the skin layers can occur in the muzzle, ears, area around the eyes, or on the body and extremities. While some of these wheals (swellings) are very itchy, others exude serum or blood. If the respiratory system is involved, the larynx and trachea can swell closed causing death from asphyxiation.

The causes of hives are varied. A partial list includes some antibiotics, various kinds of food, stings from insects and arachnids (spiders), sunlight, *Staph infections*, excessive heat or cold, *vaccines*, and *blood transfusions*. The hive reaction can be controlled with either *epinephrine* or *cortisone* injections. In severe cases, the dog should be hospitalized to watch for respiratory embarrassment. Antihistamines do not have any effect on this type of hypersensitive reaction. The prognosis for complete recovery is usually excellent with treatment and observation. Determining the cause of hives is hard. Consequently, avoiding the causative agent is equally difficult.

HOOKWORM DERMATITIS: Hookworm dermatitis is usually a disease of poor sanitation and a dirty environment. The third stage larva, especially of the *Uncinaria* hookworm species, can penetrate the hairless areas of the belly and groin region of the dog. These larva also penetrate the feet and elbows causing small, red skin lesions. The dog's chewing or licking of its feet indicates some itching is present.

The diagnosis is made by finding hookworm eggs in the feces and determining that the kennel sanitary measures are lacking. Treatment involves hookworm control both in the dog and in the environment to eliminate the infective larvae. VIP Hookworm Concentrate® or Borax™ at the rate of 10 pounds per 100 square feet of ground will kill hookworm larva. Borax™ also kills vegetation.

HORMONE HYPERSENSITIVITY: Hormone hypersensitivity is a rare itchy skin condition in which the intact dog has become reactive to its own sex hormones. While most cases occur in unspayed bitches, a male which has not been neutered can also be affected. *Testosterone, progesterone,* and *estrogen* are possible causes of the skin lesions. Clinical lesions are bilateral hair loss on the lower abdomen and groin area. This hair loss can extend up the backside of the rear legs. In chronic cases, the feet, face, and ears appear crusty and inflamed. Bitches usually exhibit enlarged nipples and vulva.

The diagnosis is made by clinical signs and skin testing the dog for sex hormones. The reaction is either immediate or delayed for 24 hours. Treatment produces dramatic improvement within seven to ten days after *castration* or *ovariohysterectomy*. The prognosis with treatment is excellent for complete recovery.

HORMONE SKIN DISEASE: A large number of hormones affect the skin and related structures. The hormones listed here are discussed individually in this chapter and in Chapter 4 on the *ENDOCRINE SYSTEM*.

While hormones have different functions and different target organs and cells, the clinical signs of hormone caused skin disease are similar. The first sign of hormone skin disease is a bilateral symmetrical (the same on both the left and right side of the body) *alopecia* (hair loss). A disturbance in pigment production in the skin generally is present in the form of *hyperpigmentation* or an increase to the skin layers. Increased skin pigmentation is noticeable in areas where the hair has fallen out. The hair coat in hormone skin disease is very dull and unhealthy in appearance. The hair can be easily epilated (pulled out). In cases where the coat has been clipped, the hair does not grow back or, at best, regrows very slowly. Generally speaking, hormone skin disease is not itchy. However, in chronic cases, *seborrhea* (dandruff) can be present producing *pruritus* (itching) from excessive flaking and secondary bacterial infections which occur on seborrheic skin.

Hormones associated with skin disease are *thyroid, glucocorticoids, growth hormone*, and *sex hormones*. Discussion of each of the individual hormones can be found within the book.

"HOT SPOT": See *ACUTE MOIST DERMATITIS.*

HYGROMA: A hygroma (*pressure point granuloma*) is the body's response to continued irritation to the skin and underlying tissue at the point of a bony prominence in the body. While the problem is more common in short-haired dogs that do not have long hair to cushion the bony points from environmental irritation, the condition does occur in the Cocker Spaniel. The most common areas for hygroma development are the elbows, hocks, and chest (keel bone).

The condition begins as a fluid-filled swelling under red, irritated skin at a bony prominence. A false sac (bursa) fills with fluid in an attempt to cushion the trauma area. Continued irritation causes the swelling to grow in size as the tissue thickens. If the inflammatory swelling grows large enough, joint function is impaired.

Early in the course of the disease, only padding the elbow and providing soft bedding are needed to eliminate the inflammatory reaction. However, as the condition becomes chronic, the use of surgical drains, antibiotics, and *cortisone* are necessary to bring this problem under control. Surgical drains can be very effective in the treatment of chronic large hygromas. The prognosis for resolution of the problem is fair to good depending on how well the hard environmental surfaces can be managed.

HYPERKERATOSIS: Hyperkeratosis, one sign of skin disease, is defined as an increased thickness in the cornified (horny) outer layer of the skin.

HYPERPIGMENTATION: Hyperpigmentation, a sign of skin disease, is an increase or excessive amount of melanin pigment in the epidermis layers of the skin. The presence of pigment is not diagnostic in chronic skin disease and hormonal imbalances. However, determining the normal level of skin pigmentation in your Cocker is important. This information will help you establish whether or not an increase in pigmentation has occurred.

HYPOPIGMENTATION: As a sign of skin disease, hypopigmentation is a decreased amount of *melanin* in the epidermal layer of the skin. Causes of hypopigmentation can be congenital or due to chemicals in plastic and rubber bowls, hormone disorders, or pigmentary disturbances in *immune-mediated skin diseases*

HYPOTHYROIDISM: Hypothyroidism can affect most body systems. Hypothyroidism signs of skin disease include bilateral hair loss, thickened cool skin, *hyperpigmentation*, itch or no itch, *seborrhea*, external ear infection, and *hypertrichosis* (retained hair so thick that it feels like a mat), and dull, dead, easily epilated (pulled out) hair coat. The Cocker Spaniel is at higher risk than the general canine public when it comes to developing a thyroid deficiency. Thyroid deficiencies take many forms each with a complex physiology. The two most important causes are *lymphocytic thyroiditis* (an autoimmune disease) and idiopathic *thyroid atrophy*.

The diagnosis of hypothyroidism requires blood tests. In many instances, the T_3 and T_4 serum values will confirm suspicions about clinical signs. On occasion, however, *TSH stimulation tests* must be performed and reverse T_3 and T_4 checked. Some veterinarians prefer to run therapeutic trials rather than blood tests. This is effective only if one can afford to wait up to six weeks to see changes in the skin.

Treatment is effective in over 90% of cases with *L-thyroxine* replacement (T_4). Treatment is administered once or twice daily for the life of the dog. *L-triiodothyronine* (T_3) is more expensive, less effective, and must be given three times a day. The prognosis for revitalizing a hypothyroid hair coat is excellent with appropriate therapy and patience.

ICHTHYOSIS: Ichthyosis is a congenital skin disease characterized by greatly increased *hyperkeratosis* involving all or part of the skin, nose, and foot pads. The life-long treatment must be done daily to keep the thickened skin hydrated and soft. Soaking baths are very therapeutic. The use of Humilac® is very beneficial because of the presence of lactic acid in a water base. Because there is no cure, controlling the symptoms is the best one can hope for with canine ichthyosis.

IMMUNE-MEDIATED SKIN DISORDERS: A list of immune-mediated diseases follows. Because most are rare, only *TOXIC EPIDERMAL NECROLYSIS* is discussed in this chapter. Other skin diseases in this group include *vasculitis*, *erythema multiforme*, *linear IgA dermatosis*, and *alopecia areata*. The triggering mechanisms of these diseases vary from drugs like antibiotics to *Staph folliculitis*. Some immune-mediated skin disorders have mild skin lesions while others like *TEN* (*toxic epidermal necrolysis*) can have a fatal outcome.

IMMUNOLOGIC SKIN DISEASES: An increasingly large number of immunologic skin disorders have been recognized in the dog. Those of importance are discussed individually and under *AUTOIMMUNE SKIN DISEASES* in this chapter. A complete list follows.

Bullous pemphigoid	Graft-versus host disease
Cold agglutinin disease	Pemphigus group
Dermatitis herpetiformis	Systemic lupus erythematosus
Discoid lupus erythematosus	

IMPETIGO: True impetigo is a superficial pustular dermatitis of young puppies most frequently affecting the skin on the abdomen. The hair follicles are not involved. The underlying predisposing causes vary from immune depression to parasitism, a dirty environment, and poor nutrition. Impetigo is usually caused by a *Staphylococcus* bacteria.

Treatment is necessary if pustular skin lesions have not spontaneously regressed within a week. A shampoo like Pyoben® or Sebalyt® used two or three times over two weeks will eliminate the infection. However, in rare instances, oral antibiotic therapy is necessary. *Culture* and *sensitivity testing* can be utilized to determine the underlying causes. If they are eliminated, the prognosis for complete recovery is excellent.

IMPRESSION SMEAR: The impression smear is a valuable aid in the diagnosis of skin disease. In this simple technique, the smear is stained with any Giemsa or Wright's stain. The smear demonstrates tumor cells, bacteria, fungi, and parasites. On rare occasions, immunologic diseases like *pemphigus* and *pemphigoid* are diagnosed by impression smears.

INTERDIGITAL CYSTS: The term interdigital cyst is an incorrect term since none of the problems which occur between and within the toes and foot pads are cystic. See *FOOT DISEASES* for a complete list of individual foot problems. Also see *PODODERMATITIS*.

IRRITANT CONTACT DERMATOSES: For a Cocker to react to a contact irritant, the offending material must have directly contacted a hairless or sparsely haired region of the body. The most easily accessible places are the abdomen and groin region, the axillae (armpits), and the area between the toes and foot pads. Cockers are less prone to various environmental contact irritants because of their thick hair coats that protect most areas of the body.

The following compounds can cause cutaneous irritation from casual or long-term skin contact: *acid* and *alkali*, soap and detergents, *flea collars*, weed sprays, and fertilizers. A more complete discussion of these compounds is found in Chapter 9 on *POISONING*.

The initial treatment of contact dermatitis is to remove the offending irritant from contact with the skin. After all residual irritant material is washed away with water, the extent of skin inflammation and damage can be determined. Treatment with Burrow's solution and *steroid* creams is continued until the skin has returned to normal.

KELOID: Keloid refers to a nontumorous growth of fibrous scar tissue, a term taken from human dermatology. However, in the dog, a keloid can occur following removal of skin tissue.

KERATOACANTHOMA: Keratoacanthoma (*intracutaneous cornifying epithelioma*) is a skin tumor common in younger adult dogs, occurring primarily in males under five. No cases in Cockers have been reported. Clinically, a claw or a nail appears to be growing out of a mass on the neck, shoulders, or back of the dog. This benign growth is generally surgically removed for cosmetic reasons. Once a dog has a keratoacanthoma, additional growths will probably appear throughout its life.

LICE: See *PEDICULOSIS* and *PARASITIC SKIN DISEASE*.

LICK GRANULOMA: See *ACRAL LICK*.

LIP FOLD PYODERMA: Lip fold pyoderma is a common skin infection associated with the mouth of the Cocker Spaniel. A complaint of severe halitosis from the fold of the lip skin is common. Because the covered tissue is kept moist, bacteria causes the skin to become infected. Various treatments exist. Benzoyl peroxide gel applied to the fold is effective. Oral antibiotics can be given for three weeks. Completely drying the muzzle and lips after drinking and eating produces results. However, all of these are only effective while being used. Cheiloplasty (the surgical removal of the lip fold) is the only permanent cure.

LIPOMA: Lipomas are common, benign skin tumors of older dogs, especially obese females over eight. Many of these masses of fat are found over the thorax. Although they are benign, they can become large enough to mechanically restrict muscle movement. The Cocker Spaniel breed is predisposed to developing lipomas.

Small growths are not removed. Most large growths peel out very well surgically. A new nonsurgical treatment involves the injection of a sclerosing calcium salt into the fatty tumor causing the fat cells to die and disintegrate. This may become an alternative to surgery. The prognosis from surgical removal or weight reduction is excellent.

LUPUS: See *DISCOID LUPUS, SYSTEMIC LUPUS*, and *AUTOIMMUNE SKIN DISEASE*.

LYME DISEASE: Lyme disease, caused by the bacteria *Borrelia burgdorferi*, is a tick-borne disease that affects several different organ systems in the body. While most cases of the disease are found in the northeastern United States and in Wisconsin, the incidence of the disease is rapidly spreading to all parts of the country. Although the deer tick is the primary vector for the disease; other ticks also carry the bacteria that causes the Lyme disease.

Signs of Lyme disease include *arthritis*, fever, and red round skin lesions. These lesions are red blotches about the size of a dime (1 to 2 cm) that suddenly appear on the abdomen. They are not raised above the surface of the skin, do not itch, and disappear shortly after medication is started.

The disease is diagnosed by *serological tests* done at state diagnostic laboratories or from *blood cultures* where the spirochete bacteria is isolated. Both humans and dogs are affected by this disease. Months after apparent recovery, heart or neurological involvement can be seen.

The treatment of choice for Lyme disease is *ampicillin* or *tetracycline* antibiotics three times a day for several weeks. A full recovery is expected if the medication is used for a long enough period of time.

MAGGOTS: See *FLY STRIKE*.

MALIGNANT MELANOMA: These highly malignant melanomas occur most frequently in male dogs nine years and older. Appearing as black growths on the skin or mucous membranes, the only treatment for malignant melanoma is wide surgical excision. Those effecting the tongue are especially malignant making early radical surgical excision necessary. Even with surgical intervention, the long term survival rate is very low with a poor to guarded prognosis. Of cases in the Cocker Spaniel, the black Cocker reports a greater increased incidence.

MAMMARY GLAND TUMORS: Mammary gland tumors technically are not neoplasms of the skin and related structures. Statistically, 60% of dog mammary gland tumors are malignant, indicating they will spread (metastasize) to the lymph nodes and the lungs. Mammary gland tumors are made up of different tumor elements with some so-called *mixed tumors* containing bone or cartilaginous tissue.

The tumor growth varies from a slow growing solitary nodule to a rapidly spreading mass not limited to one mammary gland. Most tumors spread only within the glands connected by the blood supply on one side of the body. When tumors are found across from each other, the disease has probably spread to other areas in the body. The incidence of mammary tumors in bitches spayed before their first heat is practically zero. Some mammary tumors are responsive to the *estrogen* hormone associated with heat. These tumors grow rapidly after the heat period is over.

Treatment of mammary tumors is surgical. Surgery varies from a lumpectomy to radical excision of the diseased mammary glands. The lungs should be radiographed before surgery to establish that no metastasis to the chest has taken place. The prognosis following surgery varies from excellent to poor depending on the amount of malignant tumor activity demonstrated by the neoplasm.

MANGE: A discussion of each of the following forms of mange can be found in either this chapter or Chapter 10.

> Cheyletiella mange (walking dandruff)
> Demodicosis (demodectic or red mange)
> Otodectic mange—See *EAR MITES* in Chapter 10
> Scabies (sarcoptic mange)

MAST CELL TUMOR: Mast cell tumors are generally solitary nodules of varying sizes which ulcerate early in their growth. The nodular growth is poorly defined because of the difficulty deciding where the tumor ends in the subcutaneous tissues. Mast cell tumors are found more frequently in short-haired breeds of dogs than in Cockers. Because mast cells produce the anticoagulant *heparin*, mast cell tumors are associated with poor blood clotting. In some cases, the diagnosis of a mast cell tumor is made from an appropriately stained *impression smear*.

The methods for handling each tumor depend on the clinical and microscopic appearance of the tumor. All mast cell tumors should be considered as potentially malignant! Early surgical removal is recommended. However, even with wide excision, about one-third of the tumors recur.

Four stages occur in the growth of mast cell tumors. Stage I with no evidence of spread to lymph nodes only requires surgical excision. In stage II, lymph nodes are also involved requiring both surgical removal of the tumor and radiation therapy. Stage III consists of infiltrating large multiple mast cell tumors. These are treated with *steroids* injected into the tumors and *cimetidine* to bind the mast cell histamine. The last stage, stage IV, has evidence of a spreading tumor to distant parts of the body requiring systemic *cortisone* (*steroids*) and *cimetidine*.

The prognosis for these tumors is guarded because many are malignant. The elaboration of histamine and heparin by the tumor cells causes additional problems.

NAIL DISEASES: Bacterial or fungal organisms can affect the toenails. *Paronychia*, usually caused by bacteria, is the inflammation of the tissue around the nail bed. However, systemic diseases like *pemphigus, systemic lupus*, and *demodicosis* can also involve the nail beds. Diagnosis of the cause of paronychia requires *fungal cultures* and *bacterial cultures, biopsies*, and *skin scrapings*.

Several conditions involve the nail itself. In *onychomadesis*, the hard nail is separated from the underlying nail bed. Infections, trauma, and immune diseases like *lupus* and *pemphigus* can contribute to this.

Onychorrhexis is the tendency for nails to break. The cause of the brittle nail problem is difficult to determine. If the problem becomes recurrent, the surgical removal of the defective nail may be necessary.

Onychomycosis is a fungal infection of the nail material. These infections are very difficult to clear up, requiring months of *griseofulvin* therapy to eliminate the fungus completely. If the condition recurs, surgical removal of the nail should be considered.

NODULAR PANNICULITIS: Nodular panniculitis is an uncommon subcutaneous skin condition. Multiple lumps are found over the back and sides. These lumps are less noticeable in longer-coated breeds like the Cocker. As the condition progresses, the lumps first ulcerate and then heal by scarring. Generally, the affected dog feels sick, has a fever, has no appetite, and is lethargic. The diagnosis is made by *biopsy*. Treatment is systemic *cortisone* or in some cases, *vitamin E* therapy. Once the lesions are gone, therapy is halted since most dogs will have a long-term remission.

NUTRITION RELATED SKIN DISEASE: Each of the following nutrition related skin disease subjects is discussed separately within the chapter.

Fatty acid deficiency	Vitamin A deficiency skin disease
Food allergy	Zinc responsive skin disease
Generic dog food skin disease	

OTODECTIC MANGE: See *EAR MITES*, Chapter 10.

PARASITIC SKIN DISEASE: Each parasitic skin condition is discussed separately within this chapter.

Chiggers	Fly bite dermatitis
Cutaneous leishmaniasis	Fly strike (maggot infestation)
Fleas	Hookworm dermatitis

Mange
    Cheyletiella (walking dandruff)
    Demodicosis (demodectic or red mange)
    Otodectic mange—See *EAR MITES* in
      Chapter 10
    Scabies (sarcoptic mange)

Pediculosis (lice infestation)
Rhabditic larvae dermatitis
Ticks

PEDICULOSIS (LICE INFESTATION): Two kinds of lice parasitize the dog. Both biting and sucking lice have a life cycle of two to three weeks and spend their entire life cycles on the dog. They can also transmit *tapeworm* to a dog.

Signs of pediculosis vary from none to severe agitation and itching. In rare cases, severe *anemia* occurs. Generally, the condition is easily diagnosed. Lice infestation is becoming rather uncommon because most dogs are bathed routinely in insecticide shampoos. Treatment is the use of either insecticide dips or shampoos twice two weeks apart. Reinfestation can be prevented by improving sanitation in the dog's environment.

PEMPHIGUS: See *AUTOIMMUNE SKIN DISEASE.*

PERIANAL ADENOMA: Cocker Spaniels have a higher incidence of perianal adenoma than the general dog population. This tumor affects the circumanal glands and related structures in old male dogs. These nodular growths can be either individual or multiple. While most are benign, some do grow large enough to mechanically block the rectum, making defecation difficult. When exposed to constant trauma from sitting, the growths tend to ulcerate. Because the tumor is very sensitive to male androgen (sex) hormone levels, *castration* is recommended. Over 95% of the tumors disappear within two months after castration.

PHOTODERMATITIS: Photodermatitis (*solar dermatitis*) is hypersensitivity to light. This condition is more common in regions with long days of intense sunlight. The nasal region is the most common area on the body to develop lesions. Early signs of solar dermatitis are redness and loss of hair. This progresses into crusting and scaling. Unattended, these lesions can develop into a *squamous cell carcinoma* form of cancer. The diagnosis must differentiate this problem from autoimmune diseases like *discoid lupus* and *pemphigus.*

The management of solar dermatitis involves protection from the sun. Keeping the dog out of the sun between 10 a.m. and 4 p.m. and using sunscreens on the skin protect the sensitive tissues from intense sunlight. Tattooing or magic marker application also provide protection. The prognosis is good if attention is paid to solar protection. Otherwise, after squamous cell carcinoma develops, the prognosis is poor.

PIGMENTATION DEFECTS: *Hyperpigmentation* and *hypopigmentation* are discussed earlier in this chapter.

Vogt-Koyanagi-Harada-like syndrome is a disorder caused by a rare combination of ocular disease and skin depigmentation. The same disease is found

212   COCKER SPANIEL OWNERS'

in both dogs and man. This is thought to be a response to a viral infection or an *autoimmune disorder*. The eye lesions and skin lesions are progressive and usually result in euthanasia is dogs. In some cases, early treatment with *cortisone* will stop the eye lesions and may cause reversal of the depigmentation process over a period of months. The prognosis is guarded even with an early, accurate diagnosis.

PODODERMATITIS: Pododermatitis is an inflammatory disease of the feet caused by any of several agents. Because the reason for recurrent pododermatitis is not well understood, a diligent attempt must be made to discover the cause. *Skin scrapings, bacterial cultures, fungal cultures, direct immunofluorescence, thyroid function tests, skin biopsies*, and *allergy testing* are necessary to discover the cause of pododermatitis. If a foreign body is suspected, a *radiograph* is also needed.

Inflammatory lesions on the feet are seen in Cocker Spaniels regardless of its sex. Pododermatitis treatment includes antibacterial therapy with whirlpool treatments containing antibacterial solutions. The feet are occasionally treated with topical antibacterial preparations and bandaging. If *demodicosis* is a problem, the mites must be eliminated before the feet will clear up.

The prognosis for effective treatment is guarded to poor unless the cause can be determined. If a specific cause is determined, the prognosis improves to fair to good. However, treatment may be for prolonged periods.

POSTPARTUM HAIR LOSS: See *TELOGEN EFFLUVIUM*.

PRURITUS: Pruritus, one of the signs of skin disease, is defined as itching. The following is a list of skin diseases causing pruritus.

Allergy reactions	Insect bites
Foreign bodies	Parasites
Infections	Psychogenic factors
Inflammation	Ulcerative disease

PSYCHOGENIC DERMATOSES: See *ACRAL LICK*

PYODERMAS: Deep and superficial pyodermas are bacterial infections of the skin and associated structures. The superficial pyodermas like *impetigo* and *folliculitis* involve the skin and hair follicle. Deep pyoderma affects layers beneath the skin including the subcutaneous tissues and deep sebaceous glands. A localized deep pyoderma is usually associated with foreign body (foxtails, awns) penetration of the tissues. Generalized deep pyodermas are secondary to systemic problems such as cancer, *immune deficiencies*, *hypothyroidism*, *hyperadrenocorticism (Cushing's disease)*, or *demodicosis*.

Superficial pyodermas are treated with an appropriate antibiotic and medicated shampoo. In general, the antibiotic should be continued for three to four weeks. Treatment of deep pyodermas must be directed toward correcting the underlying problem and utilization of aggressive antibiotic therapy for a minimum of six to eight weeks based on culture and sensitivity test results.

The prognosis for superficial pyodermas is good if therapy is continued long enough. Depending on the underlying cause and the type of bacteria causing the infection, the treatment of deep pyodermas has a guarded to good prognosis. Also see *LIP FOLD PYODERMA*.

RED MANGE: See *DEMODICOSIS*.

RHABDITIC LARVAE DERMATITIS: Rhabditic larvae dermatitis, also called *pelodera dermatitis*, is due to an invasion of the skin by a larva of the worm, *Pelodera strongyloides*. These parasites are found in marsh hay, straw, and rice hulls used for bedding. If a dog has direct contact with infested ground or bedding, red, raised, very itchy lesions on the abdomen develop. The hair follicles are inflamed. The lesions will become crusty from a secondary bacterial infection.

With a history of nonseasonal itching, rhabditic larvae dermatitis is diagnosed by *skin scrapings* and sometimes *biopsies*. An insecticidal dip and removal of the infected bedding results in a rapid recovery. Usually two weekly dips cure the dermatitis. The prognosis is excellent with appropriate treatment.

SARCOPTIC MANGE: See *SCABIES*.

SCABIES: Scabies is a highly contagious, extremely itchy skin disease caused by the mite, *Sarcoptes scabiei*. This mite lives on the skin, burrows into the skin layers, lays eggs in these burrows, and hatches out. This life cycle is complete in three weeks. Because the mite prefers areas of the body that are somewhat devoid of hair, early infestations are seen on the elbows, hocks, abdomen, and ears. However, as the entire dog becomes parasitized, red papules (bumps) and scaly lesions with hair loss become generalized. This mite will temporarily infest people! Many times the diagnosis is made because itchy, red bumps are found at the beltline of the owner or at other areas where clothing is tight. Dogs with scabies are extremely pruritic (itchy). Even *cortisone* has little effect at alleviating the scratching.

The diagnosis is made by *skin scrapings* although many dogs with negative skin scrapings still have scabies. The history of an intense, nonseasonal, *cortisone* unresponsive itch and human skin lesions make the diagnosis possible. Weekly insecticide dips for four to twelve weeks or for two weeks past the presence of any clinical signs compose the treatment for scabies. Although not cleared for use in scabies, *amitraz (Mitaban®)* is effective when done weekly or every two weeks for three dips. The safest treatment is lime-sulfur dipping. The odor is terrible but the dip is very safe. Little mite resistance has been observed. *Ivermectin* by injection is a new and effective treatment. Although not approved for dog use, one injection is reported to cure scabies. Normally, a complete treatment can take several months until all of the mites are dead and the life cycle is broken. All animals in contact with the infected dog should be treated. The kennel environment should also be cleaned thoroughly. Prognosis is good to excellent with adequate treatment.

SCALING SKIN: See *SEBORRHEA* and *SIGNS OF SKIN DISEASE*.

SEBACEOUS CYST: Most frequently found on the head, body, forelegs, and neck, sebaceous (epidermal) cysts are solitary skin growths containing a white cheesy material. Some sebaceous cysts are actually *sebaceous gland tumors.* Differentiation of a cyst from a tumor is important only if malignancy is suspected. Cysts should be surgically removed. If a cyst ruptures beneath the skin surface, a secondary infection and localized inflammatory reaction occurs. Antibiotics are used if secondary infection is present. While prognosis is excellent after the removal of an individual cyst, recurrence in other locations is the rule.

SEBORRHEA: Seborrhea is the most important skin disorder in the Cocker Spaniel. This chronic skin disease is characterized by a defect in the maturing process of skin cells. Actually, any process that causes the cells to mature more quickly than normal or affects the process of keratinization, skin gland (sebaceous gland) function, or the cohesiveness of the skin cells can cause signs of seborrhea. Excess scaling, which is sometimes greasy, is observed. Excess sebaceous gland activity can lead to skin infections.

The three forms of disease are classified by appearance: *seborrhea sicca* (the dry, scaling form), *seborrhea oleosa* (the greasy, waxy form), and *seborrheic dermatitis* in which both scales and greasiness are present with infections in the skin. The Cocker Spaniel is most commonly affected by seborrheic dermatitis.

After the disease is classified by cause, the distinction between the two general forms of seborrhea is made. Primary seborrhea results from hormonal dysfunctions, defects in fat metabolism, and unknown causes. All seborrheic Cocker Spaniels should be tested for *hypothyroidism.* Secondary seborrhea occurs after infestations from *external parasites* (anything from *demodectic mange* to fleas), or from *fungus infections,* cancer, *allergies, drug hypersensitivity, bacterial hypersensitivity,* and *autoimmune diseases.*

The typical seborrheic Cocker Spaniel is middle-aged, slightly overweight and rather itchy. The dog has the odor of rancid fat. Clumps of waxy skin cells cling to the base of the hair in some areas of the body. The ears contain a large amount of yellow-brown *cerumen* and smell foul. The trunk of the body exhibits large numbers of very itchy, circular, inflamed, crusty skin lesions which are a *superficial pyoderma. Pruritus* (itch) is due to the infection in the skin.

While normal skin has a turnover rate of twenty days, seborrheic skin cells turn over every three to four days. Seborrheic skin has a very high amount of free fatty acids on the surface. Normal skin has a protective covering of waxes, esters, sterols, and cholesterol, but virtually no free fatty acids. Normal skin has few bacteria while many pathogenic Staphylococcusbacteria are present on seborrheic skin.

Seborrhea therapy should include the use of medicated shampoos, nutritional supplements, treatment of seborrheic dermatitis infections with appropriate antibiotics, and possibly the use of certain hormones to decrease sebaceous gland activity. Medicated shampoos containing tar and sulfur help remove scale and debris from the skin and also decrease the amount of oil present on the surface. Tar is also antipruritic. A bathing interval of three days to two weeks helps control seborrhea. For maximum effect, lather the shampoo then leave it on the skin for 10 to 15 minutes. If the skin after removing the shampoo is very dry, use an emollient bath oil like *Humilac*® to add a light lipid protection to the surface. Clipping the Cocker coat to facilitate bathing is controversial. Some dogs do much better with a short clipped coat while others seem to have increased problems with seborrheic scaly plaques. After experimenting with both methods, settle on the most effective for your dog.

Environmental temperature and humidity are contributing factors in the flair up of seborrheic signs. Appropriate antibiotics help to control the *pyoderma* infection. To choose the best antibiotics for each case, cultures and *antibiotic sensitivity tests* are necessary. Dietary changes can play an important function in managing the seborrheic Cocker Spaniel. For instance, an obese, very waxy coated Cocker can be helped with a *low fat diet*. Adding *zinc* and *vitamin E* to the diet can also help in the control of the seborrheic dog. While *vitamin A* has been helpful in some dogs, it can be toxic so must be used with care. Also see *VITAMIN A DEFICIENCY SKIN DISEASE*. On occasion, *glucocorticoids* like *prednisolone* are necessary to decrease sebaceous gland activity. Usage should be limited to the smallest effective amount since a long term of therapy is anticipated.

Unless a primary cause of seborrhea is determined and eliminated, symptomatic treatment must be maintained throughout the life of the dog. While the prognosis for a cure is guarded, the prognosis for control ranges from fair to excellent.

SIGNS OF SKIN DISEASE: The following list of changes in the skin are signs of skin disease. Each is discussed separately within the chapter.

Acute moist dermatitis (hot spot)   Hypopigmentation
Alopecia (hair loss)   Ichthyosis
Erythema   Pruritus
Folliculitis   Scaling (See *SEBORRHEA*
Hives (Angioedema)   *& SIGNS OF SKIN DISEASE*)
Hyperkeratosis   Seborrhea (Dandruff)
Hyperpigmentation

SKIN SCRAPING: Skin scraping testing is used by the veterinarian to determine the cause of some dermatoses, especially the identification of certain types of mange. *Demodex mange mites* are easily seen while *sarcoptic mange mites* can be extremely difficult to scrape because they burrow and tunnel in the skin layers. Skin scrapings are also useful in some tumor identifications. Cutaneous *mast cell tumors* can be identified in this manner. Scraping hair and scale is also helpful in identifying fungi that cause skin disease.

SKIN TESTS: A number of skin tests are helpful in diagnosing the cause of skin disease. While general tests like *complete blood counts, urinalysis*, and chem screen blood panels help determine causes, specific skin tests may be necessary. Those listed below are discussed individually within the chapter.

Allergy testing
ANA test
Biopsy, skin
Culture, bacterial and fungal

Direct immunofluorescence testing
Impression smear
Skin scraping

SKIN TUMORS: Many tumors are related to the skin and associated structures. A list of those discussed in this text follows. The Cocker Spaniel has a breed predilection for those tumors in bold type.

Basal cell carcinoma
Cutaneous lymphosarcoma
Fibrosarcoma
Hemangiopericytoma
Histiocytoma
Keloid
Keratoacanthoma
Lipoma

Malignant melanoma
Mammary gland tumors
Mast cell tumor
Perianal adenoma
Sebaceous cyst
Sweat Gland Tumors
Trichoepithelioma
Warts (Papilloma)

SOLAR DERMATITIS: See *PHOTODERMATITIS.*

SWEAT GLAND TUMORS: Dogs are affected by a variety of sweat gland tumors. The male Cocker Spaniel eight years or older is predisposed. *Apocrine sweat gland tumors* have an affinity for the neck, head, and back. Generally benign, they appear as circumscribed solitary masses which can be mistaken for areas of *acute moist dermatitis* (*hot spots*) or *pyoderma* The uncommon *eccrine sweat gland tumors* are confined to the footpads. Treatment is a choice of either surgical removal, cryosurgery, electrosurgery, or benign neglect.

SYSTEMIC LUPUS ERYTHEMATOSUS (SLE): Approximately one-third of systemic lupus cases involve the skin. The type of skin involvement varies greatly. Excessive scaling (*seborrhea*), foot pad ulcers, *hyperkeratosis*, and ulceration at the lip-skin junction are common dermatologic signs of SLE. The diagnosis of lupus requires *ANA testing*, *biopsies*, and other lab data which must be compatible. Treatment is discussed in other chapters. Each treatment must be designed to fit the individual case. The prognosis is guarded to fair depending on the response to therapy. See Chapter 6 on *MUSCULOSKELETAL SYSTEM.*

TELOGEN EFFLUVIUM (POSTPARTUM HAIR LOSS): The phenomenon of hair loss after the birth of puppies occurs in the bitch. Telogen effluvium is not a diseased state of the hair coat. The loss is due to the action of programming hormones which causes most individual hair shafts to pass into telogen (the resting phase of hair growth). Normally, each hair shaft does this individually. The synchronized telogen hair stage causes most of the coat to fall out in a large group simultaneously. The reason most dogs have a more magnificent hair coat after puppies is because all of their hair follicles become active while growing back in a synchronized manner.

TICKS: The mouth of the tick attaches itself to dogs most commonly in the ear, under the front leg (armpit), and between the toes. Ticks can cause hypersensitive skin reactions, produce *tick paralysis*, and be carriers of a number of viral and rickettsial diseases. See *LYME DISEASE* in this chapter. Normally, ticks require three different hosts to complete their life cycle. However, the brown dog tick can complete its life cycle on the same dog making it difficult to break the life cycle of that tick species.

Tick removal is accomplished by first saturating the attached tick with rubbing alcohol and then using a tweezer or forceps to grasp the body of the tick. Steady traction will pull it out. The alcohol makes the tick release its hold as well as disinfecting the bite location. Insecticidal dips are effective in killing large numbers of ticks that can parasitize a dog during tick seasons in various parts of the country. Do not use kerosene, gasoline, or lighted cigarettes to remove ticks!

TOENAIL CUTTING: A proper, tight foot can be maintained by frequent toenail cutting or grinding. If nails are allowed to grow long, the toes spread and the foot loses its strength. Nails can be shortened by weekly cutting to the tip of the quick. This causes the quick to recede, allowing further cutting of the nails. Eventually the desired length is achieved. Radically cutting the nails causing the quick to bleed profusely is unwise since infection is a frequent sequelae. *Nail bed infections* can be very difficult to eliminate. The Dremel® hobby grinding tool can easily be used to grind the nails down to the quick. Weekly grinding takes less than five minutes after the desired length of nail has been achieved.

TOXIC EPIDERMAL NECROLYSIS (TEN): Toxic epidermal necrolysis (TEN) or *Lyell's disease* is a rare, painful ulcerative skin disease of dogs. An immune mediated response to drugs, cancer, infections, and other systemic disorders is the primary cause. The skin is painful. The dog is depressed with no appetite. While the initial actual lesion is a fluid-filled pocket, ulceration of the skin is the first observed clinical defect. A *skin biopsy* is necessary for the diagnosis of TEN. Large doses of *cortisone* and other supportive therapy are the recommended treatment. Recovery takes two to three weeks. The prognosis for recovery is guarded to fair. A death rate approaching 25% to 30% occurs.

TREATMENT OF SKIN DISORDERS: A large number of medications and forms of medications are used in the management of skin disorders. *Cortisone*, probably the most used and abused drug, comes in the form of pills, injections, salves, powders, and topical liquids. Its primary use is to control itching. While cortisone has antipruritic (anti-itch) and anti-inflammatory properties, it has some undesirable affects over the long term. Any corticosteroids taken either internally or applied topically to the skin can diminish the body's ability to fight infection. Its protein depletion effect on the body causes muscles to atrophy and the hair coat to become very sparse.

Some diseases do, in fact, require high doses of cortisone to control the effects of the disease. *Systemic lupus erythematosus* and the *pemphigus* class of skin conditions are examples. Use of cortisone for short-term seasonal allergy management is acceptable. However, repeated injections of potent corticosteroids to relieve an itchy dog create more risks than benefits.

Antibiotics are important drugs in skin disease treatment. If four to six weeks of routine antibiotic therapy does not eliminate an infection, *culture testing* and *sensitivity testing* should be considered to provide information on the most effective antibiotic on in vitro testing.

Medicated shampoos are necessary in the management of skin disease. Dogs with very sensitive skin do well with a hypoallergenic shampoo such as Allergroom®. The oxidizing agent benzoyl peroxide has a follicle flushing action in a type of medicated shampoo that is excellent in the management of *folliculitis*. Shampoos that help control excess scaling or *seborrhea* usually contain micronized tar, sulfur, and/or salicylic acid. The shampoos that contain tar are also antipruritic (anti-itch).

Hydrotherapy (soaking in water) is an excellent form of therapy for rehydrating dry skin. Combining a bactericidal liquid with warm water and adding a whirlpool action is very therapeutic for superficial skin disease.

The selenium sulfide present in some shampoos can be rather irritating even though it is a potent skin degreaser. Oils are sprayed on the coat or added to bath water to treat dry skin. While there are advantages to this form of therapy, if too much oil is used it soon becomes evident around the house. Astringent liquids are used to dry up *acute moist dermatitis* (*hot spots*). A mixture of tannic acid, salicylic acid, and alcohol makes an excellent astringent for this purpose.

The complete coverage of the subject of treatment for skin disease is too complex for a text like this. A veterinarian who specializes in skin diseases can assist you with further.

TRICHOEPITHELIOMA: The trichoepithelioma is a common skin tumor of Cockers older than five. The tumor arises from the hair follicle seeming to have a predilection for the back. Clinically, the round, raised, well-circumscribed tumor ranges from $1/4$" to 4" (0.5 to 10 cm) in diameter. Ulceration and loss of hair around the area are common but metastasis (spreading) is rare. Treatment is surgical removal or just observation.

VITAMIN A DEFICIENCY SKIN DISEASE: Two forms of vitamin A associated skin disease are observed in the dog. Although they appear the same, in one an absolute *vitamin A deficiency* exists while in the other, no actual deficiency of vitamin A is found even though the affected dog responds to oral vitamin A. Vitamin A deficiency causes *hyperkeratosis* (an increased thickness to the layers of the skin and foot pads) in addition to generalized scaling with circular thick crusty lesions. Increased hair loss may be seen.

Vitamin A responsive dermatosis has been reported in the Cocker Spaniel. See *VITAMIN A RESPONSIVE DERMATOSIS*. Today, however, with the availability of vitamin supplements and good dog foods, a true deficiency is unlikely because the liver is able to store adequate amounts of vitamin A.

VITAMIN A RESPONSIVE DERMATOSIS: A distinct skin disease which responds to moderately high doses of vitamin A is seen in the Cocker Spaniel.

This skin disorder has no sex, age, or color predisposition. A severe *seborrheic dermatitis* and *ceruminous otitis* that is refractory to medical treatment characterizes the condition. The lesions primarily found on the chest and abdomen are circular hyperkeratotic plaques with severe follicular plugging. Because lab tests including the *thyroid function test* are normal, the diagnosis can only be made from a therapeutic trial with vitamin A.

The average size Cocker Spaniel is treated with 10,000 international units of *vitamin A* daily. If a correct diagnosis has been made, a complete clearing of the skin lesions occurs in 8 to 10 weeks. Failure to continue therapy at that level of vitamin A results in recurring hyperkeratotic plaques. Because of the difficulty in measuring vitamin A body levels and because no other signs of vitamin A deficiency occur, this condition is vitamin A responsive and not a true deficiency. Since there is a breed predilection, a genetic basis for this skin disorder probably exists. Further study is necessary.

A word of caution is necessary when using vitamin A. Its capability for being stored in the body in large amounts can cause death. Doses of vitamin A at 625 I.U./kg or approximately 10,000 I.U. daily for long periods of time appear to be safe. Use of synthetic vitamin A derivatives like *Accutane*® are potentially more toxic. Dosages should not exceed 3 mg/kg of body weight.

WALKING DANDRUFF: See *CHEYLETIELLA MANGE.*

WARTS (PAPILLOMA): Cocker Spaniels have a breed predilection for warts. The skin warts (*cutaneous papillomas*) caused by a virus usually surface in young dogs. After rapid growth for several months, the warts regress spontaneously with or without treatment. The cauliflower-like growths are seen primarily on the head and feet and in the mucous membranes of the mouth. In older dogs, males are affected more frequently. This form of warts is usually singular in number. Because most warts spontaneously regress in two or three months, treatment is cryosurgery, electrosurgery, wart vaccine usage, or benign neglect.

ZINC RESPONSIVE SKIN DISEASE: Two clinical syndromes responsive to zinc occur in dogs. Differentiating the signs is unimportant. In both cases, crusting plaques appear on the chin, ears, feet, foot pads, elbows, hocks, and other joints. These thickened, circular, inflamed lesions tightly adhere to the underlying skin. A generalized unthrifty coat appearance may also occur. Many of the affected puppies are sore and have fevers accompanied by swollen lymph nodes.

The disease is caused by either decreased absorption of zinc from the intestinal tract or a tying up of the zinc with phytates in plant protein found in dog food rather than from an actual deficiency of zinc in the diet. Over supplementation of *calcium* in growing puppies can also contribute to the syndromes.

Zinc responsive dermatoses are diagnosed by *biopsy* and lack of bacterial growth from a fresh lesion culture. Secondary infections may be observed if the lesion has been present for some time. Oral zinc supplementation is recommended. A very rapid response is seen when zinc is given two times daily through the growth phase of life. After the dog reaches 14 months, an attempt should be made to stop zinc supplementation. While some dogs do not need it as adults, others require zinc for life. The prognosis for normalcy is excellent with zinc supplementation and later without supplementation if the dog's system adjusts as an adult.

UROGENITAL SYSTEM

ABORTION: The term abortion applies when the pregnancy ends early with the expulsion of one or more fetuses. Four conditions cause this uncommon problem. Intrauterine infection may cause the death of the fetuses. As the tissues deteriorate, the dead fetuses and debris are discharged. If the level of *progesterone* and its relationship with other hormones associated with pregnancy is not normal, a pregnancy may be terminated early. Usually all fetuses and tissues will be expelled. The presence of a lethal gene which occurs from the combination of the sire's and dam's genetic pool may cause whelps to be born very prematurely so that life is not possible. Most commonly, physiological crowding in the uterus causes an interruption in the viability of the placental attachment of some fetuses. In this case, some of the occupants of the uterus may be aborted while others can be carried to full term. On occasion, at normal parturition, a dead, partially formed puppy may be presented. Probably this is one that was crowded and expired earlier but could not be aborted due to its position in the uterus.

The treatment of a bitch to prevent future abortion requires a definitive diagnosis of the cause of the present abortion. Most importantly, the sire should be changed for the next litter. If a lethal genetic combination occurred, an unrelated sire should eliminate this possibility. Prebreeding *vaginal cultures* may assess the potential for intrauterine death from infection. A *canine brucellosis test* should be part of the prebreeding preparation. If a recurrence of the abortion happens after the above changes, the circulating *progesterone* levels should be measured on a weekly basis during a subsequent pregnancy. Under no circumstances should progesterone injections be given without knowing the physiologic level during all phases of pregnancy.

ANASARCA (WATER PUPPY): Anasarca is a fetal abnormality that occurs in the Cocker Spaniel. These puppies are totally filled with fluid, hence the common name *"water puppy."* The skin and all body tissues are engorged with fluid. Because of the dramatic increase in the size of the puppy, normal delivery is unusual. Its presence is found on cesarean section. Not all puppies in a litter will appear as water puppies. Some of these puppies can be saved by using *furosemide*, a potent diuretic. Water puppies, if saved, should not be used for breeding purposes.

ARTIFICIAL INSEMINATION: Artificial insemination (A.I.) may be performed for a variety of reasons. Some bitches are either temperamentally or physiologically incompatible with certain stud dogs. With the advances in *frozen semen* technology, bitches can be inseminated with semen from stud dogs that have died years before or that live halfway around the world. Artificial insemination may also protect the stud or bitch from certain venereal diseases.

Most kennel clubs around the world have regulations to follow for artificial insemination procedures. These rules and regulations are directed primarily at the control and registration of litters derived from frozen semen. Before conducting an artificial insemination procedure, a letter to the American Kennel Club, 51 Madison Avenue, New York, NY 10010, requesting the current rules and regulations on artificial insemination is necessary. Most kennel clubs require the A.I. procedure to take place in the presence of or under the auspices of a veterinarian.

Several factors play a part in the effectiveness of artificial insemination in achieving conception. Because sperm are very easily killed, absolute asepsis is mandatory. All equipment must be sterilized by heat since chemical disinfectants kill sperm. Sperm are also very susceptible to many kinds of rubber or latex collection systems and insemination tubes. In addition, cold and heat can shock sperm to render them unviable.

BIOPSY, KIDNEY: *Kidney biopsies* provide valuable information as to the degree of involvement and the prognosis of various kidney diseases. With biopsy information, exact treatment can be formulated. Because many kidney patients are gravely ill making them very poor anesthetic risks, the use of deep *sedation* and *local anesthesia* is most desirable in performing kidney biopsies. Uncontrolled hemorrhaging is a possible complication in the biopsy procedure. Because the surgeon is working through a small opening in the side, good visualization of the kidney being biopsied is impossible. Therefore, better than average surgical skill and special equipment are required for successful kidney biopsies.

BIOPSY, TESTICULAR: *Testicular biopsy* can provide important information as to causes of infertility. Biopsies can be used for *chromosome infertility* work or for examination of the usual cell type present and maturation process.

Testicular biopsy is usually done under *general anesthesia*. A small plug of testicular tissue is severed by a sharp, razor-like blade and immediately placed in fixative solution. For testicular biopsies, Bouin's fixative is recommended over the usual formalin. While some hemorrhage is associated with the surgical procedure, it usually is not a problem. Because of the manipulation of the testes, temporary sterility may be experienced. Barring unforeseen complications, any sterility initiated by the testicular biopsy is temporary.

BIRTH CONTROL METHODS: Numerous methods for preventing unwanted litters of puppies exist. While some procedures are well established, some are still in the experimental stage. Both immunologic and irradiation methods of reproduction control are still very experimental.

Birth control methods are grouped into surgical and nonsurgical methods. The most common surgical procedure in the bitch is the *spay operation* (*ovariohysterectomy*). In this procedure, the bitch is given a *general anesthesia* before removing the uterus and both ovaries through an abdominal incision. Recovery from this major surgery is rapid. All normal activities can be resumed in

10 to 14 days when the skin sutures are removed. In the Cocker Spaniel, the ideal age for this surgery is six months just before the first heat period. However, the operation can be performed at any age. Because of the prevalence of *Von Willebrand's disease*, your veterinarian may want to run some lab tests before undertaking this procedure. Since blood clotting is not normal during an actual heat period, the only bad time for the spay operation is during this three week period.

Tubal ligation can be done in the bitch but is not routinely performed. The undesirable traits of the heat period such as the attraction of male dogs and the mess associated with blood spotting during *estrus* would still be present. Also, ovaries are not normally left in place in the bitch because of the heat cycle and bloody discharge associated with heat. Most spayed bitches do not suffer from *estrogen* shortages during their lives without the *estrous cycle*. However, in a few spayed bitches, a lack of bladder sphincter muscle control may occur with advanced years. This estrogen deficiency can be controlled nicely with *DES* (*diethylstilbestrol*) once a week.

Neutering (*castration*) is the most common surgical birth control method in the male dog. While under *general anesthesia*, both testicles are removed through one incision ahead of the scrotum. Postoperatively, some swelling may occur but usually dissipates without treatment in several days. A *vasectomy* can be done in place of castration in selected dogs. Because the procedure takes almost as long as the castration surgery, a vasectomy is generally reserved for dogs that are going to be shown but for some reason are rendered incapable of producing pups. Following a vasectomy, the testicles may undergo some minor degenerative changes making some conformation dog show judges suspicious.

The use of intravaginal devices is not common in the bitch. Over the years, several have been introduced with questionable effectiveness. Because of the great variation in size of bitches, an exact fit was difficult to find.

The other nonsurgical means of birth control is through drug administration. Currently, two pharmacological compounds are licensed for use in the United States to prevent reproduction in the bitch. *Cheque*® *drops* (*mibolerone*), manufactured by The Upjohn Company as a liquid, is an anabolic and androgenic *steroid* compound. When given orally every day, it is 90% effective in keeping bitches out of heat. This drug should not be given before the first heat period. Usage should not exceed two consecutive years. The drops can be started again after 30 days or after the heat period is over if the estrous period begins after the drug has been stopped. Cheque® is well tolerated with all forms of *heartworm preventive* medication. It should not be used in bitches with a history of liver or kidney disease. Over 40% of the bitches given Cheque® drops will show one or more of the following side effects. In order of decreasing frequency, clitoral enlargement which may even protrude through the vulvar lips, a sticky white vaginal discharge, increased tearing, increased body odor, and, least common, riding behavior are present. If the side effects are objectionable, the drug should be discontinued.

The compound *megestrol acetate* marketed by Schering Corporation as *Ovaban*® is the other form of oral birth control medication. This *progestational hormone* derivative is basically designed to postpone the heat cycle but should not be used before the first heat cycle has been completed. Ovaban® is also contraindicated in pregnant bitches, in those with *breast tumors*, and in those with uterine diseases.

If Ovaban® treatment is started during the first three days of the heat period, a high dosage for eight days is given to abbreviate the heat cycle. The signs of heat diminish quickly and attraction to male dogs should cease. If the tablets have been given for three consecutive days and a breeding should occur, conception should be prevented. If the treatment is started during *anestrus* (nonheat), a low 32 day dosage schedule is administered postponing the start of heat for two to nine months.

Certain situations indicate a need for the use of *megestrol acetate* (Ovaban®). Treatment is most useful in regulating an upcoming heat for show, vacation, or hunting season purposes. Good owner compliance is necessary for proper medication. The drug is expensive and may only be used for two consecutive dosage schedules.

Injectable progestational compounds like *Depo-Provera*® are sometimes used in the control of *estrous cycles*. These are not approved for this purpose for dogs, and, hence, can be very dangerous. A much greater chance of development of *pyometra* is present after a progestational compound is injected. The drug may be long-acting resulting in bitches that will either no longer cycle normally or must be *spayed* because of an infected uterus.

A most effective form of birth control too seldom used properly is the LEASH. If a bitch in heat is on a leash and under the direct supervision of her owner, unwanted pregnancies will not occur.

BLOODY URINE: See *HEMATURIA*.

BREEDING (NORMAL AND ABNORMAL): The act of breeding domesticated dogs can be a challenging adventure. In the wild, nature may eliminate two as a breeding pair because they are not physically or possibly psychologically compatible. Man, in his infinite wisdom, determines that two of the same breed should bear offspring and sets about the task of creating a litter of puppies. Our reasons for wanting puppies are many. Some genuinely desire to improve the breed. Others hope to make money selling the offspring. The desire to show children the miracle of birth may enter into the decision. Or, a mating of convenience may take place since one neighbor may have a Cocker Spaniel bitch and another neighbor a Cocker male.

The only valid reason for bringing a litter of puppies into the world is in an attempt to improve on the genotype and phenotype of both parents. This goal requires planning and an expenditure of time and money to search out a complementary member of the opposite sex. One should never knowingly breed a dog with a serious genetically-linked medical problem. In some cases, a thorough prebreeding examination should be undertaken. Possible genetic conditions of concern in the Cocker Spaniel include *Von Willebrand's disease, progressive retinal atrophy, copper hepatitis*, medial *patellar luxation*, various other eye conditions, various other blood clotting deficiencies, and, of course, extreme variations in temperament. After a determination has been made that the Cocker bitch can be bred, a careful search for the most complimentary male is undertaken. The male should be strong in the areas where the bitch is weak, in both structural and mental properties. To breed two shy, fearful Cocker Spaniels is just as tragic as breeding two that are physically deficient in the same areas. Elsewhere in this chapter and in Chapter 4 on *HORMONES* are topics of interest to those who aspire to raise puppies.

BREEDING FREQUENCY: The frequency with which the dog and the bitch should be bred is open to conjecture. One breeding at the proper time is all that is necessary for fertilization to take place. If *smears* and *cervical glucose* are not used as criteria of *ovulation*, breeding the bitch every other day is the safest method of coordinating the meeting of sperm and ova. Recently, International Canine Genetics, Inc., 271 Great Valley Parkway, Malvern, PA 19355 has introduced a home kit for determining luteinizing hormone (LH) peak from urine. This additional tool will help determine the optimum breeding time.

In a normal *estrous cycle*, the bitch will first stand for the male dog on the ninth or tenth day after the first signs of a bloody discharge. Breeding on these days may be accompanied by some discomfort on the part of the bitch. A second breeding two days later usually does not cause any signs of discomfort in the bitch. If both partners are present, a third breeding should be consummated in 48 hours. While this spreads the due date over a six day period, you or your veterinarian can, by palpation, determine the twenty-eighth day from the successful breeding. Adding five weeks to the twenty-eighth day will accurately predict the parturition (whelping) date.

Some bitches are "breedable" for a two week period. The use of *vaginal smears* and *Tes-Tape*® to measure cervical *glucose* release are then necessary to determine the time of *ovulation* in the bitch. Also refer to the previous paragraph on determining LH peak with a home urine test. Many experienced stud dogs will not show interest in a bitch until the time she ovulates. The experienced stud dog may make lab tests obsolete.

BREEDING TIE: The physical mechanics of the tie rely on the constrictor muscles of the bitch's vagina to hold the engorged male penis. The muscles constrict behind the enlarged bulb of the penis preventing the stud from pulling away. The length of the tie can vary from five to fifty minutes. Older males frequently have longer ties. Their venous blood return is less efficient than that of a young male. A bitch should be tended to while the tie is in progress. If she rolls on her back while tied, the male may be injured. A tie is not necessary for conception to take place. While a tie does not insure conception, it does assure that most of the semen will be deposited in the forward compartment of the vagina.

BRUCELLOSIS, CANINE: Canine brucellosis is caused by the bacteria, *Brucella canis*. In 1966, a disease separate from the other Brucella bacteria that infects cows, pigs, and goats was discovered. This disease affects the reproductive tracts in both the dog and the bitch. Stud dogs may show some lymph node swelling early in the disease. Swelling of the testes follows, then atrophy (shrinkage) from the inflammatory changes that occur. While most males are then sterile, some may still produce abnormal sperm contained in semen full of inflammatory cells.

The bitch with a history of not getting pregnant or of delivering a few dead or soon to die, weak puppies is most commonly an inapparent carrier. Actual *abortions* are not uncommon between the 45th and 54th day. The vaginal discharge which follows lasts for a long time. This discharge is highly infective to any dog or person with whom it comes in contact. The disease is transmitted by breeding contact with an infected dog or contact with infected tissues or discharges following abortion or stillborn delivery. Since humans are susceptible to *canine brucellosis*, the disease has definite public health significance.

Elimination of the disease from a breeding kennel requires radical steps. All dogs in the kennel that test positive (1:200) on tube agglutination should be destroyed. If this is not possible, all of the infected bitches should be *spayed* and then placed on high levels of specific antibiotics for 60 days. They should then be tested monthly for six months to insure that they are no longer carriers. Since the organisms which isolate in the male *prostate* cannot be removed easily by surgery, all males should be destroyed. Long term high levels of appropriate antibiotics might eliminate the organism but there is no guarantee.

All dogs must be tested to keep the infection out of an active breeding kennel. Each bitch coming in for stud service must test negative before service. All studs being bred to bitches should be tested before the breeding takes place. A rapid *slide brucellosis test* is an effective screening procedure performed in the veterinarian's office.

BRUCELLOSIS TESTING: Almost every veterinarian can provide the rapid slide agglutination test for canine brucellosis. A small blood sample is required from which one drop of serum is mixed with a specific antigen tagged with a pink dye. A positive test sample is run at the same time to compare results. If agglutination (clumping) occurs in two minutes, the test is considered positive. Since false positives do occur with some frequency, don't go out and immediately shoot the entire kennel!

Send another blood sample to the state diagnostic lab where a *tube agglutination test* will be performed. Sometimes blood cultures are requested. Only after these subsequent tests confirm the slide results should you be concerned. All positive tests should be confirmed by sending serum to Baker Institute, School of Veterinary Medicine, Cornell University, Ithaca, NY 14853.

Fortunately, virtually no false negative slide agglutination tests occur. A negative rapid test means the dog or bitch is clear. The rapid slide agglutination brucellosis test is available from Pitman-Moore Company, Washington Crossing, NJ 08560.

BUN TEST (BLOOD UREA NITROGEN):   The BUN (blood urea nitrogen) or *SUN test* (*serum urea nitrogen*) is a blood test commonly done to evaluate kidney function. A rough estimation of glomerular filtration within the kidneys is obtained. In all dogs, except the Dalmatian, the end product of protein metabolism is urea which is excreted by the kidneys. Even with adequate kidney function, *adrenal gland failure, congestive heart failure,* very high levels of protein ingestion, and dehydration and shock will elevate BUN levels. The normal levels are between 10 and 20 mg/dl. Serious clinical signs are observed at levels over 40 to 50 mg/dl BUN tests should be repeated as therapy progresses to ascertain progress.

CALCULI—RENAL, URETHRAL, BLADDER: Calculi are mineral composition stones located somewhere that stones should not be found. In the urinary system, stones can be classified by their location in the system. Most commonly, single or multiple stones are found in the urinary bladder. The composition of calculi in the urinary bladder may be magnesium ammonium phosphate, calcium oxalate, ammonium urate, or cystine. *Struvite* is the crystal name of the magnesium ammonium phosphate. While most stones are smooth, the oxalate calculi can be rough. Calculi can also be located in the kidney pelvis, ureter, and urethra.

Difficulty in urinating and blood in the urine are the most common signs of urinary tract calculi. To determine the presence of stones, various diagnostic aids may be needed. If the dog is thin and relaxed, some urinary bladder calculi can be palpated through the abdominal wall. *Urinalysis* and radiographs help with the determination of bladder stones. Special radiographic techniques like *intravenous pyelography* may be necessary to outline stones in the kidney pelvis or ureters.

Treatment of calculi is the surgical removal of the stones. Most veterinary practitioners can surgically remove stones from the urinary bladder and urethra. The level of surgical skill must be quite high to remove kidney and ureter calculi. Recently, a medical option to surgical removal of struvite-type stones has been brought forward. The patient is fed *Prescription Diet® S/D®* and maintained on an appropriate antibiotic for approximately six weeks. The process is accelerated if a urease inhibitor is added to the treatment regimen. By keeping the pH of urine acid, struvite becomes much more soluble. Because of anatomical differences in the urinary tract of male and female dogs, this nonsurgical regimen is much more appropriate for bitches. Only when a single large calculus exists in the male dog urinary bladder should this form of therapy be considered. All dogs that have had urinary tract calculi removed either medically or surgically should be maintained on *Prescription Diet® K/D®* for the remainder of their lives to prevent reformation of calculi.

CASTRATION: See *BIRTH CONTROL METHODS.*

CATHETERIZATION: See *URINE SPECIMEN, COLLECTION OF.*

CESAREAN SECTION: Cesarean section (*C-section*) is the surgical delivery of puppies from the bitch through an incision in the abdominal wall. Many unnecessary C-sections are done for the convenience of the owner and/or the veterinarian. Because some bitches are very slow in whelping, the impatience of others subjects them to cesarean sections before being allowed to whelp the entire litter. The definite indications for cesarean section are *uterine inertia* (primary or secondary), history of broken pelvis in the pregnant bitch, radiographic evidence of a very large fetus, and the development of toxemia during pregnancy or delivery.

Whether or not a C-section should be done during parturition is a judgment call. With *dystocia* (difficult delivery), the bitch becomes a poorer surgical risk as time passes. To minimize chances of death to the bitch and/or the newborn whelps, early sections are most productive. Some of these, however, are not necessary. A good breeder-veterinarian team effort will know which bitch will need sectioning.

The dangers to the bitch in a C-section are from excessive hemorrhage, hypovolemic shock during or immediately after surgery, and, unfortunately, anesthesia. Your veterinarian will use the anesthesia that works best for him resulting in a live bitch and live puppies. Some use *Innovar-Vet*® and a *local* block (freezing) along the midline to avoid fetal depression. Control of the bitch may be marginal. Some are able to use *sedatives* and *gaseous anesthesia* via mask and *endotracheal tube* with little fetal depression.

Most cesarean section incisions are made along the midline from the umbilical scar to the pelvis. Rare veterinarians make flank incisions separating muscles down to the pregnant uterus. An incision is then made in the upper or lower side of the body of the uterus. All pups are delivered through that one incision. After one last abdominal inspection, the uterus is closed with *catgut suture*. The abdomen is flushed with antibiotic-saline solution and closed with several layers of sutures. One common postoperative problem is wound dehiscence (opening of the incision) because the puppies may nurse on the sutures or fetal fluids may have caused some abdominal infection. Because of this fact, the use of *stainless steel sutures* and antibiotic therapy post C-section may be indicated. All C-sections should be supported by intravenous fluid therapy during and for a short time following the surgery.

Once the bitch has recovered from the anesthesia, she should be sent home to be in her normal environment with her puppies. Unless postsurgical adhesions become too much of a problem, litters can be delivered yearly by cesarean section.

CHORIONIC GONADOTROPIN: Chorionic gonadotropin (*HCG*) has a direct affect on follicular growth in the ovary and on interstitial cells of the testes in the male dog. Some forms of hormonal imbalance or insufficiency are treated with this substance. HCG has both *FSH (follicle stimulating hormone)* and *LH (luteinizing hormone)* activity. Chorionic gonadotropin is found in human pregnancy urine and in pregnant mare's serum.

CHROMOSOME COUNTING (KARYOTYPING): *Klinefelter's syndrome* is one form of infertility in the male dog due to chromosomal abnormalities in which two or more X chromosomes exist in the male sex chromosome composition. The only way to identify this syndrome is by *karyotyping* which grows cells from the suspected dog and identifies the sex chromatin bodies in the cell nuclei. This exacting procedure can only be done in a few laboratories utilizing 10 cc of fresh heparinized blood. Contact Dr. Shirley Johnston at the University of Minnesota College of Veterinary Medicine, St. Paul, MN, for specifics on their capabilities.

CHRONIC INTERSTITIAL NEPHRITIS (CIN): When it occurs over a long period of time, the end stage of kidney disease is chronic scarring and inflammation of the kidneys. Many dogs by the age of eight or nine will experience some deterioration in kidney function. The thousands of active functional units within the kidney called glomeruli are tiny filters which are replaced by scar tissue as they wear out, reducing the size of the kidney.

In chronic kidney disease, generally an increase in water consumption becomes noticeable to the owner. As the kidney deficiency increases, the level of *uremia* in the blood stream also increases causing the dog to refuse food and to start to vomit. Unless the condition is treated and the level of uremia is decreased, the dog will develop severe electrolyte imbalances. The uremia will then become fatal.

This condition is diagnosed by a *urinalysis* specific gravity test. Affected dogs cannot concentrate urine making their specific gravity levels less than 1.030. The *BUN* and *creatinine* levels are also measured. Because of the chronic nature of the condition, a *nonregenerative anemia* is usually present.

The treatment for chronic interstitial nephritis includes free choice water, elimination of stress or hard work, supplementation with extra water soluble *B complex* and *C vitamins*, and the feeding of a restricted, high quality kind of protein diet. Adding sodium bicarbonate to the diet to alter the disturbed acid-base balance in the body may also be necessary. *Phosphate binders* like Amphojel® liquid from Wyeth Laboratories are useful in lowering high blood phosphorus levels associated with *uremia*.

The kidney degenerative process cannot be cured. With proper care, however, a relatively normal life can be maintained. The protein restricted diets are not as palatable as normal menus. Heating the canned *K/D*® or adding a small amount of chicken or turkey fat to the diet makes it more appealing. Dogs that require restricted protein diets are best when fed three or four small meals daily instead of one big one!

CLEAN OUT SHOT: After a bitch has delivered her litter, an injection of oxytocin (*POP—posterior oxytocic principle* or *PIT-Pituitrin*®) is customary. The same injection has many names. The purpose of the injection is to stimulate milk letdown and to cause the uterus to contract, expelling any fluid or placentas still present. Giving an injection AFTER all of the puppies are whelped is good practice. Unfortunately, the practice is abused when oxytocin is used by owners in an attempt to speed up the delivery of puppies. While it may be successful some of the time, the shot can be dangerous since a violent drug-induced contraction can rupture the uterus. The clean out shot is best given by the veterinarian after an examination has shown the bitch is at the end of the delivery or only has one pup to go.

CORTICAL HYPOPLASIA, RENAL: This very serious kidney disorder affects young Cocker Spaniels leading to *uremia* and death before the age of two. Most puppies will show some signs of kidney disease by six months. Puppies with renal cortical hypoplasia are poor eaters, will vomit intermittently, and will generally consume large amounts of water.

Laboratory testing should include a *urinalysis, BUN test, creatinine test,* and a *complete blood count.* Affected dogs pass much protein in the urine and fail to concentrate urine properly. Both BUN and creatinine test results are higher than normal indicating developing uremia. Chronic affects of uremia cause a depression of red blood cell production resulting in *anemia.* A definitive diagnosis can only be made with a *kidney biopsy.* Some dogs are in such poor condition that biopsy techniques could cause death. The three kinds of kidney lesions found in a biopsy are cystic areas within the kidneys, areas of scar tissue, and combinations of cystic and scarred kidney tissues.

The treatment for renal cortical hypoplasia is similar to any form of kidney disease that produces uremia and complete kidney failure. See *CHRONIC INTERSTITIAL NEPHRITIS* and *KIDNEY FAILURE.* The prognosis for recovery is poor. Affected Cocker Spaniels that reach breeding age should not be bred. The disease runs in some families of Cockers.

CREATININE TEST: The creatinine test evaluates the kidney filtration function. Unlike the *BUN test,* the creatinine level is not affected by exercise, age, dietary protein intake, or protein breakdown. To prognosticate the outcome of a kidney disease, a series of creatinine tests are run as the treatment continues. Any creatinine level that stays at a high plane warrants a guarded prognosis.

CRYPTORCHIDISM: Cryptorchidism is the failure of testes to descend normally into the scrotum. Affected dogs are more accurately identified as being unilateral cryptorchids if one testicle is not descended and as bilateral cryptorchids if both testes failed to descend properly. Whether or not a genetic component is responsible for this problem is debatable. The possibility that sibling litter mates may carry the genetic potential to produce cryptorchid offspring exists.

The American Kennel Club does not allow the showing of dogs that do not have two normal testicles properly descended in the scrotum. Also, while a unilateral cryptorchid male is usually capable of reproduction, breeding these individuals is discouraged. As a general rule, both testicles in the Cocker should be descended and in the scrotum by 12 weeks of age. On occasion, one testicle may be slow in descending into the scrotum. If one testicle is normally descended and the other can be found within one inch (2 – 2$^1/_2$ cm) of the scrotum, the puppy should be watched until he is nine months old. If the testicle is not in place by that age, it generally will not descend.

Breeders and owners have used numerous methods to encourage an undescended testicle to move down into the scrotum. Most of these methods are therapy for the owners rather than the dog. The use of the male hormone *testosterone* is not effective and may actually be dangerous by producing a rebound sterility in the dog. Stroking and stretching a testicle that is almost down might be of some benefit. It certainly won't hurt. The surgical manipulation of a testicle can be construed as changing the normal appearance of the dog and would therefore be against American Kennel Club rules. The most realistic philosophy is, "If they descend, they descend. If they don't, they don't."

From a health standpoint, a much greater incidence of cancer is diagnosed in undescended testicles. Males with unilateral or bilateral cryptorchid problems should be *castrated* before five years of age. The undescended testicles should be removed even if they are abdominal and have not developed at all.

CYSTIC OVARIES: Cystic ovaries are a cause of *infertility* in the bitch. In cases where the estrus cycle does not proceed past the point of vaginal bleeding and attraction of male dogs, cystic ovaries should be suspected. Bitches will cycle very frequently or appear to remain in *heat* continually. The term *nymphomania* is used when the *estrogen* levels remain at abnormally high planes with the bitch exhibiting continual signs of heat.

Cystic ovaries contain multiple thin-walled cystic cavities filled with fluid. Some veterinarians advocate removing these cystic structures from the ovaries. Most others feel the only reasonable method of dealing with the problem is to spay the bitch. Hormone injections have been universally unproductive in correcting the cystic ovary condition.

CYSTITIS: Cystitis refers to inflammation of the bladder possibly due to infection, *cancer*, *calculi*, or drugs. The signs of cystitis are frequent unproductive urination. The urine may contain blood and, on microscopic analysis, many cells from the bladder lining, bacteria, and *white blood cells.* Identifying the cause of cystitis is important. *Radiography*, *urinalysis*, and *urine cultures* may be required. Proper treatment can be initiated after the cause is determined. Some infections require months of medication to resolve.

CYSTOCENTESIS: See *URINE SPECIMEN, COLLECTION OF.*

DIALYSIS: *Kidney dialysis* is not routinely done in veterinary medicine. However, a technique called *peritoneal dialysis* can achieve the same cleansing effect of the blood. Several recent advances have made peritoneal dialysis more realistic for the average veterinary practice. The new concept uses the peritoneal lining of the abdomen to diffuse toxic waste products from the body into a special solution which is placed in the abdomen for a period of 45 to 50 minutes. The fluid which is removed contains one-half of the amount of toxic waste levels present in the blood. Drawbacks to peritoneal dialysis are the possibility of *peritonitis* (infection) developing, abdominal trauma from the catheter, electrolyte imbalances, and cardiovascular problems resulting from the abdomen filling with dialyzing fluid too rapidly.

The Purdue column disc peritoneal dialysis catheter®, a specialized catheter that does not become blocked, was developed at Purdue University. This allows for continuous dialysis to occur once the catheter has been placed in the abdomen. This catheter can be ordered from Hemodialysis Laboratory, Purdue University, West Lafayette, IN 47907.

Dialysis is not the answer for every kidney disorder. If the trauma to the kidney is acute and recovery could be expected if the kidneys could rest, the dialysis system can be very effective. However, if the kidneys cannot regenerate or are totally scarred down, dialysis will only prolong for a short while death from kidney failure.

DIETS: The special diets associated with dogs suffering from kidney disease are designed to provide restricted amounts of protein of a very high biological value. These diets are described in Chapter 8 on *NUTRITION*. Also discussed in Chapter 8 are diets necessary for pregnant and lactating bitches which must provide higher levels of protein and fat.

DIFFICULT BIRTH: See DYSTOCIA.

DRUGS USED SAFELY DURING PREGNANCY: None of the drugs in the following list cause birth defects when used during pregnancy.

Acetylcysteine	Doxylamine	Niclosamide
Amoxicillin	Enflurane	Nitrous oxide
Ampicillin	Ephedrine	Oxytocin
Atropine	Furosemide	Penicillin
Cephalexin	Glycopyrrolate	Pilocarpine
Chloramphenicol—	Guaifenesin	Piperazine
(last half of gestation)	Halothane	Pralidoxime
Chlorpheniramine	Heparin	Procaine
Chymotrypsin	Kanamycin	Pyrantel
Clonazepam	Ketamine	Pyrilamine
Codeine	Lidocaine	Salbutamol
Dextromethorphan	Lincomycin	Spironolactone
Dichlorvos	Mannitol	Sulfonamides—
Dicloxacillin	Mebendazole	(Short-acting)
Diethylcarbamazine	Metaproterenol	Tetracaine
Digitoxin	Methapyrilene	Theophylline
Digoxin	Methenamine	Thiopental
Dimenhydrinate	Methohexital	Tiletamine
Diphenhydramine	Miconazole	Triamterene
Disophenol	Morphine	Urokinase
Doxapram		

DRUGS THAT MAY BE USED WITH SOME RISK DURING PREGNANCY: During pregnancy, drugs from the following list should be used after weighing the risk-benefit factors and then only with extreme caution. Some of the drugs listed have caused abnormalities in at least one species of lab animal. Other drugs are listed in this group because no information is available on their activity on the fetus during pregnancy.

Acepromazine	Bunamidine	Dapsone
Aminopentamide	Cimetidine	Dichlorophene
Arsenamide	Cortisone	Dithiazanine
Aspirin	Cythioate	Fentanyl-droperidol

Hydralazine	Nystatin	Ronnel
Hydrocortisone	Phthalofyne	Spectinomycin
Iron dextran	Physostigmine	Stanozolol
Lenperone	Prazosin	Styrylpyridium
Levamisole	Prednisone	Thiabendazole
Liothyronine	Prednisolone	Thyroxin
Methylprednisolone	Procainamide	Toluene
Methocarbamol	Proparacaine	Trichlorfon
Methoxyflurane	Propiopromazine	Trimethoprim
Neostigmine	Pyrimethamine	Xylazine

DRUGS THAT SHOULD NOT BE USED DURING PREGNANCY: All of the drugs listed below have adverse effects on the fetus, either causing fetal death or leading to the development of congenital anomalies (defects). In the case of *anticonvulsants*, risking hemorrhage or congenital anomalies in the newborn is better than to chance the development of *status epilepticus* as described in Chapter 7. Their usage should be continued with this in mind.

ALL anticancer drugs (azathioprine, cyclophosphamide)
ALL anticonvulsant drugs (phenobarbital, phenytoin, diazepam,
ALL anti-inflammatory drugs (aspirin, glucocorticoids, DMSO,
  phenylbutazone)

Amikacin	Gentocin®	Nitrofurantoin
Amphotericin B	Gold salts	Propranolol
Anticoagulants	Griseofulvin	Streptomycin
Chloramphenicol (early)	Isoproterenol	Sulfonamides—
Chlorpromazine	Male hormones	(long-acting)
Cholinesterase inhibitors	Meclizine	Tetracyclines
Erythromycin estolate	Mepivacaine	Trimethoprim
Female hormones(estrogen)	Metronidazole	Vitamins A, D, K

DRYING UP A LACTATING BITCH: Drying up the milk supply from a lactating bitch can be painless to all involved when done in a sensible manner. The *weaning process* begins when the first food supplementation is given to three or four week old puppies. Any weaning process must be gradual. Remember, as the food provided for the weaning-aged puppies is increased, the food for the lactating bitch must be decreased. If the changes are made over a 10 to 14 day period, the puppies can go from eating a milky gruel on a daily basis to consuming soaked dry-type puppy food four times a day. When four times daily puppy feeding is accomplished, the bitch should be fasted one day with only a small amount of water to drink. On the day the bitch is fasted, the puppies should be totally separated from her. This separation should continue for a minimum of 10 days following.

After the one day fast, the bitch is fed a small amount once daily. The amount is increased until she is back to her prepregnant food ration level. Some behavioral benefits may be observed by allowing the bitch to have contact with the puppies for the first eight weeks.

DYSTOCIA (DIFFICULT BIRTH): Dystocia may be the fault of the pregnant bitch or of the unpresented fetus. *Maternal dystocia* is caused by an abnormality in some part of the bitch's anatomy. These irregularities may be present from birth or acquired during pregnancy or later life.

The following anatomical abnormalities may cause labor and delivery to be difficult or impossible. The pelvic canal may be too small to accommodate a normal-sized puppy. Large-headed, small-waisted breed types encounter more of a problem. In some heavily pregnant bitches, a very acute angle has formed in the birth canal and the bony pelvis. The acute angle is very difficult to ascend causing labor to be unproductive and prolonged. This form of *dystocia* can be treated by using a towel to form a sling around the abdomen. The towel sling is raised as the bitch contracts straightening the birth canal angle enough to deliver several pups in this manner. With less uterine weight, the bitch may be better able to complete the delivery process.

A broken pelvis may narrow the birth canal as it heals. Other scar tissue and adhesions make a *cesarean section* mandatory. The C-section can be planned for the 60th to 61st day of pregnancy. The bitch does not need to go into actual labor before the surgery.

Obstructions along the birth canal can cause dystocia. In unusual cases, tumors which obstruct the delivery process may be present in the vaginal vault or in the cervical area. More commonly, juvenile vulvae may make delivery of the first pup too painful. If the vulva does not dilate as the pup is presented, an *episiotomy* (surgical enlarging of the vulvar opening) may be necessary.

All of the other maternal causes of dystocia are due to problems associated with the uterus. *Primary uterine inertia* occurs when the muscular wall of the uterus fails to contract. In primary uterine inertia, the usual signs seen with all stages of labor are missing. In many cases, the only sign that the due date has come and gone is a temperature decrease which has since returned to normal. If there is to be any hope of saving the whelps, bitches with primary uterine inertia should have a *cesarean section* when their temperature drops. Because a definite genetic relationship is seen in this condition, breeders are advised to cull affected bitches from their breeding programs in the future.

Secondary uterine inertia can occur after a long delivery of most of a large litter. In this situation, the last several pups are not delivered. The bitch may appear to rest and be finished with her delivery. This type of inertia is usually secondary and a short rest period (several hours) may be all that she needs before delivering the last whelps. Too frequently, a cesarean section is undertaken when not actually necessary.

Two conditions involve the amount of fetal fluids present in the uterus. In the first instance, virtually no liquid is present around the fetus. After contractions start, an observer is impressed by how little fluid is found with contractions. Since most of these placentas fail to peel out of the uterine wall, a C-section will usually be needed with fair to poor pup livability. The other extreme, *hydrops allantois*, is too much fluid associated with the puppies. Bitches with this problem will appear overly distended during late pregnancy. This extreme build-up of fluid can cause both respiratory and cardiac difficulty because of the abnormal distension of the abdomen. To further complicate matters, bitches with this condition have very poor uterine contractions because the uterine musculature has been stretched beyond its contractile abilities. While *cesarean sections* are often needed, beware of the more guarded prognosis with hydrops allantois. Sudden relief of the built-up abdominal pressure may cause irreversible cardiac shock. Puppies delivered from the excessive fluid compartments in the bitch generally show poor livability.

The causes of *dystocia due to the fetus* can be related to its size, the position of its delivery, and to rare *fetal monsters*. An oversized puppy may not be able to be delivered through a normal-sized birth canal. Puppies in one or two puppy litters are more apt to be too large. Puppies that are presented or positioned abnormally may be difficult to deliver in a normal manner. While 40% of all puppies are born in the breech position, two rear feet with toes pointing down and a tail should be found for a normal breech position. In the Cocker Spaniel, the size of the vaginal vault allows for some manipulation and repositioning in puppies improperly presented. Although delivery of the malpostioned pup is sometimes impossible, if its delivery is successful, the remainder of the litter can be born normally without the aid of a C-section.

The most common fetal abnormalities are *anasarca (water puppies)*, *hydrocephalus*, and *Schistosoma reflexa*. All of these conditions may make a *cesarean section* necessary. In most cases, only one or two puppies in a litter will show fetal monstrosity signs. If the entire litter is affected, an infection or medication taken during pregnancy is probably the cause.

ECLAMPSIA (MILK FEVER): *Hypocalcemia, post parturient tetany*, and *milk fever* are all names for eclampsia. This condition usually occurs during delivery or shortly after whelping but may be seen during the last trimester of the pregnancy. A normally nervous high strung Cocker is more likely to be affected than one that is calmer.

Extreme panting, nervousness, muscle twitching, and an elevated body temperature are the observed signs associated with eclampsia. Fevers of 105° F are not uncommon. Affected dogs should be treated promptly since the elevated temperature can reach life threatening levels. The classical treatment is an intravenous injection of a 10% calcium solution. *Calcium* can have a profound effect on the heart muscle. If not administered intravenously, a nasty tissue slough may arise. The injection should be slow using a solution with only 10% calcium for maximum safety. *Glucocorticoids* and intravenous sugar solutions are also used in the treatment of eclampsia. Response to treatment is almost immediate. As the temperature decreases, the panting and muscle twitching cease quickly, too. Since recurrences happen, the litter should be weaned immediately and raised as orphan pups.

ENDOMETRITIS: Endometritis is defined as inflammation of the inner lining of the uterus. Classification is made by the nature of its occurrence and whether it is acute or chronic in nature.

The most serious and life threatening form of endometritis occurs several weeks after the heat signs have ceased. Signs of serious discomfort occur very quickly. The temperature is very high. The abdomen is very tense. Increased water consumption and vomiting are observed. Little or no vaginal discharge is found but that which is present will be thin and bloody in nature. Although the prognosis is at best guarded, an *ovariohysterectomy* should be attempted as quickly as possible. On surgical exploration of the abdomen, a *peritonitis* (abdominal lining infection) and a very hard, friable uterus may be found. If the bitch can stand the stress of surgery, the condition will be over on recovery from the ovariohysterectomy.

A chronic form of endometritis also occurs several weeks after the signs of heat are gone in bitches approximately five years old. At that time, the condition is usually not life threatening so may go unnoticed for a while. The usual sign is one of a constant mucoid vaginal discharge. The condition is refractory to medical treatment but is responsive to *ovariohysterectomy* at the convenience of the owner.

Another class of endometritis occurs following *parturition (whelping)*. This acute form is accompanied by a dark bloody, foul smelling vaginal discharge. The temperature rapidly elevates. The bitch increases her water consumption but refuses food. A decrease in milk supply for the puppies may also occur. The treatment of choice is a broad spectrum antibiotic sometimes coupled with *oxytocin (clean out shot)* to help the uterus expel any debris remaining from delivery.

A subacute or chronic form of endometritis can occur when the *whelping process* has taken a long time. Clinical signs are vague and may only be seen as poor mothering instincts. This condition also responds to appropriate antibiotics.

ESTROGEN HORMONE: Estrogen is a hormone secreted by the *ovaries* during the *heat cycle* and also produced in small amounts by the *adrenal glands*. Estrogen may be produced by a *Sertoli cell tumor* in the male testicle. This hormone is responsible for the signs associated with heat-bleeding, attraction of male dogs, and vulvar swelling.

When given shortly after breeding, estrogen hormones interrupt a pregnancy. The size of male hyperplastic *prostate glands* can be decreased with estrogen hormone. This is also effective in decreasing the size of *perianal adenoma tumors*. Extended usage of estrogen hormone may have a deleterious affect on the bone marrow causing fatal *aplastic anemia*.

ESTROUS CYCLE: See *HEAT CYCLE* in Chapter 4.

EXCRETORY UROGRAPHY: See *IV PYELOGRAM*.

FALSE PREGNANCY: *Pseudocyesis* is the correct name for false pregnancy. After a bitch has ovulated, she goes through a luteal phase in which *progesterone*, the hormone of pregnancy, is secreted. If this hormone level peaks but does not decline, the bitch's body thinks she is pregnant. All of the signs associated with pregnancy except an intrauterine fetus may be present. Her abdomen enlarges. Her breasts develop and fill with milk. Her appetite increases. Her attitude becomes more sluggish and she craves for affection. In later false pregnancy, slight signs of uterine contractions and nesting will occur. The bitch may also mother inanimate objects and toys.

The abdominal distension which becomes very apparent between the 42nd and 49th day (earlier than in true pregnancy) and will disappear just as suddenly as it occurred. Many breeders feel that when this phenomena occurs, the bitch has aborted or resorbed the litter. Since the bitch was not pregnant in the first place, this is not true.

No treatment is necessary for false pregnancies unless it becomes extreme. In most instances, removal of the toys that are being mothered and elimination of the nest are sufficient to cause the hormone levels to return to normal. Decreasing food and water intake may be necessary to dry up the mammary glands. In rare instances, the use of *Ovaban*®, *diethylstilbestrol*, or *testosterone* are used to reverse the affects of pseudocyesis. The use of hormones should be discouraged except in extreme instances.

Once a bitch has had a false pregnancy, others of varying intensity will occur. Only breeding the bitch will keep it from recurring. *Ovariohysterectomy* will also eliminate the condition. *Spaying* the bitch while she is producing milk is undesirable since milk production may continue for an indefinite time period even after the hormone source in the ovaries is removed.

FERTILITY LAB TESTS: The tests listed here are helpful in the diagnosis of canine infertility. Each is discussed individually in the chapter.

Biopsy, testicular	Sperm count
Brucellosis test	Tes-Tape®
Chromosome counting	Thyroid function tests
(Karyotyping)	Vaginal cultures
LH Peak urine test	Vaginal smears
Sex hormone assays	

FETAL MONSTROSITIES: Hideous monstrosities may result from the administration of teratogenic (anomaly producing) drugs during the first five weeks of pregnancy. Refer to the listing of drugs to be avoided during pregnancy. The *dystocia* produced necessitates a *cesarean section*.

FOLLICLE STIMULATING HORMONE (FSH): Follicle stimulating hormone (FSH) is a protein hormone substance produced in the anterior portion of the pituitary gland in the base of the brain. In the bitch, FSH plays a role in the development of the ovarian follicles. In males, the sperm producing cells in the testes are affected. The purified form of the hormone may be used in the treatment of infertility in the bitch. Its usage can initiate a heat period which would then be treated with *luteinizing hormone (LH)*. *Chorionic gonadotropin (HCG)* is a commercially available hormone with both FSH and LH activity.

FROZEN SEMEN: Since 1981, the American Kennel Club has allowed the use of frozen semen in the artificial insemination of dogs registered with the AKC. This procedure takes advantage of the fact that sires long dead can still have an impact on the breed, the spread of venereal diseases can be controlled, and the cost and stress of shipping bitches can be reduced.

Several factors are peculiar to frozen semen insemination. The semen extender is important in maximizing the viability of frozen sperm. The method of thawing the semen is very important because reconstituted semen is prone to temperature shock if the thaw is done improperly. Lastly, sperm from frozen semen is not as vigorous as fresh semen. These factors make it imperative that exact ovulation in the bitch be determined for good conception to occur.

Currently, two procedures are followed for artificial insemination of reconstituted frozen semen. In one procedure, the bitch to be bred is placed under anesthesia and an incision is made in the uterus. The semen is placed into the body of the uterus through this surgical opening. The second procedure relies on pinpointing ovulation and breeding with normal artificial insemination procedures at the precise time of ovulation. Both techniques are effective.

Dogs participating in this program using frozen semen must use semen collected at one of a number of approved AKC frozen semen storage stations. The current guidelines require that the semen producing dog be free from *canine brucellosis*, a copy of its AKC registration certificate be on file, and three color photographs (side and front views) for identification purposes be provided. Each frozen ampule of semen will provide from 100 to 300 million sperm for insemination. A list of approved frozen semen banks is available from The American Kennel Club, Department B, 51 Madison Avenue, New York, NY 10010.

GENITAL CANCER: Tumors or cancer can develop in any part of the reproductive tract. Each sex will be considered individually.

Tumors of the ovary are not uncommon. When these cancerous growths produce hormones, outward signs of heat, *nymphomania*, and hair coat changes are observed. If no hormones are produced and the mass grows large enough, the growth can be felt through the abdominal wall. Also, the bitch may exhibit some discomfort when she lies on her abdomen. Surgical removal, when possible, is the treatment of choice.

Rare *uterine tumors* are generally non-malignant *leiomyomas*. An ovariohysterectomy is curative. On the other hand, vaginal tumors are relatively common and are usually benign. Leiomyomas and *fibromas*, the most common tumors, while not malignant can cause *dystocia* (difficult birth). If the breeding career is to be continued, surgical removal should be attempted.

An interesting tumor that affects both dogs and bitches is *transmissible venereal tumor (TVT)*. This disease is spread only by coitus. Within seven days of transmission, evidence of tumor growth is seen. The vaginal wall and the penis are common sites for this cauliflower-like tumor growth. About 60% of these tumors will regress and disappear spontaneously within 60 to 180 days. Only a very small percentage will spread to other areas of the body. This tumor is very x-ray responsive. Should metastasis (spreading) make surgical removal impossible, TVT is also sensitive to all of the usual anti-cancer drugs.

In addition to the *transmissible venereal tumor*, the two most common sites for genital cancers are the *prostate gland* and the testicles in male dogs. *Prostatic cancer*, the same type that occurs in man, is uncommon. Being rather metastatic, the *adenocarcinoma* has usually spread by the time a diagnosis of prostate cancer is made. Surgical removal of the prostate may be successful in a small number of cases where the cancer has not yet spread to other organs. Removal of the prostate gland requires a high degree of surgical skill, usually resulting in a male dog that continually dribbles urine.

Testicular tumors are common in the dog. Three kinds of tumors occur in the testes. The least significant tumor, the *interstitial cell tumor*, does not secrete any hormones. Because it does not attain enough size to be noticed, finding is usually incidental on routine *castration*. Generally, testicular tumors do not metastasize.

The second type of testicular tumor, the *seminoma*, is also benign and does not secrete any hormones. This tumor can grow up to four or five inches (10 to 12 cm) in diameter causing some general discomfort. Surgical removal is curative. Whether the remaining normal-sized testicle is removed during the surgery is up to the discretion of the surgeon.

The *Sertoli cell tumor*, the most significant testicular tumor, secretes female hormones. In undescended testicles, this type is the most common. While its presence in a descended testicle doesn't cause much increase in size, the tumorous undescended testicle can grow to rather large proportions in the abdomen or inguinal canal. Because of the female hormone influence, many changes occur such as a pendulous prepuce, an increased nipple size, an attraction of male dogs, and a *bilateral hair loss*. A small number of Sertoli cell tumors will metastasize late in the tumor's life. If the tumor is removed before spreading, the hair and skin changes will return to normal in two to three months. Additional discussion on *SERTOLI CELL TUMORS* is found in Chapter 4.

GLOMERULONEPHRITIS: Glomerulonephritis is inflammation of the capillary loops of the glomeruli (functional units) within the kidneys. Generally, a bacterial infection or other changes causing deterioration of the kidney glomeruli bring about the problem. *Systemic lupus erythematosus (SLE)*, *pyometra*, *endocarditis*, and *heartworm disease* may also effect this situation. Determining if the kidney changes are acute is important so that with adequate rest and therapy, recovery of normal function can be achieved. If the glomerular changes are causing permanent dysfunction, recovery is doubtful. A number of blood tests, *kidney biopsies*, and *urinalysis* results will need to be tabulated to determine the prognosis and best course of treatment.

HEAT CYCLE: The heat cycle (*estrous cycle*) usually occurs for the first time after a pup reaches six to ten months of age. While most bitches will cycle two times a year, up to nine months between heat periods is not unusual. Four stages compose the cycle. *Anestrus*, the quiet period, has no outward sign of hormonal activity and may last for five months. *Proestrus* follows with vulvar swelling and bloody discharge for three to ten days. The end of the proestrus period occurs at the first acceptance of a male dog for breeding. During *estrus* (this period of acceptance), the bitch, on stimulation, shows signs of flagging her tail or moving it to the side as she lifts the vulva solidly planting her rear legs. Estrus may last from three to ten days. *Diestrus* (*metestrus*) follows, lasting about two months. In many bitches, diestrus is not distinguishable from anestrus.

All of these phases of the heat cycle are influenced by different hormones. Several weeks before signs of proestrus are seen (swelling and discharge), the *estrogen hormones* increase and then peak during *proestrus*. A strong surge of *luteinizing hormone (LH)* occurs close to the start of estrus. *Diestrus* is marked by the influence of *progesterone hormone*. After either *parturition, false pregnancy*, or a decrease in the progesterone level, *anestrus* returns. Also see *ESTROUS CYCLE* in Chapter 4.

HEMATURIA: Hematuria is the presence of blood cells in urine. Determining the origin and cause of the blood in the urine is important. Urinary bladder infections, trauma from *bladder* or *urethral stones*, trauma from accidents or injury, a side effect of the anticancer drug *Cytoxan*®, the presence of a urinary system tumor, a by-product of a blood clotting defect, or an incidental finding from a bitch in heat are some typical causes. Hematuria is a sign of disease and not a disease itself. Treatment and prognosis depend on the cause.

HERMAPHRODITE: A hermaphrodite contains both male and female gonadal tissue. A differentiation between *pseudohermaphrodites* (outwardly males with ovaries internally or outwardly females containing testes internally) and the true hermaphrodite defined above exists. Intersexuality runs in certain Cocker Spaniel families. Extensive chromosome analysis has been performed in familial hermaphrodites within the breed. Normal XY male chromosomes are replaced with XX (genetically the female chromosome indicator) but male characteristics result externally. *Karyotyping* provides important information in differentiating the pseudohermaphrodite from the hermaphrodite. In either case, these Cockers are infertile. While a hereditary basis for these conditions is indicated, the genetic mode of transmission has not been determined. Surgical elimination of gonadal tissue is desirable. A greater number of bilateral *cryptorchid* males are affected by this anomaly than other dogs.

HERPES VIRUS: The *canine herpes virus (CHV)*, a venereally transmitted viral disease, is particularly lethal to newborn pups up to two weeks old. In adult males, no clinical signs are seen. In breeding bitches, history of stillborn pups, *abortion*, or *infertility* may be observed. Newborn pups are infected within the birth canal on delivery. Puppies that die of CHV have characteristic lesions on autopsy. The kidneys of these infected pups have petechial (pinpoint) hemorrhages over the surface beneath the capsule surrounding the kidney, typical of the disease.

Infected dogs and bitches in a breeding kennel should be eliminated from future breeding programs and isolated from other dogs. No treatment for the disease exists, but the virus can be killed with any common disinfectant. Canine herpes virus does not pose a public health hazard.

HYDROCEPHALUS: Hydrocephalus is not rare in the Cocker Spaniel. This congenital anomaly occurs when the fluid-filled canals (*ventricles*) within the brain fill with enough fluid to cause the normal brain matter to atrophy. Affected puppies, if they survive birth, are very slow mentally and have a very apple-domed head with bulging eyes. The diagnosis is made on the basis of clinical signs and radiographs of the skull. If the condition is present at birth, the enlarged head will create *dystocia* which may create the need for a *C-section*.

HYPOSPADIAS: Hypospadias is the most common urethral congenital anomaly in the male dog. In this condition, the urethra opens on the bottom and behind its normal position at the tip of the penis. Because of the location of the opening, any semen would be deposited much posterior to the desired anterior section of the vagina making fertilization difficult to achieve. On occasion, surgical corrections may effectively change the opening to a more normal location. The hereditary aspects of this condition are undetermined.

INCONTINENCE: Incontinence, usually more common in bitches than in dogs, is the inability to control the elimination of urine. A number of factors cause urinary incontinence. In young dogs, a *patent urachus* (an embryonic remnant) or an *ectopic ureter* or *mislocated ureter* entering the urinary bladder can make house training appear to be impossible. In older bitches spayed before their first heat, a small percentage will develop a hormone responsive incontinence. The weekly use of *diethylstilbestrol (DES)* will control the problem. A *vaginitis* or a *urethritis* will cause frequent, difficult urination which may be construed as incontinence. The use of *radiographs* and other lab tests may be necessary to identify the cause of incontinence.

INERTIA, UTERINE (PRIMARY AND SECONDARY): Primary and secondary uterine inertia are two causes of difficult birth. Uterine inertia is discussed more completely under *DYSTOCIA*.

INFERTILITY: The topic of canine infertility is a very complex subject. Because both the sire and the dam are involved, the discussion is divided into causes of male and female infertility. Several obvious causes may affect both males and females.

Inadequate nutrition and proper vitamin and mineral intake can cause a physiologic infertility in females. Deficiencies in either *vitamin A* or *vitamin E* will cause reproductive failure. *Manganese deficiency* can cause *abortion* and impaired reproduction. A deficiency in the trace mineral *iodine* may be associated with fetal resorption and *abortion*. If *essential fatty acids* are not adequate in the diet supply, reproduction is severely impaired.

Infectious diseases caused by bacteria, viruses, *mycoplasma*, and *rickettsia* may be associated with failures in the reproductive process. The most common diseases in dogs are the bacterial disease *canine brucellosis* and the viral disease *canine herpes virus*. However, the presence of certain pathogenic bacteria in the genital tract of either the male or the female may cause failures in reproduction.

Disturbances in normal hormone levels in the body may alter normal reproductive function. The *thyroid gland* and its associated hormones are important in the normal metabolic processes in the body. Failure of the *pituitary gland* to secrete proper amounts of several different hormones will alter reproductive mechanisms in both males and females. Excesses or deficiencies of *adrenal gland* hormones have an effect on the reproductive process. Sex hormone problems specific to each sex will be mentioned under male and female related infertilities.

The other major cause of infertility in both sexes is psychological in nature. Attempting to breed a very subordinate, reserved male to an extremely dominant bitch can be a real adventure! This male is willing to take "no" for an answer. Raising a male in a home where he is not allowed to engage in male activities makes it more difficult for the dog when the owner then wants to breed him. He can't lift his leg on the piano to mark territory. He can't mount the lady of the house when she has her menstrual period. He is not even allowed to ride someone's leg to masturbate because these activities are not usually acceptable traits for a house dog. Suddenly when he reaches the age of four, the owner decides his dog should father a litter to insure the preservation of his wonderful traits. The owner who thinks that suddenly the "stud dog" will understand that it is now okay to mount this bleeding bitch when for the past four years the dog has gotten in serious trouble for attempting the same kind of activity is in for a surprise and disappointment. In most cases, the house rules and training over a period of years will keep the male dog from performing the normal breeding act.

Female related infertility causes can be divided into anatomical and hormonal. Fertility problems related to the genital anatomy can be present at birth. Others such as the formation of a cancerous growth or adhesions after a litter or an accident are acquired later. If congenital (present at birth) anomalies in the genital tract are suspected, a very complete surgical inspection of all of the related structures is necessary. *General anesthesia* and the use of dyes or stains to check on the patency of the fallopian tubes and uterine horns are required. *Uterine biopsies* may also be necessary. The term "breaking down a bitch" is used by some breeders to describe the digitally dilating and stretching of muscular rings present in the vaginal vault to make a natural breeding possible. Some of these can be relaxed with the drug *aminopropazine fumarate* (*Jenotone*® by Coopers Animal Health, Inc.) at the rate of 1 mg per pound of weight given two or three hours before the breeding is attempted. Other strictures require surgical alteration. Still others require *artificial insemination* and may later require a *cesarean section* because of dystocia from the strictures in the vaginal vault.

Female hormonal causes of infertility are usually due to improper amounts of hormones at inappropriate times in the *estrous cycle*. As expertise in veterinary endocrinology progresses, the ability to assay (measure) these hormones at various times in the cycle improves. This information helps determine where the body is deficient in normal hormone levels.

Causes of *male infertility* may be related to anatomical blockages, environmental effects on the scrotum and testicles, and those of a hormonal nature. In young puppies, congenital abnormalities in the anatomy of the penis are usually apparent on careful inspection. Abnormalities involving the testicle and duct work are less obvious.

Transient infertility may be found in cases where testes have been exposed to high temperatures of the environment or from fevers. A curious type of infertility in the male involves the creation of antibodies against sperm as an *autoimmune reaction*. This usually results from an acute inflammatory response in the tubular duct work that transports sperm. Even if the initial reaction is only involving one testicle, the autoimmune response will be bilateral resulting in complete infertility.

Chromosome abnormalities are another type of male infertility. In *Klinefelter's syndrome* in man, at least two X chromosomes in the male makeup exist. Only one X chromosome should be present. See *CHROMOSOME COUNTING*. The most common hormone abnormality in the male dog involves the *thyroid hormone*. Both libido and spermatogenesis (sperm formation) can be affected. Other hormone deficiencies or excesses will affect the fertility rate of the male dog.

Various drugs can affect fertility in both the dog and the bitch. If breeding the male is anticipated, your veterinarian should be consulted about the possibilities of stopping any medication several days before the anticipated stud service. This is not necessary with all medicines.

The identification of causes of infertility can require much testing and detective work on the part of the veterinarian. Most Colleges of Veterinary Medicine have specialists in *theriogenology*, the study of reproductive problems. These board certified specialists may be able to uncover the causes of infertility with equipment and testing not usually available to general veterinary practitioners.

IV PYELOGRAM: During the IV pyelogram, also called *excretory urography*, an organic iodide compound is injected intravenously. As it is excreted through the kidney and ureters, *radiographs* are taken. While no information of renal function is obtained, visualizing the kidney looking for cysts, *tumors*, obstructions, *calculi*, and size variations in the kidney is possible. To prepare a Cocker for an IV pyelogram, food is withheld for 18 hours. An enema is administered before taking the dog to the hospital for the procedure. The urinary bladder is emptied before the drug is injected. One or more radiographs are taken before the iodide injection. Radiographs are then taken 1, 3, 5, 10, and 15 minutes post injection. The side effects from the iodide include sneezing, vomiting, and *hives*. In extremely rare cases, cardiac arrest and *anaphylactic reactions* have been seen. The procedure is considered safe. Only rare individuals will react adversely to the injected drug.

KARYOTYPING: See *CHROMOSOME COUNTING*.

KIDNEY FAILURE: Kidney failure is classified as either acute or chronic in terms of the length of time in which the process has occurred. Further classification into reversible and irreversible groups is important from a prognostic standpoint.

Most of the signs of kidney disease are due to the rising level of urea (waste products) in the blood. Signs of *uremia* are depression, dehydration, vomiting, loss of appetite, and possible diarrhea. Long term affects cause *anemia*. Most acute kidney failures will produce smaller than normal amounts of urine or no urine at all (*anuria*). *Chronic kidney failure* usually causes increased dilute urine from increased water consumption. Some chronic cases, however, have lesser than normal urine output.

The causes of acute and chronic kidney failure are many and varied. Because acute renal failure may be treatable, tests are advisable to determine the feasibility of treating the condition. At best, chronic renal disease may be controlled but the kidney damage is not reversible. Only removing urea from the blood will alleviate signs. The build-up of uremic waste products is continuous as the body burns calories doing work. Dietary management and fluid therapy will help keep *uremia* in check. Without the luxury of kidney transplants, management of kidney failure syndromes must be tied to the prospects for curing the condition or, at least, controlling the signs produced by uremia. See *CORTICAL HYPOPLASIA, RENAL.*

KIDNEY FUNCTION LAB TESTS: The following list of kidney function lab tests are performed to diagnosis kidney problems.

Biopsy, kidney	Creatinine test
BUN test	IV pyelogram
Plasma PSP test	Urinalysis
Urine PSP excretion test	

LABOR, SIGNS OF: Labor is divided into three stages. No absolute, clear-cut lines separate one stage from another.

The *first stage of labor* is the period of preparation and relaxation. This stage smay vary in length from almost nothing to two days but probably averages 12 to 18 hours. The length of the first stage is somewhat influenced by the temperament of the expectant mother and the environment in which she has been placed to have her puppies. A mellow, laid back bitch has a shorter first stage than a neurotic house pet that isn't a dog any more. Placing the expectant mother in new surroundings like a whelping box may lengthen the first stage of labor.

The bitch experiences little pain as the cervix dilates. Clinical signs of stage I are restlessness, nest making, and panting. No true contractions are occurring. During this period the body temperature is dropping, possibly only for a short time. Taking a rectal temperature two times a day will usually catch this temperature decrease. The drop will be from the normal 101° F down to 98° F or so. Where one or two puppy litters are suspected, this temperature drop is very important. After a short drop, the temperature will edge up toward normal. If uterine contractions have not started, the bitch becomes a prime suspect for *primary uterine inertia* necessitating a *cesarean section.* As a rule, contractions producing puppies should begin within 24 hours of the temperature drop.

The *second stage of labor* initiates purposeful contractions. The bitch becomes more quiet and may lose various fluids at times during this stage. As contractions become more forceful, the bitch may arch her back as she delivers a newborn pup. The length of time to allow contractions is open to conjecture. Generally, the first pup may take up to two hours for full cervical dilation and birth canal dilation enabling delivery to take place. If the contractions occur for longer than six hours, placental separation will jeopardize the life of that pup. Subsequent pups usually come in groups of two or three over a 10 to 30 minute period. This flurry of activity is followed by a resting period of up to three or four hours. As long as the bitch rests between deliveries, concern over long whelping periods is not necessary.

The *third stage of labor* is the period when the fetal placentas and membranes are expelled. Placentas may come with each puppy delivery or they may be retained until later in the delivery process. Allowing the bitch to eat the placentas and membranes may provide some hormones that will stimulate uterine contraction and milk letdown. Consumption of one or two of these placentas is all that is necessary.

The whelping process is completed when the bitch relaxes and settles into the nest with her newborn pups. The new mother then usually falls asleep. If the whelping process was prolonged or if all of the placentas are not accounted for, your veterinarian should examine the new mother and give her a *postpartum injection*. See *CLEAN OUT SHOT* in this chapter.

The bitch's temperature after whelping may rise to 102.5° to 103° F. This is a physiological increase due to her activity and the initiation of lactation. Antibiotics are not required unless the temperature exceeds 103° F.

LH PEAK URINE TEST: International Canine Genetics, Inc. has developed a new urine test that will accurately predict *ovulation time* in the bitch. This test is an important tool in determining exact breeding times for frozen semen *artificial insemination* and for bitches with unpredictable *estrous cycles*. The test which requires 25 to 30 minutes is performed on a fresh urine sample at home. Further information can be obtained by calling ICG on their toll free number (800) 248-8099.

LUTEINIZING HORMONE (LH): Luteinizing hormone is produced in the *pituitary gland* at the base of the brain. In the bitch, LH prepares the ovary for pregnancy by initiating a corpus luteum (the place on the ovary from which the egg is discharged). In the male, this hormone causes cells in the testes to secrete *testosterone hormone*. LH is sometimes injected into infertile bitches to stimulate follicle rupture and ovum release.

METRITIS: Metritis is defined as inflammation of the uterus. Most metritis problems are actually *endometritis* involving the inside lining of the uterus and not the muscular wall or the serosal outer covering of the uterus. Inflammation of the muscular wall, inner lining, and outer covering can occur after surgery or after some natural form of trauma to the entire organ. Also see *ENDOMETRITIS* as the same facts are true for metritis.

MILK FEVER: See *ECLAMPSIA*.

MISMATE INJECTION: Unwanted pregnancies are controlled by giving the bitch an injection of *estradiol cypionate (ECP)* within three days of the unplanned mating. Estradiol cypionate, however, is not approved for mismate injections in dogs. Your veterinarian may ask you to sign a liability waiver before using the drug for this purpose. Side effects from use of estradiol cypionate include an increased length to the *estrous cycle* with further attraction of male dogs and a greater incidence of *pyometra*. In fact, if the injection is given during *diestrus*, the chance for the development of pyometra is up to 20% greater than normal. See *ESTROUS CYCLES* in Chapter 4.

The greatest danger from *estrogen* usage is to the bone marrow. Severe and even fatal *bone marrow depression* can occur from overzealous use of estrogen hormones. Under no circumstance should more than one injection of estradiol cypionate be given during any one *heat cycle*.

Prostaglandins are occasionally used to cause *abortion* in dogs. Due to the side effects seen shortly after administration, they are not too popular. Prostaglandins are not currently licensed for use in dogs. See *PROSTAGLANDINS* in this chapter.

MONORCHID: Monorchid, which technically means only one testicle present, is a misused term. The presence of one testicle in the dog is very rare. In most cases, only one testicle has descended in the scrotum and the other testicle is in the inguinal canal or the abdominal cavity. A more correct description would be unilateral *cryptorchid*.

NEPHRITIS: Inflammation of the kidneys is defined by the term nephritis. Normally adjectives are used to describe the type of nephritis and the duration and location of the inflammation. For instance, *chronic interstitial nephritis* is inflammation of a long-term nature occurring in the interstitial tissue of the kidney. Because the causes of nephritis are many and varied, the important kidney diseases are discussed individually within the chapter. See *CHRONIC INTERSTITIAL NEPHRITIS (CIN), GLOMERULONEPHRITIS, KIDNEY FAILURE,* and *PYELONEPHRITIS.*

NEUTERING (CASTRATION): See *BIRTH CONTROL METHODS.*

OVARIOHYSTERECTOMY (SPAY): See *BIRTH CONTROL METHODS.*

PALPATION: Palpation, a method of *pregnancy diagnosis*, is the act of applying light pressure to the body surface with the fingers to make a physical diagnosis. The technique of palpating the abdomen to determine pregnancy must be developed with experience. For the novice, the best time to check for pregnancy is exactly 28 days from the conception date. Begin 28 days from the first breeding date, checking again 28 days from all breeding dates.

One hand is all that is necessary in Cocker Spaniel abdominal palpation for pregnancy. The technique involves using one hand to feel and press against the abdomen, allowing the internal viscera (organs) to slide between the fingers while searching for the pregnant uterus. At 28 days of pregnancy, each fetus is enlarged to the size of a Ping-Pong® ball in most Cockers. Palpating multiple, round, firm masses is a positive pregnancy diagnosis.

The palpation technique has several shortcomings. Obese and very large bitches are extremely hard to palpate accurately. A tense, nervous bitch will usually not allow you to feel her abdomen deeply enough to feel the fetuses.

Palpation earlier than 24 days or later than 30 days from the date of breeding is not possible with any degree of accuracy. The fertilized eggs do not implant in the uterine wall until the 20th day after a successful breeding. Even at 24 days, the uterine enlargement is pea sized. By 30 days post breeding, the entire uterus is enlarged making it is difficult to distinguish a 30 day pregnant uterus from a colon full of stool.

PERITONEAL DIALYSIS: See *DIALYSIS.*

PERSISTENT PENILE FRENULUM: The persistent penile frenulum is a developmental abnormality in the male Cocker Spaniel puppy which remains undiscovered until puberty. Pain is observed either when the penis is exteriorized or upon sexual excitement.

A fine band of fibrous tissue connects the bottom surface of the penis to the back portion of the prepuce. Any attempt to remove the penis from the sheath pulls it back into the sheath causing discomfort. The penis actually bends if enough pressure is used to exteriorize it. Whether this anomaly is hereditary or just congenital is unknown.

Surgical severing of the band of tissue is a simple procedure usually accomplished with local anesthesia since the band of tissue does not have a generous blood supply.

PLACENTAL SITES, SUBINVOLUTION OF: Each fetal placenta is attached to a separate site in the endometrial wall of the uterus. After whelping, a raw zone is left where each placenta was attached. A thin bloody discharge is seen for up to six weeks as the placenta site scars. In some bitches, the placental site does not heal. While the bitch feels good, has no fever, and is eating well, she continues to have a bloody discharge for months following *parturition* (*whelping*).

Subinvolution of the placental sites is a self-limiting condition. No treatment is required unless the bleeding is considered very heavy. Healing will eventually occur if infection is not present. Treatments used for subinvolution of placental sites are antibiotics and *ergotamine.*

PLASMA PSP TEST: This plasma test will show nonspecific kidney disease before the usual kidney tests (*BUN* and *creatinine*) are elevated. After a baseline heparinized blood sample is obtained, *PSP* (phenolsulfonphthalein) dye is injected intravenously. Exactly 60 minutes later, another heparinized blood sample is taken and examined for the amount of dye excreted during the 60 minute period. Values under 80 mg/100 ml are normal.

POSTPARTUM HEMORRHAGE: Vaginal bleeding after *whelping* is normal varying from slight to heavy. In bitches with *Von Willebrand's disease*, blood loss may be more severe. In these bitches, postpartum injections of *oxytocin* may be very beneficial to contract the uterus. Normal postpartum bleeding can last up to six weeks, becoming less and less frequent.

PREBREEDING EXAMINATION: Both the dog and the bitch should have some prebreeding medical data. If the purpose for breeding the dogs is to improve the breed, assurance that dogs with serious genetic defects are not being bred is essential. All breeding stock should have radiographs on file showing normal hips (*hip dysplasia* free). They should be free from *Von Willebrand's disease, progressive retinal atrophy, glaucoma, epilepsy, Factor X deficiency, copper hepatitis,* or any other suspected genetically linked disease.

A negative *canine brucellosis test* and possibly a clear *vaginal culture* before breeding are desirable. Both sexes should be current on all vaccinations and free from all parasites prior to breeding. If there is past history of irregular *heat cycles,* evidence of systemic illness, or other information that may jeopardize the pregnancy, competent veterinary help should be sought.

PREGNANCY DIAGNOSIS, METHODS OF: Unlike other species of animals and man, no blood test assays in the bitch diagnose pregnancy. Early experimental work shows that testing urinary total *estrogen* levels at 21 days of pregnancy may show some promise. Also, decreases in serum gamma globulin (IgG) and *serum creatinine* levels are reported. A rapid, early blood test may be developed from these facts sometime in the future.

Radiography is of very limited use in pregnancy diagnosis because fetal skeletons are first seen on x-ray 21 days BEFORE delivery. In many instances, the fetal skeleton can not be seen on an abdominal radiograph before 16 to 18 days pre-delivery. Radiography is primarily used very near term to count numbers of fetuses and to determine *dystocia* possibilities. Fetal skulls, not bodies or legs, should always be counted when determining numbers of fetuses.

The effectiveness of *ultrasound* equipment in the diagnosis of pregnancy is dependent on the type of ultrasound techniques used and the skill of the veterinarian. The light-weight, portable Doppler and A-mode ultrasound instrumentation are no more effective than palpation between 20 and 35 days of pregnancy. However, the more expensive sophisticated real-time equipment may demonstrate vesicle formation as early as 20 days. More experimentation is necessary to determine its use in clinical practice.

The limitations of *palpation* have been noted under *PALPATION.* Other signs of pregnancy are bright pink nipples and *anorexia* (lack of appetite) lasting four to seven days 21 days after breeding. These signs should only be used in conjunction with other clinical evidence of pregnancy.

PREGNANCY DURATION: Almost all references refer to 63 days as the normal gestation period in the bitch. Considerable variation from this number is normal. Puppies can be born and survive as early as 55 days and as late as 70 days after breeding. Some confusion arises when multiple breedings have taken place but this can be settled by palpation. When the fetuses are palpated the size of a Ping-Pong® ball, a 28 day pregnancy is present. The breeding, if more than one took place, should be calculated to the date closest to the 28th day prior to palpation.

The *LH hormone* is important in the length of time considered to be normal gestation in the bitch. The 64 day time period is consistent from the preovulation

LH peak to whelping. Ovulation occurs two days after the LH surge. The ovum matures for several days and may remain capable of being fertilized for four to five days after the luteinizing hormone peaks. The most reliable clinical sign of ovulation and LH peak are wrinkling of the vaginal wall and a loss of turgidity to the vulva. Also see *LH PEAK URINE TEST.*

PREPUTIAL INFECTION: During their lifetime, most male dogs have a mucopurulent (pus colored) discharge from the preputial opening. If these infections are cultured, *Staphylococcus* and *Streptococcus* bacteria are discovered. The infection does not cause a febrile (fever) response and does not usually spread to the *prostate gland.*

Treating a preputial infection is a lesson in frustration. With appropriate antibiotics and preputial douches, the discharge can temporarily be eliminated. Usually, within two to four weeks of cessation of therapy, the discharge will return. This discharge should be eliminated before breeding a bitch. To keep spotting in the home to a minimum, an extremely heavy discharge should be treated. Continual douching is the only method of controlling the discharge in an ongoing basis.

PROGESTERONE HORMONE: The progesterone hormone in the bitch, also called the hormone of pregnancy, is produced by the corpus luteum (where the follicle and ovum came from) on the ovary. When not pregnant, the bitch's levels of progesterone remain fairly constant for about 84 days before dropping off. During pregnancy, the level will rise for the first 30 days and then gradually decrease until reaching prepregnant levels one to two days before *whelping.* Progesterone is the only hormone necessary in the bitch to maintain pregnancy.

PROSTAGLANDINS: Prostaglandins are naturally occurring, powerful, luteolytic drugs. The normal level of prostaglandins at *whelping* is high, playing a big role in the signs that the bitch shows in stage II of labor. *Prostaglandin F_{2a}* (alpha) is used in the treatment of *metritis* and *pyometra.* Bitches given prostaglandins for medical problems exhibit signs of toxicity to the drug similar to those in Stage II labor—panting, vomiting, nervousness, scratching and shredding paper. At the present time, prostaglandins are not licensed for use in dogs. Your veterinarian may require a release form for liability purposes.

PROSTATE GLAND: The prostate gland is a muscular secreting accessory sex gland that surrounds the neck of the urinary bladder in the male dog. The function of the prostate is not clear. Its alkaline secretion neutralizes strongly acid urine in the urethra. It also flushes sperm down the urethra while acting as a transport medium.

PROSTATE HYPERPLASIA: A common, usually asymptomatic condition of old male dogs is *benign hyperplasia* of the *prostate gland.* Because *castration* causes the enlarged gland to atrophy, hyperplasia is linked to the male hormone *testosterone.* Sometimes, difficulty in passing stool is observed. The gland grows to such a size that it pushes against the rectum making the dog strain to pass stools. Those stools that are passed are sometimes termed "pencil stools" for obvious reasons.

The enlarged prostate can be treated by female hormone injections. See *MISMATE INJECTION* for a discussion of the existing dangers. *Castration* remains the treatment of choice. The gland returns to normal size less than four weeks after surgery.

PROSTATITIS: Prostatitis is the inflammation of the *prostate gland.* While not as common as *benign hyperplasia,* prostatitis is generally seen in younger male dogs. The affected dog will walk in a stilted manner, keeping his back arched. He will be off his feed and have a fever. Rectal *palpation* of the prostate gland is painful.

A *bacterial culture* and *sensitivity test* are recommended. However, the antibiotic, *erythromycin* , is very active in the prostate so is a good choice when a culture can not be obtained. On occasion, *corticosteroids* and *estrogens* are combined with the antibacterial therapy. Your veterinarian should reexamine these cases because chronic abscessation of the prostate is an undesirable sequelae. The prognosis is guarded to good.

PYELONEPHRITIS: The inflammation of the kidney and kidney pelvis (the cavity in kidney for collecting urine) is defined as pyelonephritis. This problem is caused by many different bacteria. Decreased urine flow is a serious sequelae to pyelonephritis. Elements in the urinary sediment of the *urinalysis* test are important in diagnosing pyelonephritis.

PYOMETRA: Pyometra is a *progesterone*-mediated disease of the endometrial lining within the uterus. Usually occurring in *metestrus (diestrus),* a bacterial infection in the uterus influences its presence. Open or closed pyometra refers to whether or not the cervix allows drainage to be observed.

Most bitches that develop pyometra are at least five years old. However, cases have been reported after the first *heat cycle.* Many of these bitches have histories of *false pregnancies* or never having had puppies. While considered a disease of the intact bitch, stump pyometra can occur in the remnant of the uterine body if some ovarian tissue is left in place following an *ovariohysterectomy (spay).*

While the signs of pyometra vary, the most common clinical syndrome is depression, loss of appetite, vomiting, *polyuria* (increased urination), *polydipsia* (increased water consumption), and development of a pendulous abdomen. The body temperature varies from normal to three or four degrees above normal. Some bitches will appear lame probably due to the developing toxemia. If the cervix is open, a discharge varying from bloody to dark to thick or creamy in color is present. This may be continuous or intermittent. Closed pyometra has no discharge. The bitch also acts much sicker.

The disease complex is diagnosed from the history, *blood counts*, and *radiographs.* In rare instances, exploratory surgery is necessary to identify the enlarged uterus. In almost all cases of closed pyometra, the *white blood cell count* is over 28,000 with some as high as 75,000 (normal white blood cell counts range from 7,000 to 16,000). A *blood urea nitrogen test (BUN)* is important in determining the degree of kidney involvement from the toxemia present. Some bitches have a concurrent *sugar diabetes* problem which complicates the recovery from surgery with a greater chance of infection and slower *wound healing.*

An *ovariohysterectomy* remains the treatment of choice in pyometra. When possible, the surgery should be delayed for a few days after initiating antibiotic therapy. However, this is not always possible. The surgical procedure is supported by intravenous fluids and the use of antibiotics both intravenously and within the abdominal cavity to minimize the chances of infection from the uterine stump. Recovery is followed with oral antibiotics for seven to ten days. All of the clinical signs cease rapidly following successful surgery.

The surgical procedure is not without its dangers. *Anesthesia* is much riskier in the severely toxic patient. Many closed pyometras have a very thin-walled uterus that ruptures on the slightest manipulation during its surgical removal. The resulting contamination of the abdominal cavity makes additional procedures necessary to combat the resulting *peritonitis.* Placement of drain tubes, additional antibiotic therapy, and hospitalization may be needed.

In bitches used for breeding, the experimental use of natural *prostaglandins* may provide an alternative to *ovariohysterectomy* surgery. The use of prostaglandin F_{2a} (PGF_{2a}) will cause the corpus luteum to lyse (disintegrate) thereby lowering the *progesterone* level and reducing the endometrial lining growth. The uterine muscle contracts and is accompanied by some cervical relaxation. No clinical improvement is seen for 48 hours. The concurrent use of antibiotics is important. Serious side effects make hospitalization during treatment mandatory. *White blood cell counts* help monitor the improvement of the general condition. Bitches treated with this regimen should be bred the next *heat period.* Because this drug is not approved for use in dogs, your veterinarian may require a signed liability waiver. A higher incidence of pyometra may occur in families with an increased incidence of *primary uterine inertia.*

RENAL CANCERS: Tumors of the kidney, ureter, urinary bladder, and urethra are uncommon to rare. The *adenocarcinoma,* the most common primary kidney tumor, is more frequent in older males than in females. Generally, the cancer spreads to the lungs but can also metastasize to other body organs. In dogs less than one year, the *nephroblastoma (Wilms' tumor)* is observed, frequently spreading to the lungs. Metastatic tumors, those that have another primary site, are more commonly found in the kidneys than are primary tumors. Various diagnostic tests may be necessary to identify the presence of renal tumors. These tests include *kidney biopsies, urinalysis, IV pyelography,* and possibly exploratory surgery.

Surgical removal of the involved kidney and ureter is the suggested treatment. *Radiographs* of the lungs should be taken before the surgery is undertaken. This surgical procedure requires a high level of skill. The use of other anticancer aids in primary kidney tumors is possible, but results are variable.

Ureteral and urethral tumors are extremely rare in the dog. Surgical treatment, when possible, would be the treatment of choice.

Transitional cell carcinoma, occurring more frequently in females, is the most common *urinary bladder tumor.* The diagnosis is usually made following the observation of *bloody urine*. On occasion, tumor cells may appear in the urine on *urinalysis*. Abdominal *radiographs* may show the presence of a space-occupying lesion in the posterior portion of the abdomen. A partial surgical removal of part of the bladder wall is recommended. Catheterization for seven days keeps the healing bladder decompressed. Early diagnosis is important if a functional part of the bladder is to be saved. Prognosis on all renal cancers is guarded at best.

SCHISTOSOMA REFLEXA: Schistosoma reflexa is a congenital anomaly. The presented fetus is generally doubled over with all or most of the abdominal viscera (organs) appearing outside of the abdominal cavity. Because of the transverse presentation, *dystocia* is usually present. The Schistosoma reflexa is found on the completion of a *cesarean section*. Fetal abnormalities of this nature are euthanized rather than attempting extensive abdominal wall reconstruction.

SEX HORMONE ASSAYS: Currently, *testosterone*, *progesterone*, and *estrogen* levels can be measured from a serum sample. This sample must be shipped on ice. These tests are best run by Dr. Ray Nachreiner, Animal Health Diagnostic Laboratory, Endocrine Diagnostic Section, P.O. Box 30076, Lansing, MI 48909-7576.

SEX HORMONE INJECTIONS: Each of the following sex hormones is discussed individually within the chapter.

Chorionic gonadotropin	Luteinizing hormone
Estrogen	Progesterone hormone
Follicle stimulating hormone	Testosterone

SILENT HEAT: Some heat cycles are not obvious. No vulvar swelling or bleeding is apparent. Signs associated with heat (flagging the tail and vulvar lifting on stimulation) are very weak or unnoticed. This phenomenon called a silent heat has an unknown cause. Affected Cocker Spaniel bitches are fertile so if they are bred at the appropriate time, they will bear puppies. Often *vaginal smears* are necessary at least three times a week to follow the cycle to find the time of greatest fertility. Also see *LH PEAK URINE TEST*.

SPAY (OVARIOHYSTERECTOMY): See *BIRTH CONTROL METHODS*.

SPERM COUNT: Semen is collected by ejaculating the male dog in a quiet area, preferably after playing with a bitch in heat. The semen contains three fractions. The middle, thick, whitish fluid is the one containing the sperm. Sperm are evaluated for motility, numbers, and morphology (appearance). Minimal numbers for reproduction are 80% motile, at least 200 million sperm per ejaculate (500 million is average in a normal male), and less than 20% abnormal appearing sperm.
    Semen must be collected carefully in a glass or Teflon® tube that has been warmed to body temperature to prevent shock to the sperm. The sperm containing

fluid fraction varies from 0.5 ml to over 3 ml in volume. This portion is ejaculated within the first two minutes of fluid production.

SPLIT HEAT: A split heat is most commonly observed at the time of a bitch's first heat period. Some vulvar swelling with four or five days of a bloody discharge which ends abruptly may occur. Four to five weeks later the bitch goes into true *estrus* starting with the *proestrus* stage. In 8 to 10 days, this leads into the standing fertile heat. The split heat is related to the development of the ovarian follicles. In some bitches, follicular development causes enough *estradiol* increase to produce overt signs of heat. This follicular growth is about four to six weeks before actual *proestrus* begins. If older bitches cycle every four months, they are not ovulating. Measuring the *estrogen* and *progesterone* levels in such a bitch will help pinpoint the deficient phase of the cycle.

TES-TAPE®: Tes-Tape® is a paper tape that changes color in the presence of sugar. At the time of a bitch's ovulation, the cervical mucus contains *glucose*. Tes-Tape® is inserted into the vagina and moistened with vaginal secretions. If cervical mucus contains glucose, the change in tape color accurately indicates ovulation.

The presence of some types of *vaginitis* also cause glucose formation changing the color of the Tes-Tape®. A bitch with *diabetes mellitus* would also have *glucose* in vaginal secretions. The Tes-Tape® should be used with clinical signs of *estrus* and *vaginal smears* to determine the optimum time for breeding.

TESTOSTERONE: Testosterone is a male androgenic hormone produced by the Leydig's cells in the testes. Within an hour after these cells are stimulated by *luteinizing hormone (LH)*, testosterone is produced. Much higher levels of testosterone are needed within the testes to maintain *spermatogenesis* (the formation of sperm) than are found in the circulating blood stream.

Testosterone hormone causes the male characteristics and actions—leg lifting, deep bark, territorial guarding, luxurious hair coat, and libido. Testosterone injections increase libido but may cause a temporary sterility. While the male will now mount and breed a bitch, he may have no active spermatozoa for about five to seven days after the hormone injection.

THYROID FUNCTION TESTS: The three usual tests for thyroid function which are important in reproductive problems are the T_4 value, the T_3 value, and the *TSH stimulation test*. Additional discussion on these tests is found in Chapter 4. Many reproductive problems can be traced to poor thyroid function.

TUBAL LIGATION: See *METHOD OF BIRTH CONTROL.*

UNDESCENDED TESTICLE: See *CRYPTORCHID.*

URINALYSIS: Much valuable information can be obtained from this relatively simple procedure. Any kidney or reproductive tract work-up should include this test.

URINE SPECIMEN, COLLECTION OF: Three methods are utilized in the collection of a urine specimen. *Catheterization* can be accomplished with ease in the male and with some difficulty in the bitch. Some danger of introducing infection into the urinary bladder via the catheter exists. If the urethra is inflamed, the catheter may aggravate its sensitive lining.

The second method, *cystocentesis*, is a method of tapping the urinary bladder by inserting a long needle through the abdominal wall into the bladder and withdrawing urine into a syringe. This requires a cooperative dog that will allow its front legs to be elevated and its abdomen to be manipulated so the urinary bladder can be restrained for needle penetration. Since this is a blind penetration, slight danger of internal organ damage and internal hemorrhage exists.

The third method, the collection of a *midstream urine specimen*, is suitable for many procedures. With a little practice, your dog will not mind the use of a flat, clean pie plate to enable you to collect an ounce of urine. Confine the Cocker overnight. Exercise it in the morning on a leash. Most dogs will urinate after overnight confinement even if they are not accustomed to *leash* restricted exercise. A bitch may raise up as you slip the flat pan under her. However, the urge to micturate is great enough that she will resume the squatting position and allow you to collect a specimen. The sample is then transferred to a clean glass or plastic container and transported to your veterinarian. Collected specimens should be transported within one hour of collection or refrigerated for up to three hours before analysis. Midstream urine specimens may not be acceptable for *bacterial cultures* of urinary tract infections.

URINE P.S.P. EXCRETION TEST: The urine PSP excretion test gives a good gauge of kidney tubular function. After a catheter is placed in the urinary bladder to remove all urine, phenolsulfonphthalein (P.S.P.) is injected intravenously. All urine formed in 15 and in 60 minutes is collected. The amount of P.S.P. in each sample gives an assessment of kidney tubular function.

UTERINE HORN TORSION: Uterine horn torsion is the complete twisting of a pregnant horn or of the entire uterus. The twisting effectively cuts off the blood supply to the affected part of the uterus causing profound shock to the bitch. Even with emergency exploratory surgery, most bitches are given a poor prognosis for survival.

A great amount of rolling or jumping behavior in a bitch with a heavily pregnant uterus is the reason for this rare condition. This activity causes the uterus to turn on itself. The only clinical signs present are profound shock and abdominal discomfort. Early surgery may slightly improve the prognosis.

UTERINE PROLAPSE: Uterine prolapses primarily occur after *whelping* is complete. Some however do take place after one horn is empty and becomes evaginated with continued uterine contractions. These cases are diagnosed by the presence of abnormal tissue protruding from the vulvar lips. Manipulation and a surgical incision in the abdomen will replace the protruding tissue. Many replaced uteri will partially prolapse after subsequent heat periods. Most recurring uterine prolapses are treated with an *ovariohysterectomy (spay)*.

VAGINAL CULTURES: The use of vaginal cultures as an aid in *fertility testing* is controversial. The vaginal tract has a normal bacterial flora which includes *E. coli, Streptococcus canis, Staphylococcus aureus*, as well as a number of other bacteria considered to be pathogens (capable of producing disease). The amount and kind of bacteria in the forward area of the vagina near the cervix is the most important consideration in determining whether the bitch has a bacterial population deleterious to breeding.

Specialized instrumentation is necessary to culture the anterior vaginal compartment. With a Cocker Spaniel bitch, a 10 inch guarded culture instrument is used. A comprehensive culture would include both aerobic (requiring oxygen) and anaerobic (able to grow without oxygen) bacteria. The interpretation of *bacterial culture* results requires experience. If large numbers of bacteria are isolated from the anterior vaginal vault, they should be considered detrimental to the anticipated breeding. An *antibiotic sensitivity test* should be performed to determine the kind of antibiotic therapy to initiate.

Some bitches may be treated and bred during the same heat. Others should be treated, not bred, and cultured again on the next heat. Under no circumstances should one assume that the bacterial flora will be identical from heat to heat. The techniques of vaginal culturing can aid in the management of infertility in the hands of an experienced veterinary clinician.

VAGINAL HYPERPLASIA: Vaginal hyperplasia is caused by increased levels of *estrogen* and its effect on the tissues in the vaginal vestibule near the opening of the urethra. Most of these conditions occur in late *proestrus*. Some are seen about the time of *whelping* when the estrogen levels rise again. This condition has a hereditary basis and continued breeding of affected bitches is questionable.

The prominent sign is a round, red, moist-appearing dome of tissue protruding through the vulvar lips. No pain or discomfort to the bitch is evident. This condition will resolve itself as the heat cycle proceeds and estrogen levels drop. Both breeding and whelping can usually occur naturally in spite of the presence of the soft mass of vaginal tissue. To eliminate the passage of the genetic predisposition of vaginal hyperplasia, *ovariohysterectomy (spaying)* should be considered for affected bitches. Some surgeons recommend removal of the mass. This surgery causes much blood loss because of *estrus (heat)*. Special care must also be taken to keep the urethral orifice open. Vaginal hyperplasia or prolapse can occur at subsequent heat periods even after surgical correction.

VAGINAL SMEARS: Vaginal smears taken throughout a *heat cycle* can provide valuable information about ideal breeding times. A sterile cotton swab introduced into the vaginal vestibule is gently rubbed against the vagina wall. The swab is then rolled out on a clean glass slide and stained with any cytology stain. The interpretation of this simple technique requires some experience.

Three cell types are observed: *white blood cells, red blood cells,* and epithelial cells. As hormone levels of *estrogen* increase, the shape of epithelial cells change. Normal epithelial cells in *anestrus* are circular with a large oval nucleus within the cell. As *proestrus* begins, the cells start to develop pointed corners. The nucleus shrinks in size, becoming darker. As the process of cell cornification continues, the cells become very pointed with a dark, pinpoint nucleus. Full cornification reaches its maximum at the time the bitch stands for breeding during *estrus*. In *metestrus*, circular epithelial cells with large nuclei reappear and the cornified cells disintegrate.

While the epithelial cells are going through these changes, *red blood cells* are appearing and disappearing in the various stages of the heat cycle. *White blood cells* also disappear and reappear as the heat cycle progresses. The clinician observing serial smears will also note the presence or absence of cellular debris. As a rough, general rule, when the completely cornified cells make up 60% of the epithelial cell population, ovulation should occur. Emphasis is on the fact that this is a rough estimate. Using these smears in addition to the appearance of vaginal crenulation (wavy appearing vaginal lining) is the best means of pinpointing the *LH* peak. Ovulation occurs 48 hours after the LH peak. Also see *LH PEAK URINE TEST*.

VAGINITIS: Vaginitis is the inflammation of the vagina characterized by discomfort. In some cases, a mucopurulent (pussy) discharge is present. Other cases are asymptomatic. *Juvenile vaginitis* is not uncommon in puppies after 10 weeks of age. They may show some increase in urinary frequency and a sticky yellow discharge. Many of these infections are rather resistant to antibiotics. However, the onset of the first *heat period* is curative. Most vaginitis problems are due to superficial infections of the vaginal epithelium. These infections can play a role in *infertility*. Appropriate antibiotic therapy and in some instances, therapeutic douches are necessary to restore normal fertility.

WATER PUPPY: See *ANASARCA*.

WEANING PROCESS: See *DRYING UP A LACTATING BITCH*.

SUGGESTED VETERINARY VISITS

6 to 10 weeks
— First vaccination, fecal examination, initial veterinary health examination checking for umbilical hernia, luxating patellas, heart murmurs, dwarfism

10 to 14 weeks
— Second vaccination, second fecal examination

14 to 18 weeks
— Third vaccination—parvovirus vaccination after 16 weeks

20 to 24 weeks
— Rabies vaccination dependent on local law

24 to 28 weeks
— Ovariohysterectomy if not to be bred or shown

32 to 36 weeks
— Castration if not to be bred or shown

52 weeks
— Dental checkup for proper bite, missing teeth, retained baby teeth, and early periodontal disease

2 years
— CERF eye exam repeated yearly, OFA hip registration, Von Willebrand's disease and Factor X registration in American Spaniel Club's Health Registry

Yearly as an adult
— Revaccination, fecal examination, CERF eye exam, and periodontal teeth exam

7 years and older
— Annual physical exam including urinalysis, chem panel blood test, teeth cleaning, and a change to a senior dog food diet

8 years
— Apply for permanent registration in The American Spaniel Club Health Registry for normal eyes (progressive retinal atrophy and cataract)

CHECKLIST FOR VETERINARY EXAMINATIONS OF COCKER SPANIELS

6 to 10 weeks
— Listen to heart, examine teeth, patellas, umbilicus, ears, and tonsils

3 to 6 months
— Test for Von Willebrand's disease before major surgery, perform urinalysis to check on congenital kidney disease, discuss ear care and bathing for seborrhea control, and watch for neurological storage diseases

9 to 12 months
— Examine mouth and teeth for retained deciduous teeth

2 years
— OFA hip dysplasia x-ray, recommend CERF eye exam

7 years and older
— Complete physical exam annually including teeth cleaning, urinalysis and chem panel blood test

BIBLIOGRAPHY

CHAPTER 1

Physicians' Desk Reference. 40th ed. Oradell, NJ: Medical Economics Co., 1986.

Short, C.E. *Practical Use of the Ultrashort-acting Barbiturates.* Princeton Junction, NJ: Veterinary Learning Systems Co., 1983.

Swaim, S. *Surgery of Traumatized Skin.* Philadelphia, PA: W.B. Saunders, 1980.

Veterinary Pharmaceuticals and Biologicals–1985/1986 Edition. Lenexa, KS: Veterinary Medicine Publishing Co., 1986.

CHAPTER 2

Degen, M.A., "Canine and Feline Immunodeficiency–Part I." *Comp on Cont Educ,* 8 (May, 1986), pp. 314–316.

Dodds, W.J., "Von Willebrand's Disease in Dogs." *MVP,* 65 (September, 1984), pp. 681–686.

Feldman, B.F., "Immune-Mediated Thrombocytopenia," *Comp on Cont Educ,* 7 (July, 1985), pp. 569–576.

Jenkins, T.F. *et al.,* "Treatment of Autoimmune Hemolytic Anemia in the Dog." *Canine Prac,* 13 (May/June, 1986), pp. 39, 42, 43, 45.

Littlewood, J.D., "A Practical Approach to Bleeding Disorders in the Dog." *J Sm Anim Prac,* 27 (June, 1986), pp. 397–409.

CHAPTER 3

Ettinger, Stephen J. *Textbook of Veterinary Internal Medicine,* Philadelphia, PA: W.B. Saunders, 1975.

Lorenz, M.D., Cornelius, L.M., *Small Animal Medical Diagnosis,* Philadelphia, PA: J.B. Lippincott, 1987.

Thomas, R.E., "Congestive Cardiac Failure in Young Cocker Spaniels." *J Sm Anim Pract,* 28 (April, 1987), pp. 265–279.

Thrusfield, C.G.G., *et al.,* "Observations on Breed and Sex in Relation to Canine Heart Valve Incompetence." *J Sm Anim Pract,* 26 (December, 1985), pp. 709–717.

CHAPTER 4

Doxey, D.L., *et al.,* "Canine Diabetes Mellitus: A Retrospective Survey," *J Sm Anim Pract,* 26. (September, 1985), pp. 555–561.

Feldman, E.C., ed., "Symposium on Endocrinology." *Vet Clin No Amer,* 7, 3 (August, 1977), pp. 434–486, 497–512, 549–635.

Peterson, M.E., ed., "Symposium on Endocrinology." *Vet Clin No Amer,* 14, 4 (July, 1984), pp. 721–766, 783–808, 827–858, 927–935.

Rosychuk, R. "Management of Hypothyroidism." *Current Veterinary Therapy VIII.* Edited by R.W. Kirk. Philadelphia, PA: W.B. Saunders, 1983.

CHAPTER 5

Brunner, C.J., et al., "Canine Parvovirus Infection: Effects on the Immune System and Factors That Predispose to Severe Disease." *Comp on Cont Educ*, 7 (December, 1985), pp. 979–989.

Dillon, A.R., ed., "Symposium on Gastroenterology." *Vet Clin No Amer*, 13, 3 (August, 1983), pp. 415–460, 503–567, 627–646.

Leib, M.S., et al., "Acute Gastric Dilatation in the Dog: Various Clinical Presentations." *Comp on Cont Educ*, 6, 8 (August, 1984), pp. 707–712.

Palminteri, A., ed., "Symposium on Gastrointestinal Medicine and Surgery." *Vet Clin No Amer*, 2, 1 (January, 1972), pp. 79–98, 131–154, 181–194.

Rand, J. S., et al. , "Portosystemic Vascular Shunts in a Family of American Cocker Spaniels." *JAAHA*, 24 (May/June 1988), pp. 265–272.

Thornburg, L. P., et al. , "Copper Toxicosis in Dogs–Part 2." *Canine Pract*, 12 (September–October, 1985), pp. 33–38.

Twedt, D.C., ed., "Symposium on Liver Diseases." *Vet Clin No Amer*, 15, 1 (January, 1985), pp. 39–76, 119–196, 229–242.

CHAPTER 6

Alexander, J.W., and Roberts, R.E., eds., "Symposium on Orthopedic Diseases." *Vet Clin No Amer*, 13, 1 (February, 1983), pp. 43–54, 71–134, 163–194.

Bennett, D., Kelly, D.F., "Immune-based Non-erosive Inflammatory Joint Disease of the Dog." *J Sm Anim Pract*, 28 (October, 1987), pp. 891–908.

Chrisman, C.L., ed.,"Advances in Veterinary Neurology–Myasthenia Gravis and Diseases of the Muscle." *Vet Clin No Amer*, 10 (February, 1980), pp. 213–234.

Romatowski, J.,"Spondylosis Deformans in the Dog." *Comp on Cont Ed*, 8 (August, 1986), pp. 531–534.

CHAPTER 7

Chrisman, C.L., ed., "Symposium on Advances in Veterinary Neurology." *Vet Clin No Amer*, 10, 1 (February, 1980), pp. 3–29, 57–63, 65–130.

Chrisman, C.L. *Problems in Small Animal Neurology*, Philadelphia, PA: Lea and Febiger, 1982.

Jaggy, A., Vandevelde, M., "Multisystemic Neuronal Degeneration in Cocker Spaniels." *J Vet Int Med*, 2 (July–September, 1988), pp. 117–120.

Kern, T.J., Erb, H.N., "Facial Neuropathy in Dogs and Cats." *JAVMA*, 191 (December 15, 1987), pp. 1604–1609.

Wilkie, J.S.N., Hudson, E.B., "Neuronal and Generalized Ceroid-lipofuscinosis in a Cocker Spaniel." *Vet Path*, 19 (1982), pp. 623–628.

CHAPTER 8
Alpo Pet Center. *Canine Nutrition and Feeding Management.* Allentown, PA: Alpo Pet Center, 1984.
Lewis, L.D., and Morris, M.L. Jr. *Small Animal Clinical Nutrition,* Topeka, KS: Mark Morris Associates, 1984.

CHAPTER 9
Kirk, R.W., and Bistner, S. *Handbook of Veterinary Procedures and Emergency Treatment,* Philadelphia, PA: W.B. Saunders, 1981.
Oehme, F.W., ed. "Clinical Toxicology for the Small Animal Practitioner." *Vet Clin No Amer,* 5, 4 (November, 1975), pp. 589–622, 699–726, 737–754.
Oehme, F.W., cons. ed. *Current Veterinary Therapy VIII.* Edited by R.W. Kirk. Philadelphia, PA: W.B. Saunders, 1983.
Osweiler, G.D., cons. ed. *Current Veterinary Therapy IX.* Edited by R.W. Kirk. Philadelphia, PA: W.B. Saunders, 1986.

CHAPTER 10
Aguirre, G.D., ed. "Symposium on Ophthalmology." *Vet Clin No Amer,* 3, 3 (September, 1973), pp. 436, 453–528.
Angarano, D.W., "Disease of the Pinna–Diseases of the Ear Canal." *Vet Clin No Amer,* 18 (July, 1988), p. 882.
Barnett, K.C. "The Diagnosis and Differential Diagnosis of Cataracts in the Dog." *J Sm Anim Pract,* 26 (June, 1985), pp. 305–316.
Brooks, D.J. *Personal Communication on Contact Lenses,* 1987.
Chrisman, C., *Problems in Small Animal Neurology,* Philadelphia, PA: Lea & Febiger, 1982.
MacMillan, A.D., Lipton, D.E., "Heritability of Multifocal Retinal Dysplasia in American Cocker Spaniels." *JAVMA,* 172 (1978), pp. 568–572.
Muller, G., *et al. Small Animal Dermatology.* Philadelphia, PA: W.B. Saunders, 1983.
Peiffer, R.L. Jr., ed. "Symposium on Ophthalmology." *Vet Clin No Amer,* 10, 2 (May, 1980), pp. 399–454.
Peiffer, R.L. Jr., *et al.,* "Surgery of the Canine and Feline Orbit, Adenexa, and Globe, Part 7: The Lens." *Comp An Prac,* 2 (January, 1988), pp. 4–17.
Peiffer, R.L. Jr., *et al.,* "Surgery of the Canine and Feline Orbit, Adnexa, and Globe, Part 8: Glaucoma and Surgery of the Iris and Ciliary Body." *Comp An Prac,* 2 (February, 1988), pp. 3–15.
Slater, M.R., and Erb, H.N., "Effects of Risk Factors and Prophylactic Treatment on Primary Glaucoma in the Dog." *JAVMA,* 188 (May 1, 1986), pp. 1028–1030.
Yakely, W.L., *et al.,* "Familial Cataracts in the American Cocker Spaniel." *JAAHA,* 7 (1971), pp. 127–135.

CHAPTER 11
Ihrke, P.J., Goldschmidt, M. H., "Vitamin A Responsive Dermatosis in the Dog." *JAVMA*, 182 (1983), p. 687.

Johnston, D.E., ed. *Small Animal Dermatology in Practice,* Lawrenceville, NJ: Veterinary Learning Systems, 1985.

Lissman, B.A. "Lyme Disease," *Current Veterinary Therapy IX.* Edited by R.W. Kirk. Philadelphia, PA: W.B. Saunders, 1986.

Muller, G., *et al. Small Animal Dermatology.* Philadelphia, PA: W.B. Saunders, 1983.

Scott, D.W., "Vitamin A-ResponsiveDermatosis in the Cocker Spaniel." *JAAHA*, 22 (January–February, 1986), pp. 125–129.

CHAPTER 12
Dain, A. R., "Intersexuality in a Cocker Spaniel Dog." *J Reprod Fertil*, 39 (1974), pp. 365–371.

Dorn, A.S., *et al.*, "Sex-hormone-related Diseases Treated Surgically in Male Dogs." *Mod Vet Prac*, 66 (October, 1985), pp. 727–733.

Johnson, C.A., ed. "Reproduction and Periparturient Care." *Vet Clin No Amer*, 16, 3 (May, 1986), pp. 419–434, 453–494, 521–600.

Johnson, M.E. *et al.*, "Renal Cortical Hypoplasia in a Litter of Cocker Spaniels." *JAAHA* 8 (July–August, 1972), pp. 268–274.

Jones, D.E., and Joshua, J.O. *Reproductive Clinical Problems in the Dog*, London: P.S.G. Wright, 1982.

Osborne, C.A., and Klausner, J.S., eds. "Symposium on Urinary Tract Infections." *Vet Clin No Amer*, 9, 4 (November, 1979), pp. 645–700, 775–782, 795–818.

Osborne, C.A. "Canine Urolithiasis I and II." *Vet Clin No Amer*, 16, 1 and 2 (January and March, 1986), pp. 3–26, 227–239, 303–324, 333–407.

Rhoades, J.D., ed. "Symposium on Reproductive Problems." *Vet Clin No Amer*, 7, 4 (November, 1977), pp. 653–698, 705–714, 735–794.

Selden, J.R., *et al.*, "Inherited XX Sex Reversal in the Cocker Spaniel Dog." *Hum Genet*, 67 (1984), pp. 62–69.

Selden, JR, *et al.*, "Genetic Basis of XX Male Syndrome and XX True Hemaphroditism: Evidence in the Dog." *Science*, 201 1978, pp. 644–646.

INDEX

10% Mucomyst® 161
50% Glucose **93**, 95, 99, 102, 138
2–PAM 98, 137, 151
3, 5–diiodothyronine (T₂) 36
1080 138, 142

— A —

AAFCO **106**, 120, 122
Abortion **222**, 227, 241, 242, 247
Acanthosis nigricans **189**
Accutane® 220
Acepromazine maleate **1**, 52, 151
Acetylsalicylic acid **63**, 64
Achalasia **41**
Achondroplasia **62**
Acid 158, 208
Acid poisoning, internal and external **131**
Acne **189**
Aconite (wild) plant poisoning **131**
Acquired deafness 169
Acquired epilepsy 92
Acquired hydrocephalus 94
Acral lick **189**
Acromegaly **29**
ACT 11, 12, 14
ACTH 29, 30, 32, 36, 40
ACTH-dexamethasone suppression test **29**, 33
ACTH stimulation test 32
Actinomycosis 79
Activated charcoal 132, 134, 135, 138, 139, 140, 148, 152, 154, 156, 157, 158
Activated coagulation time 12, 14
Activated partial thromboplastin time 12, 14
Acute anal sac infection 191
Acute anterior uveitis **160**, 164
Acute blindness **160**
Acute corneal ulcer **161**

Acute gastric dilatation (bloat) syndrome 13
Acute glaucoma 183
Acute liver disease 51
Acute liver failure 44, 138
Acute moist dermatitis **190**, 200, 217, 219
Acute pancreatitis 9, 53
Acute polyradiculoneuritis 101
ACVO 161, 162
ACVS **1**
Addison's disease **29**, 40, 85, 89
Additive free diets **106**
Adenocarcinoma 17, 239, 252
  kidney 252
  lung 17
  prostate 239
Adenovirus 167
Adenovirus–1 50, 164
Adenovirus–2 164
ADH 33
Adrenal glands **36**,237, 242
Adrenal gland failure 228
Adrenal gland tumor 89
Adrenocorticotrophic hormone 36
Adriamycin® 22
Adult dog, dietary management of **106**
Adult encephalitis 95
Adult teeth eruption 58
AIHA **8**
Alanine aminotransferase 59
Albinism 1, 122, 174
Albumin 110
Aldosterone **30**, 36
Alkali 141, 158, 166, 208
Alkali poisoning, internal and external **132**
Alkaline phosphatase 71
Alkaloid poisoning **132**
Allergic inhalant dermatitis 192
Allergy 16, 18, 26, 27, 189, **190**, 215
  anaphylactic reaction 142, 244
  atopy 173, 190, **192**, 202
  bacterial hypersensitivity **193**, 201, 215
  hives 204, 244
  irritant contact dermatoses **208**

COCKER SPANIEL OWNERS'

— F —

— H —

COCKER SPANIEL OWNERS'

COCKER SPANIEL OWNERS'

COCKER SPANIEL OWNERS'

— Q —

— R —

COCKER SPANIEL OWNERS'

— S —

COCKER SPANIEL OWNERS'

Whipworm 55
White blood cell 9, 13, **16**, 176,
    232, 256, 257
White blood cell count 11, 54, 62,
    63, 251, 252
White blood cell depression 50
White muscle disease 125
Wilms' tumor 252
Wisteria plant poisoning **159**
Wobbler syndrome 80, **105**
Wobbling gait 124
Wobbly gait 137
Wound healing **7**, 114, 127, 130,
    252
Wry mouth 51, 52

— X —

X-ray 75, 160
X-ray, skull **105**
Xenodine® 171
Xylazine **3**, 22, 33, 39, 204
Xylocaine® 2, **4**

— Y —

Yeast infection in ear **188**
Yew plant poisoning **159**

— Z —

Zinc 81, 109, 111, 122, 123, **130**,
    216
Zinc deficiencies 130
Zinc deficiency skin disease 203
Zinc phosphide poisoning **159**
Zinc responsive skin disease **220**
Zolazepam 3
Zoonotic infestation 54

Breed Manual Publications Ltd.

To keep you informed about any new editions and publications, please complete this page and send it to:

Breed Manual Publications
3370-CS Jackson Drive
Jackson, WI 53037

Name of book purchased _____
Date purchased _____
Where purchased _____
How did you learn about the book?

I am interested in dogs for:
      pets   show dogs   working dogs   breeding
Other: _____

I would be interested in seeing manuals on the following breeds:

Suggestions for future editions:

Name _____
Address _____
City _____ State ___ Zip _____

Thank you for your help!